Mastering Qlik Sen

Expert techniques on self-service data analytics to create enterprise ready Business Intelligence solutions

Martin Mahler
Juan Ignacio Vitantonio

BIRMINGHAM - MUMBAI

Mastering Qlik Sense

Commissioning Editor: Amey Varangaonkar
Acquisition Editor: Tushar Gupta
Content Development Editor: Aaryaman Singh
Technical Editor: Dinesh Chaudhary
Copy Editor: Safis Editing
Project Coordinator: Manthan Patel
Proofreader: Safis Editing
Indexer: Aishwarya Gangawane
Graphics: Tania Dutta
Production Coordinator: Aparna Bhagat

First published: March 2018

Production reference: 1140318

Published by Packt Publishing Ltd.
Livery Place
35 Livery Street
Birmingham
B3 2PB, UK.

ISBN 978-1-78355-402-7

www.packtpub.com

`mapt.io`

Mapt is an online digital library that gives you full access to over 5,000 books and videos, as well as industry leading tools to help you plan your personal development and advance your career. For more information, please visit our website.

Why subscribe?

- Spend less time learning and more time coding with practical eBooks and Videos from over 4,000 industry professionals

- Improve your learning with Skill Plans built especially for you

- Get a free eBook or video every month

- Mapt is fully searchable

- Copy and paste, print, and bookmark content

PacktPub.com

Did you know that Packt offers eBook versions of every book published, with PDF and ePub files available? You can upgrade to the eBook version at `www.PacktPub.com` and as a print book customer, you are entitled to a discount on the eBook copy. Get in touch with us at `service@packtpub.com` for more details.

At `www.PacktPub.com`, you can also read a collection of free technical articles, sign up for a range of free newsletters, and receive exclusive discounts and offers on Packt books and eBooks.

Contributors

About the authors

Martin Mahler, a rocket scientist by education, is a passionate Qlik Luminary 2018 with vast experience in championing Qlik Technologies across financial services. With an MSc in engineering and IT as work experience, he advocates Qlik's self-service capabilities and democratization of data within organizations. Being an energetic individual, he also regularly shares his knowledge at presentations within QlikDevGroups across Europe. He currently serves as Vizlib's CEO.

Writing a book is not an easy endeavor—it took over 13 months to finish the title, not lastly due to Qlik's constant updates which had to be included. I would like to acknowledge the endless support and love from everyone who has been part of this journey, directly or indirectly, especially Maria, my parents, the brews, friends, and colleagues.

Juan Ignacio Vitantonio is a consultant who helps global companies thrive through the use of Qlik technologies, allowing them to gain business insights by implementing self-service solutions. Whether attending Qlik events, assisting the Qlik community, or serving as a Qlik branch moderator, he is always willing to help and learn from others. He is passionate about Qlik and data discovery. He enjoys traveling. He has a BSc in software engineering and an MSc in engineering.

Writing Mastering Qlik Sense is by far the most challenging yet rewarding thing I have ever done in my life. The feeling I had after writing each page is indescribable. I would like to thank everybody who has supported me along this journey, Julio in particular, my close friends, and colleagues, who in different ways have encouraged me to always give my best.

About the reviewers

David Alcobero is the CTO and co-Founder of Vizlib, a highly customizable, supported and feature-rich visualization library for Qlik Sense. He leads the product development team, platform design and vision strategy.

David was born in Barcelona (Spain), where he got his MSc in computer science and engineering at UAB (Universitat Autonoma de Barcelona). He was working as a Qlik developer and software engineer in Spain for 5 years until he moved to London in 2014, where he worked as a Qlik consultant for 3 years in a variety of industries, from e-commerce, through manufacturing to banking.

> *Martin and Juan made an excellent work synthetizing the must-have-knowledge in order to became a real Master in Qlik Sense. It was a true pleasure, and honor, to do one's bit on this book.*

Ralf Becher is an internationally recognized Qlik expert and long term Qlik Luminary. He has more than 25 years of experience in information technology, working as systems architect and principal consultant in business intelligence and big data, in multiple industries.

In 2004, he founded TIQ Solutions in Germany, a Leipzig-based company specialized in modern, quality-assured data management and advanced analytics.

Ralf joined Vizlib in 2017 as a technical advisor, passionate to build first-class web components and data visualizations for contemporary analytical solutions.

Dilyana Ivanova is a Director at AIG as Data Analytics & Visualization lead. The team uses data, analytics, and business expertise to provide insights across all aspects of insurance.

She was a BI consultant and enjoyed a diversity of projects, industries, and countries. She focused on Data Visualization & used Qlik's powerful set of tools to build innovative solutions.

She grew up, lived, and worked in Bulgaria for her undergrad in computer science. She moved to Scotland for her master's and developed *A Guide to Access Control for the BI system at the University of St Andrews* for her thesis.

> *I would like to thank the authors and the publisher for the opportunity to work on the book. It has been very exciting to be a part of this project.*

Karl Pover is the owner and principal consultant of Evolution Consulting, which provides QlikView consulting services throughout Mexico. Since 2006, he has been dedicated to providing QlikView pre-sales, implementation, and training to more than 50 customers. He is the author of Learning QlikView Data Visualization and Mastering QlikView Data Visualization. He has been a Qlik Luminary since 2014.

Packt is searching for authors like you

If you're interested in becoming an author for Packt, please visit `authors.packtpub.com` and apply today. We have worked with thousands of developers and tech professionals, just like you, to help them share their insight with the global tech community. You can make a general application, apply for a specific hot topic that we are recruiting an author for, or submit your own idea.

Table of Contents

Preface

Qlik Sense is a powerful, self-servicing business intelligence tool for data discovery, analytics, and visualization. It allows you to create personalized business intelligence solutions from raw data and to get actionable insights from it.

This book is your one-stop guide to mastering Qlik Sense, catering to all your organizational data analytics needs. You'll see how you can seamlessly navigate through tons of data from multiple sources and take advantage of the various APIs available in Qlik and its components for guided analytics. You'll also learn how to embed visualizations into your existing BI solutions and extend the capabilities of Qlik Sense to create new visualizations and dashboards that work across all platforms. We also cover other advanced concepts, such as porting your QlikView applications to Qlik Sense and working with Qlik Cloud. Finally, you'll learn to implement enterprise-wide security and access control for resources and data sources through practical examples.

With the knowledge gained from this book, you'll have become the go-to expert in your organization when it comes to designing data analytics solutions using Qlik Sense.

Who this book is for

Thank you very much for purchasing Mastering Qlik Sense! Both the authors are very excited to accompany you on your journey to becoming proficient and a master of Qlik Sense. Two new concepts are being introduced with the latest technology that make it different than QlikView: its improved self-service capabilities with the goal of democratizing data and data literacy within organizations, and the introduction of robust APIs that let you extend Qlik Sense using web technologies and take its analytics even further.

As such, due to the breadth of different new skill sets now required in a typical Qlik Sense project (web development, Qlik scripting, expressions, and business understanding for data analytics), it's nearly impossible to master them all. However, this book will provide you with synthesized and advanced knowledge of all relevant concepts around mastering Qlik Sense on an enterprise level.

As such, the book is specifically targeted at three groups of people:

- **QlikView gurus**: People who have extensively used QlikView in the past and are looking to transition to Qlik Sense
- **Qlik Sense beginners**: People who are new to Qlik but have had some experience using Qlik Sense in their organization and wish to bring their expertise to the next level and
- **Web developers**: Frontend and backend JavaScript developers who want to get a better understanding of the Qlik technology to leverage its rich and powerful API

Accordingly, the book is structured into three modules.

- Module 1, *The Qlik Sense Self-Service Model:* Module 1 is about understanding the essence of self-service and how Qlik Sense is facilitating this capability. This module will revolve around the various use cases in self-service, how to set up the security for this, and how to prepare an environment where non-technical users can be empowered to create their dashboards and visualizations. Emphasis will be put in this module on QlikView developers who are looking to understanding Qlik's new product and to what extent they are different and similar.
- Module 2, *Best Practices for Data Modeling and Expressions:* Albeit very similar to QlikView's best practices, it is essential that the audience knows and understands Qlik's best practices on how to correctly and efficiently use the in-memory calculation engine to master the Qlik Sense technology.
- Module 3, *Qlik Sense API:* Qlik has decided to open up the Qlik engine as well as all of their services via an API. This suggests that extensions and integrations into third-party platforms are possible, which exceeds the capabilities that come out of the box in Qlik Sense. The real power of the associative engine can be leveraged in any way desired, which will be the topic of this module.

We hope you enjoy it!

–Martin & Juan

What this book covers

Chapter 1, *Qlik Sense Self-Service Model*, is about understanding the essence of self-service, the significance of empowering the business user, and what types of use cases of self-service exist. It will teach you to identify the correct use cases for using Qlik Sense and advising the business on how and why to leverage self-service Business Intelligence.

Chapter 2, *Transitioning from QlikView to Qlik Sense*, is a comparison of QlikView and Qlik Sense, focusing on the differences and similarities between the two technologies. You will learn the differences between QlikView and Qlik Sense. You will learn how to prepare for Qlik Sense, and see what new stuff needs to be learned, differences, and commonalities between the two technologies.

Chapter 3, *Security Rules: Attribute Based Access Control*, explains that Qlik Sense has introduced a new concept of security rules for applying non-data-level permissions called Attribute-Based Access Control. This chapter will teach you this new concept and will let you become proficient with the security rules and translate permission requirements into security rules logic.

Chapter 4, *Master Items in Qlik Sense*, explains that with a new type of digital asset has been introduced, called Master Items. This chapter will focus on understanding the concept of **master items (MI)**, how to work with them and how to deploy them within the scope of a Self-Service model. It will let you become proficient with the different types of MI and advise users how and when to use MI.

Chapter 5, *Qlik Sense on Cloud*, Qlik Sense is now also offered as a solution on the cloud. This is a novel concept of deploying business intelligence solutions, and this chapter will elaborate on this model and its difference from traditional local Qlik Sense deployments. After reading this chapter, you will understand the Qlik Sense Software as a Service model, know how to deploy a cloud-based solution, and understand when to use and when not to use cloud-based solutions.

Chapter 6, *Qlik Sense Data Modeling*, offers a description of how Qlik stores its data in-memory, and what implications it has on data modeling. The chapter will look at dimensional data modeling in detail, using best practices from Ralph Kimball in Qlik Sense, while also covering optimization exercises to reduce the RAM footprint and calculation time on the front-end. After reading this chapter, you will understand many of the available data modeling techniques and you will be able to create efficient and optimized data models for Qlik Sense apps.

Chapter 7, *Best Practice for Loading Data in Qlik Sense*, educates the user about various types of data loading concepts in Qlk Sense, the concept of an ETL approach and its importance, and how to implement it in Qlik Sense (both Desktop and Enterprise). You will be able to identify data sources, know how to organize data to facilitate the loading process, develop an ETL strategy for his project, and master loading techniques such as incremental or partial reloads.

Chapter 8, *Advanced Scripting*, covers various advanced ways to script and write sophisticated ETL code within Qlik Sense to facilitate all the data modeling and data loading techniques described in chapters 6 and 7. It will show you how to load data from sources in their most efficient way, transform tables in every possible way, and write useful and resilient code using control structures.

Chapter 9, *Advanced Expressions in Qlik Sense*, shows how to leverage Qlik Sense's powerful in-memory calculation engine while understanding all the concepts of its expressions. At the same time, these expressions always need to be implemented efficiently to avoid jeopardizing the user experience.

Chapter 10, *Overview of Qlik Sense APIs*, is about giving an extensive overview of what an API is, which APIs are available in Qlik Sense, and how to usually take advantage of technology with an API. It will familiarize you with all 19 APIs in Qlik Sense. You will understand the implications of an API and recognize use cases for the API. It will also cover Qlik's open source initiatives.

Chapter 11, *Working with the Qlik Dev Hub*, Qlik has its own user-friendly Qlik Sense development environment called Qlik Dev Hub. This chapter will describe the Qlik Sense development environment, how it is organized, and how to set it up for development. It will leave you with right know-how to utilize the dev hub and organize and govern the dev-hub work and modules.

Chapter 12, *Coding in Qlik Sense*, is for Qlik developers who have never had exposure to web development. It will describe all the languages and libraries used in Qlik, extension development, the reason JavaScript is used, and considerations when developing extensions or mashups for mobile. You will internalize the concept of web development and how HTML5 and JS code are read by the browser, understand the concepts of the most relevant JS libraries for Qlik, be able to read and write underlying code written in JavaScript, and debug web development code.

Chapter 13, *Creating Extensions in Qlik Sense*, demonstrates how to leverage the Extension API to build compelling visualizations using the D3.js library and control components using AngularJS. It will emphasize teaching how to write the code, best practices, and how to structure your extensions, including their property panel. Two step-by-step guides will help you internalize the steps required to build extensions for Qlik Sense, and you will be able to work with Qlik's Generic Objects such as the HyperCube for even more amazing projects.

Chapter 14, *Integrating QS in Websites via Mashups*, Mashups are probably the aspect of Qlik Sense with unlimited possibilities, and they allow the technology to tackle almost every requirement. While building mashups becomes web development predominantly, several aspects need to be considered when integrating Qlik objects. This chapter will teach you how to set up a Mashup project, connect to the Qlik engine, and import and embed Qlik Visualizations and Objects into applications sitting outside of Qlik Sense. You will learn how to develop basic mashup HTML pages, how to read the code in a mashup, how to deploy successful mashup projects, when to use mashups, and when not to.

To get the most out of this book

Mastering Qlik Sense is part of the Mastering series in Packt Publishing and requires you to have at least a basic understanding of Qlik Sense before working with this book. You should have either already deployed a couple of Qlik Sense apps or have worked extensively with QlikView before in case you are now looking to transition to Qlik Sense. If you are coming from a web development background, in an effort to better understand the world of Qlik Sense, some aspects of this book, with the exception of Module 3, might be too advanced for you too.

To make the most out of this book, although recommended, you don't necessarily read it from the beginning until the end, but you should feel encouraged to jump between Modules 1-3 and the chapters within them. The individual chapters, and especially modules, are written in such a way to be conclusive, meaning that they can be read individually, based on your interest. Cross-references between chapters are made to ensure you know where to continue your reading if you wish to deepen your knowledge.

To closely follow the practical examples and to make the most of the code snippets, please ensure you download the latest version of the Qlik Sense Desktop client from the official website which can be found here https://www.qlik.com/us/try-or-buy/download-qlik-sense.

For the coding parts, an advanced text editor is recommended for your use, such as sublime (https://www.sublimetext.com/) or notepad++ (https://notepad-plus-plus.org/). And please, if you can, do use Google Chrome!

Happy Qlik'ing!

Download the example code files

You can download the example code files for this book from your account at www.packtpub.com. If you purchased this book elsewhere, you can visit www.packtpub.com/support and register to have the files emailed directly to you.

You can download the code files by following these steps:

1. Log in or register at www.packtpub.com.
2. Select the **SUPPORT** tab.
3. Click on **Code Downloads & Errata**.
4. Enter the name of the book in the **Search** box and follow the onscreen instructions.

Once the file is downloaded, please make sure that you unzip or extract the folder using the latest version of:

- WinRAR/7-Zip for Windows
- Zipeg/iZip/UnRarX for Mac
- 7-Zip/PeaZip for Linux

The code bundle for the book is also hosted on GitHub at https://github.com/ PacktPublishing/Mastering-Qlik-Sense. In case there's an update to the code, it will be updated on the existing GitHub repository.

We also have other code bundles from our rich catalog of books and videos available at https://github.com/PacktPublishing/. Check them out!

Download the color images

We also provide a PDF file that has color images of the screenshots/diagrams used in this book. You can download it here: http://www.packtpub.com/sites/default/files/ downloads/MasteringQlikSense_ColorImages.pdf.

Conventions used

There are a number of text conventions used throughout this book.

`CodeInText`: Indicates code words in text, database table names, folder names, filenames, file extensions, pathnames, dummy URLs, user input, and Twitter handles. Here is an example: "The `<html>` element is the root element of an HTML page."

A block of code is set as follows:

```
<!DOCTYPE html>
<html>
<head>
<title>Mastering Qlik Sense Page Title</title>
</head>
```

When we wish to draw your attention to a particular part of a code block, the relevant lines or items are set in bold:

```
<title>Mastering Qlik Sense Page Title</title>
<link rel="stylesheet" href="/MasteringQlikSense.css">
</head>
```

Any command-line input or output is written as follows:

```
$ mkdir css
$ cd css
```

Bold: Indicates a new term, an important word, or words that you see onscreen. For example, words in menus or dialog boxes appear in the text like this. Here is an example: "Select **System info** from the **Administration** panel."

Warnings or important notes appear like this.

Tips and tricks appear like this.

Get in touch

Feedback from our readers is always welcome.

General feedback: Email feedback@packtpub.com and mention the book title in the subject of your message. If you have questions about any aspect of this book, please email us at questions@packtpub.com.

Errata: Although we have taken every care to ensure the accuracy of our content, mistakes do happen. If you have found a mistake in this book, we would be grateful if you would report this to us. Please visit www.packtpub.com/submit-errata, selecting your book, clicking on the Errata Submission Form link, and entering the details.

Piracy: If you come across any illegal copies of our works in any form on the Internet, we would be grateful if you would provide us with the location address or website name. Please contact us at copyright@packtpub.com with a link to the material.

If you are interested in becoming an author: If there is a topic that you have expertise in and you are interested in either writing or contributing to a book, please visit authors.packtpub.com.

Reviews

Please leave a review. Once you have read and used this book, why not leave a review on the site that you purchased it from? Potential readers can then see and use your unbiased opinion to make purchase decisions, we at Packt can understand what you think about our products, and our authors can see your feedback on their book. Thank you!

For more information about Packt, please visit packtpub.com.

1
Qlik Sense Self-Service Model

Considering this book is called *Mastering Qlik Sense*, you have probably already been exposed to Qlik Sense and are familiar with its capabilities and functionalities. While you probably have experience on how to install the tool on a small scale, you ask yourself whether Qlik Sense is viable to be deployed on an enterprise level. This book takes the next step with you and will show and teach you how to take Qlik Sense to the next level. What needs to be considered to successfully deploy to enterprises? In order to answer that question, firstly the newly introduced self-service approach within the **business intelligence (BI)** world needs to be analyzed.

Self-service BI, abbreviated as **SS BI** throughout this chapter, is a new approach to data analytics in which users get access to the IT platform to load their data and create their own data-driven analytic reports. This model differs significantly from how traditional BI tools are deployed.

Qlik has recognized the need for self-service in the market and has decided to develop a wholly new product called **Qlik Sense**, which is also the main topic of this book. This chapter aims to take a step back from focusing on the new technology and educate and inform the reader about the new self-service approach that Qlik Sense is taking.

We will begin this chapter with a discussion on the historical background of Qlik Sense as narrated by Qlik itself (yes, the company itself!). The **self-service model** will be introduced with its key four focus points. A small excursion will be taken to the so-called **IKEA effect** and why it is relevant to Qlik Sense. With the self-service model, different user types within this space emerge, which will be described and summarized. This will allow the reader to not only identify those user types but also approach them appropriately.

To ensure the business and the organization are best advised on Qlik Sense and self-service BI, a list of benefits and challenges will be described. They will help assess whether Qlik Sense is fit for purpose in the examined use case and what can be done to mitigate the risks in order to make self-service BI a success within the organization.

Last but not least, the reader will be equipped with lots of recommendations on how to best champion Qlik Sense, all coming from the distilled professional experience of the authors deploying the same in large-scale organizations.

The goal of this chapter is for the reader to be able to understand the dynamics of self-service, how to correctly leverage them with Qlik Sense to identify good use cases for using the technology, and advising the business on how and why to invest in self-service BI.

The chapter is structured into the following sections:

- A review of Qlik Sense
- The self-service model
- The IKEA effect
- User types in self-service
- Benefits and challenges of self-service
- Recommendations on deploying self-service with Qlik Sense

A review of Qlik Sense

With the release of Qlik Sense, QlikTech decided to address a new trend in BI – the emergence of self-service BI and the need for business users to become more self-reliant. Business users wish to be in more control and get faster access to BI and their business data.

Based on their Qlik associative analytics engine, which successfully promoted the ability for data discovery in QlikView, Qlik decided to reinvent itself by building a next-generation BI tool which addressed five themes to capture the new trend:

- **Gorgeous and genius**: Within the theme, Qlik focused on making QS as slick and visually beautiful as possible, enabling the user to leverage the full power of the associative engine model and allowing for a *seamless experience across all devices*.

- **Mobility with agility**: Moving away from a local installed client, Qlik Sense is 100 percent web-based and therefore can be accessed by any device that supports web browsers. The same applies to the enterprise platform, which with the release of Qlik Sense Cloud will ensure the whole environment will be hosted outside of your users' premises, making it *accessible at all times* from anywhere in the world.

- **Compulsive collaboration**: With the focus on collaboration, new ways of consuming data can be explored if users have real-time capabilities to *either modify or enrich existing reports or easily share insights with each other* by sharing bookmarks or stories of their data.

- **The premier platform**: Short development and deployment time to market – the platform *focuses on simplifying and speeding up the SS BI supply chain* from data access to development, with access through broadened API under one unified platform interface.

- **Enabling new enterprise**: By unifying the whole platform, Qlik is offering its capabilities, including security, reliability, and scalability, not only for large enterprises but also for smaller companies. With their Qlik cloud offering, they aim to even *increase the flexibility* to address a new market: small companies or teams which do not have the resources or the time to invest in an infrastructure before deploying Qlik Sense.

Addressing the five themes earlier was not possible by releasing a new version of QlikView. Qlik had to disrupt itself and create a wholly new product almost from scratch, retaining their market-leading in-memory calculation engine and their expertise and vision around data discovery and business intelligence.

Qlik Sense is fundamentally different from QlikView in its approach to BI and the development process, as well as the user experience. What stays the same is the security model called section access, Qlik's associative engine (the driver of data discovery) and most of the front end expressions to aggregate your data, including set analysis. However, the whole approach to developing apps and dashboards is different as all of a sudden the user becomes an integral part of the process. Qlik Sense's easy-to-use approach gives them capabilities to significantly contribute to their own content even to the extent that all of the development can be done by them. This will be elaborated in Chapter 2, *Transitioning from QlikView to Qlik Sense*; however, it is important to understand Qlik Sense is not an evolution of QlikView, but a whole new concept on how to offer BI and data insights to the business.

The most common fallacy among Qlik customers is to believe an existing QlikView environment can simply be migrated to Qlik Sense, leveraging its new technology and implementing new cutting-edge visualizations. This is not the case, as guided analytics dashboards, a dominant development concept in QlikView, are not directly supported in Qlik Sense in the same way. For those who are not familiar with QlikView, its *guided analytics* aspect takes the user on a pre-canned journey through the dashboard with sometimes restricted views and constrained ways to interact and explore the data, hence *guided*.

While it is not impossible to implement something similar to the API using the approach of mashups and advanced extensions, this would require IT and the user to enter the world of web development, which is the absolute opposite of a business-friendly self-service environment. In there, possibilities are unlimited; however, new skills are required and the very value-add of sped-up dashboard development that QlikView provides gets lost in Qlik Sense when it comes to guided analytics dashboards. On the other hand, building simple visualizations is much easier in Qlik Sense, supported by the sheet canvas, the drag and drop functionality, and the suggestive dimensions and measure which is all hosted on the web, requiring no installation on the client side other than access to the platform. Also, the data loading process has been significantly simplified by offering a huge variety of connectors and user-friendly data processing interfaces.

 Understanding the strengths and weaknesses of Qlik Sense, and how to best approach them and leverage the technology within the organization, is the goal of this book. For this understanding, the concept of the self-service BI model is key in order to also understand the Qlik Sense platform.

The next section will focus on explaining the self-service BI model in Qlik Sense, its advantages, and disadvantages, as well as classic user types and working models, finishing with some considerations and recommendations on how to best deploy self-service within your organization.

The Self-Service model

Transforming data with intelligence (TDWI), an organization providing educational research material on data and BI, did extensive work in 2011 in researching and describing the dynamics of the newly emerging phenomenon of self-service BI. This is how its published report describes it:

> *Self-service BI is defined as the facilities within the BI environment that enable BI users to be more self-reliant and less dependent on the IT organization.*

Self-reliance and reduced dependency are key here, as a shift from the classic BI model is evident, where the responsibilities of developing data analytics dashboards move away from IT and closer to the business. And this makes sense as the business itself is the body within the organization that best understands how to extract value from its own data and what insights it hopes to get out of its analytics. Also, by being able to modify BI dashboards themselves, not only can users personalize their own reports but time to market is reduced significantly.

TDWI identifies four key objectives self-service BI focuses on:

- **Simpler and customizable end-user interfaces**: Communicating data in an effective way to get the insight across efficiently is key and arguably the most important objective of self-service BI. Compelling visualizations, uncomplicated dashboards, and clear presentation of data are paramount for any BI tool. Qlik Sense does exactly that and takes the user experience to another level by leveraging its associative engine and allowing the user to explore the data in their own way through filtering and truly embracing data discovery.

- **Easy access to source data**: The best analytics solution or platform will not be of any use if the user can't access the data. A big difference to traditional BI tools, though, is that not all data needs to be stored in one database in order to be consumed. Qlik Sense allows users to easily connect to various data sources using drag and drop as well as following user-friendly load wizards. Qlik's acquisition of QVSource in 2016, a third-party tool which has a collection of data connectors to plenty of platforms, underlines the importance of being able to connect data from disparate sources into one dashboard for reporting and analysis purposes. Also, by opening up the sourcing of data, new reports and dashboards can be built, which may not have been possible with an earlier architecture of technologies. Think of combining data from different departments, linking them by cost center, and being able to draw new insights of how costs are directly associated with revenue. All in all, being able to easily connect to its own data, the business can build its own bespoke reports, to its own requirements, and at its own pace:

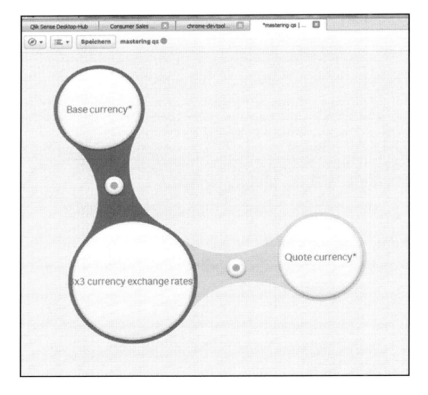

An example of a combination of different data

- **Easy-to-use BI tools**: Similar to the first point, this one focuses on the simplicity of building these dashboards. Even if it is expected that the business upskills itself to become more IT-savvy, self-service BI tools will only be adapted to the organization if they are easy to use for the layman. Hence, Qlik has focused a lot on developing a very user-friendly interface in Qlik Sense, which allows the user to create their own dashboards simply by dragging and dropping certain items to a canvas, rearranging them to their own liking, and selecting the dimensions and measures they wish to analyze. Qlik Sense is incredibly easy to use for simple analytics, with sophisticated data load and processing editors on the back end too. The capturing of this objective is best demonstrated with Qlik's release of the visual management of data associations, the so-called **data load bubbles** depicted in the diagram that precedes this bulleted list. It allows the user to create connections between different tables, creating a logical link based on the suggested key, which will then associate on the front end when filtering.

- **Quick-to-deploy and easy-to-manage architecture:** Albeit very technical, self-service BI should be as easy on the back end as it is on the front end. As will be discussed in later chapters, the management of the Qlik Sense environment has been simplified a lot, the same as the licensing model and many other things in the back end. This is done to support a fast release cycle and deployment to business users, decreasing the time to market of new apps and enabling IT and users to work in an agile way iteratively, without time-consuming release processes. The same principles have been applied to the deployment of the whole architecture: Qlik Sense is fairly easy to scale horizontally across multiple nodes if the user base increases. Installation of the technology is also well supported in cloud platforms such as Amazon Web Services, Microsoft Azure, or Google Cloud. The simplicity on the back end makes it very attractive too for the IT department to deploy self-service BI without massive training, making the technology much more cost-effective.

The relationship between those four key objectives is depicted in the following diagram:

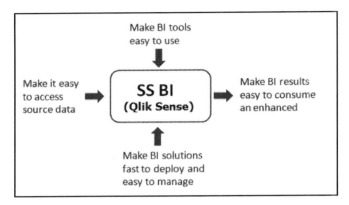

The ecosystem of self-service BI shows that there are four interdependent areas where its principles need to apply to aggregate to one successful solution. While it is the front end that is predominantly being advertised, all other aspects are equally important and need to be taken into account when taking the whole into consideration.

The freedom that comes with self-service BI, though, stands in strong opposition to IT governance principles: standards, data quality, consistency of terms and definitions, and consistency of look and feel. IT departments often resist allowing the business user to venture into the data analytics world all by themselves, believing this will lead to data anarchy and loss of control and governance over the BI environment.

 The phrase **developing in production** is unheard of, yet this is exactly what self-service BI, and Qlik Sense, is trying to postulate, which can add increased value to the organization and reduce the costs of IT. The biggest hurdle in embracing a self-service environment in large organizations is cultural as BI becomes more dynamic.

For it to be successful, a strict framework needs to be introduced to successfully deploy Qlik Sense. The key there, however, will be to introduce governance which is user-enabling and not an IT dictatorship. IT governance in Qlik Sense without impairing the users will be at the forefront of this book.

The IKEA effect

 The IKEA effect is a cognitive bias which refers to the tendency for people to value things they create themselves as qualitatively higher than identical things created by someone else.

The name IKEA derives from the Swedish furniture manufacturer and relates to their business model that allows the consumer to compile and build their furniture themselves at home, based on instructions. A working paper by Harvard Business School points out that traditional economic thinking would suggest a consumer or customer would subtract their own labor from the overall final cost of the product. In fact, the opposite effect can readily be observed and the perceived value of the product is increased the more individual labor is put into it, suggesting there is *love* in our own labor.

This relates well to a similar story about cakes. Since 1931, Betty Crocker had been espousing speed and ease in the kitchen to facilitate the life of women living in the city. Part of that was to also invent the famous cake mixture which allowed a person to promptly bake a fresh cake themselves by adding a couple of ingredients. Having to go to the bakery or confectionery to buy a cake was too simple and certainly did not impress the dinner guests. The initial cake mixture required the customer to only add water to the mix and put it in the oven. Betty Crocker struggled to get traction with their new product, even though it ticked off all the economic boxes. It was self-made, could be baked on demand, was very easy, and little could go wrong. Experimenting with variations, Betty Crocker eventually discovered that taking away the milk and the eggs from the mix, effectively asking the customers to put more effort into the baking, made the product a hit. This is where they discovered that people wanted to put their own personal touch to the cake they baked, effectively *increasing the home-made* authenticity of what they made.

This story shows two things where a clear link can be drawn between cake mixture and self-service BI:

- Firstly, there is also the presence of a cognitive bias in self-service BI, which allows the user to perceive their own reports they build as being qualitatively higher than they are in reality. This bias is a powerful aspect of successful adoption and plays a significant role in promoting self-service BI within the organization. Users will be keener to sell and promote the analytics work they create and will naturally be keen to share all insights they discover. This can eventually lead to having the self-service BI tool promoting itself, almost going viral.

- Secondly, the approach Betty Crocker eventually took is not just designing for ease and speed but focusing on designing an entire user experience. This is important in self-service BI as the architect or developer should not only focus on delivering results but put equal focus on the fashion in which the results and insights are delivered to the end user.

The fact is that with self-service BI and the close involvement of the end user in the development process, new psychological dynamics are introduced to the classic IT development process which need to be taken into account. It also reiterates the importance of forgetting some best practices in IT development in order be able to harness the new possibilities and the new approach to data analytics which come with self-service BI.

User types in self-service

With the introduction of self-service to BI, there is a segmentation of various levels and breaths on how self-service is conducted and to what extent. There are, quite frankly, different user types that differ from each other in level of interest, technical expertise, and the way in which they consume the data. While each user will almost be unique in the way they use self-service, the user base can be divided into four different groups:

- **Power Users or Data Champions**: Power users are the most tech-savvy business users, who show a great interest in self-service BI. They produce and build dashboards themselves and know how to load data and process it to create a logical data model. They tend to be self-learning and carry a hybrid set of skills, usually a mixture of business knowledge and some advanced technical skills. This user group is often frustrated with existing reporting or BI solutions and finds IT inadequate in delivering the same. As a result, especially in the past, they take away data dumps from IT solutions and create their own dashboards in Excel, using advanced skills such as **VBA, Visual Basic for Applications**. They generally like to participate in the development process but have been unable to do so due to governance rules and a strict old-school separation of IT from the business. Self-service BI is addressing this group in particular, and identifying those users is key in reaching adoption within an organization. Within an established self-service environment, power users generally participate in committees revolving around the technical environments and represent the business interest. They also develop the bulk of the first versions of the apps, which, as part of a naturally evolving process, are then handed over to more experienced IT for them to be polished and optimized. Power users advocate the self-service BI technology and often not only demo the insights and information they achieved to extract from their data, but also the efficiency and timeliness of doing so. At the same time, they also serve as the first point of contact for other users and consumers when it comes to questions about their apps and dashboards. Sometimes they also participate in a technical advisory capacity on whether other projects are feasible to be implemented using the same technology. Within a self-service BI environment, it is safe to say that those power users are the pillars of a successful adoption.

- **Business Users or Data Visualizers**: Users are frequent users of data analytics, with the main goal to extract value from the data they are presented with. They represent the group of the user base which is interested in conducting data analysis and data discovery to better understand their business in order to make better-informed decisions. Presentation and ease of use of the application are key to this type of user group and they are less interested in building new analytics themselves. That being said, some form of creating new charts and loading data is sometimes still of interest to them, albeit on a very basic level. **Timeliness**, the relevance of data, and the user experience are most relevant to them. They are the ones who are slicing and dicing the data and drilling down into dimensions, and who are keen to click around in the app to obtain valuable information. Usually, a group of users belong to the same department and have a power user overseeing them with regard to questions but also in receiving feedback on how the dashboard can be improved even more. Their interaction with IT is mostly limited to requesting access and resolving unexpected technical errors.

- **Consumers or Data Readers**: Consumers usually form the largest user group of a self-service BI analytics solution. They are the end recipients of the insights and data analytics that have been produced and, normally, are only interested in distilled information which is presented to them in a digested form. They are usually the kind of users who are happy with a report, either digital or in printed form, which summarizes highlights and lowlights in a few pages, requiring no interaction at all. Also, they are most sensitive to the timeliness and availability of their reports. While usually the largest audience, at the same time this user group leverages the self-service capabilities of a BI tool the least. This poses a licensing challenge, as those users don't take full advantage of the functionality on offer, but are costing the full amount in order to access the reports. It is therefore not uncommon to assign this type of user group a bucket of login access passes or not give them access to the self-service BI platform at all and give them the information they need in (digitally) printed format or within presentations, prepared by users.

- **IT or Data Overseers**: IT represents the technical user group within this context, who sit in the background and develop and manage the framework within which the self-service BI solution operates. They are the backbone of the deployment and ensure the environment is set up correctly to cater for the various use cases required by the above-described user groups. At the same time, they ensure a security policy is in place and maintained and they introduce a governance framework for deployment, data quality, and best practices. They are in effect responsible for overseeing the power users and helping them with technical questions, but at the same time ensuring terms and definition as well as the look and feel is consistent and maintained across all apps. With self-service BI, IT plays a lesser role in actually developing the dashboards but assumes a more mentoring position, where training, consultation, and advisory in best practices are conducted. While working closely with power users, IT also provides technical support to users and liaises with the IT infrastructure to ensure the server infrastructure is fit for purpose and up and running to serve the users. This also includes upgrading the platform where required and enriching it with additional functionality if and when available.

The previous four groups can be distinguished within a typical enterprise environment; however, this is not to say hybrid or fewer user groups are not viable models for self-service BI. It is an evolutionary process in how an organization adapts self-service data analytics with a lot of dependencies on available skills, competing established solutions, culture, and appetite on new technologies. It usually begins with IT being the first users in a newly deployed self-service environment, not only setting up the infrastructure but also developing the first apps for a couple of consumers. Power users then follow up; generally, they are the business sponsors themselves who are often big fans of data analytics, modifying the app to their liking and promoting it to their users. The user base emerges with the success of the solution, where analytics are integrated into their business as the usual process. The last group, the consumers, is mostly the last type of user group that is established, which more often than not doesn't have actual access to the platform itself, but rather receives printouts, email summaries with screenshots, or PowerPoint presentations. Due to licensing cost and the size of the consumer audience, it is not always easy to give them access to the self-service platform; hence, most of the time, an automated and streamlined PDF printing process is the most elegant solution to cater for this type of user group.

At the same time, the size of the deployment also determines the number of various user groups. In small enterprise environments, it will be mostly power users and IT who will be using self-service. This greatly simplifies the approach as well as the setup considerations.

Benefits and challenges of self-service

Knowing the advantages and disadvantages of self-service BI is fundamental to its success within the organization. It is important when you plan to introduce self-service BI and prepare a business case to assess whether it actually achieves what you hope it will. Also, organizational blockers can be recognized in time to prevent them having an adverse effect on the environment. Disadvantages are good to know because they will add credibility to the tool if you establish beforehand what it's supposed to be used for. If users only expected printed PDF files en masse, Qlik Sense might end up becoming an inadequate tool and far too expensive, disappointing stakeholders and users.

Benefits

There are several online blogs and articles discussing the benefits and challenges of self-service BI and more of them are expected to be released after publication of this book. This section will summarize the most relevant benefits which are applicable to Qlik Sense. The order of points is arbitrary and, to some extent, they reiterate content that has already been elaborated in this chapter:

- **Empowering users**: Users become self-reliant and empowered by the ability to create business intelligence apps all by themselves with little to no help from IT. They know best what they want to see and extract from their data. Self-service BI allows them to build their own personalized analytics, to their own requirements, at their own pace.
- **The speed of development**: If a proper framework is in place with setup access to various data sources and a controlled environment where publication of new and enriched apps is streamlined and automated, app development and the subsequent delivery of new insights can be significantly sped up. This not only delivers results and information in a timely fashion but also allows for a more agile and iterative approach to developing analytics with a short feedback cycle.
- **The IKEA effect**: The cognitive bias described earlier in this chapter lets users perceive the apps in which they had significant input as being much more valuable. While biased, this greatly encourages users to get involved and promotes the adoption of data analytics within the organization. As most organizations are investing to become digital and more data-driven, the adaptation of data analytics is an integral part of it and the IKEA effect certainly helps.

- **Relieving IT**: As organizations become more data-driven, the pressure on IT to deliver faster becomes evident. With applications deployed and used by the business, an inconvenient overhead emerges to support these applications, which prevents IT from doing any further development of new ideas and data sources. This bottleneck not only puts pressure on IT but also frustrates the business, which has to wait longer for the realization of its projects. With self-service BI, power users from the business can become an integral part of the development, relieving the pressure on IT. This frees them to think about more strategically and technically challenging tasks and focus on value-added development for the company rather than just *keeping the lights on.*

- **Becoming proactive rather than reactive**: By having the data readily available, and with the possibility of creating new analytics being easy, the business can start becoming more proactive in its culture. Rather than receiving reports, agreeing on actions, and getting a feedback report within the next cycles to confirm whether its strategy was the right one, the business can become more data-driven and not only receive a faster feedback but also spend more time investigating the data to make better-informed decisions. While this sounds like a sound generic benefit, it is only with self-service BI that this becomes possible in its most efficient way.

- **Reduced technology costs**: It is possible to cut down on technology costs on various ends by deploying self-service BI. For example, by reducing the involvement of IT and handing over the bulk of the development to the business user, it is not necessary to spend as much money on getting consultants on board for development purposes as with traditional BI tools. At the same time, self-service BI (with its ease of use) allows for an increased speed of development and subsequent decreased time to market, which also reduces the costs associated with deploying the technology. Lastly, due to the speed of development and the possibility of integrating agile project management with lots of iteration, as well as involving the business end user into the process, self-service BI projects can have a much higher success rate, which also effectively brings down the overall technology costs within the organization.

- **Mobile**: This is possible and a novelty. If Qlik Sense is set up correctly and the user has had some basic training, it is possible to create analytics and basic dashboards on mobile devices such as the iPad. Qlik Sense's ease to use and capability to create compelling dashboards allows for a pioneering way to develop on the go, something which has rarely been possible so far and only in a limited capacity.

Challenges and risks

Following are the challenges and risks that are involved:

- **Data Literacy:** Just as literacy is the ability to derive meaning from the written word, data literacy is the ability to derive meaning from data. In more technical terms, data literacy can be referred to as the ability to "consume for knowledge, produce coherently and think critically about data." Qlik Sense has put significant effort into making the new self-service BI technology as simple to use for the business end user as possible. Dragging and dropping functionality is omnipresent, limiting the use of keyboards required as well as the necessity of writing of code at all. While this works for very basic and simple solutions, there is no way around having to upskill in basic concepts of data modeling, data aggregation, and data presentation within Qlik Sense, or for that matter any other self-service BI tool. Qlik Sense, in particular, has a very powerful associative in-memory calculation engine, which, however, requires the data model to be set up correctly, with underlying tables linking or the right keys, for the front end to aggregate the numbers correctly. At the same time, summing, averaging, or obtaining the max or min value is easy but writing more sophisticated aggregations, for example, based on dates, deltas, or totals, requires training in set analysis. Data modeling techniques very quickly become relevant if the user wishes to load more than two or three data sources. For the user or power user, as a matter of fact, to create more than basic dashboards, the organization needs to invest in training.

- **Data quality**: Qlik Sense boasts about its capabilities to bring together various data sources into one dashboard in a user-friendly way. While powerful, it presumes the data loaded into Qlik Sense is of the highest quality, has been validated, and is coherent, and excludes the possibility of invalid combinations of the data models. This assumes the perfect scenario where the user picks various data tables like in a shop and can immediately derive insights from what has been loaded. While hypothetically possible, if the organization started using Qlik Sense since its inception, it is quite frankly unrealistic. There are disparate systems producing data, different teams have a diverse understanding of the same business and dissimilar ways of capturing meaningful and correct data across the organization. Bringing it together into one place without any validation process creates a mess and chaos which will not produce any meaningful analytics. If a proper data governance, ideally within a data warehouse, is not in place, self-service BI will not work, and will at best only be loading one data source at a time, diminishing the value-return of the technology investment.

This risk, however, is an ongoing problem of poor data management within organizations and not specifically related to Qlik Sense; Qlik Sense only brings this issue to the surface. To mitigate this risk, there needs to be an organizational layer between data within the organization and the data available for Qlik Sense to control, validate, and clean the data made available for self-service BI.

- **A constant struggle for governance**: Qlik Sense promotes empowering the user to create their very own data analytics with little to no limits. With no limits also comes no control, which is a source of chaos and frustration not only with IT but also with the users of self-service BI. Governance is required for two reasons:
    - Firstly, IT needs to guarantee that the user, while building their own dashboards, is in no position to break the system for everybody else who is using it. The bulletproof solution would be to limit the user from doing anything but this would defeat the purpose of self-service BI and diminish the value of Qlik Sense. This introduces a constant struggle between freedom and value versus control, which not only raises a lot of discussions but can initiate conflict or tension within the departments in an organization. There are a couple of areas of middle ground in this issue which will be presented in later chapters, but getting to that point will require educating both sides of the fence.
    - Secondly, with limited governance, there is a lack of testing and validation of the reports produced by the users. Using different aggregation logic and terminologies, or simply making errors, Qlik Sense is error-prone and it is dangerous if a dashboard is distributed to a wide audience, who then possibly use the results and insight to support their decisions and actions. By misrepresenting information, it is possible for a BI tool to do more damage to an organization than it could ever bring in value. Users need to be critical thinkers and now even more so. This is especially applicable to self-service BI where looser governance is required. To provide you with a suitable analogy by Karl Pover, it's like going from reading news from a few, established news organizations to reading news from your social media feed.

- **Basic dashboards and data analytics**: Whether or not this is a challenge depends on how the organization is looking to utilize Qlik Sense. Qlik Sense predominantly produces very basic dashboards with uncomplicated aggregations where a simple idea can be presented and analyzed. Doing more sophisticated analysis, even to the extent of bringing in machine learning elements, requires either training, hiring a specialist resource, or integration with external systems. This then takes self-service BI back to becoming normal BI, where the users are not able to do these things themselves. The same applies to Qlik Sense's advertised unlimited possibilities with the QS API, where compelling and super amazing mashups can be created. But this is not self-service, this is old-school web development, which not only requires a specific set of skills but also has a longer time to market and a more complicated development process.

- **Inconsistent design principles and terminology**: If everyone is able to build their own reports and dashboards in Qlik Sense, it is not unreasonable to suggest that everyone will design their apps to their own liking and style as well as use their own terminology in describing business insights. This possible inconsistency can be annoying to users and makes it difficult promote the brand of data analytics within the organization. Inconsistencies, especially in terminology, can also lead to misunderstandings. To overcome this risk, a design principle and terminology framework need to be in place and monitored by IT.

Recommendations on deploying self-service with Qlik Sense

 Whether or not Qlik Sense will be a success in the organization is not only a matter of its capability and the collection of its functionalities. Assessing its fitness for purpose goes beyond just ticking a list of boxes saying *Is this possible in Qlik Sense, yes or no?*

This section summarizes various recommendations which have been captured and collected by the authors in the course of their deployments.

As part of a successful deployment of Qlik Sense, it is important IT recognizes self-service BI has its own dynamics and adoption rules—the various use cases and subsequent user groups need to be assessed and captured. For a strong adoption of the tool, IT needs to prepare the environment and identify the key power users in the organization and win them over to using the technology. It is important they are intensively supported, especially in the beginning, and they are allowed to drive how the technology should be used rather than having principles imposed on them. Governance should always be present but power users should never get the feeling they are restricted by it. Because once they are won over, the rest of the traction and the adoption of other user types is very easy.

Here are a few of the important points on deploying self-service with Qlik Sense:

- **Qlik Sense is not QlikView**: Not even nearly. The biggest challenge and fallacy is that the organization was sold, by Qlik or someone else, just the next version of the tool. It did not help at all that Qlik itself was working for years on Qlik Sense under the initial product name `Qlik.Next`. Whatever you are being told, however, it is being sold to you, Qlik Sense is at best the cousin of QlikView. Same family, but no blood relation. Thinking otherwise sets the wrong expectation so the business gives the wrong message to stakeholders and does not raise awareness to IT that self-service BI cannot be deployed in the same fashion as guided analytics, QlikView in this case. Disappointment is imminent when stakeholders realize Qlik Sense cannot replicate their QlikView dashboards.
- **Don't assume that simply installing Qlik Sense creates a self-service BI environment**: Installing Qlik Sense and giving users access to the tool is a start but there is more to it than simply installing it. The infrastructure requires design and planning, data quality processing, data collection, and determining who intends to use the platform to consume what type of data. If data is not available and accessible to the user, data analytics serve no purpose. Make sure a data warehouse or similar is in place and the business has a use case for self-service data analytics. A good indicator for this is when the business or project works with a lot of data, and there are business users who have lots of Excel spreadsheets lying around analyzing it in different ways. That's your best case candidate for Qlik Sense.

- **IT needs to take a step back and monitor the Qlik Sense environment rather than controlling it**: IT needs to unlearn to learn new things and the same applies when it comes to deploying self-service. Create a framework with guidelines and principles and monitor that users are following it, rather than limiting them in their capabilities. This framework needs to have the input of the users as well and to be elastic. Also, not many IT professionals agree with giving away too much power to the user in the development process, believing this leads to chaos and anarchy. While the risk is there, this fear needs to be overcome. Users love data analytics, and they are keen to get the help of IT to create the most valuable dashboard possible and ensure it will be well received by a wide audience.

- **Identify the key users and user groups**: For a strong adoption of the tool, IT needs to prepare the environment and identify the key power users in the organization and to win them over to using the technology. It is important they are intensively supported, especially in the beginning, and they are allowed to drive how the technology should be used rather than having principles imposed on them. Governance should always be present but power users should never get the feeling they are restricted by it. Because once they are won over, the rest of the traction and the adoption of other user types are very easy.

- **Qlik Sense sells well–do a lot of demos**: Data analytics, compelling visualizations, and the interactivity of Qlik Sense is something almost everyone is interested in. The business wants to see its own data aggregated and distilled in a cool and glossy dashboard. Utilize the momentum and do as many demos as you can to win advocates of the technology and promote a consciousness of becoming a data-driven culture in the organization. Even the simplest Qlik Sense dashboards amaze people and boost their creativity for use cases where data analytics in their area could apply and create value.

- **Promote collaboration**: Sharing is caring. This not only applies to insights, which naturally are shared with the excitement of having found out something new and valuable, but also to how the new insight has been derived. People keep their secrets on the approach and methodology to themselves, but this is counterproductive. It is important that applications, visualizations, and dashboards created with Qlik Sense are shared and demonstrated to other Qlik Sense users as frequently as possible. This not only promotes a data-driven culture but also encourages the collaboration of users and teams across various business functions, which would not have happened otherwise. They could either be sharing knowledge, tips, and tricks or even realizing they look at the same slices of data and could create additional value by connecting them together.

- **Market the successes of Qlik Sense within the organization**: If Qlik Sense has had a successful achievement in a project, tell others about it. Create a success story and propose doing demos of the dashboard and its analytics. IT has been historically very bad in promoting their work, which is counterproductive. Data analytics creates value and there is nothing embarrassing about boasting about its success; as Muhammad Ali suggested, *it's not bragging if it's true.*

- **Introduce guidelines on design and terminology**: Avoiding the pitfalls of having multiple different-looking dashboards by promoting a consistent branding look across all Qlik Sense dashboards and applications, including terminology and best practices. Ensure the document is easily accessible to all users. Also, create predesigned templates with some sample sheets so the users duplicate them and modify them to their liking and extend them, applying the same design.

- **Protect less experienced users from complexities**: Don't overwhelm users if they have never developed in their life. Approach less technically savvy users in a different way by providing them with sample data and sample templates, including a library of predefined visualizations, dimensions, or measures (so-called Master Key Items). Be aware that what is intuitive to Qlik professionals or power users is not necessarily intuitive to other users – be patient and appreciative of their feedback, and try to understand how a typical business user might think.

Summary

Qlik struck a new path with the development of a new product called Qlik Sense. Unlike QlikView, the new technology focuses on bringing self-service BI capabilities to business users, empowering them to create their very own data analytics, to their requirements, at their own pace. The self-service BI model differs significantly from traditional BI tools in the way that it incorporates the end user into the development process and, as such, needs to be approached in its own way.

The self-service model has its own goals, aims, and dynamics. Its four main focus points are simple and customizable end-user interfaces, easy access to source data, easy-to-use BI tools, and quick-to-deploy and easy-to-manage architecture. It sets up a business-friendly environment where the users themselves enjoy the freedom of doing development in their own way. While self-service offers lots of functionality, not all users are either able or willing to leverage all of it.

Some users have a high interest in self-service while others are more interested in getting an answer in a digested and timely fashion. The different user groups can be summarized and ordered by level of sophistication into IT, power users, users, and consumers. Identifying those groups plays an important aspect in designing the architecture for a self-service environment with Qlik Sense. Especially power users are not only the most active users but they also need to be won over as advocates for the technology: they build the dashboards and promote them and the technology to the business without much input from IT. This can make Qlik Sense as a BI solution very cost-effective. This, sped-up development time, empowerment of users, the IKEA effect, and mobile capabilities are all great benefits of Qlik Sense which allow organizations to become more data-driven to be able to make better, timely, and informed decisions for their business. The challenges and risks are predominantly the lack of governance that comes along with the self-service aspect of Qlik Sense, including the required investment into training, and also that, while easy to install, reliable data sources need to be in place in order to extract the most value from Qlik Sense.

Without meaningful data, data analytics will not be much of a value-add to the business. It is, therefore, important to take into account various organizational considerations before deciding to deploy Qlik Sense. Recommendations are summarized in this chapter, with the top three being: don't assume Qlik Sense can be deployed in the same way as QlikView; introduce governance but not a governance dictatorship, and promote collaboration to create a data-driven culture with advocates of Qlik Sense.

2

Transitioning from QlikView to Qlik Sense

If you are reading this book, it is very likely that you have heard of or worked with QlikView before. You will likely be an expert in manipulating data in the load script and juggling with set analysis to perfect expressions to give you the result you wish to see in a visualization or dashboard. But since Qlik Sense has come along, how different is it to the skill set you have in QlikView and how much of that can you transition to the new technology? From a technology point of view, Qlik Sense, being web-based and predominantly run under HTML 5 and JavaScript as opposed to the .NET framework, is still the same sauce you are cooking with. The great Qlik engine has remained almost identical, to the extent that you can blindly take over loading scripts or expressions as they are from QlikView applications.

This chapter will take you through the journey from being a QlikView developer to becoming a Qlik Sense developer. In brief, it will cover the following topics:

- Typical journey from QlikView to Qlik Sense
- The different approaches to projects
- The differences in the loading script
- The differences in the frontend
- Which new skill sets are required to transition to Qlik Sense
- Qlik Sense on mobile

Journey from QlikView to Qlik Sense

What has changed from a developer's point of view?

The following chart summarizes the developer's Qlik Sense journey over the duration of one year, coming from a pure QlikView environment with limited knowledge of JavaScript or web development:

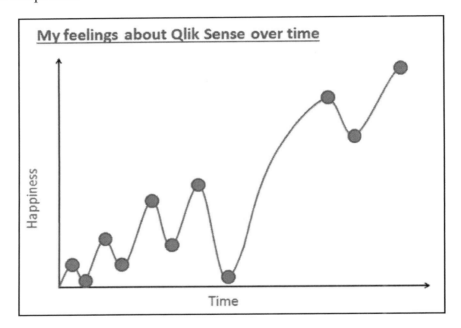

1. **Lasso experience**: Coming from a QlikView background, the very first time you saw Qlik Sense in action was probably when you were exposed to a lot of new features on how data can be visualized in Qlik, using web technologies, JavaScript, and HTML. It looks sexy, sure, but the thing that impressed you the most would have probably been the lasso functionality on the Scatter Chart, which allows you to select your values on the canvas cowboy style by dragging a lasso with your mouse, as depicted in the following image:

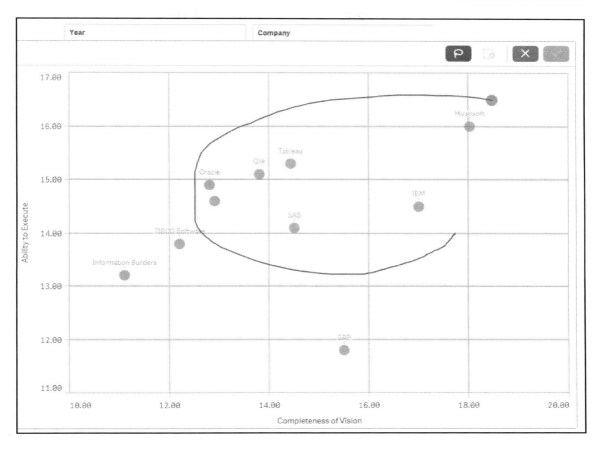

Scatter graph consisting of the lasso functionality

This, among other features, definitely shows the different kind of world Qlik Sense occupies as opposed to QlikView, and how entirely new ways of interactivity can be implemented. As a seasoned QlikView expert, this brief overview of Qlik Sense should have piqued your curiosity to explore the latest technology to bring you to the next step.

2. **First Dive**: You have seen Qlik Sense in action, and now you want to explore its capabilities on your own. The initial step to creating any dashboard is to load data onto the application. This will give you a reason to explore the edit script in Qlik Sense, rather than the loading wizards and, there, for the first time, you will experience something so familiar to you yet it feels and looks so different. While most elements of the load script are identical to QlikView, scripting on a web browser just seems alien to you and somewhat backward.

The edit script is only one of many other familiar elements in Qlik Sense that will require you to adapt, including the Expression Editor, Data Model Viewer, and its new way of organizing apps into streams.

3. **Viz-bang**: Everything new will eventually require you to adapt and to learn new things. After spending some time getting up to speed with Qlik Sense, you will now have come to grips with its basic concepts, and the disturbing fact that you will always have to have your browser open and that everything feels a bit laggy when developing. However, your first dashboards and Qlik Sense application, albeit very simple, look amazing. The Viz-bang that occurs when you click through the sheets while demoing your work to the business and clients blows them away. Everybody is sold immediately on the idea of having such a dashboard to themselves on their data. Qlik Sense is sexy, and the proof of concepts you have just delivered have given you lots of projects to work on-let's crack on!

4. **The Qlik Sense brick wall**: And this is where things become disappointing. The proof of concept went well, and the business likes the idea of using Qlik Sense and has come back to you with a comprehensive list of requirements they wish to see implemented. Colors and specific formatting options look and feel good, and, if you're lucky, they will have provided you with examples either of their existing legacy application or of things they have seen on other projects or the Internet.

Sadly, native Qlik Sense out of the box is very limited. Fundamental settings cannot be implemented, and formatting the charts and tables in the right way is either impossible or requires a workaround with complex conditional color expressions. Other things are just not possible-changing the line thickness in line charts, dynamically changing the title of the column tables, or even choosing your very own corporate brand colors. One of the coolest features in QlikView was its ability to show and hide, as well as overlap visualizations for a more guided approach to analytics.

While QlikTech, the company behind Qlik Sense, has become significantly better at working on those issues and limitations, they are still there and are to this day the biggest hurdle of successfully delivering projects in Qlik Sense.

5. **Exploring extensions**: But that's all fine. After all, what you have always been advertised is Qlik Sense's powerful and deep API, with which you can practically build anything you ever wished for using HTML5 and JavaScript. These things are called Qlik Sense extensions or mashups, the first has more JavaScript components, which can be embedded in the Qlik Sense dashboard, whereas the latter, a more standard website that loads Qlik Sense objects and functionality.

Understandably, as you are not coming from a web development background, you are not too familiar with those new coding practices: ReactJS, AngularJS, Bootstrap, RequireJS, and D3.js. You have probably read about them in a blog, or they have been dropped during discussions with colleagues, but this new world of technology was just not required when building dashboards in QlikView.

However, thankfully, Qlik have vigorously promoted open source coding in the Qlik community and have created a website called Qlik Branch (`http://branch.qlik.com`).

6. **Web Development:** The more time you spend on integrating as well as understanding these fascinating open source projects, the more you realize this is becoming more and more like web development. The speed of development decreases significantly from what you are used to with QlikView, where everything revolved around the preset framework of chart objects, loading script, and set analysis. Extensions and mashups now have so many additional dependencies: browser type and version, screen size, and libraries that are being used-all of these things sitting on top of the already sometimes challenging Qlik ecosystem. Some suggest, with opening up the API, the role of the Qlik developer is being split up into these new disciplines, making it almost impossible for one developer to understand and master all parts of Qlik going forward.

At the same time, learning JavaScript, let alone HTML5 and CSS, is not an easy endeavor, and the breadth is immense. As much as we all realize the potential of integration with those new technologies, at the same time, Qlik's fundamental value proposition, having everything in the box as a one-fits-all solution, is defeated: time to market increases, required skills are harder to obtain, and richness of coding takes the platform further away from the actual end user. This is a real problem, as well as a challenge for Qlik's market, and, at the time of writing, I am still unsure how they plan to overcome this hurdle.

But as a techy and geeky reader, we are all interested in learning more and discovering how we can take Qlik Sense even further with JavaScript, and that's where you find the time to upskill yourself.

7. **Upskilling in JavaScript:** You have decided to take the time and effort to learn new skills, and that's where the journey into the world of JavaScript takes you. ES6, AngularJS, NodeJS, RequireJS, Bootstrap, D3.js, jQuery, transpilation-all these terms sound like chaos, and I felt utterly lost in this world when I first dove into it. Don't be discouraged-most of these things are fancy-sounding libraries which are, in essence, a collection of JavaScript functions and methods that simplify development. With a couple of exceptions, most of them are compatible with one another. The most common libraries, and, most relevant, to Qlik Sense, will be described in detail in Module 3.

   While the learning curve is a bit slow at the beginning, rest assured that it will speed up significantly over time. The best way is to start with something existing and *hack* your way through it. After a couple of hours, you will be able to do slight modifications to an extension or mashup, and you will realize all your coding skills acquired so far will come in handy. At the end of the day, JavaScript mostly revolves around loops, if statements, and variables.

8. **Qlik Sense hard landing**: After a couple of months working with Qlik Sense, and spending lots of time training and upskilling in JavaScript, you will very likely end up becoming frustrated. Small and simple changes, which would not take longer than an hour in QlikView, end up requiring at least one day of effort in JavaScript. The mashups and extensions you developed naturally will experience bugs and hotfixes, or tactical solutions will become less stable. Disappointment and frustration will emerge, and you will very likely have wished to have implemented your project in QlikView.

9. **JavaScript World R&D**: But, also, while you are upskilling in JavaScript, you will start discovering the vast amount of possibilities with the new language, the open source projects that are available, as well as the sophisticated community behind all components of web development. Your enthusiasm will grow, and you will realize new ways of doing data analytics. Admittedly, time will become your only obstacle: you will realize you could achieve so many cool things if you integrated them with the powerful Qlik engine, but it would probably take you a good while to develop them. That's where you start becoming more efficient: instead of producing code yourself, you are googling for snippets of codes or available open source projects, and you spend more time on integrating pieces of code. Instead of doing classic R&D (Research & Development), you are now following a new kind of R&D: Rip-Off and Duplicate.

10. **Leveraging self-service**: Once you manage to grasp the core concepts of JavaScript and get familiar with the available open source libraries, you will see your time being spent predominantly on mashups and extensions, tasks that business users realistically will not be able to do themselves. Because you are being fully occupied, the requests by the business for changes or new apps will start piling up and, understandably, the waiting time will increase. And that's a key inflection point in a typical Qlik Sense development cycle, where your users are motivated enough to get their hands dirty and start doing some analytics themselves, embracing the self-service aspect of Qlik Sense. Your job will be to set up the self-service environment to be as user-friendly as possible and give your user basic training. If this is successful, adoption of Qlik Sense across the whole organization is almost guaranteed, as the businesses themselves, having developed their dashboards, will go around promoting the platform to everyone. Qlik Sense, with its self-service capability, is indeed breaking the limits of traditional business intelligence (BI), and you will see it reaching unprecedented territory.

11. **Enlightenment**: By the time you reach this point, if you manage to, then you will have very likely become a tremendous advocate of the Qlik Sense technology, its vast possibilities, and its immense contribution to the business by providing cutting-edge analytics on a user's desktop, iPad, or mobile phone. It has been a bumpy journey with a massive learning curve, but, once you arrive at your destination, you will genuinely embrace Qlik Sense, its engine, and its seamless integrability with all other technologies. The goal of this book is to get you there and make you a master of Qlik Sense.

QlikView and Qlik Sense comparison

It is not an easy endeavor to compare QlikView and Qlik Sense, as they are serving different use cases and are built upon two completely different technologies. However, asking for a direct comparison is the most-asked question among existing QlikView users or developers, or even among businesses that are evaluating which technology to use for their data analytics project.

This section will try to provide a like-for-like comparison both from a user perspective as well as from a technical standpoint.

The different approach to projects

Qlik Sense's primary focus is to deliver a governed environment where business users can freely create apps and analytics without needing dedicated IT developers or consultants to do it for them. Of course, some more complex apps and dashboards will continue to require a classic software development approach; however, when compared to QlikView, this shifts, and the Qlik consultant will need to change their mindset slightly.

Requirements gathering

The goal of every new Qlik Sense project is to ensure to have the business user in mind. Approach the business user themselves, not the project manager or the stakeholder, and try to understand how he or she is conducting analytics at the current stage and what the pain points they experience with it are. This may involve shadowing them or even doing their job for a day.

Understanding where the lack of efficiency lies is key to gathering requirements in Qlik Sense. In QlikView, it was always straightforward: you need a dashboard, let's design it, and there you go. If you want to empower the business to do analytics themselves, you need to start understanding how they work. It is also crucial to identify an appetite for data analytics of the business: are they happy doing analytics themselves or would they instead have everything provided for them? Usually, users in operational aspects of a company are less concerned about solving problems and figuring out insights in the data-they wish to get relevant information provided to them in the most timely and most natural way possible. For managers or analysts, this looks exactly the other way around: they want to be able to quickly and easily create analytics themselves to answer a question they have about their data.

Another important aspect is to understand the level of technical sophistication. If there is a lack of technical capabilities within a project or a company, there is no point throwing set analysis at them or introducing to them the capacity of interactively creating data models in the load script. Keep it simple for them by using managed Master Key Items. On the other hand, if you feel the users are technically advanced and have a basic understanding of coding, this has to be embraced. Introduce them to the power of set analysis and the scripting techniques, and you will see beautiful dashboards being created.

Lastly, the most critical aspect of requirement gathering relevant to Qlik Sense and missing in QlikView is to understand what devices and how the Qlik Sense app will be used. While QlikView was almost exclusively available on desktop, Qlik Sense can now be utilized on mobile devices on the go. Depending on where and how it will be used, there will be different considerations on the user experience design, the context of the displayed data, as well as the integrability with other platforms and technologies (for example, you can't export to XLS on your iPad). This is explained in more detail a little later in the *Qlik Sense on Mobile* section.

Implementation

In QlikView, the implementation phase was predominantly developer- and IT-focused. Agile development processes introduced a way to maintain a close feedback loop with the business. While the same is also possible in Qlik Sense, the question resides on whether the business will become part of the implementation as well.

If the user becomes heavily involved in the development process, the implementation of Qlik Sense projects becomes interestingly interactive. Instead of having close iterations with the business on their app, you can start actively involving the user in the development themselves. Give them the data, show them how to create a couple of basic charts, and let them do it on their own. Once they're happy with the general design and context of the app, you as a consultant/developer can take it away and beautify it and make it more robust and production-ready. Your involvement in such a scenario will revolve around building extensions for the users and be writing the data model, as well as planning the architecture of the Qlik Sense environment.

Maintenance

The maintenance phase, leaving Qlik server maintenance and user training aside, is not very pronounced in QlikView. You may need to respond to challenges around data being wrong or the occasional user question, but, beyond that, the user consumes the app, and that's it. If there are new ideas and requirements to be implemented, those are usually written down and implemented in a new version of the same app. For static apps in Qlik Sense, where users cannot add content to the app, the same applies.

When, however, the user has permission and is intended to be able to create his/her sheets and visualization objects in the app, the maintenance phase of an app becomes an integral aspect of Qlik Sense deployment. As users can create not only their sheets but also promote those sheets to a community place where all other users can see it as well, the maintenance phase quickly turns into a resource-intensive support phase, which, in a mature Qlik Sense environment, can become the daily job of a consultant. Users can create their mini-dashboards, they can duplicate existing sheets and modify them, and experiment with new aggregations by exploring the expression editor of Qlik Sense.

There are multiple implications that could raise several red flags in a governed environment, mainly when the activities are conducted in a real production environment. This requires preparing the Qlik Sense deployment with either Master Key Items or a different concept on how to facilitate self-service development without risking the performance of the app. Same time security rules need to be tight in live production environments: disabling the editing of sheets, maybe only allowing the user to utilize Master Items Dimensions and metrics. This will require you to also distinguish between the type of users: perhaps some more sophisticated users will be allowed to do more self-service analytics than others.
At the same time, a process needs to be put in place for promoting sheets and including them as part of the core app at some stage.

To conclude, with self-service in place and it being a major selling point of the Qlik Sense technology, the maintenance phase becomes an interactive support phase, where the role of a Qlik Sense consultant almost resembles the one of DevOp.

Differences in the loading script

There are plenty of commonalities between QlikView and Qlik Sense in the loading script, but this section will cover a few of the differences:

- **Data sources**: Qlik Sense does not work on absolute file paths, as it uses the concept of data connections. This allows administrators to manage permissions for each user as well as which folder and database connections the users are allowed to use and have access to. QlikView did not support the aspect of online self-service application development in production. Hence, file paths could be specified in absolute terms. The change of loading data is minimal- instead of using the file path, you will need to create a data connection based on the same and then reference the data connection using `lib://`.

While it is all is straightforward to set up and implement, caution needs to be paid to the implications of giving a user access, for example, to a database. Permissions on the database are granted to the Qlik Sense service account under which the server environment is running. This means that a user will be accessing everything the service account has permitted for. This becomes particularly interesting if you only wish to give access to a user to query one or two particular tables. The permission schema will then need to be set up on the database side.

- **Scripting expressions**: Lots of expressions are supported in Qlik Sense. Also, some expressions are still working as intended, but Qlik explicitly states they plan to remove them in the future. Hence, they suggest avoiding using them going forward.

  The following list summarizes Qlik's latest not-supported list of functions and script expressions, and it is recommended to double-check the following two links to ensure this section is up to date, as it is expected it will change going forward:

  - http://help.qlik.com/en-US/sense/3.1/Subsystems/Hub/Content/Scripting/QlikView-functions-statements-not-supported.htm
  - http://help.qlik.com/en-US/sense/3.1/Subsystems/Hub/Content/Scripting/functions-statements-not-recommended.htm

Script statements not supported in Qlik Sense

Next, you can find script statements that were working in QlikView but are no longer supported in Qlik Sense:

Statement	Comments
Command	Use SQL instead.
InputField	InputField is a QlikView statement that permits the user to change values in a given data field. This is no longer possible in Qlik Sense. Instead, variables should be used, or a more sophisticated SQL writeback solution should be used.

Script expressions not supported in Qlik Sense

This is a list of script expressions that were working in QlikView scripting but are no longer working in Qlik Sense:

- `GetCurrentField`
- `GetExtendedProperty`
- `Input`
- `InputAvg`
- `InputSum`
- `MsgBox`
- `NoOfReports`
- `ReportComment`
- `ReportId`
- `ReportName`
- `ReportNumber`

Prefixes not supported in Qlik Sense Script

The following is a list of QlikView prefixes that are not supported in Qlik Sense:

- `Bundle`
- `Image_Size`
- `Info`

Script statements not recommended in Qlik Sense

These script statements have been inherited by Qlik Sense but are not recommended to be used anymore in Qlik Sense. This is partly because they do not follow the best practice, and partly because more powerful methods have been introduced, which should be used instead:

Statement	Parameters
Buffer	Use Incremental instead of: • Inc **(not recommended)** • Incr **(not recommended)**
LOAD	The following parameter keywords are generated by QlikView file transformation wizards. Qlik Sense retains functionality when data is reloaded, but it does not provide guided support/wizards for creating the statement with these parameters: • Bottom • Cellvalue • Col • Colmatch • Colsplit • Colxtr • Compound • Contain • Equal • Every • Expand • Filters • Intarray • Interpret • Length • Longer • Numerical • Pos • Remove • Rotate • Row • Rowcnd • Shorter • Start • Strcnd • Top • Transpose • Unwrap

Differences in the frontend

There are significantly visible changes on the frontend in Qlik Sense compared to QlikView, but this section will cover most of the technical aspects of it:

- **Alternate states**: Alternate states are supported in Qlik Sense, as it's sitting on the same engine as QlikView. However, there is no supported way in the user interface to create alternate states or assign them to an object. There have been some extensions in Qlik branch, which are trying to support the direction. However, they have not been implemented robustly. Comparative analysis is one big beneficiary of alternative states, and it apparently suffers in Qlik Sense because of that. Alternate states can be used for sophisticated mashups and QAP projects, but in Qlik Sense alternate states are not available to be implemented via the user interface.

- **Variables**: Variables can be used in Qlik Sense as they were in QlikView. There are no significant differences between the two technologies, with the exception of limited possibilities to efficiently manage variables in Qlik Sense. It's still very technical; they can be loaded and declared via the script, but, for example, there is no smart way to delete multiple variables. They have to be removed one by one in the *My Work* area of Qlik Sense, which is time-consuming. At the same time, variables are not shareable objects and can hence not be created in a collaborative environment, for example, when the app has published on a stream or production node.

  They can, however, be created dynamically in the script with some technical tricks (keep the loading script with variables on a shared `.qvs` file or maintain variables in an Excel spreadsheet) and then embedded in Master Key Measures. All in all, the support for variables is still there, but maintenance of them has degraded a bit.

  An excellent blog about how variables can be used has been written by Henric Cronström at Qlik.com: `https://community.qlik.com/blogs/qlikviewdesignblog/2013/11/04/the-magic-of-variables`.

- **Bookmarks**: Bookmarks are an important feature of every frontend technology, as they allow the user to put down their bespoke view and selections of what they see to either come back to it at a later stage or to share it with other users. Bookmarks in QlikView have been a compelling feature, and they have also been implemented in Qlik Sense. But, while bookmarks can be created via both the user interface and via the API, they cannot be shared with other users, and this is a massive shortfall in Qlik Sense. Secondly, the options offered via the user interface in Qlik Sense are limited too. You can't decide whether you want to save variable values in bookmarks, if you wish to have the bookmark selections to be applied on top of current selections, or which sheet the bookmark should take you to, if at all. All in all, bookmark implementation at the time of writing is poorly implemented in Qlik Sense, and this limitation needs to be taken into account when designing a Qlik Sense app.
- **Frontend functions**: Due to the fact Qlik Sense is using the same QIX engine as QlikView, all frontend functions are working in Qlik Sense, too. There is, however, a list of expressions and functions which Qlik plans to take away in future versions, hence why they recommend avoiding using them as far as possible in new Qlik Sense apps.

The following list of recommended functions to avoid using will be changing over the course of time. Hence, it's recommended to always double check with the source at Qlik's documentation: `http://help.qlik.com/en-US/sense/3.1/Subsystems/Hub/Content/Scripting/functions-statements-not-recommended.htm`.

Frontend functions not recommended in Qlik Sense

These QlikView frontend functions are working in Qlik Sense but are not recommended to be used because they either do not follow best practice or because newer, more suitable functions were introduced:

Function	Recommendation
NumCount NumMax NumMin NumSum	Use Range functions instead

QliktechBlue QliktechGray	Use other `color` functions instead. `QliktechBlue()` can be replaced by `RGB(8, 18, 90)` and `QliktechGray()` can be replaced by `RGB(158, 148, 137)` to get the same colors
QlikViewVersion	Use `ProductVersion` instead
QVUser	Use `OSUser` instead
Year2Date	Use `YearToDate` instead
Vrank	Use `Rank` instead
WildMatch5	Use `WildMatch` instead

ALL qualifier

In QlikView, the ALL qualifier may occur before an expression. This is equivalent to using `{1} TOTAL`, and it effectively calculates the expression for the **whole** data set. If the ALL qualifier is used, a set expression cannot be used, since the ALL qualifier defines a set by itself. For legacy reasons, the ALL qualifier will still work in this version of Qlik Sense but may be removed in coming versions.

Commonalities

While this chapter focuses solely on the differences between the two technologies, QlikView and Qlik Sense, there are plenty of commonalities as well. As a matter of fact, most things have thankfully remained the same between the two Qlik technologies. While there will be a couple of areas that will require either a different way of thinking to solve problems or learn new skills, the underlying engine of both technologies is de-facto the same. Both QlikView 12 and Qlik Sense are using the same novel QIX engine, Qlik's Associative Indexing Engine, which supports the same data modeling and scripting in the backend and utilizes the same variables, bookmarks, expressions, and set analysis on the frontend.

Features as well as best practices and development techniques around them that can be used by both technologies are:

- **Set Analysis**: Set Analysis works identically in both Qlik Sense and QlikView, with all current syntax for set modifiers and set identifiers being respected by both technologies. However, due to Qlik Sense not being very good at supporting alternate states and shareable bookmarks, the use cases for the set modifier aspect of set analysis falls a bit short in Qlik Sense.

You can find more information about Set Analysis in Module 2 of this book or at Qlik's online documentation: `https://help.qlik.com/en-US/sense/3.1/Subsystems/Hub/Content/ChartFunctions/SetAnalysis/set-analysis-expressions.htm`.

- **Scripting**: Scripting techniques, expressions, and formulas used in the backend can be taken over like-for-like from a QlikView application, for example. As outlined in the previous section, the main difference lies in the source paths, called **Data Connections,** in Qlik Sense, where the source path for data needs to be updated to be relative rather than absolute file paths.

  With regard to best practices around scripting, Steve Dark, Qlik Luminary 2017, and Qlik Guru, have written a handy blog on techniques, which can be taken over from QlikView to Qlik Sense, which can be found here: `https://www.quickintelligence.co.uk/qlik-sense-scripting/`.

- **Data modeling**: As it's the same underlying engine, the same best practices around data modeling apply to Qlik Sense as they do for QlikView. This is discussed in detail in Module 2 of this book, but, in general, it is identical, to the extent that data models can be copied over like-for-like from an existing QlikView project.
- **QVDs:** QVDs, initially standing for QlikView Data File, is a compression of a loaded in-memory data model, which can be used and loaded by both QlikView and Qlik Sense. While in the past, in the original versions of Qlik Sense, there have been some issues with loading the same underlying QVDs by both technologies, these issues have now been resolved. Loading QVDs produced in QlikView can be loaded as they are by Qlik Sense, and the optimized load works as well.

  There are plenty of advantages of using QVDs, such as:

  - Increasing load speed
  - Decreasing load on database servers
  - Consolidating data from multiple apps
  - Incremental load

- **Section access**: With the introduction of the versatile security rules, some aspects of managing security with section access to the document level security have become redundant in Qlik Sense. However, dynamic data reduction can be fully leveraged like in QlikView, based on user ID or groups. As there is no desktop client or license key assigned to each user in Qlik Sense, this part of section access is dropped.

An excellent introduction to general section access can be read here on a blog post by Henric Cronström at `https://community.qlik.com/blogs/qlikviewdesignblog/2014/05/26/section-access`.

- **Data visualization best practices:** Both QlikView and Qlik Sense are data visualization tools, and, regardless of the underlying technologies, the same principles apply to how data is visualized and presented to the users. Nothing changes here, and the same approach to data visualization has to be applied. A good summary of choosing a good chart can be seen in the following image:

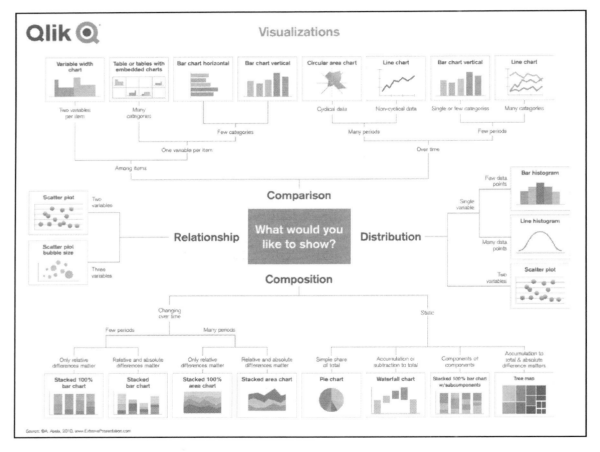

A Summary for choosing a good chart

Many blogs around that topic were posted on the Qlik Community by the visualization advocate Patrick Lundblad:

- **Data Visualization Foundations – Mapping Point Data**: `http://global.qlik.com/gr/blog/posts/patrik-lundblad/data-visualization-foundations-mapping-point-data`.
- **Data Visualization Foundations – Color By**: `http://global.qlik.com/gr/blog/posts/patrik-lundblad/data-visualization-foundations-color-by`.
- **Data Visualization Foundations – Time**: `http://global.qlik.com/gr/blog/posts/patrik-lundblad/data-visualization-foundations-time`.
- **Data Visualization Foundations – Color**: `http://global.qlik.com/gr/blog/posts/patrik-lundblad/data-visualization-foundations-color`.
- **Patrick Lundblad's Blog Page**: `http://global.qlik.com/gr/blog/authors/patrik-lundblad`.

Where to upskill to transition to Qlik Sense

During the presentation, *A year with Qlik Sense,* Martin Mahler briefly outlined the change of the role of a Qlik consultant or developer in a direct comparison between the two technologies, which is nicely summarized in the following comparative bar chart. It displays the split of the time spent as a Qlik developer in five core skill sets (**Dashboarding, JavaScript DEV** (development), **Training, Data Modelling,** and **Server Maintenance**) related to both technologies:

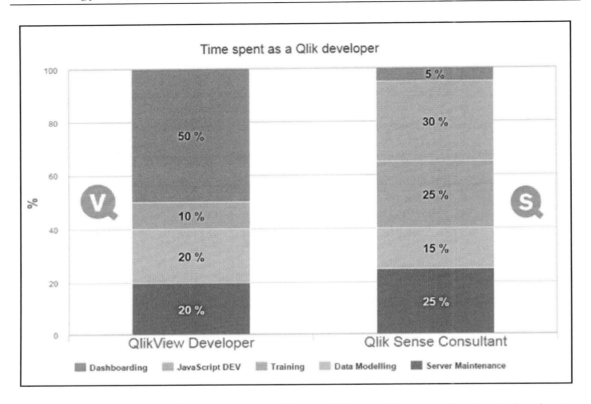

While there is a lot of overlap, the most significant difference between the two technologies is the introduction of a newly required skillset, JavaScript in Qlik Sense, which starts to occupy most of the time of the developer compared to when he or she was developing in QlikView. The second biggest change is the reduction of **Dashboarding** required in Qlik Sense. While counter-intuitive at first, it is reduced by the introduction of the core self-service capabilities of Qlik Sense. The primary person now creating the dashboards and charts is the user himself. This also explains why the amount of time spent on training the user has hugely increased, as the developer will need to teach him/her how to use fundamental set analysis, expressions, and possibly share some good practices around data visualization.

Data Modeling, on the other hand, as well as server maintenance, remains mostly unchanged. There is a slight decrease in data-modeling efforts, as various scripting techniques around facilitating guided analytics **Dashboarding** (data islands, variables, and technical fields) in QlikView are dropped in Qlik Sense. At the same time, server maintenance increases slightly due to the introduction of security rules and the more advanced publishing of Qlik Sense apps.

While Martin's conclusion is subjective, and the time spent split between the skill sets can easily vary from project to project, to a large extent, it captures the most significant gap in skills of a QlikView developer: the need to learn web development/JavaScript, and this is not to be underestimated. From understanding web development best practices to being able to write, at least in its basic form, JavaScript and utilize all relevant Qlik Sense libraries, everything will be required going forward to build mashups, extensions, widgets, and to deploy Qlik Sense on multiple devices successfully. This book will cover some aspects of coding in Qlik Sense, including introducing the reader to the most frequently used web technologies and libraries. Furthermore, it will also showcase how to build a JavaScript-based extension and integrate Qlik Sense to web apps.

The recommended sites to start learning are as follows:

- https://www.udemy.com/
- http://www.learn-angular.org/
- https://egghead.io/lessons
- https://www.tutorialspoint.com/
- https://www.pluralsight.com

With a high recommendation of the following site as it's a learning-by-coding oriented tutorial:

- https://www.codecademy.com/

Qlik Sense on mobile

One of the important selling points of Qlik Sense is its mobile compatibility-the same Qlik Sense app works seamlessly across multiple devices with an almost identical user experience. There are some limitations around interactivity (for example, there is no right-click on the iPad). However, the look and feel is very similar.

While QlikView did have an AJAX browser and an iOS app, which allowed the user to access their apps on devices other than a desktop PC, it was very limited and, quite simply, ugly. At the same time, the performance of the Qlik engine suffered when accessed via AJAX, which in summary left, a very sour user experience on mobile devices with QlikView.

Qlik Sense is all about working on mobile. While, in theory, it sounds easy to expect everything to work seamlessly across multiple devices, it is quite a big challenge. A Qlik Sense consultant/developer needs to put some thought into the design process at the beginning to ensure the end product works and is readily usable across all devices.

There are three critical aspects of mobile deployments, which will require particular attention:

- **User experience**: There is no right-click on the iPad. The functionality of user interaction is not the same on mobile as it is on the desktop client, and hence this needs to be taken into account. There is, for example, no point in offering an export to XLS button on an iPad if there's nothing more that can be done with the extract.

  Mobile devices are more app-oriented than browser-focused, and this has to be facilitated. At the same time, the screen size will vary from device to device, and you will need to ensure that the design is responsive, meaning it scales automatically, and it will not change significantly or contextually when switching devices.

- **Context**: People are using and demanding mobile integrability because they want to use their data analytics on the go. They want to be able to use an iPad in a meeting room and be able to browse their data while discussing to become more data-driven. Also, when they travel or are on the move, they want to be able to have a quick glance at what they see and not necessarily interact with the app frequently. On the other hand, when they sit on their desk browsing through the app on their desktop client, they may have more time to analyze data more profoundly and summarize their conclusions either by inviting other people to their desk or by summarizing insights in an email.

- **Integrability with other platforms and technologies**: On a desktop client, the user usually has multiple systems installed, and it's not uncommon that a Qlik Sense app will and can be used in conjunction with a different platform or system. Sometimes, it only makes business sense when you can see an integrated view of your data using multiple systems. On a mobile device or an iPad, this may be limited or not possible at all. This needs to be taken into account when designing the app for mobile usage, and at the same time providing enough information on the screen to ensure the data and visualizations sitting on top of it are meaningful by themselves. If not, then at least give some warning or information.

Mobility adds a new factor to the design process of Qlik Sense, which has its merits and needs to be considered when developing apps, both from a technical point of view and also from a business view, as well as how the users plan to consume the app.

Summary

If you are coming from a QlikView background, moving on to Qlik Sense at some point is very likely for you. While the technology is new and slightly different, there are many transferable skills, including the Qlik expression language with set analysis. But just because QlikView and Qlik Sense share the same name in parts, and the same data engine backend, it does not mean they are 100% identical. With Qlik Sense, a new way of providing data analytics using self-service is introduced. Qlik Sense is entirely web-based, and, as such, new programming languages, such as JavaScript, CSS, and HTML5 play a significant role. The key differentiator, however, is the extensibility of Qlik Sense, using the aforementioned programming languages. Building extensions, mashups, as well as integrating Qlik into other platforms becomes a stronger use case, and with it new and different skill sets are required to implement Qlik Sense into projects successfully.

To smooth the transition from QlikView to Qlik Sense, this chapter covered what a typical journey looks like, moving from one tool to another. The main differences between the two technologies are highlighted, as well as commonalities, to avoid ambiguity. With the differences in mind, this chapter outlined how the approach to BI projects changed its shape as well, with recommendations where the reader, coming from a QlikView background, should upskill to be prepared. Mobile development plays a significant role in Qlik Sense, which is also the main reason why it was (re)developed to become 100% web-based. With it, different design aspects are introduced, which have been summarized in this chapter.

Having read this chapter, you should now be much better prepared to move on to Qlik Sense and to tackle challenges and requirements that come along with the new technology. Just knowing about it won't suffice, though, and you should be very well aware of the importance of upskilling in new areas, which should not be taken lightly. Fortunately, this book, especially Module 3, will provide some valuable lessons and insights on how web-based technologies work, as well as provide you with a good understanding of how to extend Qlik Sense.

3

Security Rules: Attribute Based Access Control

Data Analytics and Qlik Sense are all about creating content for yourself or a target audience: visualizations, data models, dashboards, sheets, bookmarks, and more technical elements like data connections. By boarding business users onto the platform and inviting them to delve into self-service analytics, you, as an administrator, are creating the foundation for masses of content. Governing the content, objects, and apps are not only challenging but can also quickly get out of control if not correctly set up from the beginning. As security is not a binary setting in Qlik Sense, it has been hugely extended to serve all of the various use cases of content creation. To cater for all the use cases, and to allow for very bespoke and tailored setups of security settings and profiles, Qlik decided to offer a new way of managing security with **Attribute-Based Access Control**, abbreviated as **ACAB**.

ACAB is an access control paradigm which grants access rights by a collection of policies which can be combined using boolean logic. Policies can use any kind of attribute, from user to resource attributes, including specific environments and more. The types of rights include various actions, which extend from reading to modifying and updating existing content. To keep things simple for the summary, a typical ACAB policy follows the following principle, which can be readily formulated into a sentence:

The sentence structure of a conventional ACAB Policy: Allow a requester to perform an **action** on a **resource,** provided that a **condition** is true.

This usually results in creating multiple policies to manage the access rights to the content of a Qlik Sense infrastructure. Due to the complexity of setting up numerous policies, security rules need to be designed in advance, and they very often include the creation of security profiles/user roles. While very powerful, this is also a complex new feature which needs to be understood before you can start leveraging it.

This chapter will focus on the fundamentals of security rules in Qlik Sense and elaborate on all its technical aspects in great detail. It will provide guidelines on how to design security user roles to facilitate permissions better and will conclude with some typical use cases and examples. It is recommended to use this chapter as a reference manual and look it up each time you are working with security rules. The following are the topics we will be covering in this chapter:

- Attribute-Based Access Control
- Administrator roles
- Security rules resources
- Security rules actions
- Security rules conditions
- Auditing security rules
- Security rule use cases and examples

While it is expected that this part of Qlik Sense will remain reasonably unchanged in future releases, it is still recommended to supplement this chapter by also visiting the Qlik Sense online help page on security rules: `http://help.qlik.com/en-US/sense/1.1/Subsystems/ManagementConsole/Content/ServerUserGuide/SUG_ConfiguringSecurity_AccessRules_Overview.htm`.

Compared to creating visualizations or dashboards, security rules are comparably technical and for some, a bit boring topic. It's however, very recommended to spend the required time to understand them as the investment will quickly pay off when designing enterprise solutions with advanced security requirements.

Looking back to when I first started with Qlik Sense, I must admit that I had a bit of a tough journey with the security rules. They are very comprehensive, and there are no quick wins - if you don't want to bite yourself at a later time, you need to properly design the security rules from the beginning, especially when you have multiple projects and self-service users in your company. Once you understand their core concepts, they can then be set up reasonably quickly. Do yourself a favor and make sure you comprehend this chapter; you will thank me later.

Introducing Attribute-Based Access Control

As already outlined, ABAC is a new way of applying and dealing with security in Qlik. It is powerful, as it gives Qlik administrators full flexibility on how they want to implement security, and, more importantly, the level of freedom they wish to give to their users or groups of users.

Security rules using ABAC are the driver of governing the Qlik Sense server and its users. They allow the administrator to control how many self-service capabilities users have and, more importantly, which users. They permit the definition of user groups and security roles, which facilitates giving some more advanced users more permissions than others. As outlined in the first chapter of this book, in the section *User types in Qlik Sense*, self-service can be introduced very efficiently by categorizing users into Power Users, Users, and Consumers. This is achieved by applying ACAB security rules.

Security rules properties

In Qlik Sense, security rules, based on an ACAB policy, require some properties to be set when they are created.

ACAB policy properties

These properties are required for the security rules to take effect:

Property	Description
Resource filter	The resource ID for the rule
Actions	The permitted actions for the rule
Condition	The security rule can be enabled or disabled

Identification properties

These properties are relevant for identification purposes in the Qlik Sense environment.

Property	Description
Name	The name of the security rule
Description	Text is describing what the rule does
Tags	Tags of the security rule for looking up purposes

Other properties

Property	Description
Context	The context the security rule applies to (QMC/hub)
Status	The security rule can be enabled or disabled

Qlik Sense security rules use an attribute called **context,** which can be either the hub or the **QMC (Qlik Management Console)**. Depending on what setting the security rule is defined with, permissions in the QMC can be separated from permissions in the actual app. In other words, you can permit an admin to publish and manage apps, but prevent him from viewing the original apps themselves. Typically, though, security rules are applied to both **contexts**.

The following is the structure of an underlying security rule template, as it looks in the QMC (QS 3.2):

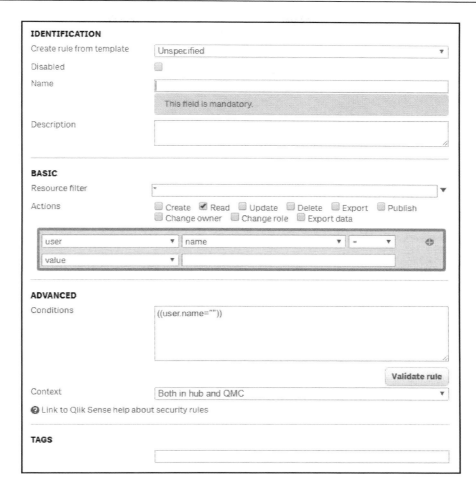

The next sections will elaborate on security rules on a more technical level. The previously described attributes will be covered in more detail and will allow you to understand all aspects of security rules, and also create new ones by yourself.

Administrator roles

Roles are a concept where **one** security rule, with a set of actions permitted on a resource, can be defined as a newly created admin role. This role can then be manually assigned to a user in the user management section of QMC.

Default administrator roles

By default, with an installation of Qlik Sense with predefined security rules, some roles are already created:

Property	Description
RootAdmin	A RootAdmin has access to everything and anything within the QMC. Upon installation, the user who successfully enters the first valid license is automatically assigned as RootAdmin. *It is paramount to ensure visibility of who is part of this role and who is not.*
AuditAdmin	Has read access to all resources to enable auditing of access rights. Has read and publish rights on the administration stream. *This security role is relevant for support users who want to be able to review permissions, typically for auditing purposes.*
ContentAdmin	Has create, read, update, and delete rights for all resources except nodes, engines, repositories, schedulers, proxies, virtual proxies, and syncs. Has read and publish rights on the administration stream. *This is technically an app administrator. They manage apps, resources, and refreshes for their user base, everything which is related to some produced content. Users in this role are unable to change any infrastructure settings on the Qlik Sense server or similar.*
DeploymentAdmin	Has create, read, update, and delete rights for apps, tasks, users, licenses, nodes, repositories, schedulers, proxies, virtual proxies, and engines. Has read and publish rights on the administration stream. *This is a typical role which would be assigned to an operational support team which manages production and does releases and deployments on behalf of developers and users.*
SecurityAdmin	Same as ContentAdmin, but with create, read, update, and delete rights for proxies and virtual proxies, and no access rights on tasks. Has read rights on server node configuration. Has read and publish rights on the administration stream. *As a security administrator, on top of having access to all content, they also manage how users can authenticate against the Qlik Sense server, including management of certificates.*

The default administrator roles are just generic roles which should help your enterprise Qlik Sense deployment get up to speed. Ideally, they should serve as a basis and you, as a Qlik Sense consultant, should modify them to cater for your own company's use case. For additional security roles, it is very easy to create bespoke ones, as well, which is described next.

Custom security roles

The default administrator roles come with the Qlik Sense server installation and will help you get up to speed with some admin roles. Depending on whether you decide to go ahead with admin roles, rather than, for example, utilizing Active Directory Groups to drive permissions, it might very well be required to either modify existing admin roles or create new ones.

Creating security roles

Creating admin roles is quite simple. On top of defining all required properties just as you would in any other security rule, you then need to specify the name of the admin role in the Security Rule Conditions:

1. Here, you can choose the `roles` attribute in the `user` resource type, as per the following screenshot:

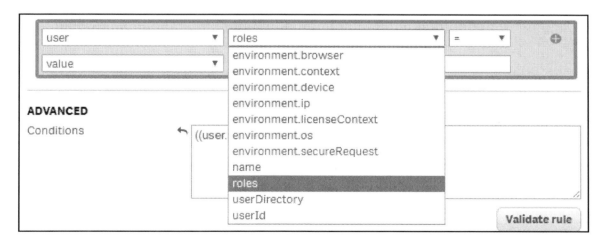

2. Once you have selected the roles attribute, you then, instead of picking one of the available ones, type in your new user role. If it's not available, it will be created automatically:

3. For more advanced users, you can type the user role specification directly into the Advanced Conditions tab by inserting:

```
((user.roles="MyCustomUserRole"))
```

Once the security rule is designed, the new security role will be available to be assigned to any user you wish.

Assigning users security roles

Assigning a security role to a user is very straightforward. Both default administrator roles or custom created ones work in the same way:

1. Navigate to the **User Management** site in the QMC.
2. In there, select the user you wish to add a new role to and move to edit.
3. In the **Edit user** mode, you will then see a dedicated section for **Admin roles**. Add a **Role** and choose from a list of available roles:

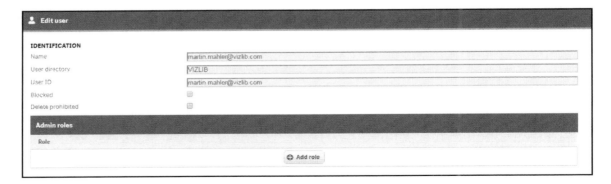

4. Once you have successfully applied a role to a user, it will appear in the user management section under the **Admin roles** column:

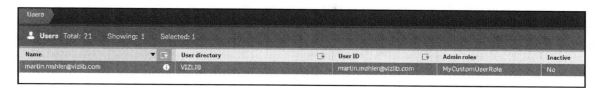

You can assign a user **multiple** admin roles.

You can assign a user an admin role even if it has not been created yet.

Security rules resources

The **Attribute-Based Access Control (ABAC)** security concept applies attribute permissions to *resources*. This section will uncover what types of resources are available in Qlik Sense and how they can be referenced, beginning with the latter.

Resource filters

Resource filters are utilized to reference one or **multiple** resources within a security rule. In technical terms, they follow the following syntax:

```
Resource Filter Syntax:
resourcetype1[*][_*][, resourcetype2[*][_*], ...]
```

The parameters described in the previous syntax can be deconstructed into the following options:

Parameter	Description
resourcetype1	Resource to be referenced. This field is **required,** and you must enter at least one resource-type name.
*	This is an **optional** wildcard. If included, the security rule will apply to all resource types beginning with the specified text. For example, App* will apply the rule to all resource types beginning with App, which means, all resources of type App and nested App.Object. If omitted, the security rule will apply to resource types with the exact name specified in the Resource field. You must supply the GUID or template for GUIDs for the rule to work. Cannot be used in conjunction with the _* option.
_*	This is an **optional** wildcard. If included, the rule will apply to all resources of the type specified. For example, App_* will apply the rule to all apps. Similarly, App.Object_* will apply the rule to all app objects. If omitted, the security rule will apply to resource types with the exact name specified in the Resource field. You must supply the GUID or template for GUIDs for the rule to work. Cannot be used in conjunction with the * option.

The real difference between the * and _* wildcard qualifiers is that the first one includes all **nested** resources (objects within an app), whereas the second **only** references the specified resource (apps, but not objects within the apps).

Naming resources in the resource filter

Based on the previous syntax, the following conventions are available when defining resource filters:

- **Explicit naming:**

    Define the resource using the resource GUID.

For example, "Stream_88ee46c6-5e9a-41a7-a66a-f5d8995454ec".

You can see the GUID for data connections, login access, and streams in the security rules overview page > resource filter, provided that you have created access rights for those resources using their respective overview pages.

- **Explicit type naming using wildcard (_*):**

  Use the "_*" wildcard to explicitly define the type of resource to apply the rule to.

  For example, "App_*" will apply the rule to all app resources only.

- **Implicit type naming using wildcard (*):**

  Use a wildcard to define the resource or resources.

  For example, "App*" will apply the rule to all resources beginning with "App." This means that this rule will apply to apps, sheets, stories, data, and objects.

- **Define multiple Resources (,):**

  Use a comma (,) and the previous explicit/implicit naming convention to define numerous resources within one security rule. This typically makes the most sense for exact definitions.

  For Example, "Stream_88ee46c6-5e9a-41a7-a66a-f5d8995454ec, Stream_12314-544a-2347-a6as6a-f5d14254ec" applies the security rule to two explicitly specified streams.

All resources are specified in the repository database using a **GUID** in Qlik Sense. **GUID** stands for **G**lobally **U**nique **Id**entifier, a unique 128-bit number that is produced by the Windows OS or by some Windows applications to identify a particular component, application, file, database entry, and user. Unless a resource is deleted, its GUID will remain unchanged, even if the resource is being updated; for example, if you publish and replace an existing app on a stream, the app GUID will remain the same.

Resource types

Now that you know what a resource is, why it is relevant to security rules, and how you can apply filters to it, this paragraph covers the different types of available resources. According to Qlik Sense's online help, the following resource filters are available. To add value to the table, it has been supplemented with commentary by the author.

App-related resources

These resource filters relate to apps and their content:

Resource filter	Filter will target	Author's commentary
App	The application	*This is the heart of all resources. If you wish to refer to a specific app, you will require defining its GUID.*
App.Content	The content stored in the app-specific content library	*This references images which are uploaded into the media library, such as sheet images or using the in-app text object*

App.Object	All App.Object resources, such as sheets, stories, script, dimensions, measures, master objects, snapshots, and bookmarks	*This is where it becomes very granular for app-specific use cases but powerful for governance purposes. Using this resource filter, you can disable the "Edit" button, the use of bookmarks/snapshots, and so on. Using App.Objects, you can also deactivate people accessing the load script, even on their apps. The types of App.Objects you can reference are:* • *app_appscript* • *appprops* • *dimension* • *embeddedsnapshot* • *GenericVariableEntry* • *hiddenbookmark* • *LoadModel* • *masterobject* • *measure* • *sheet* • *snapshot* • *story*
App.DataSegment	A representation of the data which will be loaded and used by the application	*There is no clear use case on how to utilize this resource at this stage. It can be assumed that this will become more material in a future version of Qlik Sense where users will possibly be limited to the tables within the app's data model they will be allowed to view.*
App.Internal	Parameters internal to and required by the application	*This is specific to the engine and not relevant in the context of applying security rules yet.*
Extension	The extensions installed in Qlik Sense	*This controls who can access, view, and modify extensions uploaded on to the dev-hub in your Qlik Sense environment. It's **important** not to neglect to create a security rule limiting access to extensions in your production environment. Changing the code of an extension can have detrimental effects on all applications utilizing it.*

`Widgets`	The widgets installed in Qlik Sense	*The same as with the extensions resource, however, specific for widgets.*
`WebExtensionLibrary`	The library of web extensions	*There is not much information available on this, let alone practical use cases where it can be used.*
`DataConnection`	The DataConnection resource	*Controls which data connections can be utilized by whom. This resource is vital for controlling who has access to what type of data.* *Especially with data connections to databases, the overview of the scope of data which can be read can easily be lost. Pay particular attention to the security rules of those data connections*

Task resources

Tasks revolve around updating the data of an app on a scheduled basis and form an integral part of any production deployment in Qlik Sense. These resources allow setting up control of these tasks, from who can create/access them to who can trigger them:

Resource filter	Filter will target	Author's commentary
`ReloadTask`	Tasks that perform reload on apps	*This is the most relevant resource for applying security for reload tasks.*
`UserSyncTask`	Tasks that sync users from an external user directory	*This relates to tasks which pull information from an external user directory. While not directly app-related, user synchronization tasks are essential, too, as once a new user is added to a directory, this should be reflected in Qlik Sense.*
`CompositeEvent`	Task triggers in the scheduler	*Each task can have triggers applied to it, which prompted it to reload when specific events occur. These triggers can be set within the task editor.*
`SchemaEvent`	Details for when a scheduled task will run	*These resources carry information for the triggers, like trigger details. It makes sense to allow an administrator to read this information, but not necessarily update it.*

ContentLibrary related resources

Content Library resources are usually images or other filed based documents which are uploaded and managed via the QMC.

Resource filter	Filter will target	Author's commentary
ContentLibrary	Content libraries	*This helps restrict who has access to which parts of the content libraries. It's not uncommon for a project to have its images uploaded, which it doesn't wish to share with other projects.*
FileReference	Representation of files stored on disk used by the binary sync to sync files between nodes	*FileReference is a relevant resource filter for when replication synchronization is used. It can be referenced to ensure which apps are synced across environments, for example.*
StaticContentReference	Links to files in a content library	*This resource filter is the subset of the ContentLibrary and refers to specific images/files hosted within the content library.*
TempContent	Content library for temporary content, such as files from exports	*This refers to XLS or data extracts content generated when a user exports data from a visualization. As the export data action can cover most of the permission regarding extracts, there is no real use case where TempContent can be utilized.*
SharedContent	Links to QlikView documents, Qlik NPrinting generated reports	*Applies to QlikView and nPrinting generated reports resources in the hub.*

Hub section resources

The following filter can be used to disable user access to the hub:

Resource filter	Filter will target	Author's commentary
HubSection_Home	Grants access to open the hub and view the resources you have access to. By default, on.	*Even though someone does not have access to your Qlik Sense environment or even a Qlik Sense license, he/she will still be able to view the hub and streams they have access to. This is not bad, but you don't want to mislead people about going on Qlik Sense if they don't have access to it.*

QMC section resources

The following filters are used to grant access to the different QMC sections. A user with access to a QMC section can open that section, but will only see objects according to the user's access rights:

 Unless multiple projects are onboard to your Qlik Sense environment with a decentralized administration (each project admins their nodes separately), the below should rarely be fiddled around with. It is recommended to use administrator roles instead.

Resource filter	Filter will target	Author's Commentary
QmcSection_App	The QmcSectionApp resource	*Defines if someone has access to view apps in the QMC.*
QmcSection_App.Object	The QmcSection App.Object resource	*Same as with the app, but on app objects level. Not really used.*
QmcSection_App.Sheet	The QmcSection_ App.Sheet resource	*Same as with the app, but on sheet level. Not really used.*
QmcSection_App.Story	The QmcSection_ App.Story resource	*Same as with the app, but on story level. Not really used.*

QmcSection_Audit	The QmcSectionAudit resource	*Allows admin to view and utilize Audit section within the QMC.*
QmcSection_ Certificates	The QmcSection Certificate resource	*Allows admin to access the certificates area. This should generally be inaccessible to most admins, as if someone gets access to certificates, they technically get access to everything and anything on Qlik Sense.*
QmcSection_ Certificates.Export	The QmcSection CertificateExport resource	*Even more important than accessing certificate settings, be very mindful who can export certificates. If someone has access to them, they technically have access to everything and anything on Qlik Sense.*
QmcSection_ CompositeEvent	The QmcSection CompositeEvent resource	*No documentation available for this resource. Probably a placeholder for future releases.*

`QmcSection_ ContentLibrary`	The `QmcSection ContentLibrary` **resource**	*Allows viewing and accessing the content library. This is actually quite an important aspect of the QMC, as you can prepare a library with various icons and png files which can be reused for a project. Super users should potentially have access to their own project's content library.*
`QmcSection_ CustomPropertyDefinition`	The `QmcSectionCustom PropertyDefinition` **resource**	*Custom Properties are there to help with security rules. Not everyone should have access to create those, as they're a nightmare to govern if uncontrolled.*
`QmcSection_ DataConnection`	The `QmcSection DataConnection` **resource**	*Being able to modify the connection strings of data connections can bear huge security implications. Careful on who gets access to this resource.*
`QmcSection_ EngineService`	The `QmcSection EngineService` **resource**	*Resource covering all settings revolving around engine service management.*

QmcSection_ Event	The QmcSectionEvent resource	*Resource covering all settings revolving around event management.* *No documentation available on this.*
QmcSection_ Extension	The QmcSection Extension resource	*This is a very useful resource and can help manage who can view, edit, and update extensions. Bear in mind, if this is in production, updating extensions can have detrimental effects on existing dashboards and break visualizations.* *In production, no one, beside admins, should have access to this resource.*
QmcSection_ License	The QmcSection License resource	*Resource covering all settings revolving around license management.*
QmcSection_ ProxyService	The QmcSection ProxyService resource	*Resource covering all settings revolving around proxy service management.*
QmcSection_ ReloadTask	The QmcSection ReloadTask **resource**	*Resource covering all settings revolving around reload task management.*
QmcSection_ RepositoryService	The QmcSection RepositoryService resource	*Resource covering all settings revolving around Repository Service management*

`QmcSection_` `SchedulerService`	The `QmcSection` `SchedulerService` resource	*Resource covering all settings revolving around scheduler service management.*
`QmcSection_` `SchemaEvent`	The `QmcSection` `SchemaEvent` resource	*Resource covering all settings revolving around schema event management.*
`QmcSection_` `ServerNodeConfiguration`	The `QmcSectionServer` `NodeConfiguration` resource	*Resource covering all settings revolving around node management.*
`QmcSection_` `ServiceCluster`	The `QmcSection_` `ServiceCluster` resource	*Resource covering all settings revolving around service cluster management.*
`QmcSection_` `Stream`	The `QmcSection` `Stream` resource	*Resource covering all settings revolving around stream management.*
`QmcSection_` `SyncRule`	The `QmcSection` `SyncRule` resource	*Resource covering all settings revolving around sync rule management.*
`QmcSection_` `SystemRule`	The `QmcSection` `SystemRule` resource	*Resource covering all settings revolving around system rule management.*
`QmcSection_Tag`	The `QmcSectionTag` resource	*Resource covering all settings revolving around tags management.*
`QmcSection_Task`	The `QmcSectionTask` resource	*Resource covering all settings revolving around task management.*

`QmcSection_Token`	The `QmcSectionToken` resource	*Resource covering all settings revolving around license token management.*
`QmcSection_User`	The `QmcSectionUser` resource	*Resource which makes the Qlik Sense user list visible and amendable to administrators.*
`QmcSection_ UserDirectory`	The `QmcSection UserDirectory` resource	*Resource covering all settings revolving around user sync task management. Again, a very dangerous resource to have access to - if the user sync is modified, it can exclude everyone from accessing Qlik Sense. Careful!*
`QmcSection_ UserSyncTask`	The `QmcSection UserSyncTask` resource	*Resource covering all settings revolving around user sync task management.*
`QmcSection_ VirtualProxyConfig`	The `QmcSection VirtualProxyConfig` resource	*Resource covering all settings revolving around virtual proxy management.*
`QmcSection_ PrintingService`	The `QmcSection PrintingService` **resource**	*Resource covering all settings revolving around printing service management.*

License related resources

This part covers how license resources can be referenced in security rules. There are not many use cases on why there should be security rules applied to those resources. One applicable use case, though, is to assign which type of user gets a full access token and which ones are assigned login access passes for better and more cost-effective license management.

Resource filter	Filter will target
License	The actual license entity (both Qlik Sense and Qlik DataMarket).
LicenseLoginAccessType	Login access type. CRUD for allocating tokens for login (time restricted) access and setting up the associated rule.
LicenseUserAccessType	User access type. CRUD for manually allocating tokens for user (named) access.
LicenseLoginAccessUsage	Type to keep track of login access type usage. Should not be used in resource filters.
LicenseUserAccessUsage	Type to keep track of user access type usage. Should not be used in resource filters.
LicenseUserAccessGroup	Resource for rules used for automatically assigning user access types.

Node or service related resources

These filters refer to individual entries in the associated sections of the QMC. Again, ideally, only RootAdmins should have access to the below, so it's not recommended to create specific rules using the following resources, unless, of course, you wish to set up different types of RootAdmins for decentralized management of the Qlik Sense environment.

Resource filter	Filter will target
ServerNodeConfiguration	The ServerNodeConfiguration resource
ServiceStatus	The ServiceStatus resource
EngineService	The EngineService resource
ProxyService	The ProxyService resource
SchedulerService	The SchedulerService resource

RepositoryService	The RepositoryService resource
PrintingService	The PrintingService resource
VirtualProxyConfig	The VirtualProxyConfig resource

Other resources

These filters refer to individual entries in the associated sections of the QMC:

Resource filter	Filter will target
CustomPropertyDefinition	The CustomPropertyDefinition resource
SystemRule	The SystemRule resource
Tag	The Tag resource
User	The User resource
UserDirectory	The UserDirectory resource

Security rules actions

Within security rules, **Actions** form the second part (out of four, see previous section, *Attribute-Based Access Control*) of the ACAB and determine what type of activity the user is permitted to perform on the defined resource. While read and write are common actions very familiar to traditional access control, Qlik Sense has extended them to many more, which, on one side, makes the security rules rich and powerful; but on the other side, complicated as well. This section will cover the different types of actions in Qlik's security rules and will discuss potential use cases where relevant. Each action applies to a specified resource, which forms the basis of how it can be utilized.

Permissions on actions are applied to both the Qlik Management Console and the hub, as the following image shows:

- **Create**: Create allows the user to create the defined type of resources in the Qlik Sense hub or in the app itself. Creating resources is an integral part of the newly introduced self-service capability, where users can build their dashboards and analytics. While powerful, it is also IT's governance nightmare, especially in a production environment. The more create permission a user has, the stronger his ability to impact the Qlik Sense server by creating apps, sheets, and objects. Create is governance's worst enemy. In a locked-down environment, limited users have access to a create action. The exception is usually bookmarks and stories, which typically have a low effect on performance.

  Create applies to the creation of all types of new resources in the QMC. This actions covers, but is not limited to, importing apps, duplicating apps, and copying and pasting app objects:

- **Read**: Read is the most basic and most important form of actions and permits the target user to view the underlying resource. It decides whether the object will be visible to a specific person or not. Read permission sits at the top of the hierarchy. Without it, the user might not be able to perform other actions, either, regardless of whether he was permitted to do so or not.
- **Update**: Update allows the user or admin (in the QMC context) to change/modify/update any type of attributes of **an existing** resource. This action covers elements in the QMC, as well as objects, sheets, and apps in the hub. It also includes reloading apps (by doing so, you are updating the data) or publishing apps by replacing existing ones.
- **Delete**: Delete is a straightforward action: it allows the requester to remove a resource from the Qlik Sense server.

Deleting resources is irreversible. Be very careful when doing so, and ideally, always keep a copy of the resource you plan to modify to avoid losing work.

- **Export**: The export action is only relevant in the QMC context and permits the administrator to export apps from the server. By exporting apps from the server, the user gets full access to the data and all app resources (excluding user and community sheets).
- **Publish**: Publish allows administrators to either deploy apps to a specified stream or a user to publish their personal sheets to the community sheets.
- **Change owner**: This action permits administrators to change the owners of a resource. Typically, every time a user creates a resource, he automatically becomes the owner of it. When you are the owner of an app, you usually enjoy additional permissions, including full read, update, and create actions. After a user has finished developing an app which is ready to be deployed to a production stream, it is common to transfer the ownership of the app to an administrator to restrict the access.
- **Change role**: This action applies in the QMC context and allows an administrator to change the security role of another user.
- **Export data**: Exporting data of a visualization or table is a frequent use case in dashboards. This action permits or prohibits users from exporting the underlying data. It's usually applied to control the way users consume the data and to prevent performance impacts on large underlying datasets.

Security rules conditions

The security rules conditions leverage the boolean logic. This means a collection of evaluate to either true or false and based on the combined logic, the result will end up being true or false as well, defining whether the security rule applies to a specific user. The security rules conditions follow symbolic boolean aggregation logic. While an editor exists, it's not very useful for more advanced requirements, and coding is required. This section will explain the last element of ABAC rules.

General structure of a condition

Conditions are defined using so-called property-value pairs. A property is a unique identifier for some item of data, and the value represents the description of it.

The general structure of a security rule condition looks as follows:

```
[resource.resourcetype = "resourcetypevalue"] [OPERATOR]
[(((resource.property = propertyvalue) [OPERATOR (resource.property =
propertyvalue)))]
```

A typical and condition can look like the following example:

```
resource.resourcetype = "DataConnection" and (user.roles="ContentAdmin")
```

Above, the security rule applies if the resource type is a DataConnection and, at the same time, the user accessing has been assigned the ContentAdmin administrator role.

Functions for conditions

Within the QMC, there are predefined functions for security rules which can be used to return the property values of targeted resources. These functions assist in creating more advanced security rules with special use cases:

Function	Description
IsAnonymous	A boolean function which returns true if the user requesting the resource is logged in as anonymous: user.IsAnonymous()
HasPrivilege	A boolean function which returns true if the user requesting the source has specified attribute permission on it: stream.HasPrivilege("Read")
IsOwned	A boolean function which returns true if the targeted resource has an owner: app.IsOwned()
Empty()	A boolean function which returns true if the targeted resource has any other objects or connections linked to it. This is only applicable to the app resource, as it is the only resource which has app objects (sheets, charts, bookmarks) linked to it: app.Empty()

Operands for conditions

Operands for conditions are boolean operators which are utilized to unify or combine multiple security rule conditions to create more advanced security rules:

Operands	Description

AND	Most classic operand, which combines multiple security conditions by evaluating them to true if all of the conditions also evaluate to true at the same time. The general syntax for security rule conditions looks as follows:
	`(EXPRESSION) && (EXPRESSION)`
	`(EXPRESSION) and (EXPRESSION)`

OR	The second classic operand, which compares to logical evaluation and returns true if at least one of them returns true as well. The syntax looks as follows:
	`(EXPRESSION) || (EXPRESSION)`
	`(EXPRESSION) or (EXPRESSION)`

EQUAL	This operand, not case-sensitive, compares, for example, resource attributes with a string value, and evaluates to true if they are identical: `(EXPRESSION) = (EXPRESSION)`
STRICT EQUAL	Works exactly like EQUAL; however, makes a strict comparison of the resource attribute with a value which is case sensitive. It compares not only the value, but also the value types, such as whether '1' is also an integer rather than a string. The syntax looks as follows: `(EXPRESSION) == (EXPRESSION)`
NOTEQUAL	NOTEQUAL serves the opposite purpose of EQUAL and compares whether the resource type is different from the defined value: `(EXPRESSION) != (EXPRESSION)`
STRICT NOT EQUAL	Exact opposite of what STRICT EQUAL does. It compares, strictly, whether the resource type is different from the defined value and value type: `(EXPRESSION) !== (EXPRESSION)`
NOT	This operand reverses a boolean value of an expression: `!(EXPRESSION)`
LIKE	This operand does a case-insensitive comparison and allows the use of regular expression operators, like an asterisk (*) for a wildcard: For example: `user.group` like `US.*` `(EXPRESSION) like (EXPRESSION)`

MATCHES	Typical MATCHES operand, which makes a case-sensitive comparison; however, allows the use of regular expression operators, like an asterisk (*) for a wildcard: (EXPRESSION) matches (EXPRESSION)

The full list of special query characters for the above operands LIKE and MATCHES can be found at the following URL: https://msdn.microsoft.com/en-us/library/aa976858(v=vs.71).aspx.

Basic rule editor

Security rules can get quite complex in some instances, but for simple rules, the QMC provides a basic rule editor which helps with the syntax. The editor sets the brackets required for the boolean logic to apply and, based on the template, it suggests applicable resource names in an available drop-down list:

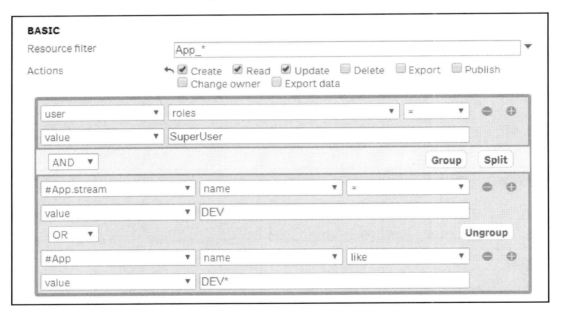

In there, you can choose from some predefined resource filter types and group them or split them into boolean logic groupings, and also apply the operators described in the preceding section. The above security rule condition simply evaluates to the following expression string, which will be inserted in the Advanced section beneath the Editor:

```
((user.roles="SuperUser") and (resource.stream.name="DEV" or resource.name
like "DEV*"))
```

The security rule applies to all `SuperUsers` and to all apps within the `DEV` stream, or apps whose names begin with `DEV*`, and allows those users to create, read, and modify those apps.

 It is important to note that the underlying editor, while very useful, does not contain the full universe of resource types, operands, and functions. It should be used for quick and basic security rules, but you should be aware of its vast possibilities to expand and not be afraid to take the produced string in the Advanced section and extend it.

Validating the security rule condition

While the basic editor helps you write syntactically correct security rules conditions, very often, when you try extending them, such as with functions like `IsAnonymous()` or when the security rule conditions become too complicated, the basic editor disappears, with the following message:

This condition cannot be displayed in the rule editor because it is too complex.

This message is very standard and does not imply the security rule is wrong, but instead that the security rule editor is not smart enough to display the advanced boolean logic. The security rule can still be valid. However, it is not up to the user to write the correct syntax in the advanced expression.

For this purpose, a validation button has been introduced, which allows the user to check whether the security rule's syntax is correct and whether the expression can be read by the QMC:

Validate rule

If the expression validates successfully, the following message will appear in the editor:

> The rule is valid.

Don't be afraid to write your own security rules without the help of the basic rule editor. While at the beginning it might appear scary, as it so often is when you attempt writing code, with the validation button and the subsequently described auditing rules, it becomes effortless to write your own. While hardcore developers will condemn me for saying this, with the natural checks in place, you can quickly and reasonably easily trial and error yourself in creating a valid security rule which fits your purpose.

Once the rule is valid, you can then check whether the permissions have been applied as intended by utilizing the security audit feature, which evaluates the security rule before even using it. This will be covered in the next section *Auditing security rules*.

Auditing security rules

Due to the complexity of ABAC security rules and the high number of rules being created in the QMC, it is very easy to lose sight of what rules have been applied and who gets access to which kind of resources. Governance and overseeing of permissions in a self-service environment are paramount, which is the reason why an auditing feature was introduced in the QMC. From experience, it is convenient, and one of the most valuable resource-monitoring tools in the QMC. In general, it serves two purposes:

- Assistance in creating new security rules, by validating whether the applied expression logic has the expected outcome. This allows for a smooth trial and error when writing security rules, with absolute confidence at the end that it works as designed.
- For auditing permission of users. When new users get added to the system, you usually check whether they have been added correctly by checking the resources they have access to. On the other side, when a user is complaining that he cannot, for example, see an app that he is supposed to have access to, you can quickly check in the auditing feature if what he is saying is true, and if it is, which permission he is missing.

Working with auditing

Auditing security rules is relatively simple. In essence, you define the target resource you wish to audit and an optional user filter, in case you don't want to retrieve the full set of users. On top of that, you can also define the environmental context of the audit—QMC or hub, that is:

Audit results

Once the filters in the Audit header are set, you can click on the **Audit** button to see the resulting audit bar, which looks like the following example:

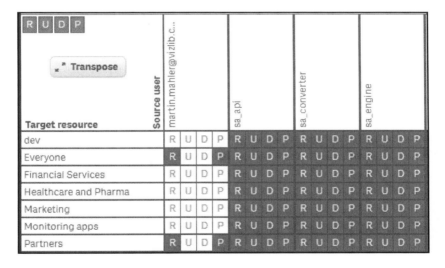

In the preceding case, you can see that the user Martin.Mahler@vizlib.com has R (read) and P (publish) access to the **Everyone** and **Partners** streams. All other streams, like **Marketing** or **Financial Services**, are grayed out, and **Martin** would be able to see neither the streams nor the apps within them in the hub. Furthermore, right next to it, all Qlik service accounts have full access to all resources, which is reflected by a full set of permissions, and expected in any Qlik Sense environment.

The abbreviated letters, R/U/D/P in this instance, stand for the types of security rule actions, which have been described in the section *Security rule actions* in this chapter. Next to lettering, the security rule audit also returns a color coding, which can be described as follows:

- **Green**: The rule is valid and in use.
- **Yellow**: The rule is valid but disabled.
- **Red**: The rule is invalid.
- **Blue**: The rule is previewed.
- **Dimmed values**: The audit result is not entirely retrieved for performance reasons. Click **Show more** to get more results.

With the above, you should be able to navigate through the auditing feature, be able to set audit filters and read the results returned.

Audit investigation

In the audit results table, you are then able to select the action you are interested in to investigate. Your selection will be highlighted on the screen, and you will be able to choose whether you wish to view details on the targeted source, the user who can see the resource or the associated security rule. The associated security rule investigation is the most important one, as it lets you know which security rule is responsible for providing permission to that user, or which security rules the user needs to have access to the targeted resource:

The earlier security rule is responsible for giving `Martin.Mahler@vizlib.com` the R and P permissions on the Partner stream.

Auditing when creating new security rules

Following up on the paragraph of validation of security rules, once you are happy with the syntax, you can preview your newly created security rule. Previewing your security rules using the audit feature helps you test how your newly created logic will change the permissions for a set of resources or users. All changes, affected by the new security rule, will be indicated with blue colored actions, similar to the audit results table described earlier in this section.

 It's not uncommon that sometimes, by accident, you will have multiple security rules applying to the same resource or user. While not ideal, it will not break anything, but will instead sequentially enforce the rules: Qlik Sense evaluates each rule in turn. If one rule provides access to a particular type, Qlik Sense provides that access.

Security rule uses cases and examples

There are no such things as generic use cases with security rules or standards which typically apply to all Qlik Sense environments. The beauty of ACAB security rules is that they can be very tailored to an environment's needs. This section will briefly outline two security rule use cases and provide context and commentary.

Security rules example:
Creating QMC stream admin roles

Sometimes, as part of a multi-project Qlik Sense deployment, it's useful giving super users advanced permissions for their own project's stream so they can manage the app deployment process themselves. While you can create a new generic admin role for streams, it is recommended to apply a bespoke security rule for each stream in this case, as each project might have different requirements on how their deployment process should look. The relevant stream in the below example will carry the name *Mastering Qlik Sense*.

Resource filter

As you wish to give each stream admin enough permission to manage his/her stream, you will want to give permission to the following resources at least:

- Stream
- App
- App.Object
- ReloadTask

To keep it generic, for this particular security rule, you will need to use the asterisk as a wildcard. The resource filter code looks as follows:

```
Stream_*, App_*, App.Object_*, ReloadTask_*
```

Conditions

Due to its complexity, and the multiple resources it should apply to, the security rule will need to be written in the advanced mode.

It's going to be segregated into the following parts:

```
user.roles = "Mastering Qlik Sense Stream Admin"
```

This part will create a new user role, called Mastering Qlik Sense Stream Admin, which you can assign to users in the user management section:

```
(resource.resourcetype="Stream" and resource.name="Mastering Qlik Sense")
```

The previous logic describes the rule apply to the resource stream, and the stream name is Mastering Qlik Sense:

```
(resource.resourcetype="App" and resource.stream.name="Mastering Qlik Sense")
```

This security statement, on the other hand, affects the rule to the resource app, and where the respective Stream name, where the app is located, is called Mastering Qlik Sense.

> **Be careful**: If you miss specifying the resource stream name, you will give the role access to all apps. Don't worry, though; previewing your security rule using the audit feature will help you catch that error in time.

```
(resource.resourcetype="App.Object" and resource.objectType="sheet" and
resource.app.stream.name="Mastering Qlik Sense")
```

Similar to the App, it gives permission to all sheets within apps found in the `Mastering Qlik Sense` stream:

```
(resource.resourcetype="App.Object" and resource.objectType="sheet" and
resource.app.stream.name="Mastering Qlik Sense")
```

Similar to the App and App.Object, this part of the security conditions gives permission for all reload tasks to apps which have been published to the `Mastering Qlik Sense` stream.

All in all, when you logically combine all the above conditions, you can get one security expression which can be added to the security rules advanced editor:

```
user.roles = "Mastering Qlik Sense Stream Admin" and
((resource.resourcetype="Stream" and resource.name="Mastering Qlik Sense")
or (resource.resourcetype="App" and resource.stream.name="Mastering Qlik
Sense") or (resource.resourcetype="App.Object" and
resource.objectType="sheet" and resource.app.stream.name="Mastering Qlik
Sense") or (resource.resourcetype="ReloadTask" and
resource.app.stream.name="Mastering Qlik Sense"))
```

Action

Depending on your governance requirements, you should apparently decide for yourself which actions you give the user role permission to, but for this example, the following ones were suggested:

```
create, read, update, delete, export, publish, changeOwner, changeRole,
exportData
```

Security rules example – Qlik Sense access rights for AD groups

In large organizations, permissions across multiple applications and services are usually applied via the use of AD groups. Qlik Sense can speedily retrieve the list of relevant AD groups and have security rules be driven by them. This makes things easier, as it delegates permissions management to a team sitting outside of the Qlik Sense administrators.

A typical use case would be to define different permissions for developers and different ones for the contributors. You might want to allow a developer to create apps, data connections, and app objects, whereas the contributors, should only be able to modify app content. These types of permissions segregations, for example, can be driven off two AD groups, uGLBDeveloper, and uGLBContributor.

Security rule for creating apps (developer)

The next example will create a security rule to permit the user group uGLBDeveloper to create apps.

Field	Code
Resource filter	App_*
Conditions	user.group="uGLBDeveloper"
Actions	create

Security rule for creating data connections (developer)

This example will create a security rule to permit the user group uGLBDeveloper to create data connections. Limiting the users who can create data connections improves the governance of what data is used in the Qlik Sense environment.

Field	Code
Resource filter	DataConnection_*
Conditions	resource.resourcetype = "DataConnection" and (user.group="uGLBDeveloper")
Actions	create

Security rule for creating app objects (developer and contributor)

Not everyone should be able to create their sheet objects, as this could impact the performance of the whole server. The next security rule will limit the ability to users in the `Developer` or `Contributor` groups:

Field	Code
Resource filter	`App.Object_*`
Conditions	`resource.App.HasPrivilege("read") and` `(user.group="Developer" or user.group="Contributor")`
Actions	`create`

The previous three security rules are created independently but work in conjunction with delivering user-type oriented permission. It's a good example of how logic can be segregated to multiple rules to keep things easy, rather than having one very complex security rule.

Summary

Security rules using access based attribute control is a new and a compelling feature to Qlik Sense. It gives a lot of flexibility, full control, and, using the audit feature, a good overview of who has access to do what within your Qlik Sense environment. It allows you, as the administrator, to apply governance to the level acceptable in your organization: from pure, open self-service to very strict and controlled deployment of applications, anything is possible.

With Qlik Sense's multi-node scalability, it is straightforward to segregate mini project environments while maintaining everything under one hood. Security rules allow for that flexibility by enabling administrators to apply different rules to different projects, user types, even to different nodes.

While robust, security rules in Qlik Sense need to be designed carefully for the platform to be scalable. Avoid creating hundreds of mini rules just as a tactical solution and try to plan ahead: How many projects will embark on your Qlik Sense environment, and how different are their use cases? What are the number of apps, the level of self-service, and the frequency of releasing updates? Capturing and assessing all these parameters can help in creating more centrally-based security rules and administrator roles.

This will not only promote governance but will also help to reduce time-to-market for new projects and Qlik Sense apps. At the same time, by educating new projects or teams new to Qlik Sense about the various established security roles and practices, they will be exposed to new ways of doing analytics they might not have thought of (self-service, for example).

All in all, planning well ahead and designing security rules properly is key to a successfully Qlik Sense deployment. And this is why it is imperative to understand all aspects of the newly introduced access based attribute control logic. Unfortunately, with flexibility in designing them, complexity is inevitably introduced. This chapter covered all the technicalities revolving around security rules, attributes, actions, conditions, and resources, and discussed how you could best design, implement, and audit the changes you have done.

While there is only so much theory that can be memorized, the best way to learn to apply security rules is to start implementing them and learn as you go.

In the next chapter, we will cover the best practices for loading data into your Qlik Sense application, always keeping our data model in mind.

4

Master Items in Qlik Sense

Master Items (MI) are a new feature in Qlik's product offering that have been introduced with Qlik Sense. They are intended to support the self-service environment by allowing the developer or app owner to create a set of predefined and reusable measures, dimensions, and visualizations. These items found on the asset panel on the left-hand side panel in a Qlik Sense app when in **Edit** mode, can be reused to build new sheets and visualizations.

The most substantial advantage of MKI is that they can be highly customized and become very bespoke: **Measures** can be defined as complex aggregations, **Dimensions** as drill-down groups, and charts as 100 percent built visualizations ready to be used straight away:

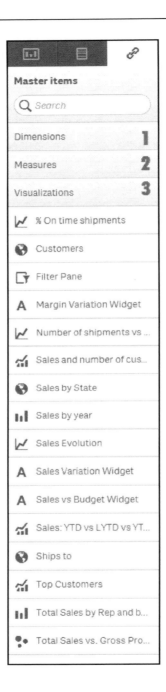

Master Items in the left-hand asset panel:

- **Master Dimensions**
- **Master Measures**
- **Master Visualizations**

Because of their **central governance** and re-usability, Master Items bring value to a governed self-service environment, and they are an integral part of mastering Qlik Sense and will be discussed in this chapter extensively.

The chapter will cover the concept in detail while discussing its technical implementation. The three different types of MKI—measures, dimensions, and visualizations—will be explained in full detail. Maintaining those items is critical, as is the idea that these will be driving the content of the application and the self-service framework.

While going into each technical detail, this chapter will elaborate on the benefits but also challenges and disadvantages that come along with using the functionality. The chapter will conclude with setting MKI up for a governed self-service environment where the users can create their sheets and dashboards without being able to either harm the Qlik Sense environment or create wrong reports.

To put it briefly, this chapter will cover:

- Understanding MKI
- The different types of Master Items, in detail
- The advantages, as well as disadvantages, of Master Items; we will demonstrate a couple of use cases where they can be successfully utilized in an Enterprise environment with or without self-service capabilities
- The technical details and the many ways of creating, editing, deleting, and maintaining Master Items

Understanding Master Items

Master Items are a new concept introduced in Qlik Sense, which allow the dashboard developer to create predefined visualizations, dimensions, and measures that can be reused throughout the app.

Utilizing this feature can be very powerful in the following three use cases:

- **Maintaining business logic**: Master Items can help with preserving business logic within an app. By being able to organize and govern aggregation logic for metrics as well as essential dimensions centrally, the dashboard owner can ensure that all sheets and visualizations are using the same expressions and efficiently aggregating data correctly and consistently across the app. The same applies to critical dimensions. Very often, data models will have a collection of various fields, but not all of them will be relevant or meaningful in the context of metrics.

- **Code maintenance**: It is not uncommon for apps to evolve. More complex aggregations are introduced to answer the surge of questions the business has, and the data model itself grows - not only in rows, but also in columns. New dimensions or tables might be added to enrich the existing data set. The challenge with every evolving app is to maintain the code, predominantly for expressions. By using Master Items, you can ensure that everything is kept in one place, and that updating, if required, can be easily changed on that one place and see the change affect the whole app. The best example is the renaming of existing dimension fields to something more meaningful to avoid ambiguity. If the app has already reached an evolved stage, using Master Items, that name change only needs to occur in one place. There is an additional level of expression governance recommended, using variables, which is described in the expression chapter in Module 2. The same also goes for visualizations that are reused in multiple places across the app – deploying them as Master Items allows changes to propagate across each copy.

- **Governance for self-service**: Coming back to the self-service model and its conflict with governance described in `Chapter 1`, *Qlik Sense Self-Service Model*, Master Items can be a great way, if not the best way, to put governance on an app in place, while at the same time keeping the freedom of self-service. By building an app-specific rich framework of permissible measures, dimensions, and especially visualizations, the user can create his bespoke reports and visualizations without risking breaking the app or presenting wrong numbers.

It ensures that aggregation logic in metrics is consistent across the app, and most relevant dimensions are also consistently used in each visualization. Using a simple drag and drop mechanism, building dashboards using the primary metrics of a data model becomes a very comprehensive exercise for the business users and prevents overwhelming them with a complicated data model structure that needs to be understood and considered. At the same time, if users are only allowed to utilize the Master Items, they will not be able to write free expressions or create a Cartesian combination of several dimensions, resulting in a possible blowout of the RAM of the Qlik Sense server.

Different types of Master Items

As discussed previously, Master Items come in three different flavors:

- Dimensions
- Measures
- Visualizations

They can all be used individually and in isolation, but it is possible to combine visualization Master Items with dimensions or metrics. Nesting dimensions within other dimensions or within measures is not possible. The different types of Master Items are described as follows.

Master dimensions

Dimensions determine how the data in visualization is grouped. In standard SQL, it is the field by which aggregation is arranged by using the GROUP BY qualifier. An example would be total sales by a salesman, with the salesman being the dimension value. Dimensions are usually qualities or categories and are characterized by discrete categorical values, rather than quantitative or continuous metrics or measures. They are typically found as slices in a pie chart or on the axis of a line or bar chart:

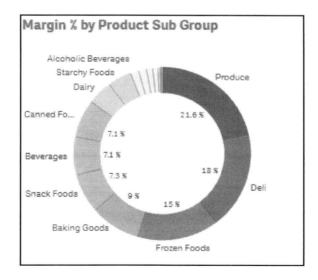

Let us see a comparison of amount over time:

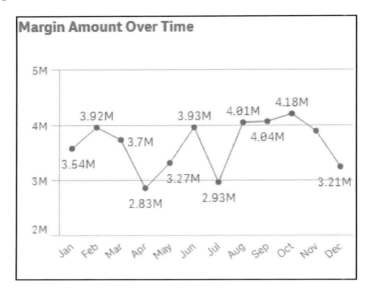

Dimensions are created from fields in the data model tables and can be:

- A single field, as is from the data model
- Calculated fields derived from one or multiple fields from the data model
- A collection of numerous only or calculated fields represented in a drill-down group
- Can have a distinct color assigned to ensure dimension values are colored consistently across charts.

Master measures

Measures and **metrics** are calculations used in visualizations to provide quantitative information about dimensions, usually expressed in numbers, intervals, or ratios. They can generally be found in columns in tables or as the *y*-axis of line or bar charts, as shown in the following two images:

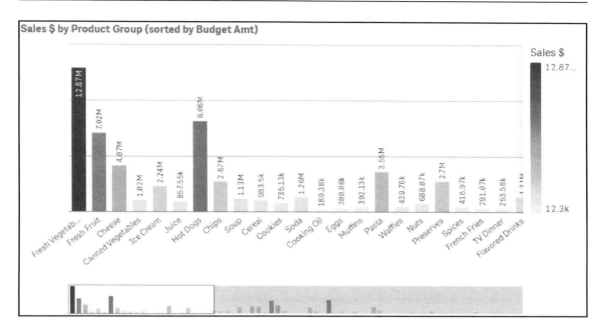

Let us have a look at the numeric data:

Sales Rep		Sales Variance	
Totals		-11.9%	
Lee Chin		946.7%	
Deborah Halmon		558.3%	
Edward Laychak		479.3%	
Don Simmons		415.4%	
Judy Rowlett		379.3%	
Edward Smith		314.1%	
Robert Kim		314.0%	

Sometimes it is of interest to not only make numerical calculations for dimensions, but to also determine calculated qualitative attributes, called *nominal ordinal values*. Examples are ratings, namely *good*, *normal*, and *bad*, summarizing one or multiple metrics into one qualitative classification for a particular dimension value.

Metrics can be very versatile, and it is not uncommon to be confused about whether to display something as a dimension or a metric. As a general rule of thumb, if aggregations are required (sum/count/divide), then it has to be achieved via measures.

While dimensions are usually straightforward in their implementation, it is necessary to be very careful when defining and utilizing measures as aggregations, and resulting numbers always need to be verified and validated. A wrongly calculated measure can do more damage to a business than a dashboard will ever be able to provide in value. It is, therefore, the most valuable use case for using Master Items, as aggregation logic can be centrally maintained, and all the business users can develop their self-service visualizations and sheets with high confidence.

At the same time, measures represent the most complicated aspect of building visualizations, as users will not only need to set up mathematical equations, but also utilize Qlik's set analysis to take advantage of more sophisticated aggregations. This is not something that the average user can do, so setting up key measures as master items alleviates the complexities of building visualizations and dashboards, while at the same time preserving the quality and confidence of the business logic.

Last but not least, self-service governance also benefits from putting measures into Master Items, as it prevents users from doing non-performing aggregations which might hurt the RAM usage of the app. This is not something that the average user can do, so setting up key measures as Master Items alleviates the complexities of building visualizations and dashboards while at the same time preserving the quality and confidence of the business logic. Last but not least, self-service governance also benefits from putting measures into master items, as it prevents users from doing non-performing aggregations which might hurt the RAM usage of the app.

Visualizations

 The point of visualizations is to communicate and present data quickly and relevantly, while maintaining the accuracy of what is being displayed. Visualizations can be created and then added to the Master Item list with predefined dimensions and measures.

The predefined dimensions and measures can be Master Items themselves.

Sitting in front of a blank canvas on top of an unknown data model can be overwhelming for new self-service users. It is therefore beneficial to create some standard (and usually the most relevant) visualizations as Master Items so that the business users can quickly drag and drop them on their sheet to create their bespoke dashboard.

It will significantly improve the self-service experience. Inserted Master Items can always be unlinked from the asset panel and provide the user with a starting point in modifying an existing visualization, including all of its settings, as well as dimensions and measures (instead of beginning from scratch).

Working with Master Items

This section is more technical and will cover all forms of working with Master Items and how to set them up in an application, including some best practices for doing so.
It is important to note in the preface of this section that Master Items can only be created, edited, and removed from an unpublished application. This might change in the future, as Qlik are gearing towards a more collaborative development approach, where multiple users can co-develop on even a published app; but as of the time of writing, this is not yet in place.

 The use of screenshots in this section will be limited, as Qlik's interface changes with each update. The asset panel is the control panel on the left-hand side of the screen when the user is in **Edit** mode.

Master dimensions

Dimensions are the air of any data model and should be easily accessible to users, as well as defined and relevant. Using master dimensions in a dashboard helps you narrow down the most used and appropriate dimensions and organize them on the left-hand panel for the user, without necessarily having to drop all over dimensions from the data model. This section will cover all of the different ways to create, edit, or remove master dimensions.

Creating master dimension from a field

Creating a new master dimension directly from the list of fields in the app is the most straightforward way. The following steps will be required:

1. While in **Edit** mode on the sheet of an app, navigate to your left-hand panel and open the **Fields** menu. In there, you will find a list of all available fields of the data model.
2. Choose the field you wish to add as a master dimension by right-clicking on it and adding it as a new dimension.
3. The following dialogue menu will pop up, where you will see the selected field added to the description. In the dialogue, you can see the whole list of dimensions on the left-hand side, and on the right-hand side, the empty attribute fields of the new dimension:

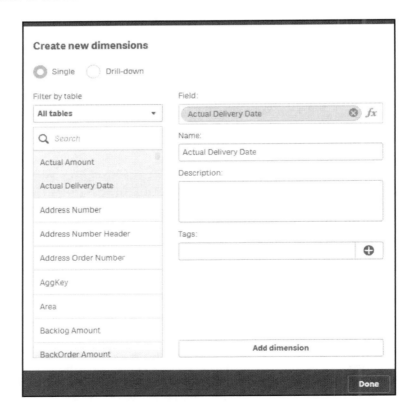

4. Enter a description which will give context to the dimension. The **Description** can be read by the user on the Master Item asset panel, so it is an excellent place to keep additional information and possible references to further documentation or contacts.

5. **Tags** are optional and utilized by the search function to identify and quickly filter the master dimensions when searching on the asset panel. While there is no cost in adding tags to it and it is helpful, the benefit is minimal, as Master Items are not introduced in masses. Each tag can contain a maximum of 31 characters, and each Master Item can have up to 30 tags. You can add tags by clicking + icon or by pressing *Enter*.

6. Click on the **Add dimension** button. Do not click on **Done** in the dialog, as it will take you back to the sheet and all work will be lost.

Creating master dimensions from the asset panel

Creating a new master dimension directly from the asset panel in the app is the second most straightforward way, right after creating it from the fields. The following steps will be required:

1. While in **Edit** mode on the sheet of an app, navigate to your left-hand panel and open the Master Items menu. In there, you will find three menu items: **Dimensions**, **Measures**, and **Visualizations**.

2. Open the **Dimensions** accordion and click on **Create new dimensions**.

3. In the following dialog menu, you will see the list of dimensions on the left-hand side, and on the right-hand side, the empty attribute fields of the new dimension:

4. Select the dimension from the list of available fields, which will be inserted into the **Field** area automatically. For a single field master dimension, no further steps are required.

5. Enter a meaningful name for the master dimension. Make sure it is relevant to the business, rather than to the developer or data modeler, as this is the stage where one can simplify the frontend of a possible more complex data model.

6. Enter a description which will give context to the dimension. The description can be read by the user on the Master Item asset panel, so it is an excellent place to keep additional information and potentially references to further documentation or contacts.

7. Tags are optional and utilized by the search function to identify and quickly filter the master dimensions when searching on the asset panel. While there is no cost in adding tags to it and it is helpful, the benefit is minimal, as Master Items are not introduced in masses. Each tag can contain a maximum of 31 characters, and each Master Item can have up to 30 tags. You can add tags by clicking **P** or by pressing *Enter*.

Creating master dimensions from the data model viewer

Master dimensions can not only be built on the frontend but also in the data model viewer, directly. For this, the following steps are required:

1. In the data model viewer, where you see a list of all available tables floating, pick the field which is of interest by selecting it, and click on the preview on the bottom-left.

2. This will pop up a preview dialog with two button options on the left-hand side, as well as some additional information about the selected field, including density and subset ratio.

3. Click on **Add as dimension**.

4. The following dialog menu will pop up, where you will see the selected field added to the description. In the dialog, you can see the whole list of dimensions on the left-hand side, and on the right-hand side, the empty attribute fields of the new dimension:

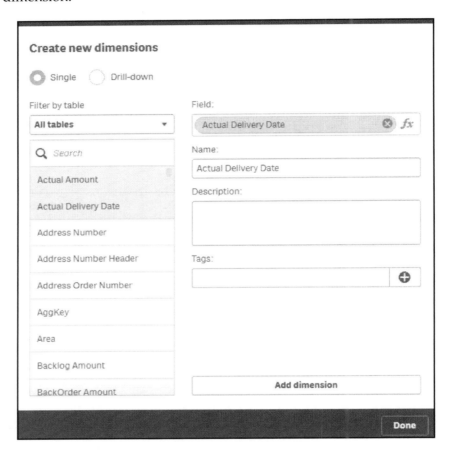

5. Enter a description which will give context to the dimension. The description can be read by the user on the Master Item asset panel, so it is an excellent place to keep additional information and potentially references to further documentation or contacts.

6. Tags are optional and utilized by the search function to identify and quickly filter the master dimensions when searching on the asset panel. While there is no cost in adding tags to it and it is helpful, the benefit is minimal, as Master Items are not introduced in masses. Each tag can contain a maximum of 31 characters, and each Master Item can have up to 30 tags. You can add tags by clicking + or by pressing *Enter*.

7. Click on the **Add dimension** button. Do not click on **Done** in the dialog, as it will take you back to the sheet and all work will be lost.

Creating master dimensions via the API

It is also possible to create master dimensions directly via the Qlik Sense API. This, however, will not be covered in this section, as it would go beyond the scope of this book. Basic concepts of the API will be included in Module 3 of this book, but for advanced methods, it is recommended to visit the Qlik Sense API documentation website online on `https://help.qlik.com/`.

Creating calculated master dimensions

Calculated master dimensions represent the more advanced way of creating new dimensions based on existing fields. Sometimes, the fields (being in the state they are) do not suffice to be used in a visualization directly. The most common use cases to create calculated master dimensions are:

- Calculated dimensional flags
- Dimensions formatted in a different way than provided by the data model
- Aggregated dimensions

With the exception of aggregated dimensions, the calculation logic for all other use cases should be pushed back to the loading script, as the frontend will take unnecessary performance hits.

To create a calculated dimension, please follow any of the top three approaches to creating a master dimension:

1. When you open the dimension dialog, an **fx** symbol (stands for function) is visible next to the field. Click on it to open the function's dialog.
2. In the popped-up function's dialog, enter the expression for the aggregated dimension. Make sure that you know and have read the second module of this book, as there are many ways to go wrong in this part.

3. Once the aggregation is added, click on **Apply** on the bottom-right, and the calculated dimension will be added as a field to the dimension dialog.

4. Enter a meaningful name for the calculated master dimension. Make sure it is relevant to the business, rather than to the developer or data modeler, as this is the stage where one can simplify the frontend of a possible more complex data model.

5. Enter a description which will give context to the dimension. The description can be read by the user on the Master Item asset panel, so it is a great place to keep additional information and potentially references to further documentation or contacts.

6. Tags are optional and utilized by the search function to identify and quickly filter the master dimensions when searching on the asset panel. While there is no cost in adding tags to it and it is helpful, the benefit is minimal, as Master Items are not introduced in masses. Each tag can contain a maximum of 31 characters, and each Master Item can have up to 30 tags. You can add tags by clicking + or by pressing *Enter*.

Creating a drill-down master dimension

The drill-down dimension is a handy feature of Qlik Sense. It allows you to add grouped dimensions into visualizations, which are then automatically drilled-through, based on filter selections in the data model.

 The drill-down mechanism switches the displayed dimension based on whether the dimension defined earlier it has only one possible value left to show.

It is handy to display hierarchies of data in a visualization, giving some additional added value in intuitive dashboard analytics.

To create a calculated dimension, please follow any of the top three approaches to creating a master dimension:

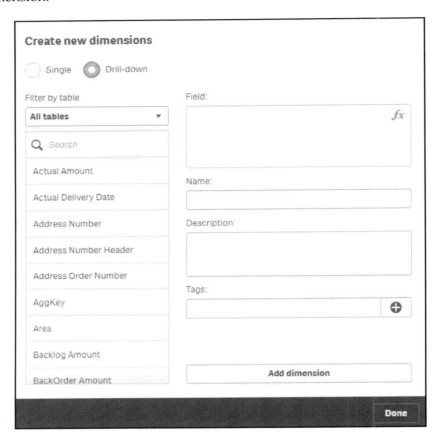

1. When you open the dimension dialog, a **Drill-down** bullet point is visible at the top-right and needs to be selected.
2. Once the **Drill-down** bullet point is selected, the **Field** text area grows bigger, allowing you to insert multiple dimensions, or even calculated dimensions.
3. Once numerous fields are added, ensure that you define the sort order, as it will become the defined order in which the Drill-down dimension group will navigate through the available fields on the dashboards, from top to bottom.

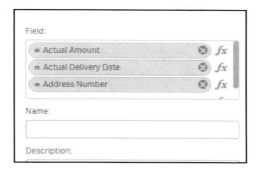

4. Enter a meaningful name for the drill-down master dimension. Make sure it is relevant to the business, rather than to the developer or data modeler, as this is the stage where one can simplify the frontend of a possible more complex data model.

5. Enter a description which will give context to the dimension. The description can be read by the user on the Master Item asset panel, so it is an excellent place to keep additional information and potentially references to further documentation or contacts.

6. Tags are optional and utilized by the search function to identify and quickly filter the drill-down master dimensions when searching on the asset panel. While there is no cost in adding tags to it and it is helpful, the benefit is minimal, as Master Items are not introduced in masses.

Editing, deleting, and duplicating master dimensions

Editing, deleting or duplicating master dimensions, be it a calculated field, a drill-down dimension, or a plain simple field, is straightforward.

 Make sure that you are working on an unpublished app, as otherwise, you will not be able to modify, delete, or create duplicates of a master dimension.

Master items can be deleted in four simple steps:

1. Navigate to the left-hand side of the asset panel and click your way through to the accordion with the list of created master dimensions. You can also edit a master dimension from its preview. You open the preview by clicking an item in the master dimensions.

2. There, pick the master dimension you wish to edit, delete, or duplicate, and right-click on it to view the options available.

3. With deleting or duplicating the master dimension, the journey ends here, while when editing it, the **Edit** dimension dialog is brought up. In there, similar to when master dimensions are created, feel free to modify any attribute.

4. After making your changes, click on **Save** to get back to the sheet.

Be very careful when deleting a master dimension, as all visualizations or objects in which it is being used will fail to render, which can result in irreversibly breaking some of the charts on the dashboard. Master dimensions are global settings which can potentially be used across multiple apps, so be very careful when editing or deleting them.

Master measures

Measures are the first thing a user looks for when he tries to answer a question about data.

What are the revenues? What is the cost? Who is the largest client? Quantifying data is the essential practice of data analytics, and also the reason why master measures can play such an important role when creating dashboards for self-service in Qlik Sense.

It is not only essential to be able to find the key measures and metrics quickly, but also to ensure that the aggregation and calculation logic applied is correct. With all of the different ways in which data can be filtered, permutated, and aggregated, it's paramount the user does not incorrectly utilize metrics, as it could then convey a wrong picture of the business and its data.

Creating master measures is part of establishing governance by containing the self-service capabilities to predefined ways of using metrics and measures.

This section will cover all of the different ways to create master measures, edit, and delete them.

Creating master measures from a field

Creating a new master measure directly from the list of fields in the app is the most straightforward way. The following steps will be required:

1. While in **Edit** mode on the sheet of an app, navigate to your left-hand panel and open the **Fields** menu. In there, you will find a list of all available fields of the data model.
2. Choose a field you wish to serve as the basis for a master measure by right-clicking on it and adding it by creating a new measure.
3. The following dialog menu will pop up, where you will see the selected field added to the **Expression**. You can then either type in the expression directly (and move straight to *step 5*), or click on the orange **fx** (standing for functions) to open the expression editor:

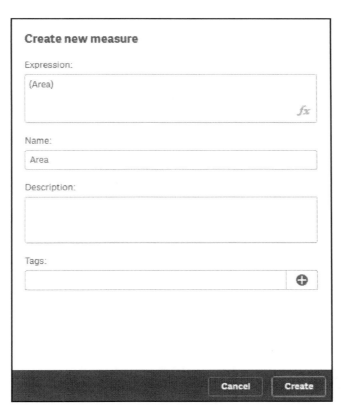

4. In the expression editor, you have an assisted aggregation wizard on the right-hand panel. At the same time as typing here, the expression and the syntax are checked and validated. Click **apply** to add the expression to the master measure:

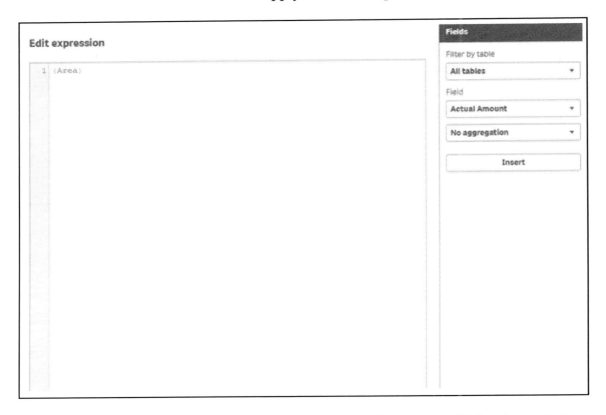

 If there is an error in the expression editor, Qlik Sense will hint about what is incorrect in the lower left-hand corner. Additional error information may be available by clicking the icon next to the **hint**.

5. In the master measure dialog, add a description which will give context to the measure. The description can be read by the user on the Master Item asset panel, so it is an excellent place to keep additional information and potentially references to further documentation or contacts.

6. Tags are optional and utilized by the search function to identify and quickly filter the master measure when searching on the asset panel. While there is no cost in adding tags to it and it is helpful, the benefit is minimal, as Master Items are not introduced in masses. Each tag can contain a maximum of 31 characters, and each Master Item can have up to 30 tags. You can add tags by clicking **P** or by pressing *Enter*.

7. Click on the **Create** button to add the master measure to the app.

You can open the online help with the full description of how to use the current function by double-clicking the function name in the expression editor and pressing *Ctrl + H* on the keyboard. This feature becomes available after having entered the first parenthesis of the expression after the function name, and only when using a computer with a keyboard.

Creating master measures from the data model viewer

Similar to how master dimensions can be created in multiple ways, master measures can also be added directly via the data model viewer. For this, the following steps are required:

1. In the data model viewer, where you see a list of all available tables floating, pick the field which is of interest by selecting it, and click on the preview on the bottom-left.

2. This will pop up a preview dialogue with two button options on the left-hand side, as well as some additional information about the selected field, including density and subset ratio.

3. Click on **Add as measure**.

4. The following dialog menu will pop up, where you will see the selected field added to the expression. You can then either type in the expression directly (and move straight to *step 5*), or click on the orange **fx** (standing for functions) to open the expression editor:

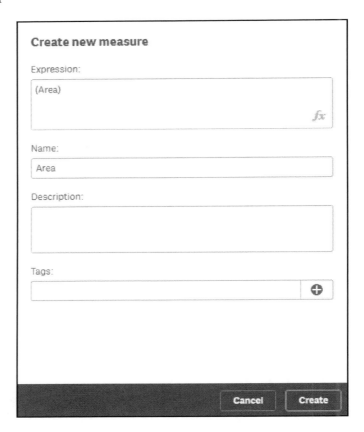

5. In the expression editor, you have an assisted aggregation wizard on the right-hand panel. At the same time as typing here, the expression and the syntax are checked and validated. Click **apply** to add the expression to the master measure:

 TIP
If there is an error in the expression editor, Qlik Sense will hint about what is incorrect in the lower left-hand corner. Additional error information may be available by clicking the icon next to the hint.

6. In the master measure dialogue, add a description which will give context to the measure. The description can be read by the user on the Master Item asset panel, so it is an good place to keep additional information and potentially references to further documentation or contacts.

7. Tags are optional and utilized by the search function to identify and quickly filter the master measure when searching on the asset panel. While there is no cost in adding tags to it and it is helpful, the benefit is minimal, as Master Items are not introduced in masses. Each tag can contain a maximum of 31 characters, and each Master Item can have up to 30 tags. You can add tags by clicking **P** or by pressing *Enter*.

8. Click on the **Create** button to add the master measure to the app.

You can open the online help with the full description of how to use the current function by double-clicking the function name in the expression editor and pressing *Ctrl + H* on the keyboard. This feature becomes available after having entered the first parenthesis of the expression after the function name, and only when using a computer with a keyboard.

Editing, deleting, and duplicating master measures

Editing, deleting or duplicating master measures is straightforward, and very similar to master dimensions.

Make sure that you are working on an unpublished app, as otherwise, you will not be able to modify, delete, or create duplicates of a master measure.

1. In **Edit** mode, navigate to the left-hand side of the asset panel and click your way through to the accordion with the list of created master measures. You can also edit a master measure from its preview. You open the preview by clicking an item in the master measure.

2. In there, pick the master measure which you wish to edit, delete, or duplicate, and right-click on it to view the options available.

3. With deleting or duplicating the master measure, the journey ends here, while when editing it, the edit dimension dialog is brought up. In there, similar to when a master measure is created, feel free to modify any attribute.

4. After making your changes, click on **Save** to get back to the sheet.

 Be very careful when deleting a master measure, as all visualizations or objects in which it is being used will fail to render, which can result in irreversibly harming some of the charts on the dashboard. Master measures are global settings which can potentially be used across multiple apps, so be very careful when editing or deleting them.

Master visualizations

Master visualizations are created to organize the most common or important visualizations used in the application. This is so that they can be reused across the app and be made available to the user on the left-hand asset panel via drag and drop. At the same time, for governance purposes, if the self-service capabilities should be limited on the dashboard, it will allow the developer to pre-create all charts, which can then be inserted by the users to create their bespoke dashboard. Also, if the data model is only meaningful if presented in a particular way, these preset charts can also assist the self-service capabilities of the dashboard by supporting

Unlike with master dimensions or master measures, there is only one way to create master Visualizations. Again, Master Items can only be created or amended when the app is yet unpublished.

Creating master visualizations

To create a master visualization, an existing chart needs to be available in the app, as you cannot create a master visualization from scratch, unlike master dimensions or master measures:

1. Ensure that you are in **Edit** mode and you have the sheet open in which the chart to be added as a master visualization is displayed.
2. Right-click on the selected chart and click on **Add to master items**.

3. The following dialog will pop up, which will inherit the existing chart title as the Master Item name.

4. In the master visualization dialog, add a description which will give context to the measure. The description can be read by the user on the Master Item asset panel, so it is a good place to keep additional information and potentially references to further documentation or contacts.

5. Tags are optional and utilized by the search function to identify and quickly filter the master visualization when searching on the asset panel. While there is no cost in adding tags to it and it is helpful, the benefit is minimal, as Master Items are not introduced in masses. Each tag can contain a maximum of 31 characters, and each Master Item can have up to 30 tags. You can add tags by clicking **P** or by pressing *Enter*.

6. Click on the **Create** button to add the master visualization to the app.

Editing, deleting and duplicating master visualizations

Similar to master dimensions and master measures, editing, deleting, or duplicating master visualizations works in the same way. However, it is not necessarily as straightforward as one would expect to be able to modify a master visualization directly in the sheet - this is not possible. In order to make changes, the following steps are required:

Make sure that you are working on an unpublished app, as otherwise, you will not be able to modify, delete, or create duplicates of a master visualization.

1. In **Edit** mode, navigate to the left-hand side of the asset panel and click your way through to the accordion with the list of created master visualizations. You can also edit a master visualization from its preview. You open the preview by clicking an item in the master visualization.
2. In there, pick the master visualization which you wish to edit, delete, or duplicate, and right-click on it to view the options available.
3. With deleting or duplicating the master visualization, the journey ends here, while when editing it, the edit dimension dialogue is brought up. In there, similar to when a master visualization is created, feel free to modify any attribute.
4. After making your changes, click on **Save** to get back to the sheet.

Be very careful when deleting a master visualization, as it will disappear from all sheets in the application, which can harm the dashboard uncontrollably. Master visualizations are global settings which can potentially be used across multiple apps, so be very careful when editing or deleting them.

When dragging a Master visualization to your canvas, you have the option to *unlink* it which creates a local copy of the master visualization for you to edit. All changes to the copy will remain local and will not affect the Master Item.

Summary

Master Items are a new feature introduced with Qlik Sense which allow a developer to democratize the data and visualizations within an app. They permit you to effectively predefine, control, and maintain metrics, dimensions, and pre-canned visualizations, to make them readily available for the end users in the dashboard.

Next, to improving the self-service capabilities of a deployed app, Master Items also provide a way to deploy governance and control on self-service. By predefining available metrics and dimensions, you can prevent an inexperienced user from creating inefficient aggregations and calculations in the frontend, which could result in a RAM hit of the underlying server.

This chapter outlined typical strategies and use cases for deploying Master Items, as well as showcasing, step-by-step, how to create them in Qlik Sense. It concluded with the advantages and disadvantages of Master Items and left you with a solid understanding of when to use Master Items, how to use them, and how to prepare them for self-service analytics.

The next chapters, especially module 2, will provide you with a good understanding of how to best define metrics, various data modeling techniques, and some fundamental education on how to create an efficient data model for consumption via Master Items.

5
Qlik Sense on the Cloud

With the emerging trend of software sitting on the cloud and the associated new concept of selling **software as a service (SaaS)**, Qlik did not miss the trend and has extended its platform by offering Qlik Sense on the cloud. Especially attractive for personal use and small businesses, Qlik Sense for business use can be available to you for as little as $15/month/user (as per 10th March 2018).

While much cheaper than buying Qlik Sense tokens, Qlik Cloud comes with some technical limitations, which this chapter will discuss. It will give you an overview of the product offerings with a list of features in comparison, including a description of how the cloud model works, its benefits, and to what extent it's different from both the Qlik Sense Desktop Client and the Server edition. It's important to note, however, that Qlik Sense's Cloud offering is still in its infancy and continuously being improved. Practical application is not yet common (at least on an enterprise level), however, with reading this chapter you will become aware of its opportunities and be able to make an educated decision whether a cloud-based solution is a suitable option for your own data analytics endeavors.

The chapter will conclude with some example use cases and scenarios where it would be beneficial for an individual or a company to use QS in the cloud or hybrid Sense environments, rather than hosting everything on-premise.

These are the topics that we will be covering in this chapter:

- Data analytics in the cloud
- Qlik Sense cloud models
- Hybrid cloud

Data analytics in the cloud

Cloud is a term which has, in the past year, become very strongly associated with software innovation, low cost, and flexibility. On the cloud, you do not run software locally on your machine, but it's hosted on a server on the web. This allows you to connect to the same instance from different devices, be it mobile, iPads, or from your laptop. At the same time, as it's accessible from practically anywhere where the internet is available, cloud solutions are encouraging the collaboration and sharing of information, in this case, data analytics.

The cloud is the future for various reasons, but at the same time, it introduces associated risks: if the data is not hosted on my premises or devices, where is it hosted? Who else has access to it, and how can I control or limit this? There are also regulatory requirements about where data is organized; take the **GDPR** (**General Data Protection Regulation**), for example, which will apply from 25th May 2018 in the European Union.

 The General Data Protection Regulation (Regulation (EU) 2016/679) is a regulation by which the European Parliament, the Council of the European Union, and the European Commission intend to strengthen and unify data protection for all individuals within the **European Union** (**EU**).

As a Qlik consultant or business user, you should be aware of the implications of how and where your data resides, and spend an appropriate amount of time understanding the technical setup. While everything will eventually look the same on the frontend, with identical user experience, you need to be conscious of how data is processed behind the scenes, and whether or not it poses a business risk to you, either by not complying with regulatory requirements or by potentially exposing your data to outsiders.

Some argue that your data, when stored in the cloud, if compliant, is much safer, as companies like Google, Microsoft, and Amazon have much stronger security teams, are more diligent making regular backups, and have fail-safe redundancy in place, providing continuous operation.

While there are no particular guidelines or bulletproof methods for determining whether doing data analytics on the cloud is appropriate for your business, asking yourself the following questions is the first step:

- Where is my data stored, technically and geographically?
- Who owns my data; do I have the right to have my data deleted?
- Do I want to have ubiquitous access to my data analytics from practically anywhere?

- Is sharing data analytics and insights a fundamental requirement for my business?
- Do I want to maintain my data analytics environment?
- Am I happy with the essential basic data analytics offering, or do I wish to have control over extending it?
- Do I have the knowledge and time to invest in my infrastructure?

Whether or not your business requires a cloud setup, it should always start with its requirements and business necessities, and not the other way around.

Qlik Sense cloud models

Qlik initially emerged from software that was installed on-premises, but has now transitioned not only to a subscription model, but also to being available on the cloud, to be consumed by businesses as well as by personal users.

This section will cover the cloud licensing model, its features, and some guidance to help you decide which model is most fit for your business, or your customers.

Depending on the requirements and the use case, Qlik is, at the moment, offering three different subscription models on the cloud:

- Qlik Sense Cloud Basic
- Qlik Sense Cloud Business
- Qlik Sense Enterprise in the Cloud

All three subscriptions provide access to the full scope of the Qlik Sense associative data engine, such as the ability to associate multiple data sources with a few clicks, visual data preparation capabilities, and the ability to create and explore analytics applications. The differences between the three models are the usage limitation, customizability, and the availability of extra features.

Naturally, over time, both the pricing and the feature offerings might change, but this chapter will cover the available options and functionalities at the time of writing, in February 2018.

Qlik Sense Cloud Basic

Qlik Sense Cloud Basic is ideal for users who wish to get started with visual analytics on the cloud. As it is free to use, all a user needs to do is to register an account on Qlik's website, `https://www.qlikcloud.com/`. The same account can also be used to download the Qlik Sense Desktop version or to participate in the Qlik community.

 Qlik Sense Cloud Basic is free to use and is a great way to explore Qlik's analytics platform.

With Qlik Sense Cloud Basic, users can:

- Upload data and connect to web files
- Create fully interactive Qlik Sense apps, based on their data
- Share their produced app with up to five other Qlik Sense Cloud users
- Access the free package on Qlik's DataMarket

For personal use, a school, or university work project, or for playing around with data or Qlik itself, Qlik Sense Cloud Basic is particularly suitable. The following is a snapshot of the demo apps:

Qlik Sense Cloud Business

Qlik Sense Cloud Business includes additional collaboration features and governance settings which allow small teams, projects, or businesses to leverage and operationalize data analytics in the cloud. Collaboration on app creation, consumption, and publishing is enabled across groups of users.

 Qlik Sense Cloud Business is ideal for small teams, projects, or businesses who are in need of a cost-effective or temporary data analytics solution which is quick to set up, with no additional investment in infrastructure required. As of March 2018, it is priced at $15 per user per month and is free to try for 30 days.

On top of the basic functionalities of Qlik Sense Cloud Basic, the Business model provides more capabilities around the organization of apps. Specifically, it offers the following added features:

- **Administer and govern groups**: Ability to invite up to 49 additional group members to collaborate, and share apps and analytics. Each additional invited member will increase the usage cost by, currently, $15 per month per user.

- **Co-develop content**: Qlik Sense Basic Cloud only allows you to work by yourself, and then share the produced app. With the business model, you are now able to create and edit apps with other group members in a collaborative workspace. Any group member can view and contribute datasets that are accessible by other members of the same group.

- **Data connectivity**: Many more web connectors are available in the Qlik Sense Business Cloud model: Facebook fan pages, Google Analytics and AdWords, Salesforce, SQL, Twitter, web files, YouTube analytics, and YouTube data. On top of that, REST connectivity is available, too.

- **Organization and governance of apps**: With the Qlik Sense Business Cloud, up to three streams are available for group administrators to publish app content to and to leverage available security rules to establish who can view the streams and the apps within them.

- **Scheduling of data refreshes**: Configure a scheduler to automatically update your app data as often as daily, so your apps are always up to date.

- **Increased data storage**: Qlik Sense Business Cloud allows you to work with much bigger datasets, permitting you a maximum app size of up to 150MB (compressed), and total data storage of 500GB.

Qlik Sense Business Cloud is the perfect choice for you if you are interested in data analytics, is accessible from anywhere, quick to set up, and will not require additional investment in infrastructure, or much technical knowledge about Qlik Sense server administration.

As it's subscription-based, the Qlik Sense Business Cloud solution can be very cost-effective; the initial upfront investment is low, and the subscription is temporary, meaning it could be canceled at any time. This makes it particularly attractive for fixed-term projects, pop-up businesses, or as a tactical solution while your company is going through the process of evaluating or setting up their strategic data analytics environment.

Qlik Sense Enterprise in the cloud

Qlik Sense Enterprise gives you the full spectrum of functionality, customizability, and features of Qlik similar to the Qlik Sense Server edition. Qlik Sense Enterprise can be bought as a solution which is hosted in the cloud on Qlik's premises, with some additional management options. It's designed for organizations that need to widely deploy governed data and self-service analytics, and build custom apps and extensions with an unlimited integration of data from different sources. It also provides guaranteed granular control, administration, and governance of deployed data, apps, and the user and user groups accessing them. Qlik Sense Enterprise, in brief, differentiates itself from the Basic and Business Cloud models by offering the following additional options:

- **Flexible deployment**: Ability to deploy Qlik Sense server in a cloud of your choice with several options provided by Qlik, which include administration services, either by themselves or by one of their accredited Qlik partners. Qlik Sense Enterprise on the cloud can also become one part of a larger Qlik Sense infrastructure using a so-called hybrid approach, which will be covered later in this chapter. You can also choose to manage and deploy a private cloud-based deployment which is fully managed by an in-house team and hosted on a secured server like AWS, Microsoft Azure or Google Cloud.
- **Customize**: By being in full control of the Qlik Sense Enterprise installation, you can also leverage Qlik's open and standard APIs to develop custom guided analytics apps (called mashups), embed analytics in operational (web) apps sitting outside of Qlik Sense, and use extensions created by others, such as the Vizlib library.

- **Event-based data refreshes**: Trigger data refreshes based on events within your business processes, or leverage the Qlik Sense scheduler, which allows you to schedule automatic reloads of your apps up to every minute.
- **Create user-specific data views**: Qlik engine supports data-level security, called section access, which reduces the available data set to the user, based on their permission.
- **Expanded data connectivity options**: Qlik Sense Enterprise has a variety of data connectors, which are either available for free or can be purchased and added to your existing platform. A full list of which ones are available can be viewed at the following link: `https://www.qlik.com/us/products/qlik-connectors`.

Qlik Sense Enterprise on the cloud is mostly relevant for organizations that are looking for a cost-efficient and quick way to invest in and scale their data analytics capabilities without necessarily having to supply the required infrastructure themselves. They can either leverage Qlik's managed hosting services, or with powerful cloud-based infrastructure providers available, such as AWS, Microsoft Azure, and Google Cloud, also manage their hosted data analytics solution themselves. Given its speed of deployment and flexible options for scaling, hosting Qlik Sense Enterprise on the cloud can be a desirable and cost-efficient solution for many organizations, small and large who prefer OPEX (operational expenditures) over CAPEX(capital expenditures).

As already discussed in the introduction to this chapter, data security and regulation are, however, serious considerations which need to be assessed before going for a cloud-based option.

Features overview

The earlier sections mostly covered the difference between the various Qlik Sense Cloud options at a high level. At a low level, this section will provide a detailed overview of the available features, as per Qlik's own Product Overview document. Given the pace of progress at which they evolve the product, more features could become available, and as such, it is strongly advised that you refer to the website for the most up to date version at `https://www.qlikcloud.com/`.

The following table will give a better idea of how different the Qlik Sense options are from one another:

Feature	Qlik Sense Cloud Basic	Qlik Sense Cloud Business	Qlik Sense Enterprise
Deployment and Management	Fully hosted and managed by Qlik	Fully hosted and managed by Qlik	Deploy on-premise or in a cloud of your choice
Create and explore apps	♥	♥	♥
Associate multiple data sources	♥	♥	♥
Share insights with others	♥	♥	♥
Share streams of content	One stream	Three streams	Unlimited streams
Codevelop content		♥	♥
Admin and govern groups			♥
Granular control, administration, and governance			♥
Governed self-service			♥
Embed analytics and extend through APIs			♥
Visual data preparation	♥	♥	♥
Scheduler data refreshes		♥	♥
Create event-based data refreshes			♥
Define user-specific views			♥
Connect to data sources	Web files	Connectivity options	Full data connectivity
Access Qlik DataMarket	Free package	Essentials package	Add any package
Maximum App Size	25 MB	150 MB	Unlimited
Total Data Storage	250 MB	500 GB	Unlimited

(Source: https://www.qlik.com/us/-/media/files/product/qlik-sense/qlik-sense-cloud/qlik-sense-cloud-product-overview-guide-en.pdf?la=en)

Hybrid cloud

As Andrew Clarke beautifully described in a blog post at http://global.qlik.com/cn/blog/posts/drew-clarke/hybrid-cloud-analytics, *Cloud is a delivery mechanism, not a solution*. As such, Qlik is working on a hybrid cloud solution available for Qlik Sense Enterprise, which will give you the choice of how you wish to release your Qlik Sense environment to your users: on-premise, on the cloud, or even a mix of both, by connecting the whole infrastructure under one roof.

 Cloud is a delivery mechanism, not a solution. The hybrid cloud analytics solution will be a customer-defined strategy, not a policy defined by the vendor.

While a hybrid solution is not yet available at the time of writing, it is still worth discussing the hybrid model as an option when deploying Qlik Sense analytics on the cloud. The key ingredients to define Qlik's approach in providing hybrid cloud analytics can be summarized as follows:

- **Transparency**: Full transparency where the data resides and where the analysis happens. The user will be presented with all available apps and data through one single universal hub based on their role and security permission, not the location of where things reside and run.
- **Location Enforcement**: For several reasons, including but not limited to industrial, or national regulation, or companies' protection of their intellectual property, customers may choose to host data and do analysis against it within their premises, behind a firewall or offline. Within the hybrid cloud, as an administrator, you will be able to designate via the management console where the data is hosted and create enforcement rules on where digital assets can and will reside based on that dataset.
- **Orchestrated Entitlement**: Entitlements and licensing will be easily managed universally for the whole platform, regardless of whether the user is accessing via the cloud or the on-premise environment.
- **Bi-directional Migration**: Migration is vital. Based on the customer's criteria, a bi-directional migration to/from one infrastructure environment to another will be seamless in the hybrid cloud deployment.

- **Single Management Console**: A hybrid cloud analytical solution will be managed as one seamless environment across infrastructure boundaries via a single console.

Example of a hybrid cloud analytics solution

The case illustrates a made-up infrastructure setup of a hybrid cloud solution:

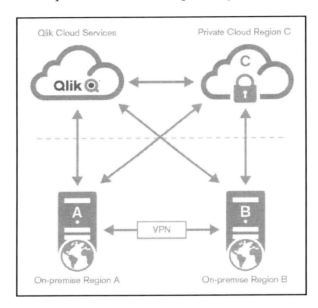

There are four environments to be seen; the top two of which are cloud-based, and the two bottom ones are hosted on-premise, in two different regions. All of the four setups are interconnected and are managed via one single management console.

On-Premise Servers: These two servers represent a typical deployment of Qlik Sense Enterprise, which is hosted within the premises of our fictitious organization. No one who is not connected to the internal network can access those servers. To ensure teams in different regions don't experience too much lag when accessing their apps, the on-premise infrastructure has been split into two regions: A and B.

Now, in some cases, analytics sitting on the cloud can be very beneficial. Take, for example, a customer analysis app utilized by the sales team, which needs to be accessible by the employees when they are on the go, meeting their customers. Mobile access via an iPad or a mobile phone is essential, and as such, a cloud solution is perfect. To ensure that no one but the sales representatives themselves can access the apps, the whole hosted cloud solution is private, requiring authentication to log on. Both the cloud and the on-premise servers are connected and, based on specific criteria, the hybrid cloud environment ensures that only the customer analysis app is published on that particular server.

Separately, the organization might also be interested in offering externally facing analytics, such as comprehensive analytics on some publicly available data. As such, to segregate this environment from everything else, a separate cloud server is created, which exclusively hosts publicly available apps.

With a hybrid cloud analytics solution, the organization can tackle multiple use cases, host data, and do analysis-enforced locations, all by protecting its data and securing where it's hosted, fully complying with regulations.

Summary

Doing Qlik Sense data analytics in the cloud has been a bold statement in the last couple of years, but it's becoming more of a reality. While still in its infancy, Qlik Sense Cloud is making a lot of progress and improvements. The most significant concerns about where data resides and regulations are being tackled with the hybrid cloud. While old QlikView customers larger, and slower, organizations will still have their reservations about this new approach to deploying analytics, new Qlik customers, and smaller companies or projects will find the value propositions of the cloud-compelling, especially the prompt setup, the low up-front investment, and bypassing the necessity to invest in infrastructure.

In my personal opinion, Qlik Sense Cloud will eventually grow to become the go-to Qlik model for doing data analytics. There are just too many benefits, both technologically and economically, for doing so, and eventually, more and more customers will migrate. While, at the time of writing this, Qlik Sense Cloud is not only too expensive, but also lacks many basic features, such as the integration of custom-made extensions, it is quickly improving, and I'm confident it will become a game-changer for the existing Qlik ecosystem. Follow it closely!

6
Qlik Sense Data Modeling

Data modeling is, from my point of view, one of the key components of every data project. From my early start as a consultant in Los Angeles and New York City, modeling was paramount to any project. I would spend 60% of my time analyzing requirements and designing the model. I learned from the beginning that a good data model saves time and headaches in the future.

A good model applies to any tool. From the old OLAP cubes to the newer tools, such as Qlik Sense, if you know modeling, you will be talking the same language like many others worldwide.

Back in the days when I was working as a business intelligence consultant in Italy, we had to migrate a project from OBIEE to QlikView (version 10 back then). Everything changed but the model. The source tables remained the same, the business rules, the logic within the ETL - all the same. The rest, of course, changed considerably, as both tools were completely different.

This book would not have a data modeling chapter if Qlik Sense did not allow data manipulation. This is a key feature where Qlik Sense stands out from other tools. Later in this chapter, you will cover the importance of doing calculations in the ETL. However, we will learn in detail how powerful the Qlik Sense engine is and how to leverage it to design a great and performing data model. The more you know about how Qlik Sense works, the better your applications will perform.

We will be giving you pointers, but it is vital that you go out there and get as much information as you can. I invite you to read my blog at `biexperience.wordpress.com`. You can also take a look at at the many other sources of knowledge such as the Qlik Community site and Qlik Branch among others.

In this chapter, you will learn how the Qlik Sense engine works. You will also learn about the different types of fact tables and dimensions you will usually find in a star schema data model, and most importantly, you will learn how to link all these tables together to have a performing data model. The list of topics that we will cover in this chapter includes:

- The engine drives everything
- What should be done upstream from Qlik Sense
- Star schema fact and dimension tables

The engine drives everything

For me, Qlik is all about the engine. What you can do with this beautiful piece of engineering is just astounding. Yes, building engaging and useful visualizations is ultimately what users need, but to me, those are just the blossom on the tree. They are seasonal and change with the wind. It is the roots, trunk, and branches that provide all the strength, power, and capabilities. A leafless tree in winter is as strong as in every other season, but – to me – even more gorgeous.

Build the data model and expressions right, and with minimal ongoing effort, your application will grow with your needs without buckling under increased load. Shortcut this stage in development, and it won't be long before the fragile trunk of your application becomes exposed for what it is – hollow and weak. Do it right the first time. Yes, it takes longer to build an application correctly, but we all should take a level of pride in our work that goes beyond throwing a working model out there quickly. The reality is, when dealing with approximately a million rows of data, you can build a terrible model, and it will still perform very fast. Not good enough! If it works well, usage will spread. What happens when your client/employer wants to triple the data and quadruple the users? Just about anyone can smash together a proof of concept, but when building for a production environment, you should allow time in your estimations to do it right.

In its very first version, Qlik Sense introduced the new Qlik engine, referred to as QIX. The name **QIX** means **Qlik IndeXing**, a new name given to the engine with the birth of Qlik Sense.

Granted, the clear majority of my Qlik experience has been in large enterprises, so this is a complete necessity if I am to truly succeed for my clients. However, even if your application will only ever be used by ten people, please consider using these best practices. Be proud of your work. The engine will open doors to possibilities you never knew existed.

OK, that's quite enough hyperbole. On to the substance.

Allow me to describe what I mean by *best practices*.

For me, *best practices* are a set of principles to employ in application development. *Principles* are not hard and fast rules. They should be adopted to appropriate degrees and adapted for your particular way of working and requirements. I have written them here as I use them – I always employ these practices, and they have served me well, so I encourage you to do the same. Many of these approaches were worked out by myself through a steep learning curve, only to find that they were already a thing. I'll present my flavors here but will refer to other, more well-known documents where I know of them.

Engine components

Before you start thinking about our new data model or whether you are planning on migrating your code from QlikView to Qlik Sense, you must understand what the QIX engine components are and how your script will interact with these and vice versa. Having a deep understanding of the engine will give you the power that allows you to create a professional, stable, scalable, and durable code.

Henric Cronström from Qlik is my source of knowledge. Whatever I know about the QIX engine is because of him. I strongly encourage you to read and follow his work in the Qlik community.

There are seven components that make up the QIX engine:

- Script engine
- Internal database
- Authorization (on opening)
- Logical inference engine
- Calculation engine
- Rendering engine
- Export features

The main components relevant to data modeling and expression building are:

- Internal database and script engine
- Logical inference engine
- Calculation engine

So, we will just focus on these for now.

The QIX internal database

The QIX internal database uses *symbol tables* and *data tables*. These two types of tables get created after the script engine executes the script. The script execution is sequential; this means that it is executed from left to right and from top to bottom.

Allow me first to describe how symbol tables are created in memory and what these tables contain.

The script engine is responsible for executing our Qlik Sense script. Whenever the script engine executes a LOAD or a SQL Select statement, it will bring into memory all the rows and columns in the data source, unless otherwise specified in the syntax. The data source can be anything from an Excel file to a table in a database.

The QIX internal database builds a separate symbol table for each field in the dataset. The main characteristic of the symbol table is that it contains a row for each distinct value of the source fields, as well as two columns: a value column and a bit-stuffed pointer.

Let's take a look at the following sample line of code:

```
SQL SELECT Customer, Customer_Country, Active_Flag FROM CUSTOMERS;
```

The script engine first connects to the database through the standard Qlik Sense database connection syntax, and then it sends whatever is between the keyword SQL and the semicolon to the database engine. The database engine, which is external to our Qlik Sense application, executes the SQL command, and finally, returns the resulting dataset to the Qlik engine.

Qlik Sense can connect to a database using one of the following syntaxes: **ODBC CONNECT TO** connect-string | **OLEDB CONNECT TO** connect-string | **CUSTOM CONNECT TO** connect-string | **LIB CONNECT TO** connection

Based on the SQL query we just saw, the dataset returned by the database engine to Qlik Sense will have three columns: Customer, Customer_Country, and Active_Flag.

I created fictional data for explanatory purposes.

The sample output will look as follows:

[CUSTOMER] *Data source*:

Customer	Customer_Country	Active_Flag
Sensei Ltd	United Kingdom	Y
Sensei Ltd	Australia	N
Magic Quadrant Inc.	United States	Y
Banda Bulevard	Argentina	Y

As previously mentioned, when the script engine executes the script, it builds a separate *symbol table* for each field in the dataset. This symbol table contains a row for each *distinct* value in the field, and two columns: the field value, and a bit-stuffed, binary index value, more generally known as the *pointer*.

In this example, the dataset contains three columns or fields. The internal database will create three different symbol tables, one for Customer, one for Customer_Country, and another one for Active_Flag.

Always load fields that you will use in your application to avoid using up memory for data you do not need.

The first symbol table will be the **Customer Symbol** table, which is the first field in the dataset. This symbol table will have two columns, the first of which contains the distinct values of the dataset field **Customer** and will look like this:

[Customer Symbol]:

Value	Customer
Sensei Ltd	
Magic Quadrant Inc.	
Banda Bulevard	

The field **Customer** in the dataset has four rows, three of which are distinct or unique values. We can see that the resulting **Customer Symbol** table contains three rows.

The second column of the symbol table is a bit-stuff binary index that univocally references each row in the symbol table.

 Remember: The index is *bit-stuffed*. This means the binary index only uses as many bits as necessary to account for all the distinct values, making it as efficient as possible.

The resulting **Customer Symbol** table with the distinct values and the bit-stuffed index will look as follows:

[Customer Symbol]:

Customer	Value
Sensei Ltd	00
Magic Quadrant Inc.	01
Banda Bulevard	10

Following the same logic, there will be a symbol table for Customer_Country, and one for Active_Flag.

Let's take a look at the resulting symbol table for the field Customer_Country:

[Customer_Country Symbol]:

Customer_Country	Value
United Kingdom	00
Australia	01
United States	10
Argentina	11

And the Active_Flag symbol table looks like this:

[Active_Flag Symbol]:

Active_Flag	Value
Y	0
N	1

Before we explain the data table used in the QIX internal database, we would like to briefly walk you through how the bit-stuffed index is populated.

A few paragraphs back, we mentioned that the bit-stuffed index is binary, and it will thus use the minimum amount of binary bits necessary to represent each of the distinct values in the symbol table.

When we have a few distinct values, it is easy to understand how this is populated. In the case of the `Active_Flag` symbol table, we have two distinct values, and consequently, it will use one binary bit to represent each row, 0 for the first value (Y) and 1 for the second value (N).

If we have three distinct values, which is the case in the Customer symbol table, but use only one binary bit per row, the engine will run out of bits by the time it populates the third and last value. To overcome this, the engine uses two binary bits per row: 00 for the first value, 01 for the second value, and 10 for the last and final value.

I bet many of you are asking why the third value cannot be represented as 11, or why the first value is 00 and not 01.

The following is a formula that will let you calculate the number of necessary bits per row that the engine needs to identify each of the distinct values.

A binary system, or base two system, uses two symbols: 0 and 1. To represent each of the rows in a symbol table, the engine uses the least amount of binary bits possible. The formula to calculate this is:

$$2^n >= [number\ of\ distinct\ values]$$

2 is the base system identifier, and n is the minimum amount of necessary bits to represent each of the distinct values.

The formula 2^n needs to meet the following criteria:

- n must be a whole integer, greater than or equal to *1*
- 2^n must be greater than or equal to the total number of distinct values to represent
- Start with $n = 1$ and increment its value by *one* until it meets the condition $2^n >= [number\ of\ distinct\ values]$

To summarize, the exponential number n represents the number of binary bits needed to represent the distinct values, and the resulting number of 2^n is the maximum amount of values that can be represented with n bits, where n is a whole number or a natural number.

Let's practice this with an example. The `Customer_Country` symbol table contains four distinct values: United Kingdom, Australia, United States, and Argentina. So, if we start putting the formula together, it will look like this:

$$2^n >= 4$$

We now have 2, which is the base system, and 4, which is the total number of distinct values we want to represent. So, how do we find out n? According to the definition, n has to be a positive whole number starting from 1, and this number must be greater than or equal to the number of total values to be represented.

If $n = 1$, we have $2^1 = 2$. Two isn't greater than or equal to 4, so we need to try the next whole positive number.

We increase the value of n by 1, now equaling 2. For $n = 2$, we have $2^2 = 4$, which is greater than or equal to 4, and it is also the minimum amount of bits we can have.

Understanding how to calculate the minimum number of bits needed to represent each value in the symbol table is as important as knowing the position of each of the bits.

The position of the bits goes from right to left. In a bit-stuffed index of *10*, the first bit is *0* and the second bit is *1*.

To understand the positioning of these numbers, we created the following matrix:

Bit position	2	1	0
$2^{[\text{bit position}]}$	$2^2 = 4$	$2^1 = 2$	$2^0 = 1$
Symbol table Value 1	0	0	0
Symbol table Value 2	0	0	1
Symbol table Value 3	0	1	0
Symbol table Value 4	0	1	1
Symbol table Value 5	1	0	0
Symbol table Value 6	1	0	1
Symbol table Value 7	1	1	0
Symbol table Value 8	1	1	1

If we take the example of the `Customer_Country` symbol table, there are four distinct values with three bits needed to represent those four values. With two binary bits, we can represent, at the most, eight values ($2^3 = 8$).

The first bit (far right) has the position *0*. So, $2^0 = 1$. For the first digit, we alternate one 0 and one 1 for as many values as we need (four, in my example).

The second bit is in position 1. So, $2^1 = 2$. For the second bit, we alternate two zeros and two ones.

Finally, the third bit is in the second position, and thus, we have $2^2 = 4$. We then alternate four zeros and four ones for as many values as we have.

The same logic applies to the digits in the other positions.

Now that we have described how the symbol tables are populated with their values and bit-stuffed indexes, we will talk about the second table that is created by the QIX internal database: the data table.

The data table contains the same number of rows and fields as the original data, but uses the binary index values instead of the clear-text values, and is therefore highly compressed.

As we have already mentioned, our example dataset has three columns (`Customer`, `Customer_Country`, and `Active_Flag`) and four rows of data.

In the data table, this same data will be represented with the bit-stuff indexes, and it will look as follows:

[CUSTOMER Data table]:

Customer	Customer_Country	Active_Flag
00	00	0
00	01	1
01	10	0
10	11	1

So, it is clear that the biggest impact on the compression is the number of *distinct values* in a field. Not only will more distinct values increase the number of rows in a field's symbol table, but the binary pointer values will be longer.

Here are a few things you can do to reduce the number of distinct values in your dataset, which will help with data compression and therefore improve your application performance:

- Split fields, if possible. For example, if you have a free text field Company Name with the values *Hedge Fund Limited, Hedge Fund Ltd,* and *Hedge Fund Ltd.,* this will account for three different, distinct values. However, if you split this field into Company Name and Company Suffix, you can have the Company Name table with one distinct value and Company Suffix with three distinct values, but it will be a lot easier to cleanse the data and convert everything to either 'Limited' or 'Ltd,' which will in return create one symbol table with one distinct value.

- Remove blank spaces. The field value 'Juan' isn't the same as 'Juan '. This will count as two different values. Use the `trim()` function to get rid of unwanted blank spaces.

- Shorten your dates. If you have a timestamp in your source but only display dates in your application, get rid of the time by using the function `floor()`. This will convert a timestamp value from '04-03-2019 10:54:22' to '04-03-2019'. If you need to show your hour, split your field into two, one for the date and one for the hour. This will drastically decrease RAM consumption.

- Replace business keys with surrogate keys: business keys are natural identifiers of values that are understandable to the business. For example, a business key for a Red Bike product could be 'BKS-RD-101928'. For the business, it is easy to understand that this product is a red bike with an identifier number of 101928. However, you could leave the product description to be used in your application front-end and convert all business keys into surrogate keys with the `AutoNumber()` function. This will create an incremental integer for each distinct value. Replacing long strings with numbers will improve RAM consumption significantly.

Use `AutoNumber(expression, AutoId)` when using it in different fields. `AutoId` allows you to name each of the counters. This keeps consistency in the counter among those with the same name.

The logical inference engine

The function of the logical inference QIX engine component is to identify which values in each symbol table are associated with user selections and which rows in the data table are in scope, based on the selections. Basically, the logical inference engine executes things at runtime, as opposed to the internal database tables that get created when the script is executed.

Whenever a user makes a selection in the front-end, all the visible charts need to be recalculated to show the new values based on the selections. The logical inference engine updates what is called **State Vectors**, which flag records and values as requiring aggregation.

No calculation is done at this stage – it is purely a logical step to identify what needs to be calculated. The work of the logical inference engine allows the QIX engine to have a very large data set, but only perform aggregations over the relevant records, ignoring all the others, thus enabling the speed-of-thought analysis we know and love.

In this section, we introduced a new concept: State Vectors. What is a State Vector?

Allow me to explain this in more detail. State Vectors are internal flags that get created when the user makes a selection in the front-end.

There are three main types of State Vectors:

- **Input State Vectors**: Has this field value been physically selected by the user? This field gets populated with 1 if the value has been selected, and 0 if not physically selected.
- **Output State Vectors**: Is this field value associated with the current physical selections? 1 if the value is possible based on current selections, 0 if not. It is this Output State Vector that ultimately determines if a record is to be included in an aggregation by the calculation engine.
- **Data Table State Vectors**: Based on the symbol table Input and Output State Vectors, is this record in the data table possible? =1 if possible, =0 if excluded.

Besides using these flags for aggregation purposes, Qlik uses these flags to associate the data and present it in the famous colors you might already know if you have used QlikView in the past: green, white, and gray.

To know what to show in green (selected values), Qlik uses the Input State Vector, as this represents what the user selects. When a row has 1 in the Input State Vector, it shows in green in the front-end. Remember that this gets flagged when the user clicks on a value or makes a selection, and the user will most probably see this in action while using filter panes.

The values in white (possible) get calculated based on the Output State Vector. If there is a 1 in the Output State Vector, the value will show in white.

Gray is everything that is not related to the user selections (excluded). So, when the Input *and* Output State Vectors are 0, the row is represented in gray.

Let us explain the previous concepts with an example. We can use the same dataset we introduced in this chapter. Remember that there are three columns coming from the Customer table: `Customer`, `Customer_Country`, and `Active_Flag`:

Customer	Customer_Country	Active_Flag
Sensei Ltd	United Kingdom	Y
Sensei Ltd	Australia	N
Magic Quadrant Inc.	United States	Y
Banda Bulevard	Argentina	Y

Let's assume the user clicks on the value Sensei Ltd in the Customer field. The symbol tables with the State Vectors would look like this:

[Customer Symbol Table]:			
Value	**Customer**	**Input**	**Output**
Sensei Ltd	00	1	1
Magic Quadrant Inc.	01	0	0
Banda Bulevard	10	0	0

You can see a 1 in the Input State Vector of the row Sensei Ltd because the user made a selection on that value, and a 1 in the Output State Vector because that same value is associated with the selection.

The `Customer_Country` table looks like this:

[Customer_Country Symbol Table]:			
Value	**Customer_Country**	**Input**	**Output**
United Kingdom	00	0	1
Australia	01	0	1
United States	10	0	0
Argentina	11	0	0

Sensei Ltd is in the United Kingdom and Australia, and therefore the first two rows will have a 1 in the Output State Vector in the `Customer_Country` symbol table. Note that the Input State Vector is 0, as the user has not explicitly selected any of these values.

Lastly, let's take a look at the `Active_Flag` symbol table:

[Active_Flag Symbol Table]:			
Value	**Active_Flag**	**Input**	**Output**
Y	0	0	1
N	1	0	1

Sensei Ltd has a row of data with the `Active_Flag = Y` and one for `Active_Flat = N`, and thus, there will be two of those lines with 1 in the Output State Vector.

Now, the data table will have the value, the bit-stuff index, and an Output State Vector, looking like this:

[CUSTOMER Data table]:			
Customer	**Customer_Country**	**Active_Flag**	**Output**
00	00	0	1
00	01	1	1
01	10	0	0
10	11	1	0

Enough with internal logic; what about the front-end? Well, in its most basic state, the user will see something like this in their application if they drag and drop a few filter pane objects in a Qlik Sense sheet:

They see their explicit selection in *green*, all associated values in other fields in *white*, and the excluded or non-associated values in *gray*.

Some of you might argue that there is an extra color, which is *light gray*, and I would say you are absolutely right. Anything in light gray color in Qlik Sense is an alternative value. *Alternative* is a non-selected value in a symbol table that is only excluded from the scope by selections in the same field. In this example, the alternative values are *Banda Bulevard* and *Magic Quadrant Inc.*

Last but not least, there is a fourth state: selected excluded. A value is selected and excluded when the user explicitly selects a value, but that same value is then excluded by a subsequent explicit selection. When available, this state will show in gray with a check-mark next to it.

Let's use an example to explain the state Selected excluded. The next image shows user selections: *Sensei Ltd* in the **Customer** field and **Australia** and the **United Kingdom** in the Customer_Country field.

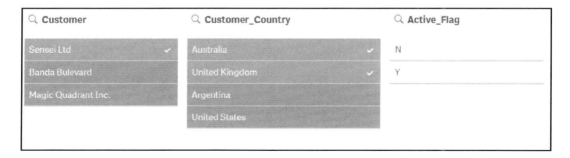

The user then selects Y from the `Active_Flag` field. This will make **Australia** become a selected excluded value, as it had been selected by the user but is now excluded from the selection after the user clicked on Y:

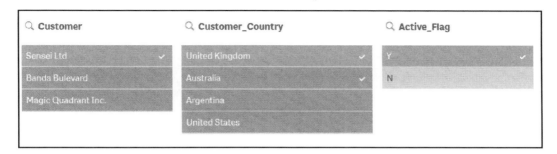

States Vectors are a very important piece of the engine, as the calculation engine will only use records that are flagged in the State Vectors. By doing this, Qlik Sense allows big volumes of data in memory; however, calculations are only performed on a reduced set of records, based on user selections or by using set analysis in the chart expressions.

We will explain set analysis in more detail in coming chapters, but it is important to know that set analysis creates another pair of State Vectors that do not necessarily respond to user selections.

The calculation engine

The calculation engine, as its name refers to, is responsible for all calculations performed in the Qlik Sense applications.

Qlik Sense is an on-demand calculation engine, meaning everything is calculated on the fly. This means that charts will get calculated or recalculated whenever the user makes selections.

One thing that is important to clarify is the fact that charts are not always recalculated. If a selection throws, as a result, a calculation that had previously been calculated, the Qlik Sense engine will get the calculated result from the cache instead of having to calculate everything again. This, as you can image, improves response speed enormously. When selections are repetitive, you will see an improvement in response time.

I would like to clarify that even though Qlik Sense stores the results based on selections, nothing is pre-calculated.

In the previous section, we explained how the logical inference engine applies the State Vectors and flags the records in the data table(s) associated with the current selections. The calculation engine is then responsible for taking those flagged records and performing the following actions, in order:

- Look for values (find values and/or combinations)
- Aggregate

First, the engine must find the rows in the data tables to aggregate. This is done by searching for the binary value 1 in the Output State Vector in the data table.

Once all rows are located, the calculation engine needs to go to the symbol table to look for the real value in the field.

A single field expression, such as sum([Gross Amount]), is a simple aggregation, as it only uses one field of one data table.

The next image shows a table with the expression field:

Data table			
Customer Q	Country Q	Gross Amount	VAT
Banda Bulevard	Argentina	55,000	1.21
Magic Quadrant Inc.	United States	123,000	1.16
Sensei Ltd	Australia	0	0.00
Sensei Ltd	United Kingdom	100,000	1.20

For a simple aggregation like Sum([Gross Amount]), only one data table is required (the one with [Gross Amount] in it), so this step is purely limited to looking up the values of [Amount] in its symbol table.

For an aggregation with multiple fields in it, such as Sum([Gross Amount]*[VAT]), the calculation engine must first get all combinations of [Gross Amount] and [VAT].

The following image highlights the two fields used in the expression:

Data table			SUM([Gross Amount] * [VAT])
Customer 🔍	Country 🔍	Gross Amount	VAT
Banda Bulevard	Argentina	55,000	1.21
Magic Quadrant Inc.	United States	123,000	1.16
Sensei Ltd	Australia	0	0.00
Sensei Ltd	United Kingdom	100,000	1.20

If both fields are in the same data table, this is straightforward, as all combinations already exist in the table. So again, it is just a lookup function, albeit with two fields instead of one. However, if [Gross Amount] and [VAT] reside in two different tables, the engine first has to build a temporary lookup table with all combinations of the two fields, as well as looking up the values.

This lookup and find combinations step is single-threaded (per object), so may be a bottleneck to performance.

As a rule of thumb, arranged fields are frequently aggregated together into the same table if the business logic allows. By doing this, performance will improve, as no temporary lookup table is needed for calculations.

Secondly, once the calculation engine has looked up the real values and created the temporary lookup table if needed, it performs the final aggregations over the records in the table.

The aggregation step is multi-threaded, and thus highly performant.

Here, we enumerate different examples of work done by the calculation engine:

- Populating a filter pane of raw values. This does not require any aggregation, as it only uses the symbol table. Only the lookup step is performed.
- Populating a chart. This requires both the lookup and the aggregation steps. The aggregation is made separately for every dimensional value.
- Calculating an `Aggr()` expression. This also requires both the lookup and the aggregation steps. The aggregation is made separately for every dimensional value.
- Using `GetSelectedCount(<field>)` in a Text and Image object. This does not require any aggregation, as it only uses the symbol table. Again, only the lookup step is performed.

Understanding the Qlik Sense engine is essential if you want to have a working application. Everything that has been explained so far will hopefully help you create an optimized data model, which will, in return, make your application more performant.

Besides understanding the internal logic of the QIX engine, there are many useful techniques to create a professional data model. Keep on reading!

What should be done upstream from Qlik Sense?

Now is a good time to discuss a perfect-world situation, and one you should aim for, even if you hardly ever reach it! Qlik Sense has an extremely powerful scripting engine that is capable of performing some extremely involved and challenging data transformations. However, just because you *can* extract, transform, and load data in Qlik Sense doesn't mean that you *should*. Qlik Sense is a visualization and data analysis tool – data preparation should be handled upstream, where it can be managed by a BAU (Business as Usual) team with more mainstream skills, and from where it can be available to multiple tools, not just Qlik Sense.

On the other hand, Qlik Sense comes with a very powerful scripting language that will make more than one colleague jealous of the development speed. Things that could take months for a database team to implement, you can do in a few hours and have it up and running in a production environment a lot sooner than old-school tools. Do use and take advantage of the Qlik Sense scripting power.

Data is very rarely available to us, and almost always needs some transformation to get it into the required shape for the business. It is also often the case that as much as you'd like one, there is no upstream team to prepare the data for you, or if there is, they probably won't have the available resources to help you; and certainly not in the time frame your business sponsors are demanding.

Let's explore in more detail what we should do in Qlik Sense, and what should be done upstream.

Things to do upstream of Qlik Sense

We call an upstream system any system that sends data to Qlik Sense or that Qlik Sense pulls data from. Examples of an upstream system could be a database, a data warehouse, flat files, and so on.

What should be done upstream depends on each business, and nothing is set in stone. However, here are a few pointers for things that would better live in an upstream system:

- All business logic and rules required to create the most granular level of data required by the application. Examples of this are:
    - If your application requires each transaction to be categorized in a particular way, maybe with a high/medium/low importance flag, the logic to decide which transactions are flagged in which way should be done upstream in the data layer, not inside the Qlik Sense script.
    - If your application only needs to show finalized monthly aggregated data and users don't need to drill down further, then aggregate it upstream, not inside the Qlik script.
- Security model configuration, this is who is allowed to see what should be defined in a central place that multiple systems can read from.
- Integrating several systems, in a way that makes sense to the business should be done in a data warehouse.
- Common tables used across the business, such us Calendar, Geography, or Location, and so on.
- Data marts, which contain a subset of data warehouse data. They are created for a specific purpose, for example, to provide reports to the finance department. Data marts should be created in a database if possible.

Things to do in the Qlik Sense script

The following is a very short list of things that I recommend should be done in the script:

- Some might say you should do as much as you can in the database. Most of the heavy lifting should be done in the database, but I would encourage you to leverage the power of the Qlik Sense script. This renders the tool unique and popular among Qlik enthusiasts.
- Any expression or variables used in your front-end application should be created and kept within your Qlik Sense environment. Call it a spreadsheet or a `.qvs` file; anything is good when maintaining variables and expressions. In Chapter 9, *Advanced Expressions in Qlik Sense*, we will tell you how this can improve performance.
- Anything that is within the Qlik Sense scope and isn't used by other systems, such as derive fields or tables from source data.

To do in the Qlik Sense UI

Using the expressions loaded in the script, the UI should perform aggregations on the finest grain on the fly; for example:

- If your application should allow users to drill into the detail of individual transactions, but you want a chart to aggregate transactions by customer, this aggregation should be done by a Qlik chart or expression.
- If you require point-in-time comparisons (such as year on year), then perform these within your Qlik Sense charts by using set analysis.
- Any calculation that would be hard to aggregate if done at a granular level. An example of this can be ratios calculations. As ratios are not additive, calculating them at the lowest grain makes it tricky to aggregate.

The previous examples do not involve applying any business logic to create new data. They simply involve taking the most granular data provided and viewing it in different ways. That is what Qlik is best at and should be used for.

It is often sensible to utilize the flexibility and rapid prototyping abilities of Qlik within an experienced team to get going, and even to get things into production. However, the goal must always be to *right-size* the Qlik script and push ETL back to ETL tools. Otherwise, your Qlik applications will often become cumbersome and require more support than should be necessary.

Star schema fact and dimension tables

Understanding the data and business you are in is essential to building a good data model. You cannot have a working and performing model unless you know in detail not only what your data means, but how you can connect it so it makes sense.

Grab a piece of paper and start writing down what you know about your data. What are you trying to communicate? What are the most relevant fields in your data source based on your requirements? How do they relate to each other? These are pointers for you to step back and think about what you want to achieve before you actually get your hands on the data.

You can even load files or tables into an application and sense the different fields and formats, and start thinking about how to reduce your data and fields.

A star schema is a logical representation of your business into facts tables and dimensions. When these tables are joined together, it will visually look like a star, and that's probably where the name comes from.

A snowflake schema is a type of star schema where the dimensions are normalized.

All is good with the definition, but what does this mean, and how do you make it happen? Keep reading to find out more!

Ralph Kimball is a legend in terms of dimensional modeling. I recommend you visit `kimballgroup.com` to expand your horizons.

Fact tables

Fact tables are the heart of your star schema. They are the centerpiece. Without a fact table, you don't have a model; that's why it is very important that you get the facts right from the beginning.

Fact tables represent measurements, or metrics, within your business scope. You can have one or many fact tables, depending on your requirements. When we say fact table, you should think about measurable things, such as sales, quantities, prices, and so on. The fact table will also contain foreign keys to your dimensions.

Foreign keys within the fact table allow linking the data to the dimensions. A primary key in a dimension is a foreign key in the fact table.

A table key univocally identifies one row within a table. When there are as many unique values in a field as rows in a table, we can say that the field is a good candidate for a primary key.

A foreign key is a primary key used in another table. A foreign key can be repeated many times across the data model.

Let's take orders in a business as an example. Orders could be your fact table, as it contains measurements such as order price, quantities, and so on. The order will have a foreign key to your customer table or dimension. This key will be the primary key in the customer table. The customer table will have one unique customer per row, and therefore, the primary key will be unique for each of the rows.

Your facts will also have a certain granularity. The granularity, or grain, defines how detailed your data is. It is acceptable to have fact tables aggregated at different levels as long as they are in different applications. If your users want to see monthly sales, why would you load the daily sales details? Aggregate when necessary and leave the details when required. Make sure your fact table caters for all users who will access the application. If one application is accessed by senior people who care about monthly sales but is also used by the analysts who use the application for data discovery, you will then need to have the most granular level of data in the application, and aggregate at the front-end using charts.

Based on your requirements, your fact table can be of the following types:

- **Transactional**: This type of fact table is probably the most granular of them all. It will contain one fact value per row, and that value is only valid for that instant. An example of this type of fact table is one holding order information. The order will be valid at a certain date, which is not necessarily the same date the transaction is loaded into the system. This fact table is usually very long (many rows).

- **Point in time snapshot**: This fact table will have data relevant to a point in time. It will store data monthly, quarterly, or for any other period useful to the business. By using this type of fact table, we can represent a point in time balance. A question such as, *What's my balance at the end of this month?* Could be answered with this type of fact table. Instead of having one transaction per row, you will have a count of your transactions and a sum of a value, such us the balance or total sales for each of the snapshots. Most probably, this table will be a lot smaller than a transactional fact; however, this does not mean these tables are small in size. If we take the example of bank accounts, if a bank has five million customers and the snapshot represents one customer account per month, we will have five million times 12 rows' worth of data per year, with end of month account balances and transactions made within that period, although a lot more can be represented per account.
- **Accumulating snapshot**: We use this fact table to represent a process that has a well-defined start and end. This table will have many date fields to represent the different stages of the process. These fields will not necessarily be populated, but are part of the process. You can also find many measures in this table. If we continue with the same example of account balances, in a transaction table, we will have one row per transaction on the account. In a snapshot fact table, we can have the month end balance per account. In an accumulating snapshot table, we can see a balance that is valid for a period of time until another transaction happens in the account. To represent this, we will have a balance start date and a balance end date. The end date will be overwritten with the current date whenever a new transaction happens.

A simplified example of the different fact tables can be found in the following image:

[Balance Transaction Fact]:	[Balance Point in Time Fact]:	[Balance Accumulating Fact]:
Transaction Date (FK)	**Trx. End of Month Date (FK)**	**Trx. Start Date (FK)**
Customer (FK)	**Customer (FK)**	**Trx. End Date (FK)**
Account (FK)	**Account (FK)**	**Customer (FK)**
Balance Amount	*Balance End of Period*	**Account (FK)**
Balance Fee	*Balance Fee End of Period*	*Balance*
		Balance Fee

Now that you know the different types of fact tables, you can model yours according to these rules.

At the beginning of this section, we mentioned the granularity of the data. Complex models can have more than one fact table, and those fact tables can have different levels of granularity needed. Let's jump directly to an example to understand this concept.

For the sake of simplicity, we will continue with the example of bank accounts. The bank applies a fee every time a customer uses the account. That fee is applied to the amount of the transaction. The bank also wants to report on balances. We can easily identify a fact table with three measures: current balance, transaction amount, and transaction fee. This table will also have foreign keys to other tables (dimensions) that will help give context to these measures.

Depending on the type of customer, the bank can apply a fixed monthly fee for each customer. Here, we identify a second, smaller fact table with a customer fee as a measure. Because this fee is applied to the customer instead of the account, the data is aggregated one level up.

This is what our two fact tables look like:

[Accumulating Snapshot Fact]:	[Transaction Fact]:
%TranStartDate	%MontEndDate
%TranEndDate	%Customer
%Customer	CustomerFee
%Account	
TransactionAmount	
CurrentBalance	
TransactionAmountFee	

Now, how do we make this work? Remember how the engine works? We first load only what we need. These facts look pretty basic, so we will load all the fields. We also need to make values as distinct as possible. These are the same, or similar, fields that we have in common between the two fact tables. We have dates in both (`TranStartDate`, `TranEndDate` and `MonthEndDate`), and we also have the customer. If we load the transaction tables separately, we will have two different data tables, and each field will have its own separate symbol table, which will make Qlik Sense store the same data type (dates) as different values. Also, the user will need to select the same date in different fields which is counterproductive. If we put the two fact tables together and make sure we rename the fields to have as many fields in common as possible, we will have fewer data and symbol tables, and performance will thus increase, and RAM usage will decrease.

The sample code looks like this:

```
Set HidePrefix='%' ;

[Accumulating Snapshot Fact]:
LOAD
        %TranStartDate                  as %Date
        ,%TranEndDate
        ,%Customer
        ,%Account
        ,round(TransactionAmount, 0.1)    as TransactionAmount
        ,round(CurrentBalance, 0.1)       as CurrentBalance
        ,round(TransactionAmountFee, 0.1) as TransactionAmountFee
        ,'TransactionFact'                as _FactType
FROM [lib://AttachedFiles/Symbol Tables.xlsx]
(ooxml, embedded labels, table is AccumulatingSnapshotFact);

Concatenate ([Accumulating Snapshot Fact])

[TransactionFact]:
LOAD
        floor(%MontEndDate)             as %Date
        ,%Customer
        ,round(CustomerFee, 0.1)          as CustomeFee
        ,'CustomerFeeFact'                as _FactType
FROM [lib://AttachedFiles/Symbol Tables.xlsx]
(ooxml, embedded labels, table is TransactionFact);
```

In this sample code, I load the two fact tables from an Excel file. I previously created my file connection, which I then invoke with the syntax `lib://<file path>`.

Now, in the first line, we set the user-defined variable `HidePrefix = '%'`. By doing this, Qlik Sense will treat all fields with a name prefix of % as systems fields, and they will therefore not be visible to the user.

I then load the first fact table. I rename the first date field, as I want it to be general so that we can also use it when we load the second fact table. This will force Qlik Sense to treat the same field types from two different tables as one field, and as a result, we will have less distinct values than having two fields with the same values.

Depending on your audience and how important accuracy to the decimal is, you can round your numbers. The technique is extremely useful if you want to optimize your RAM usage. For example, the floating numbers 12.2461 and 12.2462 are obviously different. When we round them to the nearest decimal, we will get 12.2 as the resulting number. This will decrease the number of distinct values, and by now you already know what this means. The more you round, the better. Always make sure this is acceptable to your audience.

I finally create a flag that will help me distinguish the records of the two fact tables. An expression in the front-end using set analysis to make calculations on only the first fact table would look like this:

```
sum({< _FactType = {'TransactionFact'} >} TransactionAmount)
```

I will talk more about set analysis in the coming chapters.

Continuing with the code, I then concatenate the second fact table to the first one. This makes them one logical table.

I rename `%MonthEndDate` to `%Date` so that we use an already existing field of the same type. Because the transaction fact table contains one record per customer per month, and the time when this happens is not relevant, I also make sure that the date is of a *date* format by using the `floor()` function. This truncates the `hh:mm:ss`, or hours, minutes, and seconds, from the timestamp date. For example, a date of *2018-09-11 14:58:09* will become *2018-09-11 00:00:00* when using the `floor()` function. A timestamp date value with 00:00:00 is the same as having the date, only with no hour.

You now learned what a fact table is and the different types. We also explained best practices when creating fact tables. You can now confidently define what the fact is, what fields should be pulled, and how to manipulate them to optimize your memory usage.

In the following section, we will describe another important aspect of star schemas: dimensions.

Dimensions

We previously mentioned that facts and dimensions are essential pieces of any star schema. Dimensions, as opposed to facts, contain descriptive data that helps give context to the fact values.

In general, a fact is composed of foreign key fields and measure fields. On the other hand, a dimension in its simplest form will have a primary key and descriptive fields.

Think of dimensions as things that describe your business. Examples of this could be Products, Location or Geography, Customers, Organization, and so on.

Generally speaking, star schema data models have dimensions in common. A calendar is one of the dimensions that is probably present in any model. It helps to give more meaning to the date field by adding extra attributes to it, such as month, quarter, year, and so on. These dimension fields are also used when we want to show aggregated date in the front-end without having to calculate the values in the script.

Dimensions are usually smaller in size as compared to fact tables. From a performance point of view, the same rules apply here, too. Try to make the values in each field as unique as possible. Remove blank spaces in the names using the `trim()` function. Get rid of unwanted database-related fields, such us internal IDs, audit fields, or dates related to when the rows were updated. These are usually not used in the front-end and should thus not be loaded.

Create *surrogate keys* using the `Autonumber()` function and remove all natural keys when possible, as key fields are, by nature, dense.

 The `autonumber(expr, id)` function will assign an incremental value to each distinct expression.

When it comes to dimensions, we can find a great variety of them. Dimensions can be slowly changing, rapidly changing, role-playing, among several others. I would need a whole new book to talk about data modeling in detail. However, my goal is for you to understand the basics of data modeling if you don't already. For this reason, I will only describe slowly changing dimensions and role playing dimensions, which are the most common dimensions you will find.

A slowly changing dimension is a dimension in which its attributes do not change too often over time. For example, your customer might change addresses; however, this action does not happen on a regular basis, and therefore, *customer* is a slowly changing dimension.

You can read a lot about this topic, and each author describes the types in different ways. There are eight types of slowly changing dimensions; however, the first five are the most relevant ones:

- **Type 0**: Keep original
- **Type 1**: Overwrite
- **Type 2**: Add new row
- **Type 3**: Add new attribute
- **Type 4**: Add history

Type 0 dimensions are rarely used. This type of dimension is loaded into the model once, and will not suffer any change. What this means is, the dimension is static, and from a business perspective, you will not expect any changes occurring during the life of your data model. A good candidate for this type is a status dimension, as follows:

Status Id	Status Code	Status Description
1000001	ACT	Active
1000002	CNL	Cancel
1000003	DEL	Deleted
1000004	PRG	In Progress
1000005	PND	Pending
1000006	COM	Completed

This is a table containing status information. These statuses could be used on anything in your model, from a customer to a process. This dimension table is loaded in you data model once and will not change as long as the status covers all possible situations within your business.

A **type 1** dimension will overwrite its values every time an existing value is updated. Basically, it is one in and one out. This will give us the most current records, but makes it impossible to track any history. For example:

Customer Surrogate Key	Customer Id	Customer Name	Customer Address
200000001	125824	Banda Bulevard	Calle Orono 20
200000002	13953	Sensei Ltd	Manila way 201

If our customer Banda Bulevard changes address, with a type 1 dimension, we delete the first records and we replace them with the new ones, resulting in this:

Customer Surrogate Key	Customer Id	Customer Name	Customer Address
200000001	125824	Banda Bulevard	*Calle Brown 453*
200000002	13953	Sensei Ltd	Manila way 201

With a **type 2** dimension, we can track the history in our dimension. If a customer changes address and we want to report on that change, we need to use a type 2 dimension. Modifying a dimension to track history can be achieved in two ways. The first method is to create a current record flag column. When a record in the dimension gets updated, the old record will get flagged as 'N' (No), and the most recent one flagged as 'Y'. This method can show you the changes, but it won't tell you when the changes happened. The table shows an example of this:

Customer Surrogate Key	Customer Id	Customer Name	Customer Address	Current Record Flag
2000032	4592	IndigoX	36 Cable Walk	Y

When the customer address gets updated, the record gets flagged as 'N' and the new record is now 'Y', resulting in the following:

Customer Surrogate Key	Customer Id	Customer Name	Customer Address	Current Record flag
2000032	4592	IndigoX	36 Cable Walk	N
2000033	4592	IndigoX	23 Regent's Place	Y

Note that a new customer surrogate key is also created to uniquely reference that new record in the dimension. From the moment the new records get inserted in the dimension, the new key is used in the fact table. Old fact records keep the old surrogate key to maintain integrity.

If it is important for the business to know when the change actually took place, we can have a start and end date for each record. The current record will have a *null* end date, or a fictional date, such as 9999-12-31. The example shows how a dimension with start and end dates would look:

Customer Surrogate Key	Customer Id	Customer Name	Customer Address	Start Date	End Date
2000055	0-A2D3d-xx	Parana S.A	201 Riverside Avenue	2016-10-02	2017-10-30
2000056	0-A2D3d-xx	Parana S.A	266 Riverside Avenue	2017-11-01	9999-12-31

A third method is to have only one date (effective date) and a current record flag. If we want to know how long a record has been valid for, we need the most current effective date and the one from the previous records. This dimension would look like the following:

Customer Surrogate Key	Customer Id	Customer Name	Customer Address	Effective Date	Current Record flag
44829998	34-AWRF-2	Agnes Lime Ltd	50 Battery Park	2016-11-09	N
44829999	34-AWRF-2	Agnes Lime Ltd	49th Upper West Rd.	2017-07-13	Y

A **type 3** dimension can track history by having two columns for each field for which we want to track history. This type will also hold an effective date key so we know when that record is valid from. In this dimension, will can only know the current and previous values. These values will be stored in the two columns mentioned before. An example of a type 3 dimension is as follows:

Customer Surrogate Key	Customer Id	Customer Name	Customer Address Previous	Effective Date	Customer Address Current
44829998	34-AWRF-2	Agnes Lime Ltd	50 Battery Park	2017-07-13	49th Upper West Rd.

The clear advantage of this type is that the table will not grow when values are updated, and it also allows us to keep history on the fields we really want. However, if we are planning to track history in any other field in the near future, this is not the best dimension, as we risk having to add new columns or fields and recalculate the whole dimension, even the fact table, to keep integrity.

Finally, a **type 4** slowly changing dimension will consist of two tables: one which holds the current values, and a second one which has all historical values. From a performance perspective, this is useful, as we don't necessarily have to load both if the audience is only interested in the current values. However, due to the nature of Qlik Sense, we see ourselves forced to load both tables should our users want to see the history. The reason I describe this type of dimension is because they are commonly used in other tools, and you will see them around in data marts. For tools that do not load everything into memory, this is a good solution, as you will only query the table that you need. Analyzing this from a Qlik Sense perspective, you can easily use a type 2 dimension and create logical tables, filtering by your current record flags.

Joins

So far, we have learned about fact tables and dimensions. We described facts as tables containing our measures and dimensions as tables containing descriptive information about our measures. However, we have described them as separate entities.

There is no data model without table linkage. The main purpose of data modeling is to create a performing set of tables -facts and dimensions- so we can join them together.

To understand this better, think of your fact as the structural bone of your model. You load this table first. You learn that fact tables have foreign keys to your dimensions. This means that your fact table is related to your dimensions through these unique identifiers. Fact tables and dimensions are linked through joins using their table keys.

Joins allow you to link your tables; most specifically, your facts and dimensions. Joins are statements in the script and are thus executed when the script is reloaded. In order for a join to exist, at least one table must have been loaded into memory before we use the join syntax in the script. If we don't specify to what table we want to join the next table, Qlik Sense will join it to the most recently loaded table.

Allow me to briefly describe the logical steps of the join:

1. Load table A
2. Join statement
3. Specify to what table you want to join the next table. If not specified, use table A
4. Load table B
5. Qlik Sense then joins table A to table B through a common field name

In order for Qlik Sense to know what foreign and primary keys to use, we must have one name matching in table A and table B. If we have more than one field with the same name, Qlik Sense will create synthetic keys, which are not recommended.

 A synthetic key is created as a result of a possible composite key. This means that you have two or more common fields between your joined tables.

There are four types of joins in Qlik Sense:

- Outer
- Inner
- Left
- Right

An **outer join** will result in all possible combinations of table A and table B. No condition is applied in this join. This join is not usually used within the star schema, as it will result in unrelated data; however, an outer join might be useful to create certain types of dimensions, such us calendars. The following block code shows how to use a join. If you want to try it yourself, open the *Data Load Editor* in your Qlik Sense application, type in the code, and click on *Load Data*:

```
Product:
LOAD * Inline
[
ProductId, Product Code, Product Description
111119, AOCE-1247-POX, Current Account
111120, ACRW-5098-LOK, Saving Account Premium
111121, GTRD-3422-RTY, Saving Account Standard
];

Join (Product)

Country:
LOAD * Inline
[
CountryISOCode, Country
US, United States
GB, United Kingdom
];
```

In this example, we join *Country* to *Product*. These two tables are not related and do not have a common field name. The result will be one table with the name of the first table loaded (Product), with all possible combinations. The number of rows in the joined tables is:

 # rows joined table = # of rows in [Product] table x # of rows on [Country] table

The resulting table in the Data Model Viewer looks like the following:

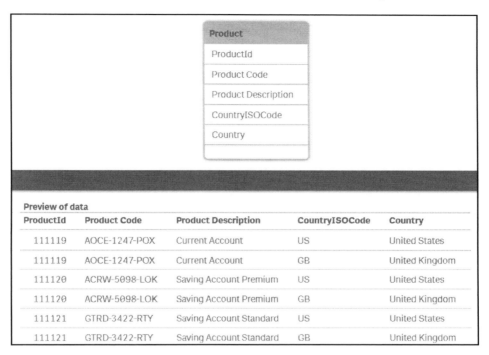

An **inner join** statement will result in a table containing records from table A matching table B. This is to say, if the value is in the first loaded table and in the second joined table, it will then be in the resulting table. This type of join is probably the most widely used.

The following code shows you the behavior of the inner join:

```
CustomerProducts:
LOAD * Inline
[
CustomerId, Customer Name, ProductId
1, Juan,111119
2, Martin,111119
3, Peter,111120
];

Inner Join (CustomerProducts)

Product:
LOAD * Inline
[
```

```
ProductId, Product Code, Product Description
111119, AOCE-1247-POX, Current Account
111120, ACRW-5098-LOK, Saving Account Premium
111121, GTRD-3422-RTY, Saving Account Standard
];
```

The resulting table will have the columns of both tables, but only those values where `ProductId` is the same in both tables. The common field name in this example is *ProductId*, and therefore, Qlik Sense will automatically join using this key field.

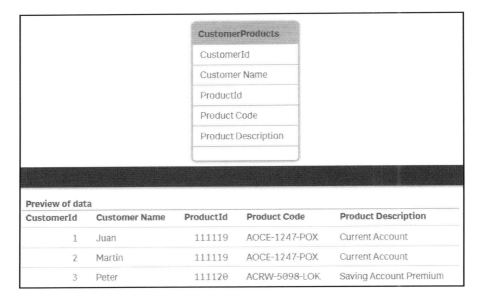

A **left join**, like the other joins, will result in one logical table. In this case, all records from the first loaded table (table A) will be kept, as well as the matching records in table B. The rest of the non-existing values in table B will be populated as null values in the resulting table.

[CustomerProduct]:

CustomerId	Customer Name	ProductId
1	Juan	99999
2	Martin	111119
3	Peter	111120

[Product]:

ProductId	Product Code	Product Description
111119	AOCE-1247-POX	Current Account
111120	ACRW-5098-LOK	Saving Account Premium
111121	GTRD-3422-RTY	Saving Account Standard

In this example, Juan has the product `999999`. However, this product does not exist in the product table. The result will be null values for all product columns for Juan. The following code shows how to implement the left join:

```
CustomerProducts:
LOAD * Inline
[
CustomerId, Customer Name, ProductId
1, Juan,999999
2, Martin,111119
3, Peter,111120
];

Left Join (CustomerProducts)

Product:
LOAD * Inline
[
ProductId, Product Code, Product Description
111119, AOCE-1247-POX, Current Account
111120, ACRW-5098-LOK, Saving Account Premium
111121, GTRD-3422-RTY, Saving Account Standard
];
```

After running the script, the final table will look like this:

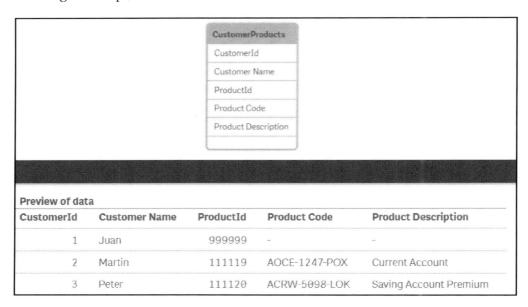

A **right join** is the same as a left join, however, all records in the second loaded table are kept, and the values on the first table are either joined through the common field or left *null* if there are no matching values.

The *left* table is the first loaded table and the *right* table is the second loaded table.

Continuing with the same example as before, all records from the product table will be kept, and records on the first table, CustomerProducts, will be matched based on the ProductId common field, resulting in the following:

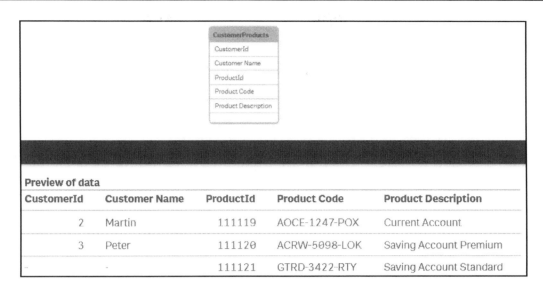

Preview of data

CustomerId	Customer Name	ProductId	Product Code	Product Description
2	Martin	111119	AOCE-1247-POX	Current Account
3	Peter	111120	ACRW-5098-LOK	Saving Account Premium
..	..	111121	GTRD-3422-RTY	Saving Account Standard

Similar to the `join` prefix, Qlik Sense also offers the `keep` prefix. This keyword can be used after `left`, `right`, or `inner`. Instead of joining two tables together and creating a final, logical table, the `keep` prefix reduces one or both tables before they are stored in Qlik Sense. These tables will show in the Data Model Viewer as two separate tables with their own names. The following code shows an example of how `keep` can be used:

```
CustomerProducts:
LOAD * Inline
[
CustomerId, Customer Name, ProductId
1, Juan,999999
2, Martin,111119
3, Peter,111120
];

Right Join (CustomerProducts)

Product:
LOAD * Inline
[
ProductId, Product Code, Product Description
111119, AOCE-1247-POX, Current Account
111120, ACRW-5098-LOK, Saving Account Premium
111121, GTRD-3422-RTY, Saving Account Standard
];
```

Summary

In this chapter, we talked about the importance of a good data model. We shared with you the techniques that will help you design a performing and future-proof model.

Data modelling best practices are applicable in any business intelligence project; however, it is important to understand how each tool works. Any model will work in Qlik Sense, but we must use its scripting power to add or remove elements that will help us make the best of the powerful QIX engine.

I encourage you to transform your relational model into a fit-for-purpose star schema, which is the standard of excellence for reporting and analyzing data.

In the next chapter, we will show you the best practices for loading data into your Qlik Sense application, always taking into account what we described in this chapter.

7

Best Practices for Loading Data in Qlik Sense

As the name of this chapter suggests, best practices can be applied anywhere throughout the life cycle of a project. From coding to test cases, there are lots of best practices one can follow to keep a data project tidy and organized.

In the previous chapter, we learned how powerful the Qlik engine is, and we also described guidelines to optimize your model.

Qlik Sense data is stored in memory so every bit of data we load counts. As well as RAM capacity, we must understand how we can load data in an optimized way. Qlik Sense scripting is extremely powerful, but with great power comes great responsibility. You, as a Qlik Sense enthusiast, must ensure your loading techniques are accurate and follow best practices within the Qlik Sense world.

In order for all of us to work and understand different projects, it is important that the majority of us follow common guidelines. The internet and books like this help knowledge and experience spread. Pick what you like from this book, mix it with other ideas out there, and create your own way of doing things. Nothing fits all. You will have to adapt the methodologies and best practices to your reality. Perhaps documenting your code will do. Or maybe adding more complex controls is necessary in your organization. Whatever it is that you do, do it right. Be clean and precise and make sure that everything in your project is easy to understand to others.

In this chapter we will learn about the following topics:

- Data loading concepts and the different ways of loading data into our application
- Data load optimization
- Loading data incrementally
- The **extract, transform, load** (ETL) approach

Data loading concepts

There are plenty of concepts regarding data loading. Yet one of the most important things we must distinguish between QlikView and Qlik Sense is that Qlik Sense finally introduced a visual and user-friendly way of loading and linking different data sources, which is called **Data Manager**. This is a massive improvement compared to QlikView, which only allows data loading by writing lines of code. Yes, you have a few *wizards* but to be honest they are not user-friendly. Although they are developer-friendly, I have never seen a business user celebrating the fact that they could load data using QlikView wizards. Instead, they would usually come to me for help.

I believe Qlik made the right choice in introducing this fantastic concept of a visual data loader and editor. It's not groundbreaking to have a visual interface, but Data Manager's simplicity and the way it associates data can make any technically illiterate user happy.

In the next section, I will describe how to use Data Manager. Nothing boring. Hands-on! We will also go into the details of how to load and optimize data loads. The more you know about scripting, the better. I usually prefer scripting but I love Data Manager too.

Data Manager

Data Manager allows you to easily add, edit, or delete your Qlik Sense application data sources using a visual interface. It also allows you to associate your data either automatically or explicitly.

Data Manager automatically generates the script that is then executed when the application is reloaded. One big flaw of Data Manager is that you cannot edit the generated script. If you do, Data Manager will not respond to your changes and from that point on, you will have to use the script editor. Qlik will hopefully make the script editor and Data Manager work hand in hand. I enjoy dragging and dropping files and automatically associating tables but the ready will most probably enjoy more having the ability to change or improve the script to their needs.

Opening Data Manager

Let's jump straight to it. To open Data Manager, create or open an existing Qlik Sense application, then click on the navigation icon in the upper-left corner and click on **Data Manager**.

 For my examples, I use Qlik Sense Cloud. It is easy to create an account and get started right away. No excuses!

The following screenshot shows where to find the menu option to open Data Manager:

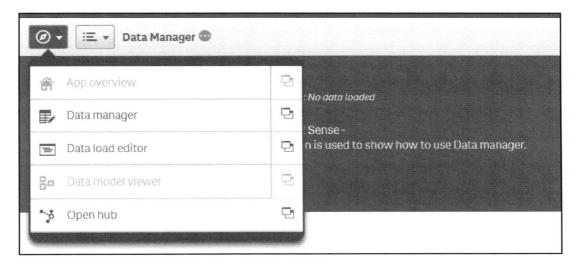

In Data Manager, you have two main sections:

- Associations
- Tables

Associations

Associations is the default view when you open Data Manager. The following screenshot shows the default Associations view of a new application:

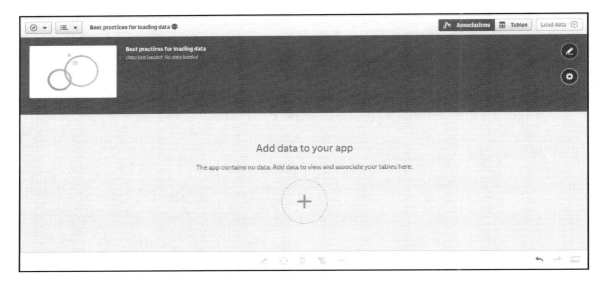

If it is a brand new application and if no data had been loaded, you will see a message inviting you to add data. It is important to highlight how easy Qlik has made it for users to interact with data. You will see a lot of redundant elements when it comes to data loading. For example, we can load data from different options within the screen. You as a user will feel welcome and will want, no matter what, to load and play with your data.

Associations and bubbles

In the Associations section, tables are shown as circles or bubbles with their names inside. Each bubble is a table and the size of it will vary depending on the size or amount of data it contains. The more rows you have, the bigger the bubble. Associations between tables are shown as some kind of a tunnel linking the two. You will have the feeling that you can flow from one table to the other through the associations. Other tools will show these associations mainly with lines and arrows. One disadvantage of the way Qlik Sense shows associations is that you cannot tell what kind of relationship exists between the tables. Is it one to many, for example, Orders and Order Items? Or many to many, such us Subjects and Students?

The Associations section simply does not give us all the information we might need. The Associations screen was created for business users, not technical people. Users don't care about data models or data cardinality. They care about their data and connecting the sources. This screen is giving them exactly that.

Adding data

You can add data to your application from many sources, such us Excel sheets, databases, and even **Qlik DataMarket**, which allows you to connect to external sources.

When you click on **Add data** within Data Manager, you will have a few options to choose from. In the examples, we use Qlik Sense Cloud; your screen may be different, depending on whether you use the Desktop, Enterprise, or Cloud version.

Allow us to briefly explain the **Add data** screen:

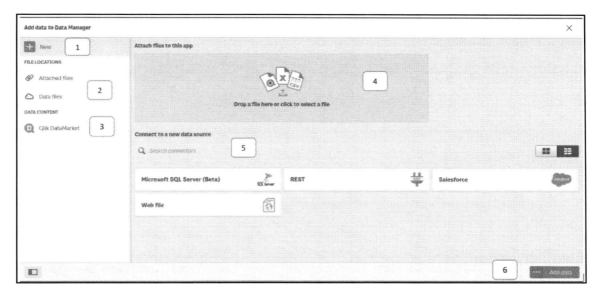

1	The **New** button [1] takes you back to the **Add data** main screen (as shown in the screenshot).
2	File locations [2] will show you connections created by you or an administrator if you are in an Enterprise environment. Do not confuse a connection with a database connection. This is a file connection, meaning there's a link between your Qlik Sense application and a folder containing files. You can see the connections by clicking on the **Attached files** option. You can also add files directly from this location. Drag and drop! If you have created connections to data sources, this will show here too. Use this section mainly after you create your connections. The Data files option will show you all files loaded to your Cloud account. You can upload files to your account by clicking on **My Data Files** in your hub accessible through this URL: `https://qlikcloud.com/hub/personal`.
3	Click on **Qlik DataMarket** [3] to choose from a variety of free and paid data sources.
4	Drag and drop files you want to upload here [4]! Choose from many formats such us Excel and QVDs.
5	Use this [5] to connect to sources such us databases, social media, and so on. Use this section to create brand new data connections that will then show in section 2.
6	When done choosing your source, click on **Add Data** [6] to add it to your application before loading it.

Now, to get started, drag and drop the sample data file into the **Attach files to this app** section. The`CountryRevenue.xlsx` source file consists of four sheets: **Revenue**, **Time**, **Location**, and **Product**. Once you drag and drop the file in the application, Qlik Sense will display a table wizard, similar to the one in QlikView.

Here, you can choose the sheets you want to load and the columns, update column names, and so on. It is simple and straightforward as shown in the following screenshot:

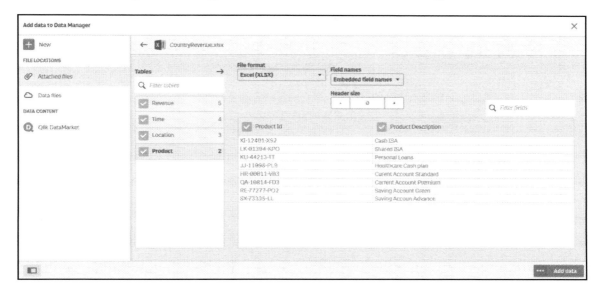

Make sure you select everything you want to load and then click on **Add data** to add the data to your application. The data will not be in the application until you reload it, but the **Add data** button allows you to preview what your tables and fields look like so you can make modifications in case you need to.

After adding the data, Data Manager will show the bubbles: one for **Revenue**, **Time**, **Location**, and **Product**. Each bubble has a different size depending on its data. The following image shows the different bubbles. The star (*) in each bubble name means the data is still to be loaded by clicking on the green **Load data** button:

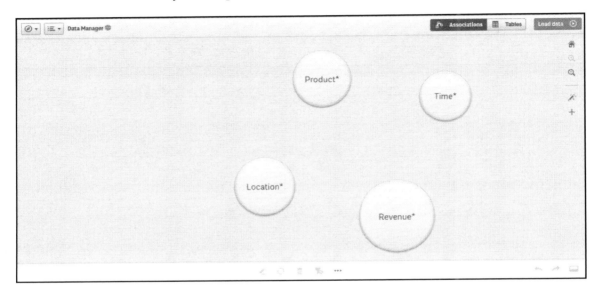

Remember that Qlik Sense joins tables through a common field name. My data source does not have any field name in common, thus none of the bubbles will be connected.

Automatic association

Qlik Sense comes with an amazing feature that allows you to automatically associate your tables based on the field names and data in those fields. To automatically associate your data based on Qlik's recommendation, click on the magic stick on the right of the screen, right above the + sign. The engine will automatically create the associations:

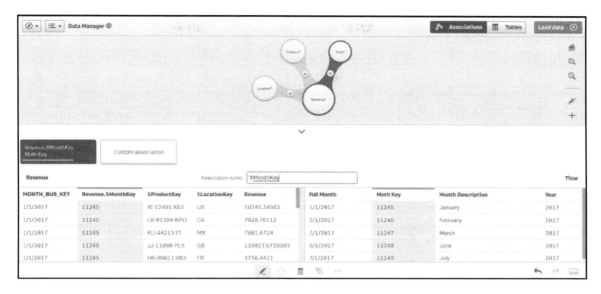

Snapshot of the associations created based on Qlik's recommendation

You can see the details of the associations by clicking in the middle circle between the bubbles. Qlik will automatically rename the associated fields so it can then join the tables through this common field name. You can change this name from within the Association name text-box as shown in the preceding screenshot.

Click on **Customer association** should you wish to use a different associating field instead of using the one recommended by Qlik Sense.

Loading data

We are now ready to load the data into our application by simply clicking on the **green Load data** button. After loading the data, all tables and fields are properly stored and saved in the application.

You can see what the model looks like either from Data Manager or the Data model viewer in the navigation menu. The data model viewer shows your tables, fields, keys, and association between the tables.

Tables

Tables section displays the tables you load from your different sources as shown in the following screenshot:

Tables from different sources is displayed in the preceding screenshot

In the top section [1], you have the already known navigation menu. You will see the navigation option on the far left and the Global Menu option. On the right side, we have the **Association** menu (which I described in the previous section), the **Tables** section (which is what the screenshot is showing), and the **Load data** button.

Tables overview

In the main section [2], you can once more see the **Add data** button. Remember when we said there are plenty of repeated elements creating redundancy? **Add data** is an example. You can also see all the tables previously loaded to your application. Section [2] shows you at a glance the name, type of data, number of fields, and name of the source file.

If you click on the tables, you will see a preview of the structure of that table as shown in section [3]. This is the same as clicking on a bubble in the **Associations** menu.

In Section [4], you have the options to edit a table, reload the table from the source, or delete the table. The edit and delete options can also be found in section 2, again creating redundancy. You just can't miss the basic commands.

Editing a table

From the Tables view, you can edit the tables by clicking on the pencil in section [2] or [4]. If you edit the Locations table, you can see the following:

The screen that appears on editing the Locations table

The first section shows again a quick overview of the table name, rows, and fields. On the right side, you have the **Unpivot** button, which allows you to swap columns by rows, the **Add field** button that you can use to add calculated fields to the table, and the last button, **Select data from source**, used to update the data from the source.

Table field types

Section [2] in the previous image, is where the fun starts. Here, you can see the table structure, column names, and data. But most importantly, you can see the data type of each column.

Fields can be of one of the following types: General, Date, Timestamp, and Geo data. Qlik Sense automatically assigns a type based on the field data. A field type can be changed by clicking on the type symbol and selecting the correct field type.

Associated fields

In the CountryISOCode field right next to the Field type symbol, you will see the association symbol. This symbol is telling us that the table is associated to another table through this field. If you click on it, you can see the transformed field name created by Qlik Sense to join to the other table. Note how we can still see the source table with the original fields but you can also see the associated fields created for this purpose.

Breaking or editing associations

You can **Break** or **Edit** the association if needed. Just click on the Association icon, and you will be presented with these two options.

The third icon in the field is the **Field** menu. By clicking here, you can Rename, Associate, or Sort the field. Field names can also be changed by clicking on top of the field name. Lots of redundancy to make your life easier.

Loading data using the script editor

In the previous section, you learned how to load data using Data Manager. This interface is user-friendly and can be useful to both business users and developers.

Sometimes we want to explore more or understand how things actually work when we create something through a visual interface. In my case, I enjoy scripting. Qlik scripting is not too hard to learn but it takes time to master. There are rules that you must follow if you want your data loads to run fast and perform well when your data increases in size.

Opening Data load editor

Earlier in this chapter, we mentioned that whatever you create through Data Manager is then translated into script lines. You can access the script editor, **Data load editor,** from the **navigation** menu, as shown in the following screenshot:

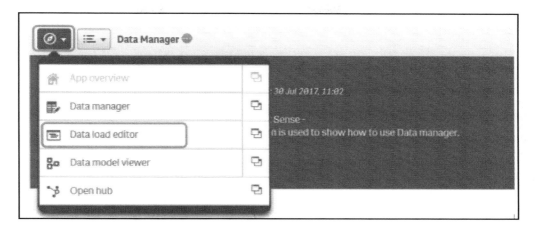

Navigation Menu

Clicking on the double window icon next to Data load editor opens the editor in a new tab.

The Main tab

If you open the same application that we used in the Data Manager section, you will see two tabs. The first tab, **Main**, is a default section with all system variables used to configure our environment. These come out of the box but can be edited by changing the values to the right of the equal (=) sign. For example, you can change the thousand separator depending on the region we are in. We take the following variable:

```
SET ThousandSep=',';
```

Then you change it to the following:

```
SET ThousandSep='.';
```

The Auto-generated section

Beside the Main section, you will see the Auto-generated section as shown in the following screenshot:

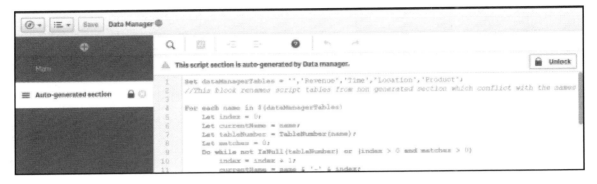

The auto-generated section beside the Main section

From a developer's perspective, I enjoy working with Data Manager mainly because I can then study the code that is automatically generated. You can learn lots of good scripting techniques as well as best practices when looking at the auto-generated script.

To make changes to the script, click on the **Unlock** button in the upper-right corner. If in doubt, you can duplicate your application by going back to your personal hub. Right-click on the application you want to duplicate and click on **Duplicate**.

Analyzing the code in the Auto-generated section

The Auto-generated section is protected as it has been created using Data Manager. This is denoted by the padlock next to the section name. Qlik is kind enough to let us make changes to this script but remember that if we do so, the changes will not be reflected in Data Manager. Once you make a change to this script, you must continue using the script to develop applications.

Geo data fields

Qlik Sense automatically recognizes that one of the tables contains geographical data, namely the Location table. Because Sense comes with an out-of-the-box map extension, whenever it identifies a field with geographical data in it, it will create either an extra field containing geopoints (for cities) or polygon data (for countries). The new fields are created within the same table where the geographical data is located in the format `<data_field>_GeoInfo`.

In my example, the Location table has two geo fields, `CountryIsoCode` and `Country`. Qlik Sense will create two fields containing polygon data with one called `CountryIsoCode_GeoInfo` and another one called `Country_GeoInfo`.

You can then use these fields to plot data on the map.

If a field is not recognized as geographical data, you can change it from the **Edit field** option in Data Manager. Alternatively, we can update the `TAG FIELD` section within the script.

Field tags

Field tags are used to add metadata to your model. It is here that you can specify the field type as well as specify whether the field is a dimension or measure, among other things. There are two types of tags:

- **System field tags**: These are generated when the script is executed. All system field tags are preceded by a dollar sign ($). System tags are reserved words and cannot be used as custom tags.
- **Custom field tags**: These are user-generated tags. You can create them with the `TAG FIELD` syntax.

The following is a list of all system field generated tags:

System field tag	Author's comments
`$system`	This tag is generated for all system fields that are automatically generated by Qlik Sense on script execution.
`$key`	A field providing a link between two or more tables.
`$keypart`	This tag is generated when a field is part of one or more synthetic key. Remember that synthetic keys are not recommended!

$syn	Tag for synthetic key fields.
$hidden	This fields denotes a hidden field. A hidden field will not appear in field selections when creating charts. These fields can still be used in expressions and set analysis but they will not show in your master items or tables fields. All tags from this point to the last one in this list can be manipulated in the script by the user.
$numeric	This tag denotes all values in this field are numeric. Excludes null values.
$integer	Same as $numeric but denotes integer values.
$text	All values in the field are of text type. No values are numeric.
$ascii	The field contains ASCII characters only.
$date	The values can be interpreted as dates. Remember that dates are in fact integer values.
$timestamp	The values can be interpreted as timestamps.
$geoname	The field contains geographical data, such as country ISO codes.
$geopoint	This field contains data in the format of [latitude, longitude] which represents a data point in the map.
$geomultipolygon	This field contains geometry polygon data which represents an area in the map, such as country borders.

Fields can have one or more tags attached to them.

The Declare and Derive fields

If you scroll down to the bottom of the auto-generated script, you will see an
autoCalendar generated by Qlik Sense. This is a new feature that is not present in
QlikView and that I welcome very much.

The Declare syntax

The `Declare` statement creates a definition for a field or group of fields. For example, Qlik Sense will automatically create extra fields whenever it finds a field containing dates. It automatically creates an `autoCalendar` using the `Declare` function.

Let's take a look at the code:

```
[autoCalendar]:
 DECLARE FIELD DEFINITION Tagged ('$date')
FIELDS
 Dual(Year($1), YearStart($1)) AS [Year] Tagged ('$axis', '$year'),
 Dual('Q'&Num(Ceil(Num(Month($1))/3)),Num(Ceil(NUM(Month($1))/3),00)) AS
[Quarter] Tagged ('$quarter', '$cyclic'),
 Dual(Year($1)&'-Q'&Num(Ceil(Num(Month($1))/3)),QuarterStart($1)) AS
[YearQuarter] Tagged ('$yearquarter', '$qualified'),
 Dual('Q'&Num(Ceil(Num(Month($1))/3)),QuarterStart($1)) AS [_YearQuarter]
Tagged ('$yearquarter', '$hidden', '$simplified'),
 Month($1) AS [Month] Tagged ('$month', '$cyclic'),
 Dual(Year($1)&'-'&Month($1), monthstart($1)) AS [YearMonth] Tagged
('$axis', '$yearmonth', '$qualified'),
 Dual(Month($1), monthstart($1)) AS [_YearMonth] Tagged ('$axis',
'$yearmonth', '$simplified', '$hidden'),
 Dual('W'&Num(Week($1),00), Num(Week($1),00)) AS [Week] Tagged
('$weeknumber', '$cyclic'),
 Date(Floor($1)) AS [Date] Tagged ('$axis', '$date', '$qualified'),
 Date(Floor($1), 'D') AS [_Date] Tagged ('$axis', '$date', '$hidden',
'$simplified'),
 If (DayNumberOfYear($1) <= DayNumberOfYear(Today()), 1, 0) AS [InYTD] ,
 Year(Today())-Year($1) AS [YearsAgo] ,
 If (DayNumberOfQuarter($1) <= DayNumberOfQuarter(Today()),1,0) AS [InQTD]
,
 4*Year(Today())+Ceil(Month(Today())/3)-4*Year($1)-Ceil(Month($1)/3) AS
[QuartersAgo] ,
 Ceil(Month(Today())/3)-Ceil(Month($1)/3) AS [QuarterRelNo] ,
 If(Day($1)<=Day(Today()),1,0) AS [InMTD] ,
 12*Year(Today())+Month(Today())-12*Year($1)-Month($1) AS [MonthsAgo] ,
 Month(Today())-Month($1) AS [MonthRelNo] ,
 If(WeekDay($1)<=WeekDay(Today()),1,0) AS [InWTD] ,
 (WeekStart(Today())-WeekStart($1))/7 AS [WeeksAgo] ,
 Week(Today())-Week($1) AS [WeekRelNo] ;
```

Qlik Sense calls this group of fields `autoCalendar`. This `autoCalendar` contains a group of different fields with date-related data. The variable `$1` will hold the value of a field and it then applies the different expressions.

In this example, the `autoCalendar` declaration has 21 fields. This is the same as applying all these formulas to your date field yourself. However, we don't always know how to do it nor remember all of the expressions, so Qlik Sense comes to the rescue and does it for us. Any fields derived from a declared statement will not show in the Data Model Viewer. Instead, they will show in the Fields section in the Sheet Editor.

The `Declare` syntax is as follows:

```
definition_name:
Declare [Field[s]] Definition [Tagged tag_list ] [Parameters parameter_list
] Fields field_list
```

The last part of the auto-generated script derives the source date fields from the previously declared structure. The `Derive` syntax can be one of the following:

```
Derive [Field[s]] From [Field[s]] field_list Using definition
Derive [Field[s]] From Explicit [Tag[s]] tag_list Using definition
Derive [Field[s]] From Implicit [Tag[s]] Using definition
```

In our example, sense derives two date fields using `autoCalendar`:

```
DERIVE FIELDS FROM FIELDS [MONTH_BUS_KEY], [Full Month] USING
[autoCalendar] ;
```

We will have a total of 42 new fields in the Sheet Edit that we can use in our charts.

The `Calendar` is the most common example you will find online to explain the `Declare` and `Derive` syntax. When you can leverage the power of the derived field is when you start mastering Qlik Sense. After all, that's the name of the book, isn't it?

Allow us to show you how the `Declare` and `Derive` functions work with an example.

We usually work with numbers which represent money. We also format these numbers in different ways within our charts. For example, we might want to show $1m instead of 1,000,000. These formats come out of the box in Sense; however, for billions, Sense uses G, which is not meaningful to many business users. Besides that, we might want to separate our amounts into buckets to show, for example, that 1,000,000 falls within the >500k bucket.

The following code will help us explain the example I just described.

Create a new application and open the Data Load editor from the **navigation** menu. Then copy the following code into the **main** section:

```
/*I load sample data using Inline load */

myDataTable:
Load * Inline
[
FullName, ProductType, Amount
Maria Johns, Personal Loan Type A, 10000
Peter Smith, Car Loan, 25000
George Thomson, Car Loan, 16000
Paula Mays, Personal Loan Type B, 55000
Patricia Gonzalez, Mortgage 5 yr fixed, 750000
];

/*I categorize my field Amount using tags */
TAG FIELD Amount WITH '$myAmount';

/* Here we declare a definition for fields with the tagged $myAmount */

[DeclaredValues]:
 DECLARE FIELD DEFINITION Tagged ('$myAmount')
FIELDS
 Dual('USD '&round($1/1000,0.1)&'K', $1) AS AmountInThousands Tagged
('$thousands', '$myAmount')
,Dual('USD '&round($1/1000000,0.1)&'M', $1) AS AmountInMillions Tagged
('$millions', '$myAmount')
 ,if(($1)>=0 and ($1)<20000, '0-20K'
 , If(($1)>=20000 AND ($1)<50000, '20-50K'
 , '+50K')) AS AmountGroup Tagged ('$amoungroup', '$myAmount')
;
/*Here we derive the files using DeclaredValues */
   DERIVE FIELDS FROM EXPLICIT TAGS '$myAmount' USING DeclaredValues;
```

In this example, we first load the sample data into an inline table. In the second part of the code, we declare the fields in a table called DeclaredValues. We declare three fields: AmountInThousands, AmountInMillions, and AmountGroup. These fields can then be used in the charts as dimensions.

The Derive syntax

The Derive function is necessary to create or derive a data field previously loaded. This function will use the table created using the Declared syntax. In my example code, I derive all fields that have been tagged with $myAmount.

To test and see the actual output generated by the Declare and Derive syntax, you can perform the following steps:

1. Run the script with the code shown in this section by clicking the **Load Data** button and then save it.
2. Using the navigation menu, click on **App Overview**.
3. Click on **Create New Sheet**.
4. Click on **Edit** to edit the sheet.
5. From the left pane, click on the first icon, **Charts**.
6. Locate the chart **Table.** Drag and drop **Table** onto the sheet.
7. Click on the Dimension button and add the **Amount** field (coming from the source) and also add the AmountInThousands, AmountInMillions, and AmountGroup fields, which are the derived fields. The following screenshot shows what the output will look like:

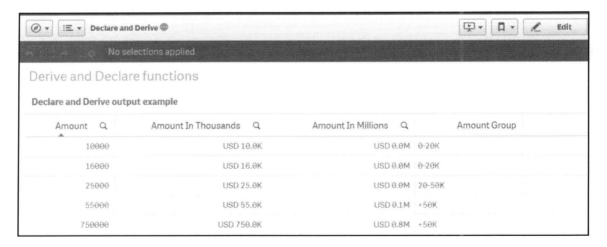

Optimizing your data loads

So far, we have shown you two ways of loading data: through Data Manager and using the Data Load Editor.

Qlik Sense has made it easy to load data by giving the user different options and making it clear and easy to understand where to go.

A good application must have a well-thought-out model. But a well-thought-out model is nothing if loading your data takes longer than expected.

In this section, you will learn how to load data faster using QVD files, and we will also explain data loading techniques that will make your script load data in a blink of an eye.

QVD files

QVD stands for **QlikView data file**. This type of file contains data stored using Qlik Sense or QlikView. QVD files can be created and read with Qlik Sense. But what's so special about these files?

QVD files have a format that makes it very fast to load when using the Sense script. When properly optimized, loading data from these files can be 10 to 100 times faster than any other source. QVD files are the core of any Qlik project. I have not seen any project not taking advantage of these files.

One QVD file will contain data from only one table. The table must be loaded into Qlik Sense before it can be stored in QVD format.

In a real-life project, you would usually pull data from a database or any other source and store it in QVD format. This allows you to be independent from the source the same moment you create the file and you also reduce the impact of hitting your source many times. When your source is a database in a live environment, the use of QVD files becomes the center of attention.

Using QVD files also allows you to bring data together from different sources. It is not uncommon that you work with different databases, spreadsheets, or online data. You can now create your data marts using QVD files.

Modifying these files is as easy as manipulating something in the script. Gone are the days where you had to wait for the slow IT department to make changes to the database so you can then show new things in your dashboards. With QVD files, you are in control and development time decreases drastically.

We mentioned in previous chapters that the best practice is to add as much as you can to your data source; however, we encourage you to leverage the power of building your own Qlik Sense infrastructure with your own QVD data sources. Not relying on others to get the job done is one of the key selling points of this tool. Own your project and data! Use Qlik Sense in the short term but always aim to have most of your calculations upstream.

Creating and maintaining your QVD files also has advantages. One of the most potent loading techniques consists of loading from your source only new or modified records instead of pulling, refreshing, or recreating your files from scratch. What's the point of loading millions of records every day if perhaps only thousands have been updated?

The first time you create the QVD will have to be, of course, a full extraction of your data source. However, once this first pull of data is done, the QVD file becomes your golden source. From here, you can pull only the modified or new records and append them to your existing QVD file. I will explain more of this in the following section.

Creating and storing QVD files

There are two ways of creating QVD files using Qlik Sense:

- Utilizing the STORE syntax: With this syntax, we can store any previously loaded table or part of it into a QVD file.
- Using Buffer: This syntax is used before any Load or Select statement. The files are automatically stored and maintained. The QVD files are stored in different locations depending on your installation.

The following example shows one way of storing data in QVD format:

```
CitiesCountries:
Load * INLINE
[
City, Country
London, United Kingdom
Manchester, United Kingdom
Leeds, United Kingdom
New York, United States
Miami, United States
Berlin, Germany
```

```
Munich, Germany
Rome, Italy
];

STORE CitiesCountries INTO 'lib://myConnection/CitiesCountries.qvd';
```

In the preceding example, we first create an `inline` table. We use this table so you can try it yourself. Most of you will not have a database installed locally so using these tables is easiest. Remember that you need to create your data connection before you can store anything using the LIB syntax.

The `STORE` syntax will save a previously loaded table into a format specified by the user. In this case, we store the data in the file `CitiesCountries.qvd`, which is in QVD format.

 Saving QVD files from Qlik Sense Cloud is not available at the time of writing. Use the Desktop or Enterprise version instead.

Loading data from a QVD file

If you would like to load data from the recently created file, you can use the following line of code:

```
LOAD * FROM 'LIB://myConnection/CitiesCountries.qvd';
```

Optimized loads

Whenever you load data from a QVD file, the load will be optimized. This means that loading the data will be from 10 to 100 times faster than any other source. However, if you make any operations within the load statement, Qlik Sense will have to uncompress the file to make those operations, losing speed.

There are two things that you can do within the load statement and still have an optimized and fast load:

- Rename the fields using the `AS` operator.
- Using the `Exists()` function in a `Where` clause. This function checks whether a specific field value has already been loaded in the script.

Examples of optimized loads

The following are examples of optimized loads:

```
Optimized_1:
LOAD
    City,
    Country
FROM 'LIB://myConnection/CitiesCountries.qvd';

Optimized_2:
LOAD
    City        AS    Cities,
    Country     AS    Countries
FROM 'LIB://myConnection/CitiesCountries.qvd';

Temp:
Load City INLINE
[
City
New York
Munich
];

Optimized_3:
LOAD
    City        AS    Cities,
    Country     AS    Countries
FROM 'LIB://myConnection/CitiesCountries.qvd'
Where Exists(City);

Drop Table Temp;
```

An example of a non-optimized load

The previous examples show three different load statements that will be performed in an optimized way. Any other operation will render the load non-optimized as shown here:

```
Non-Optimized:
LOAD
    City        AS    Cities,
    Country     AS    Countries,
    pick(match(Country, 'United States','United Kingdom','Germany'), 'US',
'GB', 'DE) AS CountryCodes
FROM 'LIB://myConnection/CitiesCountries.qvd'
Where Exists(City);
```

In this example, I create an extra field matching three countries to their country ISO codes. This will make the load non-optimized.

Incremental loads

Incremental loads is a technique used with QVD files. This technique allows you to extract and store in a QVD file only new or modified records. Your source QVD will contain a replica of your source or sources and each time you execute the script, instead of regenerating the file from scratch, you have the possibility of only loading and storing those records that have been modified or are new.

For small sources, incremental loads might not make sense. However, most of the data nowadays is what we call "big". Loading and storing millions and millions of records on a daily basis is not convenient and it is in these cases where incremental loads play a starring role.

Incremental loads are typically used to perform one of the following operations:

- Append
- Insert
- Insert and update
- Insert, update, and delete

Append

Append is the simplest scenario when using incremental loads. Append will only be used when records are not deleted nor updated but only inserted and no comparison in dates must be done. An example of an append scenario is that of a log file where rows are appended but no other operation is performed.

Using the prefix `Buffer` in the `Load` statement for this type of scenario is best as Qlik Sense will keep track of the number of records in the QVD file created and will automatically append any new records in the log to the QVD file.

A downside to this approach is that the source file, either a text file or a database table, must not change its format, such as the number of columns, names, and so on, otherwise the `Buffer` prefix will create a new temporary QVD file.

The following code shows what an append-only scenario would look like:

```
Buffer (Incremental)
LOAD @1 as LogField
FROM
[C:\AppenOnly.txt]
(txt, codepage is 1252, no labels, delimiter is '\t', msq);

MyAppendOnlyResults:
Load * from
C:\Users\localUser\Documents\Qlik\Sense\Buffers\*.qvd (qvd);
```

In this example, we use the prefix Buffer (Incremental). Qlik Sense will check the number of rows in the generated QVD file and if the source incremented the number of records, it will append the new records to the QVD file. You can test this yourself by creating a simple .txt file, running the script once, adding new rows to your .txt file, and running it again. You will see how the output automatically appends the new rows in your .txt file to your QVD file.

Insert only

In this scenario, we must have a last modified date field in our source. The source can be any source supported by Qlik Sense, such as databases, spreadsheets, text files, and so on.

Every time you execute the script, you will check when the last record was last modified and load only records with a date greater than the last modified record date.

As an example, let's use the following table as the source:

%Id	Country	LastModifiedDate
1	United States	42972
2	United Kingdom	42972
3	Canada	42972

The source table has three columns: **%Id**, **Country**, and **LastModifiedDate** in Qlik Sense date format.

In Qlik Sense, dates have a serial number assigned to them, which is the number of days that have passed since December 30, 1899.

In the following code example, we will first check the most recent LastModifiedDate and we will then load all records with dates greater than LastModifiedDate:

```
/*I treat my table keys as system fields by hiding them. We do not want to
use the keys in the front end and therefore we shouldn't show them.
*/

set HidePrefix='%' ;

/* I check if the file exists. If it doesn't I do a full load, if it does I
perform the incremental load. */

IF IsNull(QvdCreateTime('C:\myQVD\Countries.qvd')) THEN

TRACE Performing full load of data source;

Countries:
SELECT * FROM COUNTRY;

STORE Countries INTO C:\myQVD\Countries.qvd (qvd);

ELSE
TRACE File exists. Performing incremental load;

maxDate:
LOAD max(LastModifiedDate) AS MaxModifiedDate
FROM c:\myQVD\Countries.qvd (qvd);

TRACE Storing the most current modified date into a variable.;

LET vMaxModifiedDate = peek(MaxModifiedDate);

TRACE Loading new records from the source.;

Countries:
SELECT * FROM COUNTRY
WHERE LastModifiedDate > $(vMaxModifiedDate)
;

TRACE Appending stored records to  new ones.

Concatenate
```

```
LOAD * FROM c:\myQVD\Countries.qvd (Qvd);

TRACE Storing modified qvd file.;

STORE Countries INTO c:\myQVD\Countries.qvd (Qvd);

ENDIF
```

Note that we now start using variables. We will explain more about variables in the next chapter. We also use the `Trace` syntax. This will log messages in the output window to make it easier for you to follow the execution script.

You can try this example by creating a simple `.txt` file and then adding more records.

Remember that the `LastModifiedDate` can be formatted using the `date()` function but for scripting, it is recommended to have a numeric date format to avoid clashing.

 Make sure you know exactly what your date format is in the source. If you can, use the Qlik Sense numeric format. Be consistent with date formats throughout your script. Otherwise, it might not work.

Insert and update

This scenario is the same as the one before, but we will also consider updated records.

In the previous example, if you modified an existing record, you will have it duplicated as we concatenated all records from the existing QVD file to the new extracted records.

To consider new and updated records, we must add a line of code to the concatenate load statement as follows:

```
TRACE Appending stored records to  new ones.;

Concatenate
LOAD * FROM c:\myQVD\Countries.qvd (Qvd)
WHERE Not EXISTS(%Id);

TRACE Storing modified qvd file.;
```

In this example, we added the following line of code:

```
WHERE Not EXISTS(%Id);</span>
```

This will make sure that we load from the previously stored QVD file only records that having been pulled from the source, preventing duplicate records.

For this to work, we must have a unique key or ID in our source. New records will have a brand new non-existing ID, but the modified records will keep the same ID or key that we can then disregard using the `not exists()` function.

Insert, update, and delete

Finally, the most common scenario is the one where we fully manage the source by checking for new, modified, or deleted records.

The script will be the same as the one used in the insert and update scenario; however, we must add a join to the source to eliminate from our QVD those records that have been deleted after we saved the QVD file.

The following block of code inserts, updates, and deletes records from the source:

```
/* I treat my table keys as system fields by hiding them. We do not want to
use the keys in the front end and therefore we shouldn't show them. */

set HidePrefix='%' ;

/* I check if the file exists. If it doesn't I do a full load, if it does I
perform the incremental load. */

IF IsNull(QvdCreateTime('C:\myQVD\Countries.qvd')) THEN

TRACE Performing full load of data source;

Countries:
SELECT * FROM COUNTRY;

STORE Countries INTO C:\myQVD\Countries.qvd (qvd);

ELSE
TRACE File exists. Performing incremental load;

maxDate:
LOAD max(LastModifiedDate) AS MaxModifiedDate
FROM c:\myQVD\Countries.qvd (qvd);
```

```
TRACE Storing the most current modified date into a variable.;

LET vMaxModifiedDate = peek(MaxModifiedDate);

TRACE Loading new records from the source.;

Countries:
SELECT * FROM COUNTRY
WHERE LastModifiedDate > $(vMaxModifiedDate)
;

TRACE Appending stored records to  new ones.;

Concatenate
LOAD * FROM c:\myQVD\Countries.qvd (Qvd)
WHERE Not EXISTS(%Id);

TRACE We join the final table with all the current keys in the source to
remove the delete records.;

INNER JOIN
SQL SELECT %Id FROM COUNTRY;

TRACE Storing modified qvd file.;

STORE Countries INTO c:\myQVD\Countries.qvd (Qvd);

ENDIF
```

ETL – extract, transform, load

You might have heard about the ETL technique as it is widely used in most current Business Intelligence projects. Having said that, I am usually surprised how often experienced consultants avoid approaching projects in a systematic way and instead use one application to do absolutely everything, from extracting data from a database to data cleansing to creating visualizations.

An ETL approach helps you have an understandable and easy-to-manage project. Think of it as a chest of drawers. You put your T-shirts in one drawer, your underwear in another drawer, and your accessories in a different one. It will be a lot easier for you to know if something is missing by splitting your clothes into compartments and it is exactly the same in a Qlik Sense project.

Always think of your project as a global one. If you do everything in one place, there will be no room for someone else to help you. Instead, having your project part separated will allow more than one developer work on a given project.

The approach we will describe here is one that we have been using for a while now and it works. However, you may want to add your touch to the structure or naming conventions. This is only a guide for you to have an idea of what a real project looks like.

When not to use the ETL approach

Even though every modern project has some kind of an ETL technique, we would like to first explain a few ideas.

In Chapter 6, *Qlik Sense Data Modelling*, we said that most of the business logic should, if not must, be in the source and not in Qlik Sense. This is because having your business logic in Qlik Sense would prevent other tools in the organization from using the output generated. You may also find lots of different results when analyzing the same data but from different sources because each source may apply different business rules.

In small organizations, it is easy to choose only one self-service tool and stick to it. If that is the case, you may have the flexibility of heavily using Qlik Sense to extract and transform your data by applying business rules. You need to consider, though, how this can be sustained in the future. What if Qlik Sense stops existing? Or, what if Qlik comes up with a different tool and they stop supporting Qlik Sense scripts?

In medium-sized to big organizations, however, it is impossible to have only one tool. You will have several tools that will go from reporting, to self-service analytics, to guided analytics. In this case, you must force your business logic to be in the data source, which will generally be a database. All tools will then pull data from the golden source, which will contain all the business logic, and thus all output throughout all platforms will be consistent.

When to use the ETL approach

One of the powerful features in Qlik Sense is its scripting capabilities. The ability to modify your data is something the puts Qlik Sense ahead of other tools.

Qlik Sense scripting simplicity and the fact that you build your applications in a live environment—which I will explain later on—makes the tool ideal for fast development and prototyping. And prototyping is key when we talk about the ETL approach.

The reality is that you will never have everything you need to display in your dashboards in your data source. This is because, most of the time, the interest of the team managing the golden data source isn't the same as the team building dashboards. You, as a Qlik Sense seasoned developer, must enforce business rules to be built in the source. Nevertheless, there is always going to be some kind of transformations to your source.

For example, you might want to create extra fields in your calendar that are only useful in Qlik Sense as it will make your charts render faster. Or something that is very common, that we will cover in the next chapter, is the ability to create flags in your data model to make expressions calculate faster when users interact with the dashboard. These are examples of things your database team might not want to add to the source as these aren't necessarily business rules but they are more things you use to make your dashboards perform better.

The old approach to ETL

It is important I explain how an ETL approach was implemented in projects before Qlik Sense came into play as they will be different and should be planned differently too.

In an IT project, it is very common to have at least three different servers, one for development, one for testing purposes or **user acceptance (UAT)**, and one production server. You may call them different things or might have an extra server, such us preproduction. What matters here are the concepts. The structure might change slightly.

In a conventional project, you would develop in your development server. Your data sources would point to the development server. Most of the time, you wouldn't have access to live data or data source from a development environment.

Once your development is done, you would deploy your files to a UAT server where testers would try to crash what you built and find issues. So far, the development and UAT servers are in different infrastructures, and they may point to different data sources.

Once everything is approved in UAT, you would deploy your project on your production server. Your application would point to a database with live data, and it is here the end users will access the application.

The following screenshot shows what the approach to an old ETL architecture would look like:

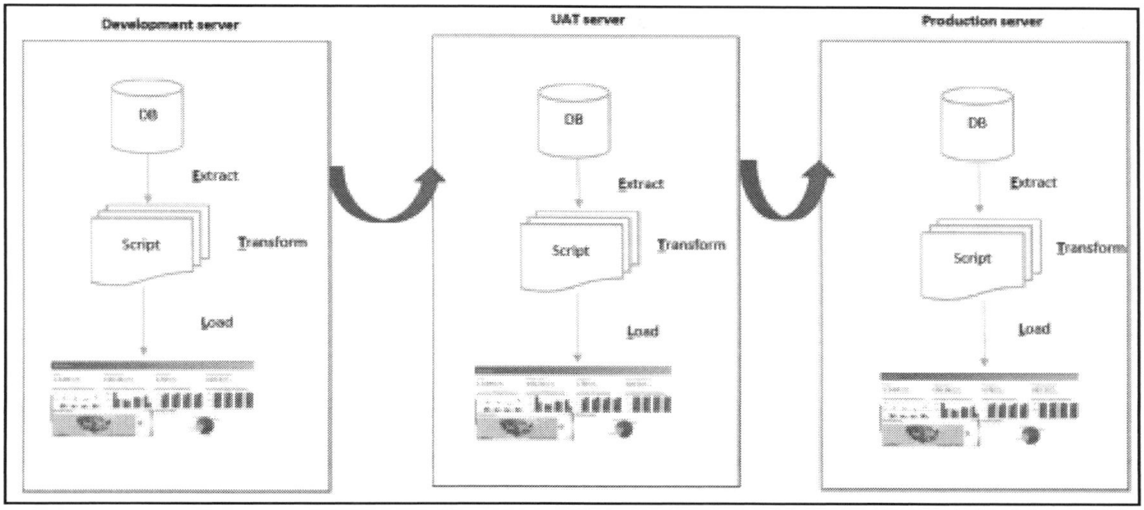

This screenshot represents the standard waterfall ETL approach: everything protected and divided into compartments. Now, take all this and throw it in the bin as things have changed considerably with Qlik Sense.

The Qlik Sense approach to ETL

With Qlik Sense, you should care more about building dashboards with live data. This means you can build amazing self-service applications in your build node, which is connected to the production node through a master central node. This brings a whole new meaning the old IT approach, which is usually very static and slow to change.

Developers can create applications under "My Work" space. Anything created in this section will be visible only to the developer. Once the application is ready to be promoted, the administrator can create a copy by duplicating the application and deploying it to a specific stream within the same build note. This stream can be used by testers or selected business users to test the application before promoting it to a stream in the production node.

You can configure who has access to each stream using the Security Rules described in Chapter 3, *Security Rules: Attribute Based Access Control*.

The superuser can also help develop applications. The best approach here would be to limit the superuser to visualizations, measures, and dimensions created in the master items. By doing so, you make sure to have proper control over what is used in the applications and ensure all elements are previously tested.

Collaboration puts the power in the hands of the business. The business will promote the use of Qlik Sense and the use of the applications. Whatever is created by a superuser will not replace anything in the published application. Instead, it will appear in a different area of the Hub. End users can have access to the guided dashboard but they can also access the more flexible dashboards created by the superuser.

This defines a whole new meaning to the Qlik Sense consultant role as they will now spend more time training end users and superusers on how to best use Qlik Sense as well as answering any questions related to the tool. The Qlik Sense developer will also be the one who creates and maintains the data model along with the master items.

Pros and cons of the new ETL approach

The use of streams is by no means new but it gives the analytics world a lot more flexibility than ever before. Even IT departments feel comfortable with streams as they can manage them but they still allow developers to create their magic in a live environment.

Of course, this approach isn't perfect and might not be useful to some types of industries.

A big con of this approach is the fact that any person of a stream within the live environment can have access to live data. For data-sensitive industries such as healthcare, this approach is dangerous, and it will most probably be prohibited. After all, you wouldn't want a random consultant accessing your health history while developing dashboards, would you?

But for many other industries, privacy isn't necessarily a problem and this approach is excellent as developers will be able to see precisely what dashboards will look like in a live environment and testers will be able to test the applications with real live and meaningful data.

If data privacy is a problem, though, you can always talk to whoever is in charge of the data source and see whether it is possible to mask sensitive data such as names or addresses. By doing this, you still have the power of live data in your hands while protecting privacy.

Summary

Qlik introduced a whole new way of loading data with the introduction of Qlik Sense. It is now much easier not only for developers but for any type of user to load and manipulate data from different sources. In this chapter, we described why Data Manager is a key feature that will keep improving and will stay for a long time. We also explained how to load data using the Script Editor and how this compares to Data Manager.

Qlik scripting continues to be very powerful and widely used among technical users. With the introduction of new syntax and function, Qlik has again made the statement that it is here to cater to all types of users.

In the next chapter, we will cover advanced scripting concepts, and you will learn how to create scripts from scratch.

8
Advanced Scripting

As we described in previous chapters, Qlik Sense makes it easy to manipulate and load data from different sources through a visual interface called **Data Manager**. Nevertheless, Qlik Sense comes with a very powerful scripting language that is shared with its father, QlikView, mostly in its totality and making these tools unique in the market.

Qlik Sense inherited most of the script elements from QlikView. Most of the functions found in QlikView can still be used in Qlik Sense. Other new functions, such as `declare` and `derive`, were introduced with Qlik Sense and are not available in QlikView. These two functions are described in `Chapter 7`, *Best Practices for Loading Data in Qlik Sense*, so I recommend you refer to them after reading this chapter if you have not done so already.

There are tons of functions in Qlik Sense, however, my intention is to describe the functions that, from my experience, are frequently used.

In this chapter, we will learn about:

- Formatting settings through variables
- Script control statements
- Table statistics
- Data security with Section Access
- Advanced sample script

Everything that is showed in this chapter will be done within a script. As a reminder, to open the script editor, you have to:

1. Create a new application using Qlik Sense Desktop, Enterprise, or Cloud
2. Click on the **Navigation** button
3. Click on **Data load editor**

The following image shows steps 2 and 3:

Formatting settings through variables

Before we start coding, we should first set the foundations that will allow us to properly set up formats as well as ways of handling values, for example, nulls or dates. This is important because different regions have different formats. Let's take the United States as an example. Numbers in the United States use commas to represent thousands and dots to represent decimals. For example, one thousand and thirty hundredths in its numerical form is 1,000.30. However, most of the countries in Latin America would use dots as a thousand separator and commas for hundredths separators: 1.000,30.

Another very important value where the format changes depending on the region is the date. Dates can be represented in different ways. For example, 2018-08-08 where we have four digits for the year, two for the month, and two for the day, or 30-01-2019 and 01-30-2019 to represent the same date in a different format.

This is only one example of things we can set up before we start scripting. Other things such as names of months and days can also be set up.

All of these formats can be set from the script using variables. Whenever we create a brand new script, we will see the following variables in the **Main** section:

```
SET ThousandSep=',';
SET DecimalSep='.';
SET MoneyThousandSep=',';
SET MoneyDecimalSep='.';
SET MoneyFormat='£#,##0.00;-£#,##0.00';
```

```
SET TimeFormat='hh:mm:ss';
SET DateFormat='DD/MM/YYYY';
SET TimestampFormat='DD/MM/YYYY hh:mm:ss[.fff]';
SET FirstWeekDay=0;
SET BrokenWeeks=0;
SET ReferenceDay=4;
SET FirstMonthOfYear=1;
SET CollationLocale='en-GB';
SET CreateSearchIndexOnReload=1;
SET MonthNames='Jan;Feb;Mar;Apr;May;Jun;Jul;Aug;Sep;Oct;Nov;Dec';
SET
LongMonthNames='January;February;March;April;May;June;July;August;September
;October;November;December';
SET DayNames='Mon;Tue;Wed;Thu;Fri;Sat;Sun';
SET
LongDayNames='Monday;Tuesday;Wednesday;Thursday;Friday;Saturday;Sunday';
```

Variables are defined as follows:

```
SET|LET variableName = 'variable value';
```

Even though the prefixes SET and LET are allowed when defining variables, we will only use the prefix SET when setting:

- System variables
- Value handling variables
- Number interpretation variables

In the following sections, I will explain these three important topics.

 The SET prefix will assign whatever is on the right of the equals (=) sign as a string. The LET prefix will evaluate whatever is on the right of the equals sign and assign the value of the evaluated expression to the variable.

System variables

Qlik Sense comes with reserved system variables. The content of these variables can be redefined by the developers making them flexible.

System variables provide information about Qlik Sense applications such as the location of the application in a machine as well as system information.

Throughout this chapter, I will only describe the functions that I consider are often used in most scripts and are useful to know and understand. There are, however, a lot more system variables that can be found in the Qlik Sense help site. For further information, you can visit `https://help.qlik.com`.

HidePrefix and HideSuffix

These two variables are used to hide fields from the selection bar. Whenever a field starts or ends with the character set in these two user-defined variables, the fields will be hidden the same way as the system fields are. If values are selected in these fields, they won't be shown in the selection bar. However, they can still be used when creating front-end expressions.

The following block of code shows an example of how to set these variables:

```
SET HidePrefix = '%';
SET HideSuffix = '_';
```

In this example, all the fields in our model that start with the character `%` will be hidden. This is a great example of when we work with our table keys. Table keys are usually used to join tables, however, they are hardly used in the front-end and thus I recommend to hide them by setting the `HidePrefix` variable.

Also, in this example, all fields finishing with `_` will be hidden and treated as a system field.

Other scenarios where I recommend you hide fields are when creating data islands with field values using toggle-like functions, such as a language or currency selector. We will most probably want these fields to be clickable in the front-end, yet, we do not necessarily want them to show in the selection bar.

 As good practice, set up all system variables at the beginning of the script.

include and must_include

The `include` and `must_include` variables are used to call a file which contains text that must be executed as code as part of the script. These are usually **QVS (QlikView script files)** or the famous TXT files.

This is very useful for when we want to reuse code created in other applications. It is a great way of sharing and reusing code.

Also, exporting script code into files is a great way to version control the scripting logic and to track changes.

The following is the syntax for these variables:

```
$(include=filename);
$(must_include=filename);
```

A blank space right after the equal sign in the `include` or `must_include` variables will throw an error.

The difference between these two variables is that `include` does not throw an error if the file specified in `filename` is not found. On the other hand, `must_include` will generate an error if the files do not exist in the specified location.

I strongly recommend you use `must_include` to improve debugging.

Even though I would encourage the use of `must_include`, I would personally use `include` when importing files generated by users or the business. These files are usually add-ons and are non-essential to our data model. If the file gets mistakenly deleted by the user, it would prevent our scripts from running properly.

On the other hand, files or scripts that are critical to our data model, such as an external file containing Section Access script, must always be loaded using `must_include`, otherwise there is a risk that someone could delete the file and thus the application would load without any section access in it, allowing access to anyone with a token.

As opposed to other structures in the script, these two variables allow the file name to be specified as part of an absolute file path. For example:

```
$(must_include=C:\MyDocuments\IncludeFile.txt);
```

However, it can also be called from a folder connection:

```
$(must_include=lib://myFiles\IncludeFile.txt);
```

Even though they are both acceptable, in Qlik Sense, I recommend you use the latter through the use of folder connections.

Remember, the contents of the files that are included using `Include` and `Must_Include` are executed as code, so make sure they comply with Qlik Sense script syntax.

CreateSearchIndexOnReload

I often experience a delay when I search in my application. This is because nothing is indexed when the data is reloaded unless we force it.

`CreateSearchIndexOnReload` does just that. Every time we reload the script, Qlik Sense will generate search index files. If nothing is specified, the index is created after the user performs the first search.

 If `CreateSearchIndexOnReload` is omitted, indexes will not be created on reload.

One thing to consider is the longer script execution time due to the index file creation process.

To set this to *on*, set the variable to 1, as shown in the following code block:

```
set CreateSearchIndexOnReload=1;
```

I recommend setting `CreateSearchIndexOnReload` in those applications which need to reload fast, or in on-demand applications, near real-time applications, and in those applications with write-back functionality which require you to reload after you have updated a record.

Value handling variables

Value handling variables are used to tell Qlik Sense how to handle certain data values, such as null values. This is very important when we want to display null values as something different that isn't null and when we want to be able to select those null values.

NullDisplay

The `NullDisplay` value is used to tell Qlik Sense how we want to show any value that is coming from the source that is *null*. A null value isn't a blank value, but a value that doesn't exist.

Whenever `NullDisplay` is set, the null value is replaced by the value set by the user.

The following is an example of how to use this variable:

```
SET NullDisplay = 'Null Value';
```

 This variable works when pulling data with ODBC and connectors.

NullInterprete

This variable is used when we want to define a non-null value coming from a text file, Excel, or an Inline table as null.

The following example shows how to use this variable:

```
set NullInterprete='NULL';

Table:
LOAD
  DataField
  ,'NULL' AS NullField
Inline
[
DataField
Value 1
Value 2
Value 3
];
```

In the preceding example, any `NULL` coming from the source will be treated as a null value. This variable is also very useful for replacing blank field values with null. Remember that blank is still a value and thus consumes RAM and storage. To replace blank spaces with null values, set the variables as follows:

```
SET NullInterprete='';
```

NullValue

`NullValue` is used together with `NullAsValue`. All null values in the fields listed after `NullAsValue` syntax will be replaced with the string set in the variable `NullValue`.

This is very useful when we want to make null values searchable. For example, if we want to easily spot how many customers have not entered a phone number, we can create something like the following example:

```
NullAsValue Telephone;

SET NullValue='%NULL%';

Customers:
LOAD
    Customer
    ,Telephone
 FROM [LIB://MyFiles\Customers.csv];
```

Number interpretation variables

So far, we have seen variables that can be modified by the users. Those variables are called user-defined variables.

Number interpretation variables, on the other hand, are system-defined variables which are automatically generated when a new application is created.

The number interpretation variables are shown in the **Data load** editor in the section Main of the script. Even though these variables are automatically generated, they can be deleted or edited by the user.

For example, if the Qlik Sense desktop you use to develop is in a region where thousands are separated by commas, you can still modify the variables for thousands to be separated by dots.

DecimalSep

This variable sets the decimal separator as follows:

```
SET DecimalSep = '.';
```

ThousandSep

This variable sets the thousand separator as follows:

```
SET ThousandSep = ',';
```

DateFormat

This variable sets the date format. This format applies to all timestamps or date fields. When loading data, Qlik Sense will automatically tag date and timestamp columns with the $timestamp and $date tags, which are the ones that will inherit this formatting.

While in Europe, we would set this variable as follows:

```
SET DateFormat = 'DD-MM-YYYY';
```

In the United States, we would have to set the variable as follows:

```
SET DateFormat = 'MM-DD-YYYY';
```

My favorite, however, is the ISO date format, which makes it the clearest version of them all:

```
SET DateFormat = 'YYYY-MM-DD';
```

MonthNames and LongMonthNames

These two variables contain the short and the long version of the months. You can replace the strings within these variables with whatever you wish.

For example:

```
SET MonthNames = 'Jan;Feb;Mar;Apr;May;Jun;Jul;Aug;Sep;Oct;Nov;Dec';
SET LongMonthNames =
'January;February;March;April;May;June;July;August;September;October;November;December';
```

DayNames and LongDayNames

Same as with the months, the short and long day names can be set using these two variables. The following example shows how you would change the variables to contain day names in Spanish:

```
SET DayNames = 'Lun;Mar;Mie;Jue;Vie;Sab;Dom';
SET LongDayNames='Lunes;Martes;Miercoes;Jueves;Viernes;Sabado;Domingo';
```

As these variables replace the regional setting in the operating systems when the application is published, a person in Germany will still see names in Spanish, as set in my example.

To dynamically change these, you either need one application per regional setting which is not recommended, or you can dynamically format names and dates in the front-end by using expressions.

Script control statements

Control statements are used to control the flow of the script. Without the control statements, our script would be executed sequentially from top to bottom and every single line of code would be executed.

A script is formed by a group of statements. These statements can either be regular or control statements.

Regular statements are usually used to manipulate data. A LOAD statement is an example of a regular statement as follows:

```
MyTable:
LOAD * FROM [LIB://MyFolder\Sales.qvd] (qvd);
```

By using control statements, we can force the script to execute certain code based on certain conditions.

Control statements end with a semicolon or with an end-of-line.

Keep on reading to learn more about these powerful statements.

Organizing your script

A tidy script is always well-received for maintenance, governance, version control, and debugging purposes. Scripts can be organized by using sections and control statements.

I like to organize my script into compartments. A part of the script will set variables, another part of the script will load data, another part will transform it, and so on. Control statements make it a lot easier to debug scripts in case of errors.

Using subroutines is, in my opinion, necessary and highly recommended.

Sub ... End Sub

This control statement is used for subroutines. Subroutines are code blocks that are only executed when the subroutine is called. Subroutines can be used more than once within the same script and among other applications!.

Subroutines are very useful and widely used in most scripts as they can also be parameterized, which can render them powerful functions. This is key when creating reusable code. Create different functions, save them separately in QVS or TXT files, and then include them in your script whenever needed. You can also re-use the code in any application.

The following is an example of a subroutine that sets a couple of variables:

```
Sub SetVariables

SET vBookName = 'Mastering Qlik Sense';
LET vCurrentYear = Year(Today());

End Sub
```

The subroutine `SetVariables` will only be executed when it is called with the `call` statement.

Subroutines also accept parameters. Each parameter must be separated by a comma. Parameters can be used as variables in the script with the dollar sign ($). The following example shows how to use subroutines with parameters:

```
Sub LoadYear(UserYear)

Table:
LOAD
*
Inline
[
Year
2015
2016
2017
]
where Year = $(UserYear);

END Sub
```

The following is an example of a subroutine that stores a table into QVD format and then drops the table. This can easily be used in any application:

```
Sub StoreAndDrop(vMyTable, vFileName)

STORE $(vMyTable) INTO [lib://FolderConnection/$(vFileName).qvd] (QVD);
DROP TABLE $(vMyTable);

END sub;
```

Call (subroutines)

The `Call` control statement is used to call subroutines. Call also accepts parameters that are sent to the subroutines. The `Call` syntax is shown as follows:

```
Call subroutineName(Parameter 1, Parameter 2, Parameter n);
```

The following script shows the complete example of a subroutine and the call of it:

```
Sub LoadYear(UserYear)

Table:
LOAD
*
Inline
[
Year
2015
2016
2017
]
where Year = $(UserYear);

END Sub

Call LoadYear(2017);
```

In the preceding example, the code within the subroutine will only populate the `Year` field with `2017` data.

As of way of organizing our script, we can have one section per main subroutine—for instance, the load of the fact table—and then one last section where we call all the different subroutines. Within the main subroutines we can call supportive subroutines such us a subrouting that stores and drops a table.

The following image shows a sample script with three different sections and a fourth section calling the different subroutines:

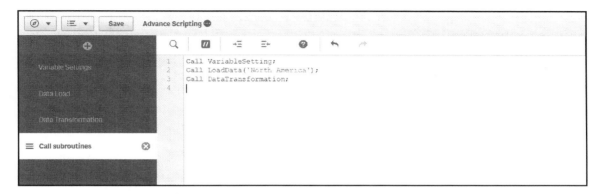

Looping

Sometimes, it is necessary to create loops in our scripts. These loops can be either run a fixed number of times or they can run until a certain condition is met.

A real scenario where loops are useful is that of a decentralized environment with multiple databases, and thus multiple database connections. If each database contains the same table structure but the data is different—for example, each database contains data for a specific region—to extract or pull the data, we would need to execute the same SQL statement for each of the databases.

Instead of having *n* different database connection calls with the same SQL code to extract the data, we can use loops that will contain one call to the database and one SQL code to pull the data.

In the following sections, the different loops syntax is regularly used in Qlik Sense.

Do... Loop

This control statement iterates one or more times until a condition is met. The condition is evaluated once the control statement and the code in it have been executed.

The syntax for Do... Loop is as follows:

```
Do [ ( while | until ) condition ] [statements] [exit do [ ( when | unless
) condition ] [statements] loop[ ( while | until ) condition ]
```

Do... Loop has several constructions. The first one is driven by Do, which means a condition is evaluated before the code within Do... Loop is executed. For example:

```
LET vCount = 1;

DO while vCount <= 5

TRACE Loop will continue until variable vCount is less or equal to 5
$ (vCount);

LET vCount = $ (vCount)+1;

Loop;
```

In the previous example, the vCount <= 5 condition is evaluated before the first loop. When the condition is no longer met, the loop ends.

Do until... Loop also evaluates the condition before the first loop, however, the loop will keep going on until the condition is true, which is contrary to Do... while, which runs until the condition is false.

The following code shows an example of this:

```
LET vCount = 1;

DO until vCount = 5

TRACE Loop will continue until variable vCount equals 5;

LET vCount = $ (vCount)+1;

Loop;
```

The same way we use Until and While with Do, we can use Until or While right after Loop. In this case, the condition will be evaluated after the first loop. This means the loop will execute at least once.

For complex code, within this control statement, we can use the Exit Do clause. This statement allows us to exit the loop at the point we place it. When used with While or Until, we can then exit the loop based on certain conditions, as shown in the previous examples.

Be careful when creating loops. Make sure to review the condition before executing the script, otherwise, you risk creating an infinite loop.

For... Next

The For... Next control statement is used when we know in advance the number of iterations we would like to perform. As with the Do... Loop control statement, For... Next also allows us to exit the loop at any point when using Exit Next. The syntax of this control statement is as follows:

```
For counter = expr1 to expr2 [ step expr3 ]
  [statements]
  [exit for [ ( when | unless ) condition ]
  [statements]
  Next [counter]
```

The expressions in the For statement are evaluated before the loop starts and only once. The Step statement will make the counter skip step expr3 (see syntax) number of positions. If step is a negative number, it will reverse the incremental iteration.

The following example shows how to use a For... Next control statement with a one-by-one countdown:

```
SET vBookName = 'Mastering Qlik Sense';
SET vBookNameBackwards = '';
/*
We loop through the string contained in variable vBookName.
Step -1 will make the loop count down one by one.
*/

FOR ForCounter = len('$(vBookName)') to 1 Step -1

/*
We get the each letter in the variable vBookName but backwards.
*/

LET vLetterPosition = mid('$(vBookName)',$(ForCounter),1);

LET vBookNameBackwards = vBookNameBackwards & vLetterPosition;

Next;

TRACE The word "$(vBookName)" is "$(vBookNameBackwards)" backwards.;
```

For Each... Next

Contrary to the control statement `For... Next`, `For Each... Next` will iterate a number of known times but instead of iterating through numbers, it will iterate through a list of values.

The syntax of `For Each... Next` is:

```
For each var in list
  [statements]
  [exit for [ ( when | unless ) condition ]
  [statements]
  next [var]
```

As with the `For... Next` control statement, `For Each... Next` also allows exiting the loop by using the `exit for` statement.

The `list` argument can have values separated by a comma, but it can also have the following syntax:

```
list := item { , item }
item:=constant | (expression) | filelist mask | dirlist mask |
fieldvaluelist mask
```

Where:

constant	Any number or string. Note that a string written directly in the script must be enclosed by single quotes. A string without single quotes will be interpreted as a variable, and the value of the variable will be used. Numbers do not need to be enclosed by single quotes.
expression	An arbitrary expression.
mask	A filename or folder name mask which may include any valid filename characters as well as the standard wildcard characters, * and ?. You can use absolute file paths or `lib://` paths.
condition	A logical expression evaluating to True or False.
statements	Any group of one or more Qlik Sense script statements.

`filelist mask`	This syntax produces a comma-separated list of all files in the current directory matching the filename mask. This argument only supports library connections in standard mode.
`dirlist mask`	This syntax produces a comma-separated list of all folders in the current folder matching the folder name mask. This argument only supports library connections in standard mode.
`fieldvaluelist mask`	This syntax iterates through the values of a field already loaded into Qlik Sense.

The following example shows a practical example of how to replicate the Qlik Sense functions `Crosstable` using the `For Each... Next` control statement:

```
/*We make sure our variables are empty.*/

SET vFields = ;
SET vNoOfFields =;


/* we load our sample data */
[Sales]:
LOAD *

Inline
[
Country, Jan, Feb, Mar, Apr, May, Jun, Jul, Aug, Sep, Oct, Nov, Dec
United States, 100, 103, 108, 103, 103, 99, 115, 113, 118, 120, 128, 125
United Kingdom, 160, 165, 165, 148, 177, 151, 149, 132, 136, 146, 140, 170
];

/*Create a variable with the number of fields in our source.*/
LET vNoOfFields = NoOfFields('Sales');

/* We create a a variable with comma separated values that we will use in
For Each... Next */

For counter = $(vNoOfFields) to 2 Step -1

/* We create the variable vFields which contains a string with all the
months columns. */

LET vFields = '@'&FieldName($(counter), 'Sales')&'@'&',' &vFields;
```

```
/* Replacing character holder "@" by single quotes */
LET vFields = replace('$(vFields)', '@',chr(39));

Next counter

/* We start the crosstable function.*/
For Each value in $(vFields)

[SalesCrossTable]:
Load
  Country,
  '$(value)' as Month,
  $(value) as Sales
Resident Sales
;

Next value

DROP Table Sales;
```

Another good example of when to use this control statement is when loading data from databases that are logically or physically in different locations. In my next example, I have 4 database connections called ASP, MENA, AMER, and EUR, each representing a region. One same fact table exists in the four databases, however, each fact table contains data for one of the regions.

Instead of connecting to the database in four different lines of code and creating the same SQL statement four times, we can use For each as follows:

```
/*
This script will only execute if the 4 DB connections ASP, MENA, AMER and
EUR are created in the server
or machine running the script.
*/

For each vDBConnection IN 'ASP', 'MENA', 'AMER', 'EUR';

LIB CONNECT TO '$(vDBConnection)';

TRACE Loading data from database in $(vDBConnection);

Fact:
SQL
SELECT * FROM QS_FACT_TABLE;

STORE Fact INTO [lib://Source/QS_FACT_TABLE_$(vDBConnection).qvd] (qvd);
```

```
DROP TABLE Fact;


Next;
```

Switch... Case... Default... End Switch

This control statement executes the `Case` that matches the expression. Switch is generally used when we want to avoid the use of nested `IF` statements.

The syntax is as follows:

```
Switch expression {case valuelist [ statements ]} [default statements] end
switch
```

The following example checks the environment in which the application is hosted by including a file which contains the variable with the environment. After this, we load a file from a folder connection created in the server. The load will point to the file in the current environment:

```
/*
The following code includes a file containing a variable definition with
string Live, UAT or Development.
Folder connections with name ConnectionLive, ConnectionUAT and
ConnectionDevelopment must be setup
in the server. Each server will have the file Environment.txt.
*/

$(must_include=lib://Environment/Environment.txt);

Switch vEnvironment
CASE 'Live';
SET vFolderConnection = 'ConnectionLive';
CASE 'UAT';
SET vFolderConnection = 'ConnectionUAT';
CASE 'Development';
SET vFolderConnection = 'ConnectionDevelopment';
End Switch;

LOAD * From
[lib://$(vFolderConnection)/Customers.txt]
(txt, codepage is 28591, embedded labels, delimiter is '\t', msq);
```

In the former example, I used three connections. This is useful when working with single node environments in which we access Development, UAT and Live data sources from the same node. If, however, each server node has access to its own environment, it is recommended to name the folder connection with the same name. Qlik Sense will automatically pick up the file using the same folder connection but will be pointing to the source where the application is currently running.

Conditional statements

Conditional statements help perform different actions based on boolean conditions evaluating to true or false. In Qlik Sense, a condition evaluating to true is represented by the value -1 and false is represented by the value 0.

Some examples of boolean conditions include:

- `1 = 1` evaluates to true or -1 in Qlik Sense
- `1 < 2` evaluates to true
- `2 <> 3` evaluates to true
- `'Qlik Sense' = 'Qlikview'` evaluates to false
- `0 = false()` evaluates to true
- `null() = null()` evaluates to null

If... Then... Elseif... End If

The `If` conditional statement forces the script execution to follow a certain path based on a condition returning true.

An `If` statement is usually used when creating flags while loading data.

The syntax is as follows:

```
If condition then
[ statements ]
{ elseif condition then [ statements ] }
[ else [ statements ] ] end if
```

The use of `elseif` is recommended when nested `If` is needed.

If the condition in the `If` statement isn't met, the code after `else` is executed.

The following example defines a variable in which we assign the current environment. If it is `Development`, we load a file with test sample data, otherwise, we load live client data:

```
SET vEnvironment = 'Development';

IF vEnvironment = 'Development' THEN

LOAD
    *
FROM [lib://Mastering Qlik Sense Dev\Sample Data.xlsx]
(ooxml, embedded labels, table is Sheet1);

Else

LOAD
    *
FROM [lib://Mastering Qlik Sense Prod\Client Data.xlsx]
(ooxml, embedded labels, table is Sheet1);

End If;
```

In the previous example, `If` is used outside the `Load` statement. In this case, `If` will be evaluated only once and follow one path based on a true/false result.

`If` can also be used within the `Load` statement, for example, when creating flags that we can then use in the frontend:

```
Data:
LOAD
    *,
if(not isnull([Balance]), 1, 0) AS _flagHasBalance
FROM [lib://Mastering Qlik Sense Prod\Client Data.xlsx]
(ooxml, embedded labels, table is Sheet1);
```

Table stats

When building your application, stats and **KPIs (key performance indicators)** are very important to understand how much data we work with, its density, its uniqueness, and so on. The Data model viewer provides great insight on the data loaded, but this is not available to end users if this is needed. For example, we may have a person controlling our ETL process from the source to the frontend application. We must expose to this person the nature of the source such as table names, the number of records in the source, the number of records after loading the script, and the load times, among other useful KPIs.

Verification and validation are essential to any application. Knowing what we load, how long it takes, how big our data is, and how this data will have an impact on the RAM is critical to maintaining a healthy enterprise environment.

Keep reading to learn how to use functions to create more powerful, insightful Qlik Sense applications.

RecNo

The RecNo() function returns the position of the source records and takes into account any where clause that may affect the number of records returned.

RecNo() is particularly useful during debugging when we want to trace values back to the source.

This function works with the source table instead of the target logical table created in Qlik Sense. This means that the number returned by RecNo() will not be affected by any where clause.

RowNo

RowNo works with the resulting internal Qlik Sense table after a load instead of the source table. This means that anything affecting the number of records loaded in a Load statement will also affect this function. For example, if my source table has 10 rows of data, but we then use a where condition that returns five rows, RowNo() will return numbers 1 to 5 while RecNo() will return values from 1 to 10 depending on the records returned.

The code shows in a simple way how RowNo() and RecNo() work:

```
MyData:
Load
  WeekDay,
    RecNo() AS RecNo,
    RowNo() As RowNo
Inline [
WeekDay
Monday
Tuesday
Wednesday
Thursday
Friday
Saturday
```

```
Sunday
]
where WeekDay <> 'Tuesday';
```

The source table in the example contains 7 rows, however, the output contains 6 rows as we filter out `Tuesday`. The output after executing the scripts looks as follows:

WeekDay	RecNo	RowNo
Monday	1	1
Wednesday	3	2
Thursday	4	3
Friday	5	4
Saturday	6	5
Sunday	7	6

NoOfRows and NoOfFields

These functions return the number of rows and fields of a previously loaded table, respectively.

The following example shows the use of these functions:

```
MyData:
Load
  WeekDay,
    RecNo() AS RecNo,
    RowNo() As RowNo
Inline [
WeekDay
Monday
Tuesday
Wednesday
Thursday
Friday
Saturday
Sunday
]
where WeekDay <> 'Tuesday';

LET vNoOfRows = NoOfRows('MyData');
LET vNoOfFields = NoOfFields('MyData');
```

```
TRACE NoOfRows() returns 6;
TRACE ;
TRACE NoOfFields() returns 3;

Exit Script;
```

Data security with Section Access

From Regulatory Compliance to protection of confidential information, securing data is the first concern of any organization. It is in fact so important that data leakage or data accessed by an unwanted source could cause companies to close.

We can split securing our applications into two parts. The first one is securing the file itself. Contrary to QlikView, we create Qlik Sense applications are created on the server through a web browser. However, an application is a file that resides on the server and thus should be protected as any other sensitive file on a server. The second part is securing the data within the file by using Section Access. Section Access describes what each of the authorized users who can access the application can see.

Authenticating a user means that the Qlik Sense Proxy will define who the user is and it will then authorize access to the application if the user is meant to have such access. After the user is authenticated, Section Access will handle what the user is authorized to see.

Most applications will contain lots of data catered to different people, for example, a CEO as well as an analyst. But also, the users can be sitting on a different region which can give us a horizontal view of our security model—this is, what regions can the access—as well as a vertical view—depending on the role, what data can they see—.

Users on different organization roles could you the same application, for example, Finance. However, if you need to cater to different areas, you will most probably need to create different applications. Whether is one or many, applying Section Access in all your applications is a must.

 Section Access is not supported in Qlik Sense Cloud as of Q1 2018.

For example, you may have users who need to access sales data for the United States. However, the Regional Sales Manager will have to access data not only for the US but also for all the countries in his/her region.

As another example, Supervisor Tom should only see data related to people in his team. Tom must not see any data from Robert's team.

The preceding examples are situations where we must control the type of data access using Section Access.

 An application with a binary load will inherit the security applied in said application.

Section Access and Section Application

Data security through Section Access can be applied at row-level or column-level. Row-level Section Access will define what rows from our data model are visible to each authorized user. Column-level Section Access defines whether certain columns from our data model should not be visible to users.

A Qlik Sense application can be logically split into two main sections:

- Section Application
- Section Access

Section Application will contain all the lines of codes which help extract, transform, and load our data. This section of the script is where we load our tables and create the data model. Everything we do in the Script Editor or Data Manager is implicitly done within the Section Application section. There's no need to explicitly define the application section when we don't define section access security.

Section Access, on the other hand, is the section where we specify our user's access. It is here where we tell Qlik Sense who should access what. We must explicitly tell Qlik Sense we are creating a section access by typing the syntax `Section Access;`. Whatever code is under this will be part of section access. To finish the section access code, we must type `Section Application;`.

Qlik Sense uses section access to automatically authenticate and authorize a user to access a file and dynamically reduces the data, allowing users to see what they should see.

Fields in section access

To create the section access, Qlik Sense provides four fields that we can use to manage data security. The fields are:

- ACCESS: This field defines what type of access the user should have. It could either be ADMIN or USER. A person defined as ADMIN can access and see all the data in the application. A person defined as a USER can see only the data he or she is assigned to.
- USERID: This is the string containing the Qlik Sense username. The proxy is used here to get the username, and then this username is compared to the value in the field.
- GROUP: Contains a string corresponding to a group in Qlik Sense. Qlik Sense will resolve the user supplied by the proxy against this group.
- OMIT: This is used to omit or remove (logically) fields for certain users. You should have one line per field and the user you want to omit.

One thing to take into account is that all the field names and values used in section access must be written in upper case. To avoid problems, the upper() function can be used in all the fields.

The next block of code shows a simple application secured by section access. The example does not reduce any data, but only secures access to the file:

```
Section Access;
LOAD
    UPPER(ACCESS) AS ACCESS,
    UPPER(USERID) AS USERID
inline
[ACCESS,USERID
ADMIN, DOMAIN\Juan
USER, DOMAIN\Martin
];
Section Application;
LOAD
*
[LIB:\\Myfiles/Sales.csv];
```

Data reduction

Besides securing access to the file, we may want to show a subset of the whole data to certain users. This is achieved by reducing the amount of data shown when a user is authorized and authenticated.

Although the data is reduced and hidden from the users, it will still remain in the application. This means the data doesn't get deleted, but it is only shown to whoever is supposed to have access to that dataset.

To understand this better, let's work with the following example. We have a list of sales managers. Each manager has access to one or more country sales figures, as shown in the following table:

Sales Manager	Country	Sales
Peter	Germany	100
John	United Kingdom	100
John	Germany	50

Peter is a sales manager in Germany and should only see his or any other sales made in Germany. John can sell in Germany and the United Kingdom and thus should be able to see any sales generated in those countries by any sales manager. Based on these rules, we must use section access to authenticate and authorize access to John and Peter to our application, but once they are in, we should reduce the data so John can see data for Germany and the United Kingdom and only Germany for Peter.

> The user ID populated in the USERID field in section access should be in the form of DOMAIN\UserId.

Reducing rows

As I mentioned previously, section access can be used to reduce either rows or fields. If we want to reduce rows—this means to hide rows of data from certain users—whenever a user accesses the application, we first need to find the field we want to reduce.

In the example in the section *Data Reduction,* I said John can access data from Germany and the UK and Peter can only access data from Germany. This means the field we want to reduce is *Country.* We know this because we want to hide data related to the country to certain users and thus the Country field becomes our field to be reduced and used in section access.

In a real scenario, we would first load our data and then apply section access.

You must remember that the name of the field and values we want to reduce must be in upper case.

The following code shows a Load statement and a COUNTRY field, which is the one we are going to reduce using section access:

```
MyData:
Load
  [Sales Manager],
    Country,
    Sales,
    upper(Country) AS COUNTRY

Inline
[
Sales Manager, Country, Sales
Peter, Germany, 100
John, United Kingdom, 100
John, Germany, 50
];

// Start of Section Access
Section Access;

LOAD
  UPPER(ACCESS) AS ACCESS,
  UPPER(USERID) AS USERID,
  UPPER(COUNTRY) AS COUNTRY

Inline
[
ACCESS, USERID, COUNTRY
USER, DOMAIN\Peter, GERMANY
USER, DOMAIN\John, UNITED KINGDOM
USER, DOMAIN\John, UNITED KINGDOM
];
//End of section access.
Section Application;
```

If Section Application; is only needed after Section Access; only if we wish to continue adding Section Application code.

 Make sure you always use uppercase in the values and field names used in section access to avoid any problems.

Reducing fields

By reducing rows, we can hide data from certain users. But section access also allows us to hide fields from users altogether.

For example, let's assume that our source, apart from having sales-related figures, also contains bonuses percentages. These figures shouldn't be seen by any sales manager, and only by the regional manager. If we only reduce rows from our data, the values in the bonus column will still be visible to any user. But, we can omit certain fields to be shown to certain users.

We need to be careful when using this feature, as charts using the omitted fields may not be able to render properly.

The OMIT field is used in the section access table to list the fields that should be hidden for a given user. If there is more than one field omitted for a given user, then we must create a new line in the section access table for that user. However, a best practice would be to have a separate table with all the fields to omit by user profile so we could then assign users to profiles and later join the profile to the fields to omit.

To illustrate this, let's have a look at the following two source tables:

Sales Manager	Regional Sales Manager	Country	Sales
Peter	Martha	Germany	100
John	Martha	United Kingdom	50
John	Martha	United Kingdom	100

Sales Manager	Bonus
Peter	5%
John	5%
Martha	5.2%

The first table contains sales figures for each sales manager. Each manager is managed by a regional manager. The regional manager can see the sales figures for all countries in their region and they can also see the **Bonus** column in the second table.

The sales manager, however, should not see any figures shown in the Bonus column. This means we must omit or hide this column from the sales manager and only leave it visible to the regional sales manager.

The following code shows the different sections to create a simple security model that can handle the security rules described:

```
/*Loading Sales data. As I want to reduce the data based on country, I
create an upper cased field with the country in it that it is used in
section access. */

[Sales]:
LOAD
  [Sales Manager],
  [Regional Sales Manager],
  Country,
  upper(Country) AS COUNTRYSECTIONACCESS,
  Sales
Inline [
Sales Manager, Regional Sales Manager, Country, Sales
Peter, Martha, Germany, 100
John, Martha, United Kingdom, 50
John, Martha, United Kingdom,100
];

/* Loading bonus data and automatically joining through field [Sales
Manager] */

[Bonus]:
LOAD
 [Sales Manager],
 upper([Bonus]) AS [BONUS] /*Everything linked to section access goes in
upper case. */
Inline [
Sales Manager,Bonus
```

```
Peter, 5%
John, 5%
Martha, 5.2%
];

//Beginning of Section Access;

Section Access;

LOAD
    upper(ACCESS) AS ACCESS,
    upper(USERID) AS USERID,
    upper(COUNTRYSECTIONACCESS) AS COUNTRYSECTIONACCESS,
    upper(OMIT) AS OMIT

Inline [
ACCESS, USERID, COUNTRYSECTIONACCESS, OMIT
USER, MYDOMAIN\Peter, Germany, Bonus
USER, MYDOMAIN\John, Germany, Bonus
USER, MYDOMAIN\John, United Kingdom, Bonus
USER, MYDOMAIN\Martha, Germany,
USER, MYDOMAIN\Martha, United Kingdom,
];

//End of section access
Section Application;

Exit Script;
```

Remember to use upper case in field names and values for those fields used in section access.

Advanced sample scripts

Creating a good script takes time and knowledge. In this section, I will show how a real script is put together in a real scenario for your reference. It is good to describe functions and best practices, but I believe showing everything come together in an example is even more valuable.

The following code example will show you in a very simple way how to:

- Split your code into different sections
- Create a simple stats table
- Check if your source file exists and create one if it doesn't use control statements
- Apply section access to the application

The sample script is split into sections that you can create in **Script Editor.**

For the script to work, you need to create a **Create a new Connection** in one **Folder** called `Environment` and another called `Source`.

In the `Environment` location, create a text file called `Environment.txt` with the following line of code in it:

```
SET vEnvironment=Live;
```

In the *Source* folder, create an Excel file called `SectionAccess.xlsx` with two columns, `ACCESS`, and `USERID`. You can add your own user to run the example.

You are now ready to copy the following sections into the **Script Editor.**

[Variable Setup] section:

```
/*
In this section we initialize all variables used in the script.
*/

SET ThousandSep=',';
SET DecimalSep='.';
SET MoneyThousandSep=',';
SET MoneyDecimalSep='.';
SET MoneyFormat='£#,##0.00;-£#,##0.00';
SET TimeFormat='hh:mm:ss';
SET DateFormat='DD/MM/YYYY';
SET TimestampFormat='DD/MM/YYYY hh:mm:ss[.fff]';
SET FirstWeekDay=0;
SET BrokenWeeks=0;
SET ReferenceDay=4;
SET FirstMonthOfYear=1;
SET CollationLocale='en-GB';
SET CreateSearchIndexOnReload=1;
SET MonthNames='Jan;Feb;Mar;Apr;May;Jun;Jul;Aug;Sep;Oct;Nov;Dec';
SET
LongMonthNames='January;February;March;April;May;June;July;August;September
;October;November;December';
```

```
SET DayNames='Mon;Tue;Wed;Thu;Fri;Sat;Sun';
SET
LongDayNames='Monday;Tuesday;Wednesday;Thursday;Friday;Saturday;Sunday';

//Including variable containing current environment (Development/Live);

$(Must_Include=lib://Environment\Environment.txt);

TRACE Current environment is $(vEnvironment);
```

[Stats Table] section:

```
/*Creating the statistics base table */

[Stats]:
LOAD
    *
Inline [
Stats.Table, Stats.Description, Stats.Records, Stats.Start, Stats.End
];

/*Creating subrouting that we will call when we create a new table. */

sub Stats

concatenate(Stats)
LOAD
    *
Inline [
Stats.Table, Stats.Description, Stats.Records, Stats.Start, Stats.End
$(vTable), $(vTableDescription), $(vRecords), $(vStart), $(vEnd)
];

End Sub
```

[Main Script] section:

```
sub Main

/*Variables used in the stats table. */
LET vTable = 'SourceTable';
LET vTableDescription = 'This table contains main source data';
LET vStart = Timestamp(Now());

/* If source file doesn't exist I create it by loading and storing the
data. */

If FileSize('[lib://Source\MyData.qvd]') THEN
```

```
TRACE Source file exists. Load data from source;

[$(vTable)]:
LOAD * FROM [LIB://Source\MyData.qvd] (qvd);


ELSE
TRACE Source file doesn't exist. Create source and store it.;

[$(vTable)]:
LOAD
   *
Inline [
Month, Sales
Jan, 100
Feb, 110
Mar, 90
Apr, 95
May, 103
Jun, 99
Jul, 102
Aug, 130
Sep, 135
Oct, 132
Nov, 115
Dec, 102
];

TRACE Storing file...;

STORE $(vTable) INTO [LIB://Source\MyData.qvd] (qvd);

ENDIF;

/* We call the Stats subrouting to store table stats. */

LET vEnd = Timestamp(Now());
LET vRecords = NoOfRows('$(vTable)');

Call Stats;

End Sub
```

[Section Access] section:

```
Sub SectionAccess

Section Access;

LOAD
  UPPER(ACCESS) AS ACCESS,
    UPPER(USERID) AS USERID
FROM [lib://Source/SectionAccess.xlsx]
(ooxml, embedded labels, table is Sheet1);

Section Application;

End Sub;
```

[Script Execution] section:

```
Call Main;
Call SectionAccess;
```

The block of code presented in this section is simple but powerful. I encourage you to add your own touch and make it grow with more functionalities. Use this code as a base and expand it. With Qlik Sense, the sky is the limit!

Summary

In this section, we learnt how to create and structure a script in Qlik Sense. I also talked about functions that you will find in many scripts and that you should be using in your own. These functions will allow you to control your script and make it more powerful. This is only a small list of the very vast list of functions you can find in Qlik Sense. If you want to learn more, you can find the complete list of script functions in the Qlik Sense Help official site.

In the next chapter, *Advanced Expressions in Qlik Sense*, you will see how to produce powerful visualizations by using advanced expressions. This is only possible after a good model is created. Script and expressions go hand in hand, so keep on reading to learn more!

9
Advanced Expressions in Qlik Sense

Expressions are an essential part of any chart. There would be no output without expressions, and the results of any output will be conditioned by the accuracy of the expressions.

We usually find expressions in the script as well as in any chart. We described script expressions in Chapter 8, *Advanced Scripting*, and we will cover chart expressions in more detail in this chapter.

An expression can be defined as a group of functions, fields, and operators that, after being evaluated, will return a number or string. We can find expressions not only within the measures of any chart but also in labels, titles, and so on. If you see the icon *fx* in a chart, it means that not only a string but also an expression can be used.

The following is an example of an expression:

```
SUM( [Gross Sales] * 1.2 )
```

The previous expression contains three elements:

- The function: SUM()
- The field: [Gross Sales]
- The mathematical operator: *

After the mathematical operator, we also have a constant number, 1.2. This expression will return a number for Gross Sales + VAT of 20%.

Simple expressions are not always enough to analyze complex datasets. Set analysis allows us to talk to the Qlik engine and manipulate datasets to obtain results beyond the user's selections.

In this chapter, you will master expressions by learning about the following:

- **Set analysis**: What it is and how to use it.
- **Variables**: How to correctly create, use, and maintain variables throughout an application to make your dashboards powerful and flexible.
- **Maintaining expressions:** How to efficiently maintain expressions in a project.

Set analysis

Every time you make selections in an application, Qlik Sense filters the data, creating a set or group. If nothing is selected, then it means that the whole data model is part of the set.

Set analysis allows you to analyze data different to the set created by your selections. The subset analyzed by set analysis of data could be inside the main dataset or outside.

For example, when displaying in a chart the number of customers by product type for 2018 compared to the total number of customers, set analysis will help get the total out of the selection from 2018.

Parts of set analysis

Analyzing sets of data different to the user's selections can be achieved by defining a set expression within an expression. An example of set analysis is the following:

```
count( {1-$<Product = {"Current Account"} >} Distinct [Customer Id])
```

Here, `{$<Product = {"Current Account"} >}` is the set expression.

Set expressions

Set expressions allow you to define field values. A set expression must do the following:

- Be used in an aggregation function such as `sum()`, `count()`, `min()`, and so on
- Start with { and end with }

In the set expression `{1-$<Product = {"Current Account"} >}`, three distinctive parts can be defined:

- **Identifier**: `$`
- **Operator**: the minus sign in `1-$`
- **Modifier**: `<Product = {"Current Account"} >`

Identifiers

Identifiers define the relationship between the set expression and the field values or expression being evaluated.

The following values can be used as identifiers:

Identifier	Description
`1`	Represents the full set of all the records in the application, irrespective of any selections made. This means the whole data model.
`$`	Represents the records of the current selection. The set expression `{$}` is thus the equivalent to not stating a set expression. For example: `sum({$} [Product Value])` is the same as `sum([Product Value])`.
`$n`	Represents the n previous selections. Example: `count ({$1} [User Id])` disregards the current selection made by the user and instead counts the `[User Id]` in the user's previous selection.
`$_1`	Represents the next (forward) selection. This is only valid when more than two selections have been made.
`BM01`	You can use any bookmark ID or bookmark name.
`MyAltState`	You can reference the selections made in an alternate state by its state name. Alternate states aren't available out of the box in the Qlik Sense September 2017 release or before.

Operators

Operators are used to include, exclude, or intersect parts of or whole datasets. All operators use sets as operands and return a set as a result.

The following table shows operators that can be used in set expressions:

Operator	Description
+	**Union**: This binary operation returns a set consisting of the records that belong to any of the two set operands. **Example:** `count({$<Product = {"Current Account"} > + 1-$ <Year = {2018}> Distinct [User Id])` This example counts the distinct users of the product `Current Account` and also counts all the users of the set excluded by user selection for `2018` across all products.
–	**Exclusion**: This binary operation returns a set of the records that belong to the first but not the other of the two set operands. Also, when used as a unary operator, it returns the complement set. **Example:** `sum({$< [Invoice Item] = {"*"} – {"Red shoes"} >} [Item Amount])` This example returns the sum of all `Item Amount` but `Red shoes`.
*	**Intersection**: This binary operation returns a set consisting of the records that belong to both of the two set operands. **Example:** `avg({$< Year = {2017, 2018}>*<Product = {"Business Credit Card"}>+<Year = {2018}, Product ={"Personal Credit Card"}>} [Credit Limit])` This example returns the average of the sum of credit limits on business credit cards in `2017` and `2018` and the credit limits of personal credit cards in `2018`.
/	**Symmetric difference (XOR)**: This binary operation returns a set consisting of the records that belong to either, but not both, of the two set operands. **Example:** `count({$< Product / = {"H*"} >}[Product])` This example returns the count of all products in the current selection that do not start with `H`.

Modifiers

Modifiers are used to add or change a selection. Modifiers consist of one or more fields followed by the values we want to assign to those fields in the following format:

```
< [Field] = {value 1, value 2} >
```

Here, `Field` is the name of a valid field in the data model and `value` is the value in the field that we want to add to the selection. If the value is a string, then it should go between " ".

The modifiers change the selection of the set identifier:

```
max({< Role = {"Manager"} >} Salary)
```

The preceding example shows the maximum salary of the current selection but with `Manager` as the employee role. Note that when the identifier is omitted, the current selection (`$`) is the default.

Set modifiers dive in

Set modifiers are key in any set analysis. It is what makes set analysis so flexible and powerful. To make things more visual, let's load the following data into a new application and use it as an example. You already know what to do:

1. Open Qlik Sense and create a new application
2. Open **Data load editor** from the navigation menu
3. Copy the following code and paste it into the Main section of the script
4. Load the data:

```
ModifiersSample:
LOAD * inline
[
Product Id, Product Description, Month, Year, MonthYear, Sales Manager,
Sales
1, Shoes, 1, 2016, Jan 2016, Mary, 544
1, Shoes, 1, 2017, Jan 2017, Mary, 235
1, Shoes, 1, 2018, Jan 2018, Mary, 1000
1, Shoes, 1, 2018, Jan 2018, Joe, 500
1, Shoes, 1, 2018, Jan 2018, Michael, 700
1, Shoes, 2, 2018, Feb 2018, Mary 560
1, Shoes, 2, 2018, Feb 2018 Kathy, 890
2, Tops, 1, 2018, Jan 2018, Mary, 60
2, Tops, 1, 2018, Jan 2018, Michael 200
3, Shirts, 3, 2018, Mar 2018, Michael, 1580
3, Shirts, 1, Jan 2018, Kathy, 759
];
```

After loading the sample data, you can create a table chart with all the fields as dimensions but leave the Sales field out. Then, in the same table chart, add the expression sum({$< [Year] = {"201*"} − {2016} >} Sales) and have a look at the resulting output.

In the following section, we will give you a few expressions to add to your table chart that will help you understand how set analysis works.

I recommend adding only one expression at a time so you can clearly see the results.

Set modifiers with set operators

The values that we want to assign to the fields in our set modifiers can use set operators in the different element sets. The following set analysis explains this:

- All sales from 2010 to 2019 but excluding the year 2016:

    sum({$< [Year] = {"201*"} − {2016} >} Sales)

As we include a non-numerical character (*) in a value that must be numerical (Year), you must enclose the values in double quotes.

In this example, the wildcard * can be replaced by ?. The star returns any character of any length while the question mark ? returns any character of length *1*. As years have four digits, using * or ? would throw the same result.

- Sales for the current selection in the Product Id field but adding product code 3 if this is not yet selected:

    sum({$< [Product Id] = [Product Id] + {3} >} Sales)

- Number of products sold in 2018 by all sales managers but Mary:

    count({$< [Year] = {2018}, [Sales Manager] = {"*"} − {"Mary"} >} [Product Id])

Set modifiers using assignments with implicit set operators

In the second example of the previous section, we showed you how to add a value on top of the current selection by adding the field name, the set operator, and the values we want to add, as shown in the following example:

```
sum({$< [Product Id] = [Product Id] + {3} >} Sales)
```

This same expression can be shortened by using implicit set operators. Instead of writing the long form `<Field = Field + {Values1, Value2}>`, you can write it as follows:

```
<Field += {Value1, Value2}>
```

After applying implicit set operators, the example would look like this:

```
sum({$< [Product Id] += {3} >} Sales)
```

The operators *, /, =, or + go to the left of the equals (=) sign and the additional values go to the right of the equals sign, as we have seen in other set modifiers.

The following examples serve to explain this:

- Sales of the current selection excluding sales for sales manager Mary:

  ```
  sum({$< [Sales Manager] -= {"Mary"} >} Sales)
  ```

Set modifiers with advanced searches

Sets can also be defined by using wildcards (*) or complex aggregations.

I showed the use of wildcards in the previous section. We can, for example, show the sales of all the products starting with the letter S:

```
sum({$< [Product Description] = {"S*"} >} Sales)
```

The wildcard * can be used anywhere in the string, and it is a replacement of any character or string of any length. The preceding example can return Shoes, Shirts, or any other string starting with S.

Within our set modifiers, we can use complex aggregations. For example, we may want to know the sales of those who sold more than two products in the year 2018:

```
sum({$< [Sales Manager] = {"=count({1<Year = {2018}>} distinct [Product
Id]) > 2" } >} Sales)
```

Note how a function is placed in the set modifier value. This works as a condition. If the distinct count of products for 2018 for each sales manager is greater than 2, then the aggregation `sum(Sales)` will happen.

Set modifiers with implicit field value definitions

An **implicit field value** definition is used when we want a possible or excluded value of another field assigned to the field in the set modifier.

In this type of expression, we must use the functions `P()` and `E()`. An example of this is as follows:

```
sum({< [Sales Manager] = p({1} [Supervisor])>} Sales)
```

The preceding example will return the sales of the sales managers who have the same name as a supervisor. The following example returns the sales of the sales managers who have never sold `Shoes`:

```
sum( {$<[Sales Manager] = E({1<[Product Description] ={'Shoes'}>}) >} Sales
)
```

Set modifiers with expressions

As well as using strings, numbers, or functions such as `P()` and `E()`, you can also use expressions as set modifier values.

To use expressions as values, you must enclose the expression in `$(= )` which is called **dollar-sign expansion**. The expression must go between `$(=` and `)`, for example:

```
$(=max(Date))
```

Now, let's have a look at the following expression:

```
SUM({$< [Year] = {2018} >} Sales)
```

The preceding example returns the sales for 2018. If by 2018 we mean the current year, you could replace the value 2018 with a function that returns the current year such as `year(today())`.

This will prevent you from having to change the expression for every new year. The modified expression with the set modifier using an expression as value looks as follows:

```
SUM({$< [Year] = {$(=year(today()))} >} Sales)
```

 Make sure your expression returns a value of the same type of the field being modified.

Comparing to other fields

So far, you have seen examples where the modifiers in the set expression assign values to the fields. However, it is often necessary to compare field values to other field values and not to particular strings or numbers.

Field-to-field comparison

To compare a field to another field, we can use a field name to the right of the arithmetic comparison in the set expression, for example:

```
sum({< [ProductId] = [ItemId] >} [Sales])
```

This set analysis will only take into account values selected in the fields ProductId and ItemId.

P() and E() functions

The P() and E() functions refer to what is **Possible** and **Excluded** respectively. These functions are used in the set modifier expression. The field to the left of the arithmetic comparison will be assigned with all the possible or excluded values to the right of the field used in the P() or E() functions. To understand these functions better, let's consider the following example. The next table consists of three columns: Product Id, Product Status Id, and Product Status Description.

Product Id	Product Status Id	Product Status Description
1	1	Active
2	1	Active

3	2	On Hold
4	3	Inactive
5	3	Inactive
6	3	Inactive

The following screenshot shows the **Product Id** selection of **1**, **2**, and **3**:

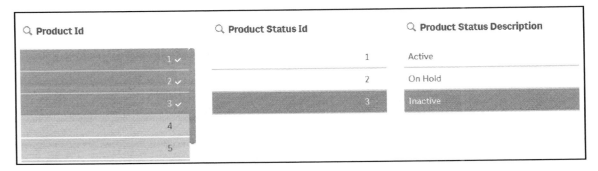

Let's recap on the QIX colors: green for user selections, white for possible values, and gray for excluded values.

Now let's consider the following expression using the P () function:

```
count({$< [Product Id] = P([Product Status Id]) >} [Product Id])
```

This would count the Product Id for all possible values of Product Status Id. In this example, the possible values of the field Product Status Id are represented by white, that is to say, 1 and 2.

The result is 2 as the possible values of Product Status Id after the selections are 1 and 2.

Now let's consider the following expression with the E () function:

```
count({$< [Product Id] = E([Product Status Id]) >} [Product Id])
```

The excluded value of Product Status Id is 3 - dark gray - so Product Id would get a value of 1 resulting in 1 as the result of the expression.

Variables

Variables are an essential part of any application. Variables hold values that can either be constant or that can change while executing a script or at runtime.

Variables can be found in scripts or in an application front-end. In the next sections, we will explain how to create, use, maintain, and delete variables.

Using variables in your script

The use of variables in your script is always necessary. It would be impossible to create complex scripts without the use of variables. Variables can contain anything from strings to functions. The definition of a variable in the script is given by the prefix SET or LET followed by the variable name and the equals sign to the right of it. Whatever is on the right of the equals sign will be assigned to the variable. A semicolon will denote the end of the variable definition.

The next line is an example of a definition of a variable in the script:

```
SET vMyVariable = 'Mastering Qlik Sense';
```

Another example of a variable definition is the following:

```
LET    vMonth = monthname(today());
```

The difference between SET and LET

You can define variables using the SET or LET prefix.

The SET prefix will assign whatever is on the right of the equals (=) sign as a string.

On the other hand, the LET prefix will evaluate whatever is on the right of the equals sign and assign the value of the evaluated expression to the variable.

Creating variables

The following structure can be used to create variables in the script editor:

```
SET | LET variableName = variable value ;
```

The following lines are examples of a variable definition using SET:

```
SET vMyString = 'This is a string';

SET vAnotherString = today();
```

 When using SET, any value to the right of the equals sign will be treated as a string.

The variables vMyString and vAnotherString contain strings even if the second line has a form of function inside.

If you want a variable to hold the result of a function after it is evaluated, use LET:

```
LET vToday = today();
```

In this example, vToday will hold today's value returned by the function today() instead of the string 'today()'.

Reading the value of variables

To read the value of the variables created in the script, you can use the Debug Panel in the script editor. Let's use an example to explain this better. Perform the following steps to create a sample application:

1. Create a new application using **Qlik Sense Desktop** or **Cloud**.
2. Open **Data load editor** using the **Navigation** button:

3. Once in **Data load editor,** click the + button to create a new section and give it a name:

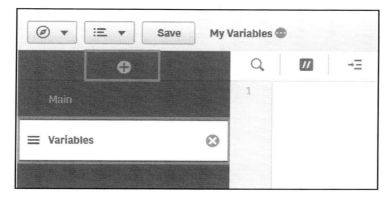

4. Copy the following code into the new section:

```
//These variables will hold strings '2+2' and
'month(yearstart(today()))' respectively

SET vSumString = 2+2;
SET vMonthString = month(yearstart(today()));

//These variables will hold values 4 and the short name of the
first month of the year respectively

LET vSumResult = 2+2;
LET vMonth = month(yearstart(today()));
```

5. Click on the **Show Debug panel** button ⚓ .
6. In the **Debug** panel, click on **Variables** and select **Show user-defined variables.** This will show you only variables created by us.
7. Click on Run to see the results.

The following screenshot shows these steps:

After executing the script, you can see four variables—vSumString, vMonthString, vSumResult, and vMonth—with their values. Those variables that were created using the syntax SET will contain strings, and those created using LET will have the result of the function after being evaluated.

Dollar-sign expansion with variables

Dollar-sign expansion is used to read or use the value of a variable in the script. In the previous section, we showed you how you could see what a variable contains; however, variables would not be useful if we could only read their values but not make use of them.

The dollar-sign expansion starts with $ (and ends with) at the end of the variable name, for example:

```
$(vSumResult)
```

To illustrate this better, let's have a look at the following example:

```
SET vMyInterestRate = 0.02;

Balance:
LOAD
AccountId
```

```
,Balance
,Balance * $(vMyInterestRate) AS [Interest On Balance]
,Balance * (1+$(vMyInterestRate)) AS [Final Balance]
FROM
[lib://MyFiles/CustomerBalances.qvd]
```

 Note that numbers assigned to variables can be used as a string or number. Adding single quotes will make no difference.

In this example, we first create the variable vMyInterestRate and assign it a 2% interest rate.

We then load my data and create two more fields. Interest On Balance applies 2% of the balance by using a dollar-sign expansion on the variable we previously created.

Final Balance contains the balance plus its interest.

So, the dollar-sign expansion is replaced with the same value assigned to the variable or with the result of an expression once it is evaluated. We mention this because it is important to consider strings when making comparisons.

For example, consider the following code:

```
SET vBookName = 'Mastering Qlik Sense';

BookTable:
LOAD * INLINE
[
Book Name
Mastering Qlik Sense
];

IF peek([Book Name]) = $(vBookName) THEN
TRACE True;
ELSE
TRACE False;
ENDIF;
```

In this example, we assign the string `Mastering Qlik Sense` to the variable `vBookName`. We then compare the field `[Book Name]` with the variable. However, this will throw an error because the value of `vBookName` when we use dollar-sign expansion is `Mastering Qlik Sense` and not `'Mastering Qlik Sense'`. As the single quotes are missing, Qlik Sense thinks we are comparing the value of `[Book Name]` with another field called `Mastering Qlik Sense`.

What we want to do is to make sure our book name is enclosed in single quotes. The following correction to the code will make it work:

```
...
IF peek([Book Name]) = '$(vBookName)' THEN
...
```

User-defined functions

Apart from strings, numbers, and system functions, variables can hold user-defined functions.

A user-defined function is a group of calculations with parameters that are stored in variables. These variables can then be used throughout the script or in any application. As the variables hold functions or calculations, the user can pass parameters that will then be used to calculate the output.

User-defined functions are stored in variables and thus must be created with the prefix SET or LET when using script code or from the Variable overview in the application edit mode.

Let's use the following user-defined variable as an example:

```
SET vFormatNumber = if($1 >=0 AND $1 <=999, round($1,0.1), if($1 >=1000 and
$1 <=999999, round($1/1000,0.1) & 'K', if($1 >=1000000, round($1/1000000,
0.1)&'M', $1)));
```

In the preceding example, we created a user-defined function `vFormatNumber` that formats numbers in thousands (K) or millions (M) and rounds them to the nearest decimal. The parameter `$1` will hold the numbers that are sent to the function when it is called.

The following block of code shows a clear example of how to use a user-defined variable within a script:

```
SET vFormatNumber = if($1 >=0 AND $1 <=999, round($1,0.1), if($1 >=1000 and
$1 <=999999, round($1/1000,0.1) & 'K', if($1 >=1000000, round($1/1000000,
0.1)&'M', $1)));


DataTable:
LOAD
$(vFormatNumber(Sales)) AS SalesFormatted,
Sales
INLINE
[
Sales
-1500
1875
180000
1570000
];
```

Note how we call the function we first defined within the LOAD statement. It's as easy as that. The great thing about user-defined variables is that you can store them in a file so you can reuse them in any script.

In the example, $1 represents the first parameter; however, user-defined functions can hold more than one parameter. The second parameter is replaced with $2, the third with $3, and so on.

Deleting and reusing variables

Qlik Sense does not allow you to delete variables from the script. However, you can reuse them or assign new values as shown in the following block:

```
SET vMyFirstVariable = 'First value';

SET vMyFirstVariable = 'Reassigning a value';
//Assigning an empty variable most probably means we don't use this
variable anymore.
SET vMyFirstVariable = '';
```

Even after assigning an empty value to the variable, it will remain in the application. You can only delete variables from the Variable overview in the application.

Keep reading to find out more about variables and how to use them in your application.

Using variables in your application

Now that you know how to create and use variables in the script, it's time to describe how you can use them in the application. Many variables will only be used in the script and are only needed while the script is executing; however, the use of variables in the front-end is heavily used and recommended as they render the application more flexible and easy to maintain.

Variable management is done through the Variable overview in the application.

Opening the Variable menu

To open the Variable overview, first open the app overview from the **Navigation** menu. To explain the steps, we will use the same application we used in the user-defined variables example:

1. Once in the application, create a new sheet or open an existing one.
2. The variable menu can only be seen in edit mode. Click on **Edit**.

3. At the bottom-left corner, you will see the menu option ▦. If you click on it, you will be presented with the Variable overview.

This menu presents all variables created in the script. The variables created in the script have a little papyrus icon next to them. The following shows what the menu option looks like:

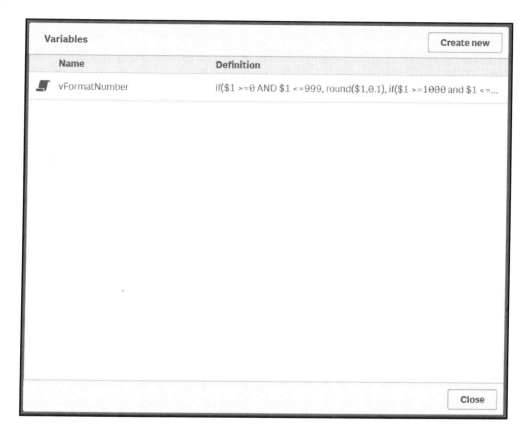

Creating a variable

To create a new variable, simply click on the **Create new** button in the top-right corner.

You will see the following screen:

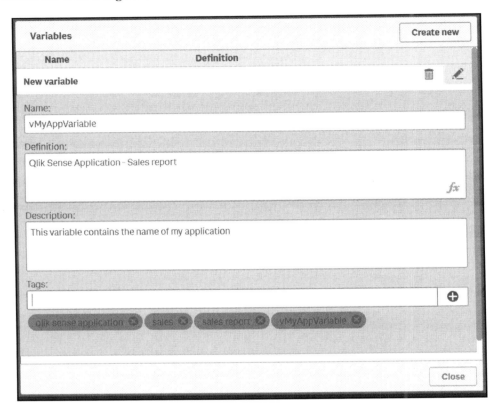

The screen that pops up on clicking the Create new Button

In this screen, we find the following options:

- **Name**: This is the name of the variable
- **Definition**: This is what the variable holds. It can either be text, numbers, or functions
- **Description**: This description is for reference only
- **Tags**: Add tags to easily find your variables when searching

Dollar-sign expansion in expressions - reading a variable

The same way you can use dollar-sign expansion in the script, you can also use it in the application. To reference a variable in the application that is either created in the script or using the Variable overview menu, you can use dollar-sign expansion as follows:

```
$(vMyVariable)
```

In the front-end, this variable will go in the expression of any chart or even dimension. For example, you could create a `Text and Image` object, and in the expression, you could type the following:

```
$(vMyAppVariable)
```

In the previous section, we defined `vMyAppVariable` to hold the string `'Qlik Sense Application – Sales report'` and that is exactly what you will see if you use the dollar-sign expansion.

Deleting a variable

Although variables cannot be deleted from the script, they can be deleted in the front-end. Any variables deleted in the front-end will be recreated if there are variables defined in the script and the script is executed.

Perform the following steps to delete a variable:

1. Open the Variable overview
2. Click on the variable you want to delete

3. Click on the **Bin** icon:

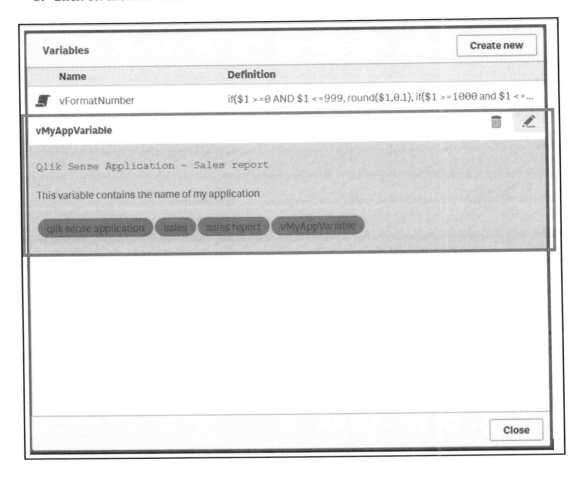

Using variables in expressions

Variables can be used anywhere, including in expressions. Variables can hold an entire expression, but they can also contain parts of it.

To use a variable that contains part of an expression, simply use the dollar-sign expansion within the expression. Say you had the following variable created in the script:

```
LET vCurrentYear = year(today());
SET vMySalesField = '[Sales]';
```

You could create a chart that calculates sales for the current year using the variable
vCurrentYear:

```
sum(if([Year] = $(vCurrentYear), $(vMySalesField)))
```

This expression returns the sales for the current year.

 Using an IF statement inside the aggregation will make the aggregation
work only when the condition within the IF statement is true.

Variables can also contain the whole expression, which makes it very easy to maintain if the
same expression is used in different charts within an application. The following script code
shows an example:

```
SET vExpression = count(distinct [Customers]);
```

After a script reload, the vExpression variable will hold the expression as a string that can
be directly used in any chart expression as follows:

```
$(vExpression)
```

Using variables in set analysis

We have already explained set analysis and its different parts. Variables can also be used
within set analysis. Simply replace part of the set analysis with the variable you want. It is
recommended to use variables in set analysis in the modifiers.

Say you had a variable that contains today's date:

```
LET vToday = today();
```

You can replace the following chart expression with the vToday variable:

```
sum({$< Date = {$(vToday)} }> Balance)
```

Not only can you use variables to replace values in set modifiers but you can also replace
the whole set with variables. For example, you may calculate the sales of a certain region for
the current year in different charts. Instead of replicating the same expression chart over
and over, you could store the whole set analysis in a variable and use it in any chart:

```
SET vCurrentYearNAM = '[Year] = {2018}, Country = {"Mexico", "United
States", "Canada"}';
```

This script variable contains the necessary set modifiers to return values for the year 2018 and the countries in the North American region.

You can then use this variable in any expression as follows:

```
count({< $(vCurrentYearNAM) >} DISTINCT [Product Id])
```

Use variables to replace parts of or whole expressions.

Using variables to replace strings

As we have mentioned throughout this chapter, variables can hold strings. The values in the set modifiers can then be placed by the variables.

Say you had the following expression:

```
sum({$< [Product] = {'Current Account'} >} [Balance])
```

You can make this expression more flexible and dynamic by replacing the Product value with a variable. Let's create a variable in the script containing the value of the product:

```
SET vMyProduct = 'Current Account';
```

To replace the value in the set analysis, replace the value Current Account with the variable name using a dollar-sign expansion. The expression looks as follows:

```
sum({$< [Product] = {'$(vMyProduct)'} >} [Balance])
```

Whenever Qlik finds a dollar-sign expansion, it will do the following:

- Resolve the dollar-sign expansion
- Evaluate the expression with the dollar-sign expansion replaced by the variable value

Based on this, Qlik Sense will first return the value of vMyProduct. The expression will look like this:

```
sum({$< [Product] = {'Current Account'} >} [Balance])
```

Once the dollar-sign is resolved, it will evaluate the expression, which in this example will return the sum of the balances for the current accounts.

Remember to always add single or double quotes to enclose the dollar-sign expansion when the variable holds a string.

Using variables to replace numbers

The same way you can use variables to replace string values in set modifiers, you can use variables to hold numbers if the field is of a number type. An example of a field of number type is `Year`.

The following example returns the sales for the year `2018`:

```
sum({$< [Year] = {2018} >} Sales)
```

The Year field is of a type number, and thus the values in the set analysis must not be enclosed in single or double quotes.

Assuming we create two variables in the script, one for the `year` and one for my field `Sales` as follows:

```
LET vCurrentYear = year(today());
SET vMySalesField = '[Sales]';
```

We could now make the expression use the two variables as follows:

```
sum({$< [Year] = {$(vCurrentYear)} >} $(vMySalesField))
```

Note that `vCurrentYear` will return `2018` which will be selected in the field `[Year]` which is of a number type. The aggregation `sum()` will be performed on the field `[Sales]`. `vMySalesField` contains a string, but because we omit the single or double quotes, Qlik Sense will consider it a field and not a string.

Maintaining expressions

In small applications, maintaining expressions isn't a problem. Every time you want to modify something, you can open each chart and change the expressions. However, when you have many applications using the same or similar expressions, changing them one by one can become challenging.

A very simple and good way of maintaining expressions is to have them all in a centralized file. This can be an Excel file that you can then read. If anything changes, you must only change things in one place. The file also gives you a place to explain each of the expressions for further clarity.

Each expression will be stored in a variable, and the variable will then be used directly in the chart expressions.

The following is an example of an Excel file format containing the application expressions:

Variable name	Environment	Expression definition	Active flag	Comments
vToday	Live	'today()'	Yes	Contains today's date
vBookName	Live	'Mastering Qlik Sense'	Yes	Book name
vSalesCurrentYear	Live	sum({< Year = {2018} >} Sales)'	Yes	Calculates sales for year 2018

This sample Excel file has five columns:

- **Variable name**: This contains the name of the variable to be used in the expressions.
- **Environment**: This column provides the flexibility to have different variables for different environments. This is useful if you want to test an expression while developing without affecting the live applications.
- **Expression definition**: This is the expression or value to be assigned to the variable.
- **Active flag**: With this flag, you can make expressions active or inactive.
- **Comments**: This explains what each variable and expression means.

You can then paste the following code into the script, which automatically creates the variables for you. In the following example, the file is called `Variables.xlsx`:

```
[Variables]:
LOAD
    "Variable Name",
    Environment,
    "Expression Definition",
    "Active Flag",
    Comments
```

```
FROM [lib://AttachedFiles/Variables.xlsx]
(ooxml, embedded labels, table is Sheet1)
WHERE [Active Flag] = 'Yes' AND Environment = 'Live';

FOR i = 0 to NoOfRows('Variables')

LET vTempVar = peek('Variable Name',$(i), 'Variables');
LET $(vTempVar) = peek('Expression Definition', $(i), 'Variables');

NEXT;

Drop Table Variables;
```

In the previous code, we first load all the fields from my `Variables` file. In a real situation, you wouldn't need to load all the fields but only those containing the variable name and the expression value. We also give the table a meaningful name: `[Variables]`.

Let's analyze the code in parts:

```
[Variables]:
LOAD
    "Variable Name",
    Environment,
    "Expression Definition",
    "Active Flag",
    Comments
FROM [lib://AttachedFiles/Variables.xlsx]
(ooxml, embedded labels, table is Sheet1)
WHERE [Active Flag] = 'Yes' AND Environment = 'Live';
```

Note that I only loaded active expressions and those that I want in my live environment. If you are working in a development environment, simply change the WHERE clause as needed. For example, if you want to use only variables that we are testing while developing, use the following WHERE clause:

```
...
WHERE [Active Flag] = 'Yes' AND Environment = 'Development';
```

What we do next is to loop through the values of the `Variables` table. Inside the control statement loop, we will do the following:

1. Read each table record
2. Create the variables
3. Assign values to the variables:

```
FOR i = 0 to NoOfRows('Variables')

NEXT;
```

Here, we use the function `NoOfRows('Table_Name')`, which returns the number of records in a previously loaded table. We will then loop through all the values in the table.

Within this loop, we then create a temporary variable that will hold the name of the final variables coming from the`Variables.xlsx` file. The following line of code shows how it can be done:

```
LET vTempVar = peek('Variable Name',$(i), 'Variables');
```

The `peek()` function returns the value of the field `[Variable Name]` in table `[Variables]` in the `i` position. The value of `i` increases with every loop.

We then create the final statement that creates the variable and assigns the expression or value to it:

```
LET $(vTempVar) = peek('Expression Definition', $(i), 'Variables');
```

After assigning the expressions to variables, you no longer need the table containing such expressions and thus we can delete the table. The following command shows how to delete a table:

```
Drop Table Variables;
```

Summary

Expressions are the backbone of Qlik Sense applications. We use them in scripts as well as in charts. But expressions would not give you much if it wasn't for the powerful QIX engine. Set analysis sets Qlik Sense apart from other tools on the market. With it, we can achieve beyond powerful analysis throughout our data model.

Variables also help us create dynamic and easier-to-maintain expressions. Use it to store part of your expressions, such as values in your set modifiers or full expressions. Dollar-sign expansion allows you to return the value of a variable.

Use user-defined functions for repetitive tasks. These variables, which are in essence functions, allow you to easily reuse code in new applications. Store your user-defined functions in a centralized file and reuse them when needed!.

In the next chapter, you will learn about Qlik Sense APIs which allow you to communicate with the Qlik Engine as well as its services.

10
Overview of Qlik Sense APIs

Qlik's vision, even before releasing Qlik Sense, has been making its powerful associative data engine more easily accessible so it can be leveraged in any form or capacity a customer or project requires. As such, developers have invested heavily in the past couple of years in developing comprehensible **application programming interface (APIs)** to allow developers to communicate with the Qlik engine and its associated services.

With an API in place, developers can leverage the Qlik product in their way and build customized solutions on top of it or integrate it with existing platforms. There are practically no limits to how Qlik can be used, making it a tremendously powerful technology. At the same time, building solutions on top of an API requires notable development effort compared to Qlik Sense's user-friendly way of creating dashboards, using drag and drop.

This module of the book is mostly techy in order to address the questions and queries of developers coming from a web development background. Classic Qlik developers will still find benefit from reading the following chapters, as they will be able to understand, at least on a high level, how a Qlik API is designed, how it can be used, and what kind of methods it is using.

This chapter, in particular, will provide an overview of all available Qlik APIs that have been introduced with Qlik Sense and the Qlik Analytics Platform. It will guide the reader on which APIs to use for which purpose and how to navigate through the rich library of available methods. It is, however, important to note it is not intended to give you the same breadth and depth as comprehensive documentation. For this purpose, and for a deeper dive into the respective APIs, with many more rich examples, it is recommended to visit the official Qlik help page (`https://help.qlik.com/`) and the Qlik community (`http://community.qlik.com/`).

The topics that we will cover in this chapter include the following:

- What is an API?
- Description of Qlik APIs
- Extension API
- Backend API
- Capability API
- enigma.js
- Leonardo UI
- halyard.js

What is an API?

We are connected with the world, and with each other, like never before. You can purchase goods, post feeds, upload pictures, or make a restaurant reservation via a mobile device or your computer. All that connectivity is enabled by the use of so-called APIs. According to Wikipedia (`https://en.wikipedia.org/wiki/Application_programming_interface`), an API is a set of subroutines, definitions, protocols, and tools that can be utilized for building applications. It's a collection of building blocks that abstract the underlying implementation of a technology by only exposing specific objects or actions a developer can perform, and simplifies programming by doing so. In the example of a Qlik Sense API, the querying of the underlying technology, the Qlik data engine, is abstracted by the use of predefined calculation and aggregation expressions (`sum`, `avg`, `count`). The engine can read those commands and returns the corresponding aggregated result.

To speak plainly, the API is a messenger that takes requests and tells a system what you want to do and then returns the response back to you, as shown in the following figure:

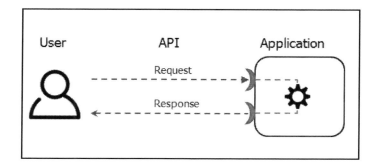

For a more familiar example, think of an API as a waiter in a restaurant. When you arrive at a restaurant to have dinner with your partner or your family, you are seated at a table and given a menu by a waiter. A menu is a list of choices you can order from, and the kitchen is the part of the system that can prepare those dishes. What is missing is the critical link to order your menu choice from the kitchen and deliver your food back to your table. That's where the waiter, or the API, comes into play. He's the messenger taking your requests from a list of available commands, or API calls, that he then takes to the kitchen, to deliver the kitchen's response, food, back to you, once it is prepared.

Think of an API as a waiter in a restaurant, who takes your order from the menu, passes it along to the kitchen, and then serves you the meal when it's ready.

A real API example is a typical flight-booking platform. Each airline nowadays has an online portal where you can search for prices, destinations, and dates to inquire about flight availability and itineraries. An example of such a search form can be seen in the following image, which is more-or-less consistent across all airline websites:

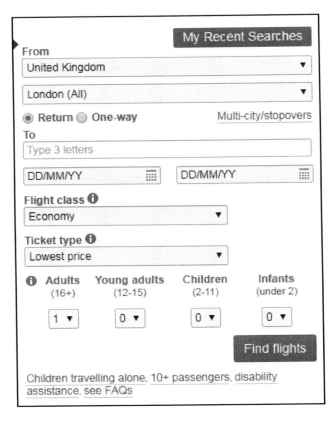

Users put in the details of their information request, and an API call goes to the flight database and scans available flights and returns the results to the user. The resulting list of available flights, prices, and itineraries is the response that is provided to you via an API sitting on top of their flight-booking engine:

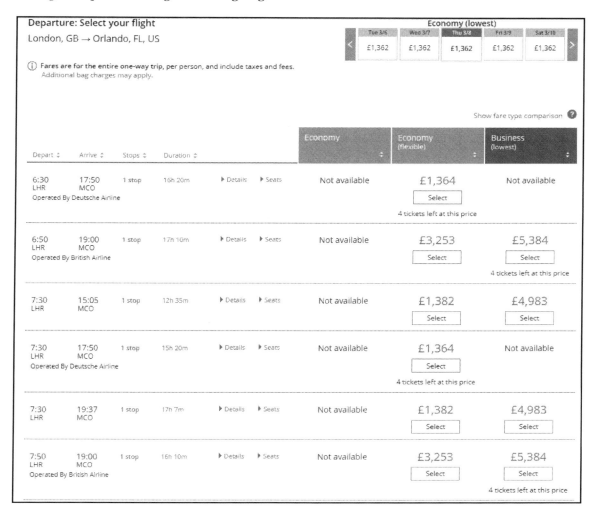

While this might look straightforward, the real power of a programmable API comes to life when you wish to send the same requests to multiple airlines, to compare prices, or to find better flight times. Travel comparison websites, such as Skyscanner.net, Opodo.com, and similar, are leveraging precisely those APIs of the airlines to offer their price comparison services. What's happening is you are formulating a request, and they send multiple API requests to available airlines to retrieve flight information and then present them to you in a consolidated view for comparison purposes:

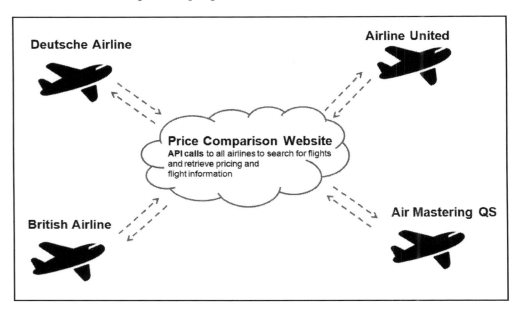

In short, an API creates connectivity by enabling the simplified and abstracted communication between devices and applications. When you think of an API, think of a waiter running back and forth between databases, websites, and devices to deliver data and create the connectivity that puts the world at our fingertips.

Qlik has invested heavily in building a comprehensive API for end users and developers to communicate with its powerful data engine, which is also one of its essential elements that makes Qlik Sense such a strong product.

In our world of Qlik, typical API requests communicate with the data engine and ask it to provide aggregation results based on filters. Furthermore, almost every part of the Qlik Sense technology has been exposed via an API. You can automatically create and load applications, schedule task reloads, retrieve system status or metadata information, and much more.

As a matter of fact, as of the November 2017 version, Qlik has 19 different available APIs, excluding open source initiatives, such as enigma.js, halyard.js, Leonardo UI, and Picasso.js. It is safe to assume that there's an API call for every task or option that is available via the Qlik Sense user interface and its **Qlik Management Console (QMC)**, with many more that have not been exposed to the UI, from applying filters, changing settings, and creating/copying/moving objects, to setting up security rules, and more. If you can manually do it in Qlik Sense via the UI, it will also be possible to automate it via an API call. More importantly, Qlik is actively working and enriching its API offering, so expect more cool stuff to come from it in the future.

The various types of available APIs, what they do, when to use them, and how they work will be seen in detail in the upcoming sections.

Description of Qlik APIs

The high number of 19 available APIs sounds scary, but the number is also a bit of an overstatement. They are all interconnected to some degree and can be considered subcategories of APIs. As a matter of fact, 10 of them are summarized under the so-called Capability API, which forms one of the core Qlik API libraries.

The following are the core Qlik APIs:

- Engine API
- Extension API
- Backend API
- Capability API (includes 10 subcategories of APIs)

Based on Qlik's API reference guide (`https://help.qlik.com/en-US/sense-developer/September2017/Content/APIs-and-SDKs.htm`), the following table shows the full list of available Qlik APIs. The following icons indicate roughly what they are used for and how they can be used to build:

- : Widgets
- : Mashups
- : Extensions

- </> : Custom components:

APIs	Libraries	Extensions	Widgets	Custom components	Mashups
Engine API	JSON RPC	✦			▦
Extension API	JavaScript library	✦			
Backend API	JavaScript library	✦			
Root API	JavaScript library (Capability API)	✦		</>	▦
App API	JavaScript library (Capability API)	✦	◈	</>	▦
Bookmark API	JavaScript library (Capability API)	✦		</>	▦
Field API	JavaScript library (Capability API)	✦		</>	▦
Global API	JavaScript library (Capability API)	✦		</>	▦
Navigation API	JavaScript library (Capability API)	✦	◈	</>	
Selection API	JavaScript library (Capability API)	✦		</>	▦
Table API	JavaScript library (Capability API)	✦	◈	</>	▦
Variable API	JavaScript library (Capability API)	✦		</>	▦
Visualization API	JavaScript library (Capability API)				▦
Custom Component API	Web component			</>	
App Integration API	URL integration				▦

Single Integration API	URL integration				⊞
qlik-visual	Web component		♣		⊞
enigma.js	JavaScript library (open source)	✦		</>	⊞
leonardo-ui	UI library (open source)	✦	♣	</>	⊞

API Stability

As the Qlik platform evolves and new functionality and API methods are introduced, Qlik uses three categories to describe the stability, support level, and likelihood of a change of methods, structs, and functions:

- **STABLE** means that the method is officially supported and not subject to any change going forward. You can entirely rely on using those methods and reach out to Qlik Support if you run into any issues.
- **EXPERIMENTAL** means that the API function or method is new, less stable, and subject to change in the future more often than other components. They can, however, be used.
- **DEPRECATED** means that the components should not be used anymore and may be removed in a future version of Qlik Sense.

Qlik is hosting a handy governance website, API insights, which allows you to quickly check which methods, definitions, and general things have changed between updates and version upgrades (http://api-insights.qlik.com/).

Engine API

The Qlik Engine API is a WebSocket protocol that uses JSON to pass information between the Qlik Sense Engine and the clients. To explain this sentence a bit further, a WebSocket is a both-ways communication protocol that allows the Qlik Engine API to communicate with the web browser of a user. The communication is both ways (*full-duplex*), which means that the user can, for example, pass a selection to the Qlik Engine API but also the Qlik Sense Engine can push updated data to the user's browser, without the user having to accept or do anything.

The format in which the WebSocket communicates is **JSON**, which stands for **JavaScript Object Notation**. It's a data structure in a string format following a specific syntax using brackets, colons, and double quotes, which can easily be interpreted by JavaScript. JSON is characterized and defined using the following set of core rules:

- Data is in name/value pairs
- Data is separated by commas
- Curly braces hold objects
- Square brackets hold arrays

The following is an example of a JSON structure:

```
{
    "id": 1,
    "name": "A green door",
    "price": 12.50,
    "tags": ["home", "green"]
}
```

Using the preceding structure, the client and the Qlik Engine API send data information that is then processed by the browser or the engine itself. To put this a bit more technically, all communication protocol follows the JSON RPC specification. This means the Engine API can be used in every programming language that supports sockets and JSON.

The Qlik Engine API consists of a set of objects representing apps, lists, fields, objects, and so on, which are organized in a hierarchical structure. This means you first need to call the app before you can call the list.

Using the Qlik Engine API, you can perform actions on these objects, such as the following:

- Creating apps and loading data
- Building stories
- Getting system information

Using the Qlik Engine API, you can communicate with the Qlik Sense Engine directly without needing to open Qlik Sense (it needs to run in the background though). This allows you to build custom web apps or mashups, or to retrieve a piece of aggregated information from the Qlik Engine API to pass it on to a different system to consume the results.

Furthermore, as you can also copy, reload, and publish apps using the Qlik Engine API, it can therefore also be used to automate repetitive or complicated updates or changes to an app.

Using the Qlik Sense .NET SDK (`https://help.qlik.com/en-US/sense-developer/`
`September2017/Subsystems/NetSDKAPI/Content/Introduction/Net-Sdk-Intro.htm`), you
can also build Windows applications that leverage the Qlik API directly.

Fortunately, Qlik has provided a handy platform to explore the Qlik Engine API to better
understand the collection of methods and the possible outputs directly on an existing app.
This is available in the **dev-hub** under the **Engine API Explorer** section, as shown in the
following screenshot:

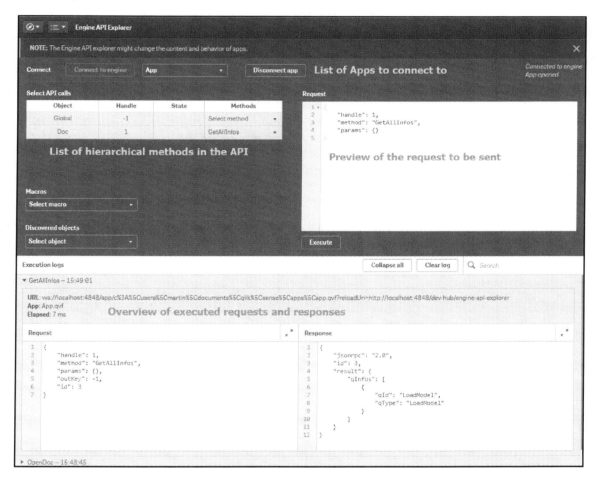

The Engine API Explorer

Request syntax

The request object follows the JSON-RPC 2.0 specification and has the following members:

Member	Description/value	Mandatory?
jsonrpc	Version of JSON-RPC. Equals 2.0.	Yes
id	Identifier established by the initiator of the request. If this member is not present, the RPC call is assumed to be a notification.	No
method	Name of the method.	Yes
handle	Target of the method. The member handle is not part of the JSON-RPC 2.0 specification.	Yes
delta	Boolean. If set to true, the engine returns delta values. The default value is false. Example of use: The delta member is set to true to get the delta of the layout or the delta of the properties of an object. For more information, see Get the delta of the layout (https://help.qlik.com/en-US/sense-developer/September2017/Subsystems/EngineAPI/Content/WorkingWithAppsAndVisualizations/RenderLayout/get-delta-layout.htm) and Get the delta of properties (https://help.qlik.com/en-US/sense-developer/September2017/Subsystems/EngineAPI/Content/WorkingWithAppsAndVisualizations/SetGetProperties/get-delta-properties.htm).	No
params	Sets the parameters. The parameters can be provided by name through an object or by position through an array.	No

Response syntax

The response syntax is the JSON object which is returned by the Qlik Engine API, with each method call.

The response object follows the JSON-RPC 2.0 specification and has the following members:

Member	Description/value	Mandatory?
`jsonrpc`	Version of JSON-RPC. Equals 2.0.	Yes
`id`	Identifier. This identifier must be identical to the identifier in the request object.	Yes
`result` or `error`	The member result is required on success. In case of failure, the member error is displayed.	Yes
`change`	Handles of the objects that have been updated.	No
`closed`	Handles that have been released (following a remove, for example).	No

The best library to communicate directly with the engine using promises is Qlik's open-source enigma.js, which is described later in this chapter.

Enigma is a promise wrapper around the Qlik Sense Engine API, which simplifies the coding significantly.

> Using a promise-based wrapper dramatically simplifies asynchronous programming, which will be elaborated later in `Chapter 12`, *Coding in Qlik Sense*.

`Chapter 14`, *Integrating QS in Websites via Mashups*, shows several of examples on how to connect and communicate with the Qlik Engine API.

Extension API

The Qlik Extension API consists of methods and properties to create custom visualization extensions in Qlik. This is a very powerful API, as it allows you to efficiently embed any JavaScript code, visualizations, or custom components into Qlik Sense and, using the property panel, to configure certain aspects of that extension.

Basic examples of use can be found as follows, which can help you get a better idea of how the Extension API can be leveraged within Qlik Sense.

Hello World using the Extension API

To illustrate an underlying implementation of an extension using the Extension API, the following example will print a `Hello World!` HTML element on to the screen:

```
define ( [
],
function ( ) {
        return {
                paint: function ($element, layout) {
                        $element.html( "Hello world! I learned how to write
this using Mastering QS");
                }
        };
} );
```

Setting initial properties

The `initialProperties` property specifies the properties the object should have when created. These are required for the extension to load with the correct settings before the user has the chance to modify them. In particular, `qInitialDataFetch` needs to be defined, which tells the extension how much data to load initially, once dimensions and metrics are set by the user.

The following is an example of setting initial properties:

```
define ( [
],
function ( ) {
        return {
                paint: function ($element, layout) {
                        $element.html( "Hello world! I learned how to write
this using Mastering QS");
                },
                initialProperties : {
                    qHyperCubeDef : {
                        qDimensions : [],
                        qMeasures : [],
                        qInitialDataFetch : [{ qWidth : 2, qHeight : 50}]
                    }
                },
        };
});
```

A more comprehensive tutorial on how to build custom extensions using this API is outlined in `Chapter 13`, *Creating Extensions in Qlik Sense*.

Exporting and printing

Each extension built for Qlik has the option to support the ability to export the visualization into different formats:

- Export as an image
- Export to PDF
- Export story to PowerPoint
- Export story to PDF

To activate the exporting functionality, you will need to enable it in the code, right after the `initialProperties` section, using the following attributes:

```
support: {
    snapshot: true,
   export: true,
    exportData: true
}
```

Backend API

Similar to the QSocks example, Qlik's Backend API is a wrapper around selected Qlik Engine API methods, but with the difference that the Backend API is aware of the context, which is a WebSocket user session with the current Qlik Sense app.

This means, for example, that if you were to leverage the Backend API to pass on a selection within a visualization extension, the Backend API would utilize the current WebSocket connection and the app in which the extension is used to pass on the selection, for example, via the `selectValues` method:

```
var self = this;
$element.find('li').on('click', function() {
    if(this.hasAttribute("data-value")) {
        var value = parseInt(this.getAttribute("data-value"), 10), dim
= 0;
        self.backendApi.selectValues(dim, [value], true);
    }
});
```

Using the `this` context (named as `self` within the function), the Backend API immediately assumes the existing app and the WebSocket connection to pass on the selection to the Qlik Engine API.

Typical examples of use are the passing on of selections using the following methods:

- `selectValues`
- `selectRange`
- `clearSelections`
- `hasSelections`

Another example is when working with search in list objects:

- `search`
- `acceptSearch`
- `abortSearch`

An overview of all available functions and methods that can be leveraged by the Backend API can be found on the Qlik Sense help website at `http://help.qlik.com/en-US/sense-developer/September2017/Subsystems/APIs/Content/backend-api-reference.htm`.

Capability API

The **Capability API** is a collection of Qlik JavaScript APIs that allow you to easily embed Qlik Sense objects and content into a web page or mashup. It can be subcategorized into the following sub-APIs:

- Root API
- App API
- Bookmark API
- Field API
- Selection API

- Variable API
- Visualization API
- Global API
- Navigation API
- Table API

It's important to note that the Capability API is dependent on RequireJS and AngularJS (1.5), and those libraries need to be loaded as well as to be able to use it.

 Each API will be introduced by its **namespace**. Namespacing is a technique employed to avoid collisions with other objects or variables in the global namespace. It's also extremely useful for helping organize blocks of functionality in your application into easily manageable groups that can be uniquely identified.

To use the Capability API, you will need to load the Qlik Sense implementation of RequireJS, and two CSS files to ensure visualizations and objects are styled as expected.

RequireJS (Qlik version), includes the following before the closing `</body>` tag, which loads the RequireJS library directly from Qlik Sense:

```
<script type="text/javascript" src="https://<qlik server>[:port]/<virtual proxy>/resources/assets/external/requirejs/require.js"></script>
```

In CSS, include the following in the `<head>` section of your page:

 To avoid any surprises during Qlik Sense upgrades or similar, you should never take a copy of the following files but always reference them from your local Qlik Sense instance.

```
<link rel="stylesheet" href="https://<qlik server>[:port]/<virtual proxy>/resources/autogenerated/qlikui.css"> <link rel="stylesheet" href="https://<qlik server>[:port]/<virtual proxy>/resources/assets/client/client.css" media="all">
```

 The virtual proxy may be omitted if you are connecting to the default virtual proxy. The same applies to the port if you are using the default ports for the current protocol (HTTP - 80, HTTPS - 443).

The Capability API is a reference in the code by loading the Qlik module via RequireJS. This is the case both for extensions and mashups, as in the following example:

```
require(['qlik'], function(qlik) {
    var app = qlik.currApp();
    app.field(Date).selectMatch('01/02/2017', true);
    console.log(I've made a selection in the data model!)
});
```

Once you've successfully loaded the dependencies, you can then leverage the full list of sub-APIs.

Root API

Namespace: qlik

The Root API is the external interface to Qlik Sense—it provides methods to open apps, get a reference to a current app, or set the specific language. In summary, it's the root of all other subsequent hierarchical API calls. Two examples will illustrate how it works:

- **Set a specific language**: This example showcases how to programmatically set a particular type of language within Qlik Sense:

```
require(['qlik'], function(qlik) {
    //set the language to something else than default language
    qlik.setLanguage('es-EN')
});
```

- **Get a list of available apps**: This example retrieves a list of all available apps and writes them on to the console log:

```
require(['qlik'], function(qlik) {
    qlik.getAppList(function(list){
        var str = "";
        list.forEach(function(value) {
            str += value.qDocName + '('+ value.qDocId +') ';
            });
            console.log(str);
        });
});
```

App API

Namespace: `qlik.app`

The App API allows accessing all objects and fields within an app, including the following:

- Making selections in an app
- Reloading an app
- Searching an app

An app must be opened using the Root API before the App API can be used, as in the following example:

```
require(['qlik'], function(qlik) {
        //open current app
        var app = qlik.currApp('');
        //insert Qlik objects into the HTML page DIV which has ID = LB01.
        app.getObject(document.getElementById('LB01'), 'uPyZavD');
});
```

Bookmark API

Namespace: `qlik.app.bookmark`

The Bookmark API contains methods to work with bookmarks on the Qlik Sense app you are connected to. It can be called only once an app has been opened using the Root API. Using the Bookmark API, you can do the following:

- Create and remove bookmarks
- Modify bookmarks
- Apply bookmarks

A bookmark, when created, has the following attributes that can be set:

Name	Type	Description
`title`	String	Bookmark title.
`description`	String	Bookmark description.
`sheetId`	String	Optional. Bookmark sheet ID.

Here is an example of creating a bookmark. This example retrieves a specific app and then, using the Bookmark API, creates a new bookmark with the name `Test`, the description `Test bookmark for Mastering Qlik Sense`, and the unique ID `fmcJkH`:

```
var app = qlik.openApp('c31e2aba-3b46-4b13-8b87-c5c2514dea1d');
app.bookmark.create('Test','Test bookmark for Mastering Qlik
Sense','fmcJkH');
```

Unfortunately, as you can see, there is no way to specify whether a bookmark and its selections can be shared by multiple users in the same way as QlikView. Also, you can't specify the alternate state ID of the bookmark.

Field API

Namespace: `qlik.app.field`

The Field API is the interface to all available data model fields within a Qlik Sense app and contains methods for field-level commands, such as the following:

- Selecting values in a field
- Getting available data from a field
- Clearing selections from a field

For example, you can use the following to select all values in the `LastName` field:

```
var app = qlik.openApp('c31e2aba-3b46-4b13-8b87-c5c2514dea1d');
app.field('LastName').selectAll();
```

The added benefit of using the Field API compared to the Backend API is that you can pass selections to dimensions that are sitting outside the context of an object using a HyperCube, possibly even on a different app.

Selection API

Namespace: `qlik.app.selectionState(state)`

The Selection API has not much to do with selections itself, but rather with selection states. Alternate states allow leveraging different selection states for a given app. This way, you could, for example, perform a comparative analysis of different selections. While a very prominent feature in QlikView, it's not as heavily promoted in Qlik Sense.

Its only method is `QSelectionState`, which allows you to create, retrieve, set, clear, and lock different alternate states.

Variable API

Namespace: `qlik.app.variable`

The Variable API provides an interface to create, modify, and set Qlik Sense variables within an app.

A variable in Qlik Sense has the following property parameters:

Name	Type	Description
`qInfo.qId`	String	Optional. Variable ID.
`qName`	String	Variable name.
`qComment`	String	Optional. Comment.
`qDefinition`	String	Optional. Variable definition.
`qNumberPresentation`	Object	Optional.
`qIncludeInBookmark`	Boolean	Optional. Include in bookmark flag.

 Variables can be deleted using the `DestroyVariableByName` method in the Engine API.

Visualization API

Namespace: `qlik.app.visualization`

The Visualization API allows you to create Qlik Sense visualization on the fly, based on a session object. It's important to note session objects are not persisted in the app and will be destroyed once the session times out. Furthermore, on top of creating new visualizations, you can also fetch **existing** visualizations from an app using the API.

This is a new way of embedding new and modifying existing visualizations. Until now, you had two levels to work on to integrate visualizations into your web page or mashup:

- Taking a visualization that has been created in the app and injecting it to your web app, using the `getObject` method
- Programmatically creating a generic non-Qlik visualization (using a third party, for example) after you've received the data from the Qlik Engine API.

With the first one, each time you want to make a change in the visualization, you will need to go back to the Qlik Sense app and modify the object, and the charts will need to be available in the Qlik Sense app. The second one might be compelling but equally difficult to implement.

The Visualization API introduces a third method, which dynamically creates Qlik Sense visualizations on the fly, by passing a set of parameters and returning the visualization.

For example, you can use the following to create a bar chart with a custom title:

```
app.visualization.create(
    'barchart',
    ["Case Owner Group","=Avg([Case Duration Time])"],
    {"title":"On the fly barchart"} )
    .then(function(vis){
        vis.show("QV03");
    }
);
```

The Visualization API only defines two methods:

- `app.visualization.get(visid)`: This is identical to the `getObject` method, but you need to show the visualization yourself, with the new show method.
- `app.visualization.create(type, cols, options)`: This call allows you to dynamically define a chart in your JavaScript code, reuse the existing visualizations (built-in or extensions), supply the dimensions and measures, and set other options for the chart.

The Visualization API is one of the most relevant APIs in the Capability API. The fact that you can easily modify and recreate charts by programmatically defining its settings allows you to potentially build a new visualization client.

Global API

Namespace: `qlik.global`

The Global API is, similar to the Root API, the entry method to Qlik's list of methods that can access global information of the client, such as the following:

- Getting authenticated user info
- Obtaining a list of apps
- Retrieving the progress of a reload

For example, use the following to obtain information about an authenticated user:

```
var global = qlik.getGlobal(config);
global.getAuthenticatedUser(function(reply){
console.log('User:'+reply.qReturn);
});
```

Navigation API

Namespace: `qlik.navigation`

The Navigation API allows you to navigate within a Qlik Sense app programmatically. As such, it will not work in a mashup or web app use case.

With the navigation API, you can do the following:

- Move to a specific sheet
- Get the current sheet ID
- Switch between edit and analysis mode
- Open up a story

The Navigation API is handy when you are trying to build simple widgets or components to navigate to a specific sheet, such as a simple sheet menu or navigation panel.

Table API

Namespace: `qlik.table`

The Table API is a way for developers to create a table using dimensions and metrics, which are returned in a standard table format of rows and columns. Unlike the qHyperCube format, which returns the data in object format, the Table API can simply be leveraged to, for example, do the following:

- Prepare extracts to Excel
- Render simple tabular information in an Angular template

The `qlik.app.createTable` method is the entry point to the Table API. It creates a `table` object that wraps the qHyperCube and returns a table object of type QTable.

The properties of a QTable object are as follows:

Name	Type	Description
rows	Array.QRow	Data rows
headers	Array.QHeader	Header information
totals	Array.QMeasureCell	Total information for measures
rowCount	Number	Total number of rows for the qHyperCube, including rows not fetched from the server
colCount	Number	Total number of columns for the qHyperCube

It is initially empty but will eventually contain data. The table object will be updated when selection state changes, and a notification is sent when data is available and will be triggered by each update. To receive a notification, bind a listener on `OnData` of the `QTable` instance.

The following is an example of creating a table and rendering it using a simple AngularJS template, as it's optimal for rendering dynamic tables on the screen:

Step 1: Create the table and add a listener to it:

```
var table = app.createTable(["FirstName", "LastName"], ["Count(Case
Id)"],{rows:200});
var listener = function() {
    var rowCount = table.rowCount;
    var colCount = table.colCount;
    table.OnData.unbind( listener ); //unregister the listener when no
longer notification is needed.
};
table.OnData.bind( listener ); //bind the listener
```

Step 2: Add the following code snippet to the main controller script:

```
if ( !this.$scope.table ) {
    var app = qlik.currApp();
    this.$scope.table = app.createTable(["FirstName", "LastName"],
["Count(Case Id)"],{rows:200});
}
```

Step 3: Define the AngularJS template using the following HTML code:

```
<tr ng-repeat="row in table.rows">//Render rows
    <td ng-repeat="cell in row.cells"> {{cell.qText}} </td>; //Render cells
within row
</tr>
```

enigma.js

enigma.js is an open source client library released by Qlik that communicates with Qlik Sense's Engine.

enigma.js is an unsupported library and delivered as EXPERIMENTAL by Qlik and may be subject to change or removed in future releases. While it would make sense to start using it, you must be aware that Qlik support will not be able to assist you if you run into issues.

enigma.js can be used both in a Node.js environment, as well as in a browser. As it's an exportable module, unlike Qlik's native APIs, which are hosted on your Qlik Sense server, it allows you to create projects that are portable and behave similarly on top of enigma.js.

As such, the configuration has to be a bit more detailed, which is explained on its open source documentation page that can be found at https://github.com/qlik-oss/enigma.js/blob/master/docs/api.md#configuration.

Using enigma.js in Node.js apps

enigma.js can be installed on your project using npm. Prerequisites are a Node.js installation of a version higher than 4.0 and a Git bash if you're running the example on Windows:

```
npm i -S enigma.js ws
```

 npm stands for **node package manager** and represents a command-line interface program to manage Node.js (JavaScript) libraries, effectively a package manager. It consists of a command-line client and an online database of public and commercial private packages, which you can easily install by running npm install (-i) commands.

Next, you can create an example file (test.js):

```
const enigma = require('enigma.js');
const WebSocket = require('ws');
const schema = require('enigma.js/schemas/12.20.0.json');

// create a new session:
const session = enigma.create({
  schema,
  url: 'ws://localhost:9076/app/engineData',
  createSocket: url => new WebSocket(url),
});

// bind traffic events to log what is sent and received on the socket:
session.on('traffic:sent', data => console.log('sent:', data));
session.on('traffic:received', data => console.log('received:', data));

// open the socket and eventually receive the QIX global API, and then close
// the session:
session.open()
  .then((/*global*/) => console.log('We are connected!'))
  .then(() => session.close())
  .then(() => console.log('Session closed'))
  .catch(err => console.log('Something went wrong :(', err));
```

(This example is taken from enigma's official repository documentation, which can be found at https://github.com/qlik-oss/enigma.js/.)

The last thing you need to do is to run the Node.js command line:

```
node my-file.js
```

Using enigma.js for your project requires a good understanding of JavaScript, promises, and WebSockets. It is recommended that you read `Chapter 12`, *Coding in Qlik Sense*, if those keywords don't ring a bell.

Using enigma.js in extensions

You are also able to leverage enigma when building extensions utilizing the Extension API. By default, when you are building an AngularJS-based extension, as opposed to a paint-based one, enigma.js is shipped within the `$scope` of the extension:

```
// Enigma until 3.2.2
$scope.component.model.enigmaModel;
// Enigma from 3.2.3
$scope.component.model;
```

Using enigma.js, you can access the App API and perform similar methods to the Capability API, such as getting an object and its properties:

```
scope.enigmaModel.app.getObject('HXasde1').then(function (obj) {
 return obj.getProperties()
}
```

Full documentation of enigma.js can be found on their GitHub account at `https://github.com/qlik-oss/enigma.js/blob/master/docs/api.md#api-documentation`.

> As it's an open source project, and subject to continuous delivery by the community via pull requests, it's highly recommended to visit their official repository to ensure the latest version and documentation is utilized.

Leonardo UI

Leonardo UI was introduced in Qlik Sense 3.0 as an open source project of Qlik's native styling components and look and feel. It's a user interface component framework, designed to be used as a complement to other frameworks (for example, bootstrap). It is non-obtrusive in the sense that it does not conflict with other libraries or your page defaults; it does not use global stylings.

Furthermore, you can also use Leonardo UI as a standalone with a CSS reset to get consistent styling of your components.

In the following example, you can see the standard styling of various components, such as buttons, input boxes, labels, functions, radio buttons, and switches:

This section will attempt to summarize the concept of Leonardo UI and give you the list of possibilities. There are, as always, many more examples and use cases to be found on the official website of this open source project at ;https://qlik-oss.github.io/leonardo-ui/.

Using Leonardo UI with Node.js

As in the example with enigma.js, you can install Leonardo UI using npm install by running the following command:

```
npm install --save leonardo-ui
```

You can then reference the downloaded .js library and styling sheet to your HTML page on your Node.js web app:

```
<head>
  <link rel="stylesheet" href="node_modules/leonardo-ui/dist/leonardo-ui.css" type="text/css"/>
</head>
<body>
  <!-- Page content -->
  <script src="node_modules/leonardo-ui/dist/leonardo-ui.js" type="text/javascript"></script>
</body>
```

Instead of using npm install, you can also manually download the Leonardo UI repository and host the reference files on your web page. Make sure to reference them correctly.

 In Qlik extensions, Leonardo UI's CSS will be loaded by default when you are building extensions using the Extension API. You will immediately be able to reference the icons, buttons, style, and classes effectively.

LUI icons

Leonardo UI also allows you to use the palette of icons available in Qlik Sense. They are being imported via a font family and can be used by assigning a <span> HTML element a class following their naming convention:

```
<span class="lui-icon lui-icon--play" aria-hidden="true"></span>
```

The following are some examples of LUI icons (a full list can be found at `https://qlik-oss.github.io/leonardo-ui/icons.html`):

Standard icons

lui-icon lui-icon--image	lui-icon lui-icon--back	lui-icon lui-icon--forward	lui-icon lui-icon--history	lui-icon lui-icon--help
lui-icon lui-icon--info	lui-icon lui-icon--toggle-left	lui-icon lui-icon--toggle-right	lui-icon lui-icon--text	lui-icon lui-icon--group
lui-icon lui-icon--search	lui-icon lui-icon--zoom-in	lui-icon lui-icon--zoom-out	lui-icon lui-icon--export	lui-icon lui-icon--import
lui-icon lui-icon--field	lui-icon lui-icon--lock	lui-icon lui-icon--unlock	lui-icon lui-icon--database	lui-icon lui-icon--calendar
lui-icon lui-icon--bookmark	lui-icon lui-icon--library	lui-icon lui-icon--star	lui-icon lui-icon--print	lui-icon lui-icon--remove
lui-icon lui-icon--handle	lui-icon lui-icon--handle-horizontal	lui-icon lui-icon--menu	lui-icon lui-icon--list	lui-icon lui-icon--unordered-list
lui-icon lui-icon--clock	lui-icon lui-icon--puzzle	lui-icon lui-icon--table	lui-icon lui-icon--filterpane	lui-icon lui-icon--plus
lui-icon lui-icon--minus	lui-icon lui-icon--triangle-top	lui-icon lui-icon--triangle-bottom	lui-icon lui-icon--triangle-left	lui-icon lui-icon--triangle-right

Icon sizing can be determined using the following classes:

- **lui-icon--large** 12px
- **lui-icon--small** 20px
- **no class** (default) 16px

Depending on which class they are assigned, their font size will assume the respective size in pixels.

LUI buttons

Using Leonardo UI, it's fairly easy to create a button with Qlik's native look and feel:

```
<button class="lui-button lui-button--rounded">Default</button> <button
class="lui-button lui-button--rounded lui-button--info">Info</button>
<button class="lui-button lui-button--rounded lui-button--
danger">Error</button> <button class="lui-button lui-button--rounded lui-
button--warning">Warning</button> <button class="lui-button lui-button--
rounded lui-button--success">Success</button>
```

This will create the following buttons:

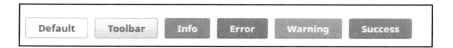

Also, you can also leverage the status (active/disabled/success) of a button using Leonardo UI:

```
<button class="lui-button lui-active">Active</button> <button class="lui-
button lui-button--gradient lui-active">Active</button> <button class="lui-
button lui-button--success lui-active">Active</button> <button class="lui-
button lui-disabled">Disabled</button> <button class="lui-button lui-
button--gradient lui-disabled">Disabled</button> <button class="lui-button
lui-button--success lui-disabled">Disabled</button>
```

This will create the following buttons:

Other LUI components

There are plenty of LUI components available, and more documentation on how they can be created can be found on the official website. Some of them are as follows:

Switches	
Labels	
Radio button groups	
Drop-down lists	
List items	
Menu tabs	

Dialogs and popups	 **Dialog title** Bacon ipsum dolor amet ham hock pork short loin, cow bacon doner jerky pork loin hamburger. Pork chop biltong chuck turkey, cow meatloaf corned beef fatback pancetta drumstick landjaeger jowl. Cancel　OK
Tooltips	Markup　JS This is the tooltip text to be displayed Hover me (top) Hover me (right) Hover me (bottom)

 It is recommended to use Leonardo UI when building mashups and especially extensions whenever possible to preserve Qlik's look and feel, and also to speed up development. Having different stylings for buttons within an app can confuse the user and will affect the design and user experience.

halyard.js

halyard.js is one of the latest open source libraries released by Qlik and is a library to support the loading of data into Qlik Sense apps, without the need for API developers to learn how to script within Qlik Sense. If you're a Qlik Sense or QlikView developer, you can consider halyard.js as a technical library that replaces the load script editor.

The library is split into two pieces to make it more flexible and extendable: one part that generates script and connection artifacts, and a second that takes those artifacts and feeds them to the QIX-engine through enigma.js.

One of the most powerful features in halyard.js is the capability to inline load data without using a connector. This empowers the user to import their raw data into a halyard.js table before the actual reload of the Qlik Sense app occurs. This gives the users the choice of any tool to access their data, without having to depend on various custom connectors. One example could be protected web data resources that currently aren't accessible with the webfile-connector.

In addition to that, halyard.js includes additional features, such as the following:

- Field transformations, such as renaming fields or creating new fields based on existing ones
- Data/time formatting
- Calendar templates

As this open source library is very new, there are not many sample use cases yet available to illustrate its utility. However, one fundamental example is to load a sample dataset using halyard.js and its `addTable` method and create a session (temporary) app using enigma.js (`createAppUsingHalyard` method):

```
require(['halyard','enigma'], function(halyard, enigma) {
    function loadData(data){
        var halyard = new Halyard();
        var table = new Halyard.Table('c:\\data\\Sales.csv');
        halyard.addTable(data, { name: 'Sales' });
        Enigma.getService('qix', enigmaConfig).then((qix) => {
            var appName = 'Sales-App';
            qix.global.createAppUsingHalyard(appName,
halyard).then((result) => {
            console.log('App '+appName+' created with data loaded from
source`);
            });
        });
    })
```

Summary

This chapter in *Mastering Qlik Sense* gave the reader a comprehensive understanding of the breadth of available Qlik Sense APIs, which can be utilized to build compelling extensions, widgets, mashups, and web apps. In particular, the four core Qlik APIs have been described, which are the Engine API, Extension API, Backend API, and Capability API, which includes 10 subcategories of APIs.

With those, the reader should be able to leverage the associative Qlik data engine and implement almost any functionality that is also possible in Qlik Sense, but in a different context for a custom implementation. While not difficult per se, utilizing the API still requires a basic understanding of HTML, JavaScript, AngularJS, and WebSockets, which are described in Chapter 12, *Coding in Qlik Sense*. This, however, should not be discouraging for Qlik developers who do not have a JavaScript background. It's equally important to be able to understand the APIs and potentially work with a seasoned developer.

While the provided overview can be handy, it's only a distilled summary of the APIs. For more in-depth examples, and comprehensive documentation, it is always recommended to visit the official Qlik help page.

Furthermore, next to Qlik's native and supported APIs, there are several open source initiatives which have been released by Qlik itself. While not officially supported, the goal of those libraries is to provide additional, more powerful, interfaces to communicate with the engine, such as enigma.js, Leonardo UI, halyard.js, and the most recent one, picasso.js.

Except for Leonardo UI, they are mostly used for very technical implementations and most likely are not going to be needed in the day-to-day activities of a Qlik developer. It is, however, relevant to understand what they are and in which cases they can be useful. It is important to mention that there are two more open source libraries available from Qlik that are not captured in this chapter: after-work.js and Picasso.js. The first library mostly revolves around the automated testing of web apps and, in the author's opinion, is not really related to Qlik itself. The second, Picasso.js, is a visualization-charting framework, which will become very relevant to the world of Qlik Sense visualization development; however, at the time of writing, little information and documentation were available.

As with everything, the only way to learn a Qlik API is to start working with it. Practice makes perfect and, eventually, once you get to grips with its powerful methods, you will genuinely embrace how easy it can be to leverage the Qlik Engine API and build practically anything you can imagine on top of it. It is worth mentioning Qlik Playground, `http://playground.qlik.com/`, which is a developer-friendly platform to explore the APIs.

The next chapters will dive a little bit deeper in to how you can leverage the Qlik APIs to create fantastic web apps and dashboards. You'll learn about all the basics of coding in Qlik Sense, which you will then leverage to build extensions and mashups via code examples and step-by-step guides.

11
Working with the Qlik Dev Hub

Mastering Qlik Sense is about learning new skills or upgrading the ones we learned in the past when using tools such as QlikView. In this book, we refer to QlikView as little as possible because it is important that you get used to the idea that even though there are similarities between the tools, they are different, and new skills must be learned.

This, however, does not mean that you must become an API expert, or change what you like doing most in a business intelligence project to become a web developer. On the contrary, any skill that you have learned in the past is still useful. This book gives you the tools to discover what's out there in the Qlik Sense world. It is up to you to grab what you like most and deepen your knowledge by adding more reading and training.

To make the transition and to introduce you to Qlik Sense as smoothly as possible, Qlik has created a developer's hub, which provides you with a selection of user-friendly editing tools to play around with the APIs, and gives you the ability to extend Qlik's code in a much more guided way.

In this chapter, we will cover the following topics:

- Dev Hub
- The Single configurator
- The Extension editor
- The Mashup editor
- The Widget editor
- QlikView converter

As a word of warning, this chapter only provides an overview of the Qlik Dev Hub, which will help you understand its potential. The examples provided in this chapter are simple, easy to follow, and concise. The next chapters will cover programming in more detail.

Dev Hub

The Dev Hub combines different tools that developers will enjoy. The Dev Hub is only available in Qlik Sense, so anyone who worked with QlikView in the past will find this a new and exciting topic.

Dev Hub allows developers to create and edit extensions, mashups, widgets, and convert QlikView documents into Qlik Sense documents. There is also an API explorer, which comes in very handy when creating extensions.

Contrary to other features in Qlik Sense, the Dev Hub is aimed at developers. This is the place where geeks can play and have fun. However, the content in this chapter is simple enough for everyone to follow.

In this chapter, I will not be covering the details of programming. You should have a very basic understanding of HTML, CSS, and JavaScript. But, don't worry! if you don't, I will make sure you understand everything here. This chapter is a good warm up for Chapter 12, *Coding in Qlik Sense*.

If you are using a Qlik Sense Enterprise environment, make sure you have *Content Admin* rights from Dev Hub to be able to create new mashups, visualization extensions, and widgets. You can find more on this in Chapter 3, *Security Rules: Attribute Based Access Control*.

Opening Dev Hub

Dev Hub comes with your out of the box Qlik Sense Desktop or Enterprise installation. It is free, and it brings sample extensions, widgets, and so on, which I will use to explain the potential of Dev Hub.

Follow these steps to open Dev Hub:

1. Open **Qlik Sense Desktop**. You will be presented with the **Qlik Sense Desktop hub**.
2. Click on the three dotted icon **[1]**.
3. Click on the **Dev Hub** menu **[2]** to open it.

The following image shows the steps I just described:

The image describing the steps with the step number highlighted in a box

Alternatively, open up a web browser and type in: `http://localhost:4848/dev-hub/`.

If you are using Qlik Sense Desktop, make sure it is running before accessing Dev Hub through the URL.

Dev Hub overview

Once we open Dev Hub, we are presented with the following screen:

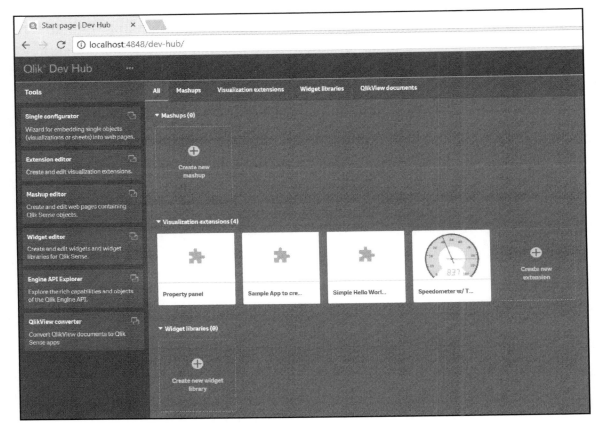

Qlik Dev Hub screen

On the left, you can find all the tools accessible through Dev Hub. The tools include:

- **Single configurator**: Allows you to call a single Qlik Sense chart or sheet using a URL.
- **Extension editor**: Allows you to create or modify existing extensions.
- **Mashup editor**: Allows you to create and modify mashups. Mashups are used to embed Qlik Sense objects (charts, sheets, and so on) into web pages.

- **Engine API explorer**: Lets you explore the capability of the Engine API.
- **QlikView converter**: Helps you convert QlikView applications - with the file extension .qvw - into Qlik Sense applications - with the file extension .qvf.

At the center of the page, you will be presented with any existing Extensions, Mashups, and Widgets.

The Single configurator

To open the **Single configurator** tool, just click on the **Single configurator** menu option in the main Dev Hub screen.

This tool allows you to create mashup pages without having to write a single line of code! You can choose the application containing the objects you want to include in your mashup. The configurator will do all the heavy lifting for you. Drag and drop the objects to the main screen, select the desired settings, and **Single configurator** will return:

- A URL that will point to the object.
- An <iframe> code that can be used in an HTML file. This is useful when embedding objects into web pages.

The following simple but jaw-dropping example will be enough for me to show you how powerful this tool is.

Once you are in the **Single configurator**, select an existing application from the drop-down list on the left. I will use Customer Sales.qvf for my example. After this, all the sheets and objects from the Customer Sales application will populate in the left section, **Sheets and objects**. Select the sheet or object that you would like to include in your mashup, and drag and drop them in the center pane. I will drag and drop the visualization **Sales Rep Variance (TY vs LY).**

 Remember, the Single configurator allows only one object.

The following image shows what the **Single configurator** screen will look like after dragging and dropping the object:

Single configurator screen

The center pane previews the object you selected and right, above it, the URL and iFrame code that you can use within your HTML file. To preview it, click on the **View** icon on the right, or copy the URL and paste it into a browser.

To the right-hand side of the object preview, you will find the **Options** menu. Use this to define whether you want your chart to be clickable, among other options. The Single configurator also allows you to pre-define selections in the charts by using the **Apply selection** option in the **Selections** menu on the right. Each option you select or deselect will modify the URL and iFrame. Make sure you always use the latest version.

Now, what do we do with this? Anything you want! You can use the URL to link it to your blog, for example, as long as all the licenses and permissions are in place, or you can share it internally with work colleagues, or anything else you can think of.

You can also integrate the iFrame code in a web page. To achieve this, create a blank Notepad document and name it `Mashup.html`. You then copy the following code:

```
<!DOCTYPE html>
<HTML>
<HEAD>
<TITLE> My first mashup using Single Configurator </TITLE>
</HEAD>
<BODY>
<DIV style="height:500px;">

<iframe height="500"
src='http://localhost:4848/single/?appid=C%3A%5CUsers%5Cjuan_%5COneDrive%5C
Documents%5CQlik%5CSense%5CApps%5CConsumer%20Sales.qvf&obj=prgzES&select=cl
earall' style='border:none;'></iframe>

</DIV>
</BODY>
</HTML>
```

Save the file, then double-click on it to open it with a web browser. You should now be able to see your mashup with the Qlik Sense object in it.

 You will find more on this and other ways to integrate Qlik Sense into web apps or mashups in `Chapter 14`, *Integrating QS in Websites via Mashups*.

The Extension editor

This useful tool helps you create and modify extensions that can be used in your Qlik Sense application. The editor lets you work with HTML, CSS, JavaScript, and QEXT files. These files are the core of any extension in Qlik Sense, but not necessarily the only ones that you will see.

Extensions will be appropriately covered in the following chapters, but this section will show you how to create and modify an extension by simply using Dev Hub.

To open the **Extension editor** while in Dev Hub, click on **Extension editor** from the menu on the left:

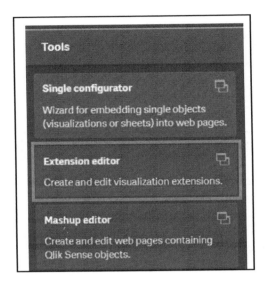

A welcome window will be shown. Click on **Create new project**. In the Create new extension window, type in the name MyQSExtension, and choose **Basic visualization template** from the **Template** drop-down list. When done, click on the **Create & edit** button.

The first file is MyQSExtension.qext, which contains metadata. Let's update the description by updating the following line:

```
"description": "Basic empty visualization template",
```

With:

```
"description": "This is my Qlik Sense extension",
```

Now we can click on the MyQSExtension.js tab, which includes the JavaScript code that creates and renders the extension. I want my extension to create a table with three rows, and each row will contain one of the words from the book name, *Mastering Qlik Sense*. The first row will contain *Mastering*, the second row *Qlik*, and the third row *Sense*. To achieve this, I will:

1. Create an array of the words Mastering, Qlik, and Sense.
2. Iterate through the array using a For loop and create the HTML code on the fly.

The following block of HTML code shows how to populate a title with a 3- row table:

```
<HTML>
<BODY>
<H1>My first extension</H1>
<TABLE border=1>
<TR><TD>Mastering</TR></TD>
<TR><TD>Qlik</TR></TD>
<TR><TD>Sense </TR></TD>
</TABLE>
</BODY>
</HTML>
```

HTML uses opening < > and closing < /> tags. The previous code creates the body of an HTML file by using `<html><body>` tags. We also add a leading header, or title, by using the `<H1>` tag. Finally, we create a table with a border of 1 using the tags `<table>`, `<tr>`, and `<td>`.

If we create a blank file, copy this code in it, and rename the file extension to `.html`, then double-click on the file, it will show us a table with three columns.

To automate this process and make it work in our extension, we must create the same content, that is, the same code I just explained, into a variable, and automatically append it to our extension using JavaScript. By doing so, we will be able to adjust the number of columns and arrays of text used to fill the table.

The following block of code shows how to achieve this:

```
    var book = [
    'Mastering',
    'Qlik',
    'Sense'
];
var content = "<html><body><H1>My first extension</H1><br><table border=1>"
  for(i=0; i<3; i++){
      content += '<tr><td>' + book[i] + '</td></tr>';
  }
  content += "</body></table></html>"

$element.append(content);
```

In the preceding code, I first created a variable that contains an array of three words. My variable content holds a long string with the HTML code I previously explained. However, this has to be dynamic, as I want to loop through my array and automatically add the values in a table.

I used a `For` loop to iterate through the values and appended the result to my `content` variable. When exiting the loop, I made sure to close the main tags `</body>`, `</table>`, and `</html>`.

The content now contains the necessary HTML code to render a table with three rows, each one with the words Mastering, Qlik, and Sense, respectively.

To integrate this code into the code of our extension, within our project in the Extension editor, go to the tab or file `MyQSExtension.js`, and within the `Paint` method, copy the code. The final version of the `.js` file looks like this:

```
define( [ "qlik"
],
function ( qlik) {

  return {
    support : {
      snapshot: true,
      export: true,
      exportData : false
    },
    paint: function ($element) {
      //add your rendering code here
      var book = [
        'Mastering',
        'Qlik',
        'Sense'
        ];
var content = "<html><body><H1>My first extension</H1><br><table border=1>"
  for(i=0; i<3; i++){
      content += '<tr><td>' + book[i] + '</td></tr>';
    }
    content += "</body></table></html>"

$element.append(content);
      //needed for export
      return qlik.Promise.resolve();
    }
  };

} );
```

To test the extension, first **Save** the changes. In Qlik Sense Desktop, create a new application and sheet. In **Edit** mode, navigate to **Custom objects** and drag and drop **MyQSExtension** to the sheet. The following image shows the resulting extension:

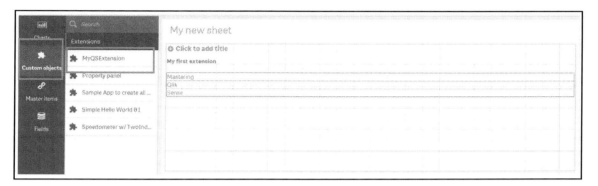

The resulting extension after dropping MyQSExtension to the sheet

More in-depth examples on building extensions in Qlik Sense can be found in `Chapter 13`, *Creating Extensions in Qlik Sense*.

The Mashup editor

The concept of Mashups isn't new to Qlik. QlikView also allows the integration of an application into websites. However, the integration of QlikView applications into sites is hard to achieve as its API isn't as open and varied as other Qlik Sense APIs.

Qlik Sense mashups help to easily integrate application objects or sheets into websites. Qlik has made it so easy that it is very common to see charts embedded in sites instead of the out-of-the-box look and feel Qlik Sense provides.

Mashup editor allows you to easily create or edit mashups. To open the editor, click on **Mashup editor** on the left-hand menu in Dev Hub:

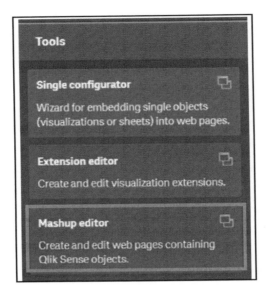

In the welcome pop-up window, click on **Create new project**. Type in the name MyQSMashup and select **Basic mashup template** from the **Template** dropdown. After clicking on the **Create & edit** button, we are presented with the main screen.

At the top, we will see tabs with the main file extension present in most extensions: .qext, .html, .js, and .css.

We can either manually change these files, or we can choose an application from the **Select an app** drop-down, and drag and drop the objects into the main pane.

The following image shows the **Mashup editor** screen with its main elements:

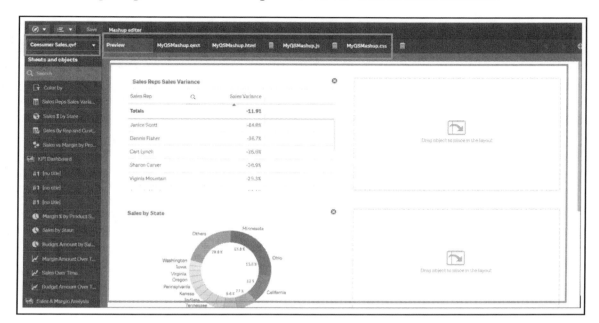

Mashup editor screen

Once we have drag and dropped the object, **Save** the project. To see what our work looks like, we can either click on **View** in the lower right-hand side corner or use the following URL:

```
http://localhost:4848/extensions/MyQSMashup/MyQSMashup.html
```

Remember that for the mashup to work, either Qlik Sense Desktop must be running, or the Qlik Sense services should be up and running-if you are working in an Enterprise environment.

The good thing about **Mashup editor** is that it gives you the base of the integration, which you can then scale up.

From within the .html file, you can add titles, tables, text, and so on. Edit the .css file to change any styling. It takes a bit of time to get familiar with all these terms, but in Chapter 13, *Creating Extensions in Qlik Sense*, we will go into more detail on how all these files work and what they mean.

The Widget editor

The Widget editor allows you to create and edit widgets, which are basically objects that customize the behavior and appearances of sheets and charts.

Contrary to extensions, widgets only use HTML and CSS code, so you will find it a lot easier to create and understand widgets, but what you can achieve with these is very limited.

As widgets only use HTML code, you can create very simple visualizations, but you can also create objects that affect the behavior of the application, such as clearing selections, locking them, jumping from one tab to another, and so on.

As with any other extension, widgets will show up in the **Custom Objects** menu while editing the application in Edit mode.

To explain the extent of widgets a bit more, I will show you how to create a simple button that can clear a user's selections. The Qlik Sense Widget editor comes with code snippets that we can reuse.

From within Dev Hub:

1. Click on **Widget editor**
2. In the **Welcome** window, click on **Create new library** to create a library to store the widget
3. Type in the library name `MasteringQSWidgets` and click on the **Create** button

The previous steps should take you to the Widget editor. Here, we have two main panels, one for HTML and one for CSS. The following image shows the editor screen:

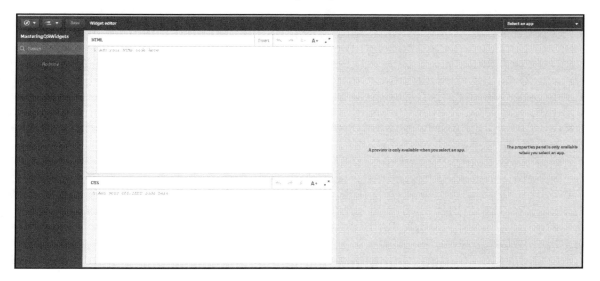

A screenshot depicting what the editor screen looks like

In my example, I use a block of sample code that comes with Qlik Sense and I can edit to my liking.

Next, click **Insert,** located on the HTML panel. From the **Snippets** list, choose **Buttons with actions** and click on **Insert** when done.

The following image shows how to insert a snippet into our widget:

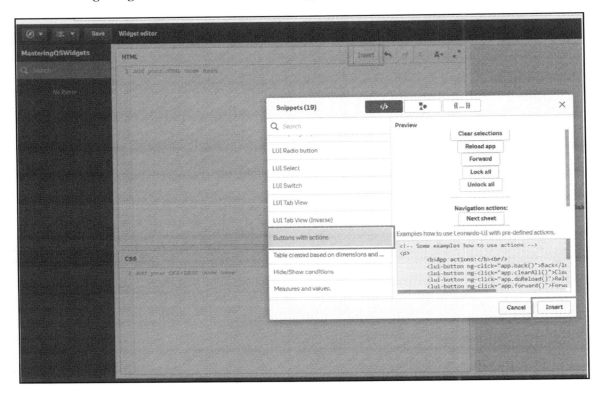

A screenshot depicting how to insert a snippet into a widget

Once you are back to the editor screen, you will see lines of HTML code populated in the HTML panel.

To preview the result, choose an application from the top dropdown,which will let us see the different buttons that the HTML code generates.

For my widget, I only want one button that clears the selections. So, let's simply remove all lines of code that are not related to `Clear selections`.

The final code should look like this:

```
<!-- Some examples how to use actions -->
<p>
  <b>App actions:</b><br/>
  <lui-button ng-click="app.clearAll()">Clear selections</lui-button><br/>
</p>
<hr/>
```

If you like what you see in the **Preview** screen, **Save** the changes and name it `MyQSWidget`. Choose **Other** in the **Widget type** dropdown and click on **Save**.

To test our widget, open an existing application or create a new one with some data, drag and drop the widget **MyQSWidget** from the **Custom Objects** section, and you now have an awesome `Clear selections` button that you can use anywhere.

You can now modify the button by choosing a different font size or color. A lot can be achieved with CSS, so follow your imagination!

QlikView converter

The QlikView converter, as its names suggests, converts QlikView application applications into Qlik Sense applications.

This very simple to use tool allows you to automatically convert most objects and scripts in a `.qvw` file into the Qlik Sense format. As not every object or syntax in QlikView is supported in Qlik Sense, there will be things that you will not be able to automatically convert. Using the converter is usually better than creating your application from scratch. Personally, I have used QlikView converter in several projects, and was impressed by how easy to use and straightforward it is.

To show how the converter works, I am going to use the `Movies Database.qvw` file that comes with any QlikView installation. The steps to convert your QlikView application into a Qlik Sense one are:

From within Dev Hub:

1. Click on **QlikView converter**.
2. Locate the `.qvw` file you want to convert. Drag and drop it into the main screen pane.

Once the converter is done processing the file, you will see five tabs at the top: **Visualizations**, **Dimensions**, **Measures**, **Variables**, and **Unconverted objects**.

By clicking on the first four tabs, you will see all the objects, dimensions, measures, and variables converted into Qlik Sense. The last tab, **Unconverted objects**, is a list of all the objects that exist in QlikView but are not supported in Qlik Sense, for example, Mekko charts.

 All the **Measures**, **Dimensions**, and **Visualizations** will be available as master items in the converted application.

The following image shows a preview of what my QlikView converter screen looks like:

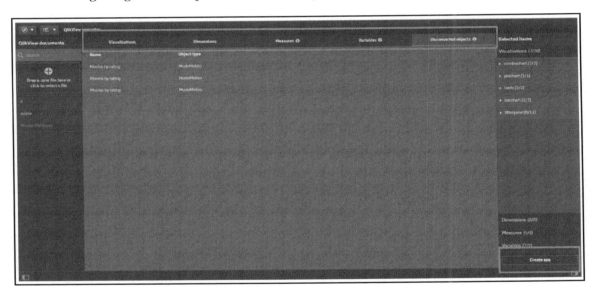

A preview of the QlikView converter screen

To finish the process and create the application, click on the **Create app** button at the bottom right-hand side of the screen. The application will be available in the Qlik Sense Hub.

Summary

Dev Hub comes out of the box with any Qlik Sense installation. It is the go-to place if you are a beginner and want to start creating mashups, extensions, and widgets, or to convert QlikView files into Qlik Sense applications. It is, however, not recommend to use Dev Hub for advanced projects, and you should instead use all the recommendations covered in the following chapters.

Dev Hub also provides an Engine API explorer, which comes in handy when developing extensions.

Whether you are new to Qlik Sense or a seasoned developer, there is a lot you can learn from Dev Hub by dragging and dropping objects, and inspecting the code behind it.

Many developers will prefer to use external **integrated development environments (IDE)** to create what Dev Hub offers, but I advise you spend a good amount of time exploring all of the possibilities it offers.
In the next chapter, *Coding in Qlik Sense*, we will get our hands dirty and learn the foundations of developing extensions in Qlik Sense.

12
Coding in Qlik Sense

Basic Qlik Sense is self-contained and allows you to solve many business intelligence use cases with the use of its load script editor, Qlik expressions, set analysis, and variables. With the full opening up of the Engine to third-party integrations via APIs, there are now unlimited possibilities for how native Qlik functionality can be extended or leveraged by other systems and applications. The world to communicate with the API, though, is with classic programming languages, with .NET and JavaScript in particular. While both frameworks (and many more web languages which support web sockets) are available, this book puts a stronger emphasis on JavaScript. Most examples and implementations are mostly transferable, regardless of which one you choose for your project.

This chapter will discuss and outline the most important JavaScript libraries and code languages required to build extensions and mashups or to integrate Qlik into a separate web app. To warn advanced web developers, the topic will probably be covered on a fairly basic level to allow people with non-development backgrounds to better grasp how these libraries work and why they are important for Qlik projects. As such, this chapter will be very valuable to former QlikView developers who are looking to transition to Qlik Sense but are daunted by JavaScript or any coding languages. While coding is always necessary, it's natural that JavaScript appears to be very complex and difficult at first sight. It's not the intention of the chapter to demystify a legend; JavaScript and its libraries are not a piece of cake, but they can be fairly easy and straightforward if kept on a basic level. Complexity increases as the code becomes more powerful, but on a low level, it's still a sequential execution of a script, with classic conditional statements (if statements), variables, and loop functions, similar to how the Qlik load script works (See `Chapter 8`, *Advanced Scripting*).

This chapter aims to give the reader a good understanding of the basic concepts of web development and how **HTML5**, **Cascading Style Sheets (CSS)**, and **JavaScript** (or **JS**) code is read by the browser. Furthermore, it will introduce the most commonly used libraries. It will help you understand the concepts of the most relevant JS libraries for Qlik, enable you to read and write basic code written in JavaScript and show you how to debug web development code in the browser. In particular, it will cover the following topics:

- HTML5
- CSS
- JavaScript
- D3.js
- RequireJS
- AngularJS

After reading this chapter, the goal should be for the reader to be able to identify the purpose of different code snippets in Qlik code, to be able to speak the language of web developers, and to know where to start looking if there's interest to extend the knowledge on these topics or specific libraries even further.

HTML5

HTML stands for **HyperText Markup Language** and it's a standard language to create website contents. It was first released in 1993 and has ever since dominated the World Wide Web. Most websites to this date have code based on HTML to display their content. Some basics were already covered in `Chapter 11`, *Working with the Qlik Dev Hub*.

HTML is a semantic language which allows you to organize and denote the structure of a website using tags such as `<header>`, `<body>`, and `<footer>` or more structural elements such as `<img>`, `<section>`, or `<p>`. It's very rich in its offering and in combination with CSS and JavaScript forms the three core cornerstones of the World Wide Web.

 If you think of a human person as an example, you could compare the HTML structure of a web page to his/her skeleton, muscles, and organs.

The so-called structural tags in HTML all follow a simple principle and require the following four things:

- An opening tag

- A specified element
- Content
- A closing tag

Take the following snippet for example:

```
<b>This is a bold Text</b>
```

The beginning `<b>` tag represents the opening tag of the code; b stands for bold and instructs the browser to format text within the tags as bold. `This is a bold Text` is the content which is specified to be formatted in bold. To indicate the end of the instruction, a closing tag, `</b>`, always characterized by a backslash, is used.

To create an HTML website, all you need to do is to open a text editor of your choice—even Windows Notepad would work—write a basic HTML code structure, and save it as a `*.html` file. `.html` files can then be opened and displayed by a web browser of your choice (Internet Explorer, Firefox, Google Chrome).

Take the following code as an example:

```
<!DOCTYPE html>
<html>
<head>
<title>Mastering Qlik Sense Page Title</title>
</head>
<body>
<h1>This is a Heading</h1>
<p>This is a paragraph.</p>
<a
href="https://www.packtpub.com/big-data-and-business-intelligence/mastering
-qlik-sense">Link to buy this book!</a>
<br>
<img
src='https://www.packtpub.com/sites/default/files/B04080_MockupCover.png'
width="40%"></img>
</body>
</html>
```

A detailed description of each element in the previous code looks as follows:

- The `<!DOCTYPE html>` declaration defines this document to be HTML5
- The `<html>` element is the root element of an HTML page
- The `<head>` element contains meta information about the document

- The `<title>` element specifies a title for the document
- The `<body>` element contains the visible page content
- The `<h1>` element defines a large heading
- The `<p>` element defines a paragraph
- The `<a>` element defines a clickable hyperlink which takes you to the URL defined in the `href` attribute
- The `<br>` element introduces a line break, the equivalent of hitting *Enter* on a keyboard when in Microsoft Word
- The `<img>` element is used to display an image

The preceding syntax will provide the following output when opened in a normal browser:

The HTML tags are located as follows:

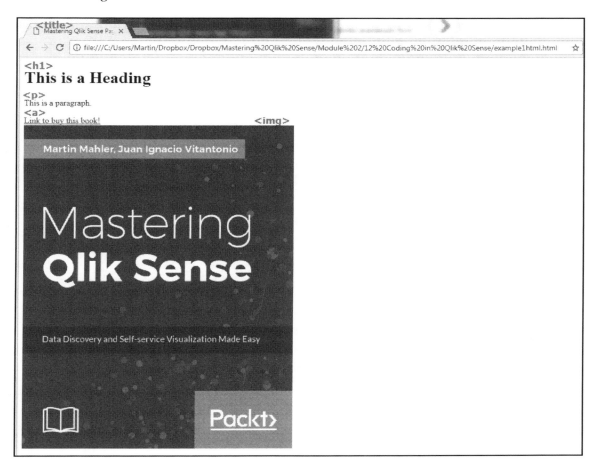

HTML5 is the newest version of HTML. It was released in October 2014 and improves former versions by introducing new tags to handle multimedia content, such as `<video>`, `<audio>`, or `<canvas>`. In particular, the last tag, the canvas element, is a very important aspect of data visualization as it introduces a different way of drawing charts compared to classic **SVG (Scalable Vector Graphics)**. Both of these methods and their differences will be introduced in the *D3.js as a visualization library* section in this chapter.

Structural tags can also be enriched and include so-called attributes. Attributes contain additional metadata information on how the content should be displayed.

Take for example the following HTML snippet:

```
<img
    class="maintext"
    src="image.png"
    height="150px"
    width="100px"
    alt="Image">
</img>
```

As you have already seen in the previous example the `<img>` tag instructs the browser to display an image. Furthermore, the element has been enriched with the following attributes:

- `class="maintext"` assigns the image element a class. Classes are used to identify elements for styling purposes or for additional code processing via JavaScript.
- `src="image.png"` tells the browser which source to use to display the image.
- `height="150px"` explicitly specifies the height of the image, in pixels.
- `width="100px"` explicitly specifies the width of the image, in pixels.
- `alt="Image"` is used to create an alternative placeholder for the image when the image is not available.

All in all, basic HTML is pretty straightforward and can be picked up quite quickly. There are several online tutorials teaching the basics. A free and good one is `https://www.w3schools.com/`, which also allows you to code while you see the output in the same window in parallel.

HTML, in combination with CSS and JavaScript, is what makes Web Development end up being so powerful. With CSS and JavaScript, you are able to access, modify, and manipulate HTML elements called **DOMs**, standing for **Document Object Models**. This is where it becomes interesting, as your web page can then become interactive and dynamic. Before getting into the JavaScript part, it's useful to understand what CSS styling does and how it can be used to change the look and feel of a website.

CSS

CSS, standing for **Cascading Style Sheets,** is a simple way to organize the styling attribute options for the HTML elements used on a page. Typically stored in a .css file and loaded at the <head></head> part of the web page, it applies all definitions and options to the whole document in just the same way you would decorate your flat. Styling can be applied either on DOM elements directly, on classes, on IDs, or on event triggers such as clicking or hovering.

Looking at the official logo of CSS, it closely resembles that of HTML5, which indicates they are meant to work in conjunction. The latest version of CSS is CSS3, but the version number, in this case, is immaterial as it's a simple extension of its older versions with some additional attributes which are compatible with HTML5.

 Continuing on the example of a human person, whose skeleton, muscles and organs are compared to the HTML structure of a web page, CSS can be considered as the look and clothes of the body. You can specify the eye color, hairstyle, clothes, and height of the person.

As discussed, CSS can be applied to a web page either by creating a separate .css file and loading it into the head or by including the CSS styling to the <head></head> by wrapping it in a <style></style> tag. Luckily, the syntax convention is fairly straightforward: you specify the element/class/id, called **selectors**, and then define your styling options in curly brackets { }, called the **declaration box**, for example:

```
p {
color: red;
font-size: 12px;
font-family: Arial;
}
```

In the preceding example, we are styling all paragraphs of our web page in red, Arial, and a font size of 12 pixels. Specifically:

- p, standing for a paragraph, is the **selector**
- Then follows the **declaration box** starting with { and ending with }
- color, font-size, and font-family are all styling **properties**
- red, 12px, and Arial are the respective styling values

Different styling properties need to be separated using a semicolon. If you forget to add it to each line, the styling won't work. It is, in my personal experience, my most common error.

Continuing from the previous web page example, if you want to style all paragraphs of the web page using the paragraph styling, the HTML and CSS code would look as follows:

```
<!DOCTYPE html>
<html>
<head>
<title>Mastering Qlik Sense Page Title</title>
<style>
p {
    color: red;
    font-size: 12px;
    font-family: Arial;
}
</style>
</head>
<body>
<h1>This is a Heading</h1>
<p>This is a styled paragraph.</p>
<a
href="https://www.packtpub.com/big-data-and-business-intelligence/maste
ring-qlik-sense">Link to buy this book!</a>
<br>
<img
src='https://www.packtpub.com/sites/default/files/B04080_MockupCover.pn
g' width="40%"></img>
</body>
</html>
```

Alternatively, you would also be able to store the CSS information in a `*.css` file and load it in the header using the `link` tag:

```
<!DOCTYPE html>
<html>
<head>
<title>Mastering Qlik Sense Page Title</title>
<link rel="stylesheet" href="/MasteringQlikSense.css">
</head>
<body>
<h1>This is a Heading</h1>
<p>This is a styled paragraph.</p>
<a
href="https://www.packtpub.com/big-data-and-business-intelligence/maste
```

```
ring-qlik-sense">Link to buy this book!</a>
<br>
<img
src='https://www.packtpub.com/sites/default/files/B04080_MockupCover.pn
g' width="40%"></img>
</body>
</html>
```

 The `<link>` tag requires the location of the `*.css` file, and the attribute `"stylesheet"`.

 If you have two or more CSS styling files which potentially even style the same element, the latest loaded file takes precedence in styling the element, on attribute level. Such typical conflicts happen unintentionally when loading additional JS libraries together with their respective styling sheets and are called **CSS clashes**.

CSS selectors

As already discussed, many types of selectors can be used to select elements on the web page to apply the styling to. While they can also become very advanced, this chapter should at least address the most common selectors.

Element type selectors

Also referred to as the type selector, the styling is applied to one or more HTML elements with the same name. The previous example with styling applied to the `<p>` element is an example:

```
p {
    color: red;
}
```

While very useful to apply a general theme to your web page, these type of selectors are not generally used to style segments of the page individually.

ID selectors

ID selectors overcome the problem of general styling, by selecting elements by their `id`. Element IDs have the benefit, but also the restriction, that they need to be unique in the HTML:

```
<!DOCTYPE html>
<html>
<head>
#mainparagraph {
    color: red;
}
</head>
<body>
<p>This is a styled paragraph.</p>
<p id="mainparagraph">This is a styled paragraph.</p>
</body>
</html>
```

The previous example will style only one paragraph based on the `id`.

> You always need to add the # prefix when selecting ids, both in JavaScript and in CSS.

Class selectors

Similar to the ID selector, the class selector allows you to style elements with a given class, regardless of their element type. This means one or more elements and element types can be styled using it and hence it's the most practical one:

```
<!DOCTYPE html>
<html>
<head>
#redcolor {
    color: red;
}
</head>
<body>
<h1 class="redcolor">This is a Heading</h1>
<p>This is a styled paragraph.</p>
<p class="redcolor">This is a styled paragraph.</p>
</body>
</html>
```

In the preceding example, both the <h1> and the second <p> class element font color will be red as a result.

Attribute selectors

The attribute selector works in conjunction with the previous selectors, but one goes one level deeper and queries the element for a specified attribute:

```
a[href="https://packt.org"] {
 color: green;
}
```

The preceding example will select all links on the web page and color them in green if they are redirecting the user to the https://www.packtpub.com/ website.

Combining different selectors

This is where it becomes advanced, and also very powerful—combining multiple selectors and applying advance logic to what exact elements are styled. Next, like for example to mention a few child combinators:

```
body > p { color : red;}
```

All paragraph elements which are direct children (one level) within the body.

 Parent, Children, and Siblings are a way to reference the relative position within the HTML DOM hierarchy, so-called node relationships. See here for more information on this topic: https://www.w3schools.com/js/js_htmldom_navigation.asp

Siblings combinators combine elements which are on the same level in the DOM hierarchy:

```
h1 + h2 { color : red;}
```

All <h2> elements placed immediately after <h1> elements.

Descendant combinators combine two elements which are one below the other in the DOM hierarchy:

```
div p { color : red;}
```

All paragraphs which are embedded within a div (divisor) element.

Unfortunately, this chapter will not go into too much detail on this and the reader is urged to delve into an additional reading material, such as Packt's recommended *Mastering CSS* book (https://www.packtpub.com/web-development/mastering-css).

One challenge around combining different selectors is the fact that too much logic is introduced into CSS styling. While it would work, and sometimes would be the best approach, it's recommended to instead work with a smart architecture of predefined classes.

JavaScript

JavaScript, also abbreviated as **JS**, is the third core technology of the triangle of web development and the World Wide Web, and the main programming language of modern web browsers. Qlik Sense, leaving the Qlik engine, services, and the repository database aside, is fully based on JavaScript.

Within the world of software development, JS has the following classification attributes as a programming language:

- It's **high-level**, meaning it's highly abstracted
- It's **dynamic**, for example, variables can become strings from numbers and vice versa during the execution of the code
- It's **weakly typed**, meaning it will *allow* some missing declaration or typos to go through
- It's **prototype-based**, meaning you can, for example, create prototype objects, and then augment them in due course, adding or remove attributes of an object
- It's **multi-paradigm**, meaning it supports multiple types of programming paradigms (for example, object-oriented, procedural) even at the same time

As such, JavaScript is very flexible and friendly for beginners to programming. As you don't need to build or compile code before you can run it (the website does this for you), development speed can be much more agile and the feedback loop becomes shorter.

Programming languages which are not **compiled** languages are called **interpreted** languages.

With HTML and CSS, continuing the example of a human person, the skeleton and styling have been defined. But so far, it is only a motionless human being. What keeps it going, functioning, dynamic, and responsive is the human brain, and in this example, JavaScript represents exactly that.

Coding with JavaScript

JavaScript code is usually declared in an HTML page within `<script></script>` tags. It's also possible, although a bit messy, to embed code directly within elements on the web page. Best practice is to outsource the JavaScript code to a separate file and to load it dynamically, but how to best modularize JS code will be discussed later in this chapter around RequireJS.

The positive thing about JS is that it can entirely interact with the HTML page by manipulating the objects, or DOM, visible on the web page. It can also receive input from forms and with versatile libraries and APIs available, discussed later in this chapter, it can turn into a very powerful and performant language to achieve almost anything on the web.

A basic example of how to calculate a number and output it to an HTML page using JavaScript is as follows:

```
<!DOCTYPE html>
<html>
<body>
<h2>Mastering Qlik Sense JavaScript</h2>
<p>Resulting Number is:</p>
<p id='demo'><p>
<script>
var x, y, z;
x = 5;
y = 6;
z = x + y;
document.getElementById("demo").innerHTML = z;
</script>
</body>
</html>
```

What the preceding code does is declare two variables, x and y, and then sum them to calculate z, which is then displayed on the HTML element with the ID called demo. It's a perfect example of how logic is calculated under the hood, and the result presented on the frontend. While the example is trivial, it's the true essence of how HTML and JavaScript work in conjunction.

> Plainly written JavaScript code which has not been extended by additional libraries or frameworks is called **Vanilla JS**.

JavaScript follows typical programming conventions, such as loops or if statements.

A classic conditional statement can be seen in the following example, which obtains the current hour of your time zone and changes the greeting depending whether it is evening or not:

```
<!DOCTYPE html>
<html>
<body>
<h1 id='greetobject'><h1>
<h2>Welcome to Mastering Qlik Sense JavaScript</h2>
<script>
var d = new Date();
var greeting = '';
var hour = d.getHours();
if (hour < 17) {
   greeting = "Good Day";
 }else{
   greeting = "Good Evening";
}
document.getElementById("greetobject").innerHTML = greeting;
</script>
</body>
</html>
```

While unable to provide the reader with a full introduction of what JavaScript is and how it works in the context of Qlik Sense, it is useful and important to understand some basic concepts around JS which are typical to that kind of programming language, outlined as follows.

JavaScript is code and not data or a markup language

It's technically possible to mix up JS with an HTML page, even to the extent of embedding code into specific DOMs as follows:

```
<button onclick="return confirm('Are you sure you want to
remove?');">Remove</button>
```

While it would technically work, there are some serious drawbacks to this once your code base becomes bigger and the logic complicates. It's best practice not to mix up UI elements with the code, and instead, to separate your JavaScript code either into the `<script></script>` tag, or ideally into a separate `*.js` file which is loaded to the web page in the headers, for example:

```
<!DOCTYPE html>
<html>
<body>
```

```
<h2>Mastering Qlik Sense JavaScript</h2>
<button id="examplebutton"></button>
<script>
document.getElementById("examplebutton").onclick=function(){
    return confirm('Are you sure you want to remove?');
}
</script>
</body>
</html>
```

Everything in JavaScript can have a property

JS, by default, has only three simple data types: number, string, and boolean. Everything else can have a property assigned to it:

```
//Define an array
var book = [];
book.title = 'Mastering Qlik Sense';
//Book now has a property!

//Define an object
var book = {};
book.author= 'Martin Mahler & Juan Vitantonio';
//Book object now has an author property!

//Define function
var book = function() {
    return 'Hello'
};
book.version= 'v1.1;
//Book function now has a version property!
```

This is an interesting concept, and while possible, it's not necessarily recommended to use to its full extent; for example, arrays should not be inadvertently used as objects with properties. But what is interesting is that functions themselves in JavaScript are technically objects as well and can be treated as values.

Variable scoping

With JavaScript being a weakly typed programming language, a variable declaration is very flexible and almost impossible to get wrong.

Simply declare a variable with a `var` prefix without having to worry about its type—JavaScript will interpret the type depending on the value it holds:

```
var variable = 'Mastering Qlik Sense';
//variable is a string
var pagenumber = 1;
//pagenumber is an integer
var iLikeTheBook= true;
//iLikeTheBook is a boolean
```

As you can also change the value of a variable during the execution of the code, the type automatically changes as well, without any complaints or runtime errors. Automatic type conversion is pretty convenient as it reduces the number of required declarations beforehand:

```
var variable = 'Mastering Qlik Sense'
//variable is a string
var variable = 1
//variable is now an integer
```

Interestingly, if you omit the `var` prefix during your variable declaration, this will work too. What will happen then is that JavaScript will create a variable for you as if you were using `var`, but it will declare it as a global variable:

```
function () {
var local_var = 'Mastering Qlik Sense'
global_var = 'Mastering Qlik Sense'
}
//global_var can be read outside of the function, local_var can't be.
```

 Weakly typed programming languages are very convenient for beginners as you can quickly write code without having to worry too much about syntax errors. At the same time, though, you will need to be careful as the automatic interpretation will just work without throwing an error message. Some unwanted effects can occur, such as automatically defining a global variable which is also used by another library, which can accidentally overwrite each other's values.

JSON

JSON stands for **JavaScript Object Notation** and is a lightweight data-interchange format which is represented as a string. It is very popular in web development for receiving and posting data to different services and is also very relevant to Qlik Sense as its connectors can read data provided in a JSON format. A basic JSON structured data collection looks as follows:

```
{
  "title": "Mastering Qlik Sense",
  "type": "book",
  "properties": {
  "firstName": {
  "description": "Martin",
  "type": "string"
  },
  "lastName": {
  "description": "Mahler",
  "type": "string"
  },
  "age": {
  "description": "20",
  "type": "integer",
  "minimum": 0
  }
  },
}
```

JSON is built on two structures:

- A collection of name/value pairs
- An ordered list of values

JSON structure can then be effectively used to transmit data from one system to another, even millions of rows, with, however, the downside that the transmitted data is not compressed and, as such, consumes a lot of memory.

AJAX

AJAX stands for **Asynchronous JavaScript And XML** and represents a set of web development techniques to create asynchronous web applications.

Asynchronous means that the execution of the JavaScript code does not run in sequence. This is especially helpful and required when working with different services where data is sent to, and a response is expected for consumption. The execution of the code should not pause during this process, facilitating the firing of multiple requests at the same time. Those requests are typically categorized into POST and GET requests. For example, POST requests are required to communicate with the Qlik Engine API.

 If some of you QlikView developers remember, when QlikView was used in web view instead of the IEPlugin, the term ajax was always present in the URL of the QV app. Ajax was used to make all those API calls to the QlikView Server to obtain the calculated objects.

Asynchronous can sometimes be tricky to work with if you are expecting a response from a separate server or service, and you wish to execute code depending on the response. To solve this effectively, promises are typically used, which allows you to handle the response and run additional code depending on the result, and the result status.

JavaScript libraries

The cool thing about JavaScript is its vast and versatile ecosystem of open source libraries which can be used and integrated with your existing code base. A JavaScript library is a collection of useful code snippets which can extend your code or greatly simplify your life. **jQuery** is one of the most prominent libraries, annotated with a $, which allows you to manipulate the DOM much easier on your web page with less code.

Using jQuery, the following example is greatly simplified:

```
//Classic JS command
document.getElementById("greetobject").innerHTML = greeting;

//Using jQuery
$('greetobject').html(greeting)
```

JavaScript libraries are very easy to integrate. Usually, they are provided with a *.js file which needs to be included in your code. To include the code, just reference the filenames in your web page <head> and feel free to use existing functions. A smarter way to load JavaScript libraries and dependencies is using RequireJS, which will be covered in this chapter.

Including jQuery, many libraries have become an integral part of web applications and modern web development can't be thought to exist without them, hence why they are so important. Even the Qlik Sense platform is based on several open source libraries such as underscore or loadash. The most important ones will be covered in this chapter.

JavaScript is not just for browsers

We are talking about HTML, UIs, and web browsers, but a world exists where JavaScript is also used for backend development. Most prominent for this is Node.js, which allows you to build lightweight backend services using the same programming languages as web apps or websites. Also, you can create building tasks with JavaScript using tools such as grunt.

RequireJS

As already highlighted, JavaScript libraries play an integral role in web app development. While they can be loaded in the HTML one by one, when you start using multiple libraries, this can become a little bit tricky when they become dependent on each other.

RequireJS solves this elegantly by providing a library to load JavaScript files in a modular way, which improves the speed and the quality of the code.

So far we were loading JavaScript files by referencing them using a dedicated <script src="library"></script> tag.

A typical structure of loading files using RequireJS looks as follows:

```
define( ["./jquery",
        "css!./css/layout.css"
      ],
      function($) {
      //jQuery was loaded and can be reference using $ in the code.
      //a layout CSS files was loaded as well. As it's using the prefix
CSS!, it's being treated as such and automatically appended to the HTML
head
      }
);
```

 css! and text! are AMD loader plugins and loaded together with RequireJS in Qlik Sense. If you plan on using RequireJS on your own project outside of Qlik Sense you might need to specifically load those as well. You can find them here https://github.com/requirejs.

Since the library only considers JavaScript (.js) files, all file extensions are omitted, hence jquery did not require the .js suffix in the previous example.

When loading JavaScript code from multiple files, there sometimes can exist dependencies. The classic way of loading files is illustrated in the following example:

```
<script src="library1.js"></script>
<script src="library2.js"></script>
<script src="library3.js"></script>
<script src="main.js"></script>
```

The code base in main.js depends on libraries 1 -3 to load first. Managing the dependencies, especially in large projects, can quickly get out of hand. RequireJS uses **Asynchronous Module Loading** (**AMD**) for loading files, meaning that each file will load asynchronously in the defined order.

The previous loading example translated into RequireJS code, embedded in main.js, looks as follows:

```
//Main.js file
require(["library1","library2","library3"],
    function(a,b,c){
    //You can now use library a, b and c for your code
    }
);
```

To break the asynchronous loading for strong dependencies (for example, library 2 requires library 3 to be loaded first), a shim function can be used to configure the module loading process and specify the sequence of files to be loaded:

```
requirejs.config({
  shim: {
  'source1': ['library1','library3'],
  'source2': ['library2']
  }
});

require(["library1","library2","library3"],
    function(a,b,c){
    //You can now use library a, b and c for your code
    }
);
```

Source 1 will be loaded before source 2 to resolve dependency issues.

In RequireJS, it's important to understand its two most relevant functions, which are define() versus require(). The difference between those two is that require() is used to run immediate functionalities and code, while define() is utilized to define modules for use in multiple locations. So in the previous examples, libraries 1-3 would use the define() function to declare any relevant dependencies (such as CSS files), whereas the place where all the libraries come together to be executed in a relevant matter is where require() is used.

As illustrated in the previous examples, RequireJS greatly simplifies and organizes your code base, which is the reason why it's being so heavily used by Qlik and is a pillar of the framework for Qlik Sense extensions.

RequireJS takeaways

RequireJS is not rocket science. It's a simple and controlled way to load modularized JavaScript code. You don't necessarily need to become an expert in RequireJS as in most cases in Qlik Sense API development will be straightforward; however, you should understand why and how it's being used and how to solve simple challenges around loading library dependencies.

AngularJS

AngularJS is a structural framework for building dynamic web applications in JavaScript. It extends the classic HTML syntax by embedding dynamic angular expressions which update or modify the DOMs based on the code. It's very handy in dynamically binding data in and out of your HTML web page, which is why, for example, Qlik Sense's native straight table has been developed on an Angular basis.

It's a whole different concept to jQuery, which is elaborated further in this chapter.

As with every useful library, AngularJS simplifies application development by presenting a higher level of abstraction of writing code to the developer.

AngularJS has two distinct versions running available on the net. Angular 1.X and Angular 2.X, called simply AngularJS and Angular 2 respectively. These two versions are not simple upgrades, but fundamentally different concepts of frameworks. Qlik is built entirely on Angular v1.5 and any reference in this book to Angular will always be about v1.5 as well.

It's difficult to highlight the benefits and advantages of using Angular without becoming too technical but this part of the chapter will attempt to provide you with a basic overview of why AngularJS is used in Qlik Sense and what the key principles and components of the framework are.

It's all about bringing structure to JavaScript

Before AngularJS became popular, jQuery was the core library which was used to develop web apps and to dynamically interact with the HTML DOMs. Using jQuery is referred to as imperative programming, meaning your code specifies not just *what* you want to happen, but *how* you want it to happen as well. As a result, you would end up with many internals to make the code work properly, most likely ending up in a massive collection of code snippets and losing the overview of how it all connects to each other. With imperative programming, you might end up having a lot of behaviors and animations that are wired up behind the scenes, which are not apparent when looking at the code.

The solution to this problem is to start using declarative programming, which only specifies *what* you want to happen, and leave the how it will happen to AngularJS, the framework of our choice. By declaring the UI and placing the markup directly in HTML, you maintain the logic for the presentation in one place and you separate it from the rest. Once you also understand AngularJS's extended markup, it's clear how and where data is bound and it becomes easy to manipulate the UI.

 Not all of AngularJS is necessarily beneficial to building simple Qlik Sense extensions or mashups, but it's the framework on which Qlik was built and hence it is important to understand why and how it works.

A simple case of a Vanilla web application based on AngularJS can be seen as follows:

```
<html>
<script
src="https://ajax.googleapis.com/ajax/libs/angularjs/1.6.4/angular.min.js">
</script>
<body ng-app="MasteringQS">
<div ng-controller="myCtrl">
    <button ng-click="myFunc()">OK</button>
    <p>The button has been clicked {{count}} times.</p>
</div>
<script>
angular.module('MasteringQS', [])
.controller('myCtrl', ['$scope', function($scope) {
    $scope.count = 0;
    $scope.myFunc = function() {
        $scope.count++;
    };
}]);
</script>
</body>
</html>
```

When read by the browser, the code then creates a button on the `.html` page which, when pressed, increments the numbers of clicks dynamically, as the following screenshot shows:

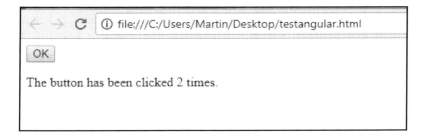

To elaborate on the code, as a starter, the AngularJS library is being loaded (in Qlik Sense, this is done by default). What can then be identified are the various `ng-`, which stands for Angular, attributes which extend the classic way of writing HTML with declarative AngularJS code, called **directives**. There are several built-in `ng-directives` available in the library, but you can also write your own ones.

`ng-app` is one of the built-in directives and initializes an AngularJS application, in this instance called **MasteringQS**. As we are passing data from a function to the HTML DOM, a controller is required, called `myCtrl` in this instance, which holds the code logic and *controls* the data in the app. To run the code controller, an `ng-click` directive is added to the button on the page which executes the `myFunc()` function to increment the counter. But when the counter is incremented on-click, how does the resulting value appear on the HTML DOM as per the screenshot? That's where the two-way data binding magic comes into play. The resulting counter value is stored in the `$scope`, which is the binding part of the controller and the view. Object values and attributes can be passed vice versa using the $scope: to embed values and expressions into the DOMs on the view, double curly braces are utilized `{{}}`. So, in the example, once `$scope.count` is updated, it's automatically evaluated in the view within the paragraph where `{{count}}` is positioned. Simple as ABC!

Following the preceding quick crash course on how all those AngularJS components come together, it is now a good point to go into the detail in each one of them to provide a better understanding of what they are and how they can be used.

Scope

Scope, or `$scope`, is the glue between the application controller (JavaScript) and the view (HTML). It allows for a two-way data binding and, using `$watch` expressions, constantly monitors for changes of the data either on the view or on the controller. It's a JavaScript object which can hold properties and methods. The scope is unique to a specific controller, so if you have multiple controllers on an app, such as in the case of different Qlik Sense extensions, the scope will only be local to that particular extension.

To add properties or update values to a `$scope`, simply update it in the controller code as you would with any other JavaScript variable:

```
$scope.name = "Martin Mahler";
```

To retrieve the scope in the view, simply reference the property `name` in the HTML:

```
<h1>My name is {{name}}</h1>
```

Controllers

Controllers are defined by JavaScript code and are used to augment the AngularJS scope. It's effectively a way to control the data that is flown between the view (HTML) and the code within the web application. Controllers are used to generally achieve two things:

- Set up the initial state of the $scope object and the view
- Add behavior to the $scope object

It should not be used for any presentation logic and mainly contains the business logic of an app. It should also not be used to filter an output, format the input, or to share code between different controllers. The controller can be loaded within a segment of the UI by using the attribute ng-controller as in the following example:

```
<html>
<script
src="https://ajax.googleapis.com/ajax/libs/angularjs/1.6.4/angular.min.js">
</script>
<body ng-app="MasteringQS">
<div ng-controller="myCtrl">
    <h1>My name is {{name}}</h1>
</div>
<script>
angular.module('MasteringQS', [])
.controller('myCtrl', ['$scope', function($scope) {
    $scope.name = "Martin Mahler";
}]);
</script>
</body>
</html>
```

While large web applications can have multiple contextually separate controllers, it's generally common to have few controllers.

Templates

In AngularJS, a template is HTML code, sometimes a snippet, which contains AngularJS-specific elements and attributes and is often linked to a specific controller. Templates can be reused multiple times with different values or texts in AngularJS. It's particularly relevant when building Qlik Sense add-ons or extensions, as this will be the basis on which the controller will apply its rendering logic to. In its most basic case, the template can be considered to be a simple HTML web page.

Directives

Directives belong to one of the most important concepts in AngularJS and are effectively what extends the basic HTML markup by teaching the browser new HTML. These special attributes always start with and can be recognized by its `ng-` prefix. A single directive may handle many HTML elements and a single HTML element may be managed by multiple directives.

By default, AngularJS comes with some standard directives, such as the following:

- `ng-model`: This directive binds the values of AngularJS application data to HTML input controls. Taking the example from before, we've now extended the HTML with an input box where value can be added by the user. Using `ng-model`, the value is bound to the `name` variable in the `$scope`. As it's a two-way binding, in this case, the same variable is later updated in the header:

```
<div ng-app="myApp" ng-controller="myCtrl">
    Name: <input ng-model="name">
    <h1>You entered: {{name}}</h1>
</div>
```

- `ng-repeat`: This directive repeats HTML elements for each item in a collection. In the following example, `ng-init` initializes the list of names which are passed on to `ng-repeat` directive to loop through them and generate list points:

```
<div ng-init="names=['Martin','Juan', 'David', 'Dilyana']">
  <ul>
    <li ng-repeat="x in names">
      {{ x }}
    </li>
  </ul>
</div>
```

  `ng-repeat` is very popular when building widgets or extensions around list boxes or basic tables.

- `ng-if`: The `ng-if` directive removes or recreates a portion of the DOM tree based on an `{expression}`. It's important to note that `ng-if`, unlike `ng-show`, does not just hide but entirely removes the DOM element:

```
<div ng-if='true'>
  <p>I'm visible</p>
</div>
<div ng-if='false'>
```

```
    <p>I'm not being rendered at all.</p>
</div>
```

- ng-class: This directive allows you to dynamically set one or more classes to an element, which can then be styled using CSS. In the following example, we are also making use of ng-model for a two-way binding. Within the select element, the user is able to choose from two values, in this case representing the coloring style. The selected value is then, using ng-model, propagated to the divisor, where it defines the class of it.

```
<style>
.sky {
    color: blue;
}

.tomato {
    color: tomato;
}
<style>
<select ng-model="color">
    <option value="sky">Sky Blue</option>
    <option value="tomato">Tomato REd</option>
</select>

<div ng-class="color">
    <h1>Welcome Home!</h1>
    <p>I like it!</p>
</div>
```

- ng-style: This directive lets you change the styling of an element as follows:

```
<div ng-controller="myCtrl">
    <h1 ng-style="style">My name is {{name}}</h1>
</div>
<script>
angular.module('MasteringQS', [])
.controller('myCtrl', ['$scope', function($scope) {
$scope.name = 'Martin'
$scope.style = {
        "color" : "red",
        "background-color" : "blue",
        "font-size" : "60px"
    }
}]);
</script>
```

There are many more native directives provided with AngularJS which can be discovered on the official homepage of Angular here: `https://docs.angularjs.org/api/ng/directive`.

In Qlik Sense, it is not required to declare an `ng-app` in your templates as the code is embedded in a Qlik Sense AngularJS app already. This is not straightforward—but we will elaborate on this in the next chapters.

Creating your own directives

It's possible to create your own bespoke directives as well to extend the HTML functionality with your own code. New directives are created by using the `.directive` function, and to invoke them, a new HTML tag using the directive name needs to be introduced. The following code can be used as an example:

```
<body ng-app='myApp'>
<mastering-qlik-directive></mastering-qlik-directive>
<script>
var app = angular.module("myApp", []);
app.directive("MasteringQlikDirective", function() {
    return {
        template : "<h1>Mastering Qlik Sense made by a directive!</h1>"
    };
});
</script>
</body>
```

When naming a directive, you must use a camel case name, `MasteringQlikDirective`, but when invoking it, you must use a dash separated name, `mastering-qlik-directive`. It doesn't make sense, but that is how it works. From the official documentation:
Angular normalizes an element's tag and attribute name to determine which elements match which directives.

"We typically refer to directives by their case-sensitive camelCase normalized name (e.g.ngModel). However, ***since HTML is case-insensitive, we refer to directives in the DOM by lower-case forms, typically using dash-delimited attributes*** on DOM elements (e.g. ng-model)."

You are able to invoke your custom-created directive using one of the following four types, based on the `MasteringQSDirective` example:

- **Element name**: `<mastering-qlik-directive></mastering-qlik-directive>`
- **Attribute**: `<div mastering-qlik-directive></div>`
- **Class**: `<div class="mastering-qlik-directive"></div>`
- **Comment**: `<!-- directive: mastering-qlik-directive -->`

Restrictions can be applied to how the directive can be invoked to avoid unintentional misuse of the same directive elsewhere:

- **E** for element name
- **A** for attribute
- **C** for class
- **M** for comment

> By default, EA restriction is applied, meaning the directive can be invoked by both elements and attributes.

The following code snippet shows how a restriction can be declared:

```
app.directive("MasteringQlikDirective", function() {
    return {
        template : "<h1>Mastering Qlik Sense made by a directive!</h1>",
        restrict : "E"
    };
});
```

AngularJS takeaways

If you're used to HTML, jQuery, and classic web development, AngularJS approach will seem a bit unusual to you. However, once understood, the library introduces a lot of structure to web development and the benefits of using a framework will pay off. While there are many other popular and, for some use cases, more suitable JavaScript frameworks, such as Vue.js or ReactJS, Qlik Sense itself is built in AngularJS and as such you are unfortunately bound to it if you would like to develop code which is meant to run within Qlik Sense.

For mashups, things are obviously different and in essence a personal choice, but then again, you could just leverage the existing AngularJS framework used in Qlik Sense rather attempting to combine two worlds in your web app. Either way, you should be familiar with the library, what it stands for, and how the basic concepts and principles work. This chapter scratches the surface of how AngularJS works and while further reading is recommended, it is important to be careful with available reading material on the internet and tutorials as they can quickly become very technical.

D3.js as a visualization library

We are now introducing the author's favorite library, a very powerful and cutting-edge visualization library for JavaScript called **D3**, standing for data-driven documents. D3 is the state of the art when it comes to creating custom interactive data visualizations in the web browser using SVG, HTML, and CSS, from basic ones such as bar or pie charts to more complex ones as well. It's important to note that D3 does not introduce new visual representations but solely makes use of existing ones and focuses exclusively on transforming them.

Before starting to describe the library in detail, it's paramount to understand some fundamentals around visual representations and why the library leverages SVGs to create data visualizations.

SVG

D3.js makes heavy use of **SVG**, which stands for **Scalable Vector Graphics**. SVG is a way for web browsers to render images on the web. While not an image itself, it scales vectors to recreate visual components which, if using different screen sizes, scale accordingly. Data visualizations make a good use case for SVGs and, as such, are the main driver behind D3.js. To start off, a new SVG canvas needs to be created on which various elements can be drawn:

```
<svg width="400" height="400"></svg>
```

To draw a circle on top of the newly created SVG canvas, simply add the `<circle>` element to it:

```
<svg width="400" height="400">
   <circle cx="200" cy="200" r="50" fill="red">
</svg>
```

This will create a red circle on the middle of the newly created canvas, with cx and cy being the coordinates of the circle's center point, r the radius, and fill the color of the circle. The red circle will look something like the following screenshot:

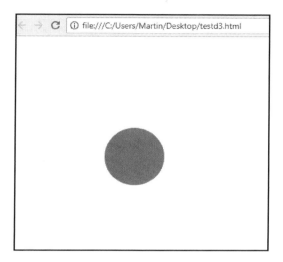

As well as a circle, the following other shapes are also supported within SVG:

- rect: Rectangle element
- ellipse: Ellipse element
- line: Line element connecting two specified points on the canvas
- polyline: A set of connected straight line segments
- polygon: A closed set of connected straight line segments

The special thing about D3 now is that it allows you to bind arbitrary data to SVG elements and thus creates data-driven visualizations.

Selections

Before a transformation can be applied, elements on the template need to be selected in D3, hence selections are a very important aspect of D3 and the first step before applying any logic. Luckily, similar to AngularJS, D3 uses a declarative approach, meaning you can select elements collectively:

```
d3.selectAll("p").style("color", "red");
```

If the D3 library is loaded in the web page, the example would color all paragraph elements in red.

Selecting elements can be done using either d3.select(this) or d3.selectAll(this) where this is the specific element(s) you are attempting to select. The first method, .select(), will just select the first element that matches to the criteria specified in document traversal order. The second method, .selectAll(), will simply select all the elements that match the criteria specified and return them as an array of elements.

enter() and exit()

This is where the magic happens around binding data. In D3.js, once you have selected elements, with the enter() method you are creating nodes (referenced as d in function(d)) for incoming data and with exit() you remove those nodes if they are no longer needed. Taking the following example, all paragraphs are selected and an array of data is entered into the selection. Once the data has been entered, a node is created for each single array element which allows it to loop through each node and apply some logic to it as shown in the following code:

```
<html>
<body>
</body>
<script
src="https://cdnjs.cloudflare.com/ajax/libs/d3/4.13.0/d3.js"></script>
<script>
d3.select("body")
  .selectAll("p")
  .data([4, 8, 15, 16, 23, 42])
  .enter().append("p")
  .text(function(d) {
     //d represents each data node in the array
     return "I'm number " + d + "!";
  });
</script>
```

In the previous example, a new paragraph <p> element is created (by using .append("p")) for each value with the text saying which number it is.

This can, of course, be extended by creating SVG elements based on the available data:

```
<html>
<body>
</body>
</html>
```

```
<script
src="https://cdnjs.cloudflare.com/ajax/libs/d3/4.13.0/d3.js"></script>
<script>
var svg = d3.select("body").append('svg').attr("width",
1000).attr("height", 1000)

 svg.selectAll("circle")
   .data([4, 8, 15, 16, 23, 42])
   .enter().append("circle")
   .attr('cx', 200) //x offset
   .attr('cy', 200) //y offset
   .attr('r', function(d) { return d })
   .style('fill', 'purple')
</script>
```

The code will create six circles with a radius size which is dependent on its array value. And this is how data visualization is created!

 Note we had to select an SVG element first before appending the circles to it, as otherwise, it would not know where to append the circle to and it would not render.

In the current example, our data is fixed, but if it were to dynamically change or update, you would expect circles to be added, or removed, using the exit() method. To create these kinds of interactive data visualizations, a common pattern of update, enter, and exit is used, which can be illustrated as follows:

```
// update...
var p = d3.select("body")
 .selectAll("p")
 .data([4, 8, 15, 16, 23, 42])
 .text(function(d) { return d; });

// Enter...
p.enter().append("p")
 .text(function(d) { return d; });

// Exit...
p.exit().remove();
```

Using this kind of separation makes it easier to specify what kind of actions to take in each scenario, and also illustrates the power of D3: it lets you transform documents based on data, which includes both creating and destroying objects. Also, once the data has been bound to the document, you can omit the data operator going forward; D3 will retrieve the previously bound data and this allows you to reuse properties without rebinding.

Dynamic properties

A fairly familiar concept for readers who have been using jQuery in the past, D3 also allows you to specify properties on elements dynamically. This is an extremely powerful and essential feature of it, as it permits you to apply different styling, positioning, and content to each data node, depending on the values that are passed along:

```
d3.select("body")
 .selectAll("svg")
 .data([4, 8, 15, 16, 23, 42])
 .enter().append("circle")
 .attr('cx', 200) //x offset
 .attr('cy', 200) //y offset
 .attr('r', function(d) {
    //dynamic radius based on data
    return d })
 .attr('fill', function (d) {
    //dynamic coloring based on data
    if(d>15){
     return 'green'
    }else{
     return 'red'
    }
 })
```

Expanding on the example from before, where multiple circle radiuses were created based on their array values, the fill color of each of those circles can be evaluated dynamically based on its value. If the circle value or radius is larger than 15, it will color in green, otherwise in red.

Despite their apparent simplicity, these functions can be surprisingly powerful.

Transitions

Transitions in D3 gradually interpolate styles and attributes over time, giving the change of state in the data visualization a more natural feeling. As you can see how things change, you get a better user experience when interacting with the visuals dynamically. The so-called tweening can be controlled in D3 using different types of animations, such as linear or elastic.

D3's transition method makes it easy to animate transitions of all sorts, from colors to position to the styling of a DOM of the screen. For example, to change the color of a selected DOM element instantaneously, you can apply a styling attribute:

```
d3.select("p").style("color", "blue")
```

Instead, what you can do is animate the change over time using a transition:

```
d3.select("p").transition().style("color", "blue")
```

Transitions can also be applied to positions or shape of SVG elements:

```
d3.selectAll("circle").transition()
.attr("r", function(d) { return Math.sqrt(d); });
```

The preceding snippet will create circles from scratch, resembling dots, and slowly let them grow to their original radius size using the square root of node valued.

D3 takeaways

All in all, D3 is the most popular and core JavaScript library which is used to create compelling visualizations from scratch in Qlik Sense. It helps that it has a massive follower base and open source community, which makes working with the library easier. There are several examples available on the web, such as the famous official D3 Gallery available here: `https://github.com/d3/d3/wiki/Gallery`.

While this book is not meant to teach you proficient D3.js, it will showcase how to integrate a simple D3 visualization into Qlik Sense in `Chapter 13`, *Creating Extensions in Qlik Sense*.

Recommended reading material can be found either on D3's official website, `https://d3js.org/`, with its comprehensive documentation, or Packt even provides useful books on the topic as well, for example, `https://www.packtpub.com/web-development/mastering-d3js`.

Debugging

Debugging is the routine process of identifying, locating, and removing program errors, bugs, or abnormalities. Debugging itself, and finding the issue in the code, is one of the most tedious and challenging tasks in web development. Luckily, most modern browsers now provide comprehensive debugging tools to assist with the development of web code. As it's not trivial to use them though, especially for beginners or developers with no web development background, part of this chapter is dedicated to helping navigate through the debugging process, focusing on the most relevant tools for developing on top of Qlik Sense.

While most browsers provide debugging tools, the author's personal and recommended choice is Google Chrome's Developer Tools.

Diving into the world of F12

Using Google Chrome, you open a website of your choice, wait for it to load, and you press *F12* to get into the Chrome Developer Tools. A window on the right-hand side will appear, squishing your screen a bit:

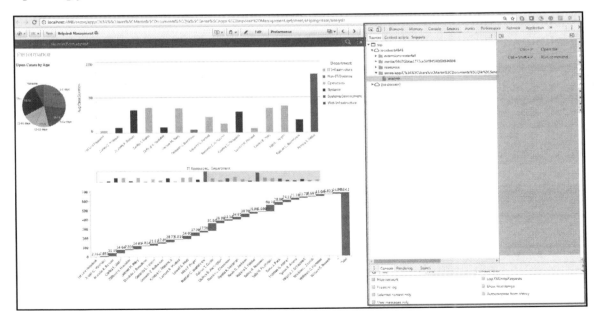

The highlighted box on the right is the Chrome Developer Tool

In there, the first thing you usually see is the **Sources** panel open, which gives you an overview of all loaded files in your current view. It provides you with the folder structure loaded from the server and the underlying files as shown in the following screenshot:

The next most relevant tab is **Elements**, which give you a full overview of the fully rendered HTML code of the current page for inspection. More about this tab is written later in the *Inspecting the DOM* section.

The **Console** tab is where the JavaScript magic happens. It allows you to run JavaScript code to, for example, manipulate the DOM, update the styling, or test various code snippets. Furthermore, errors, `console.log()` output, and warnings will be output in the console log for your information, which is very helpful for identifying and spotting basic issues and bugs with the code:

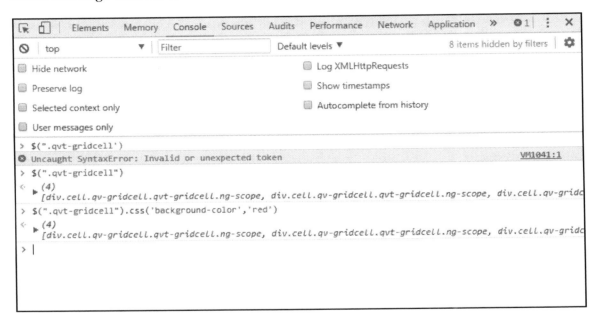

In this example, the first line, a jQuery selector, was invalid due to a syntax issue and the `console.log()` provided information about the error. The next line selected those DOM elements in the correct way, and the third line selected the same DOM elements and updated their `background-color` to be `red`. Changes and updates executed in the console are only temporary: on website refresh, everything will be reset.

The useful thing about the console log, as already mentioned, is the error logging. When the code of the website, or parts of it, won't run, errors are thrown in there, as can be seen in the next example. It not only highlights the underlying JavaScript file where the code is failing but also provides you with the exact line of code. When clicking on it, Chrome's Developer Tools automatically jumps you to the faulty file and line as the following screenshot shows:

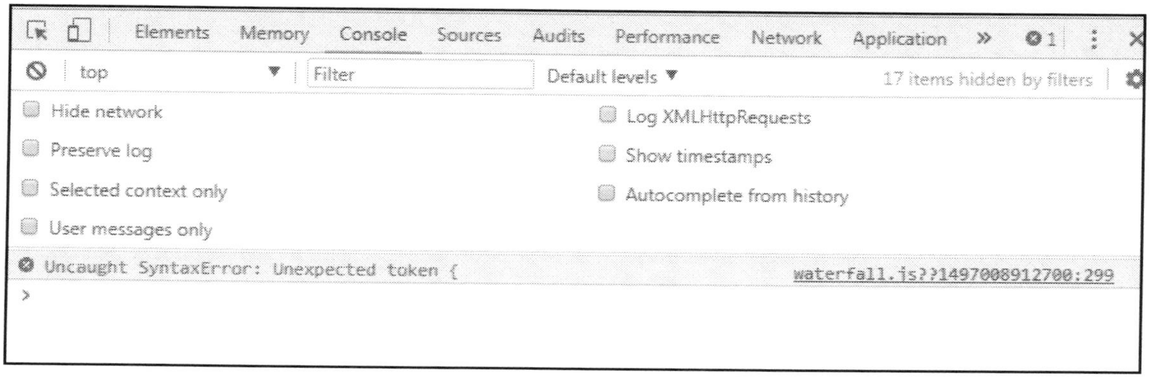

The **Memory** panel helps you conduct memory profiling of your website if you ever ran into memory issues. Especially for data visualization, where memory-consuming data is graphically visualized, memory performance can play an important role, because it solely relies on the end user's browser memory, not the one of the server.

A very similar one is the **Performance** panel, which checks the time required to load a web page, memory consumption, and many more performance aspects, thoroughly scanning every single file and interaction that is being made on the web page. The results are displayed graphically as shown in the following example:

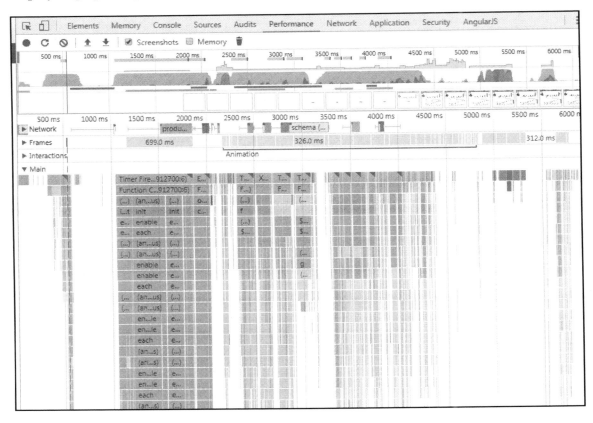

Results displayed using the Performance Panel

The **Network** panel allows you to analyze performance, including traffic which goes in and out of your web application, such as the time to download an external file, WebSockets or classic network latency. The **Application** panel permits you to inspect all resources that are loaded on the web page, including IndexedDB or Web SQL databases, local and session storage, cookies, Application Cache, images, fonts, and style sheets. Lastly, the **Security** panel will help you troubleshoot security-specific problems such as issues with certificates and more.

While lots of features are available in Chrome DevTools, not all of them will be used regularly or at all in the context of developing mashups or extensions for Qlik Sense. Nevertheless, it's recommended to also visit the official website of Chrome DevTools to familiarize yourself with the different settings and possibilities: `https://developers.google.com/web/tools/chrome-devtools/`.

> Make sure you are **disabling the cache** when debugging your code to avoid old changes to persist after you refresh the page.

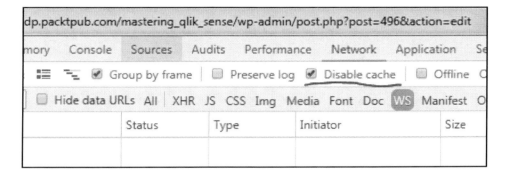

Inspecting the DOM

Inspecting the DOM using the Chrome DevTools represents one of the most important exercises not only for debugging but also for development purposes. As mentioned, the **Elements** panel lets you access the resulting web page and inspect every single element and DOM, up to the extent of allowing you even to modify it, add new tags, or remove parts of it.

> It's important to note that this will only be the resulting DOM structure of a web page at a given time: with different actions and events, the structure can and will always change. Furthermore, copy pasting the HTML code will not allow you to run a copy of the website locally unless you also download all corresponding CSS files.

In this example, we have visually selected a legend marker and the corresponding HTML tab is highlighted in the DOM:

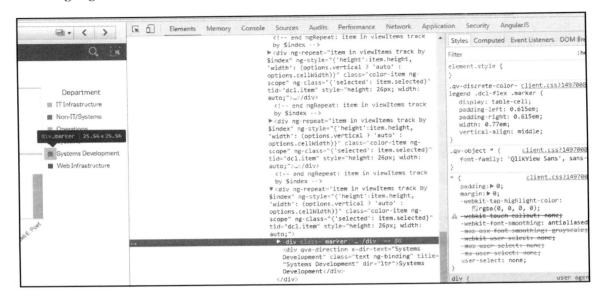

In there, you can now also see the applied CSS styling on that particular DOM. By adding new styling options in on the right-hand side, within the `element.style {}` section, you can update the marker on the fly. This is a useful exercise to see how the styling is changed with certain settings, before adding it to your CSS file.

 You can see many `ng-repeats`, `ng-style`, and `ng-class` directives in the DOM when inspecting a Qlik Sense app. That's AngularJS!

Furthermore, you can also directly fiddle with the HTML code: just right-click on it and it will allow you to move, remove, and update the elements and their attributes:

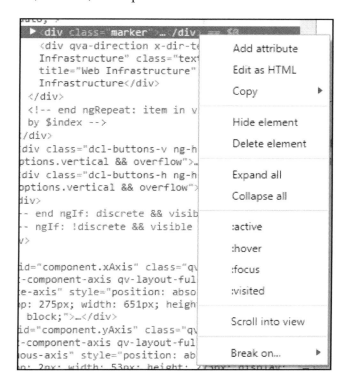

When developing visualizations for Qlik Sense, you'll very likely spend a lot of time on this panel working out issues, testing out new CSS styles, and debugging behaviors when users interact with your objects.

This is actually an interesting point with web apps. As your web browser is effectively the device which renders and executes the code on your screen, you have, in theory, full access to how the website is displayed for you. There are no secrets on the web, as they say, and as such it's very easy to copy templates, ideas, styling, and frontend development code. Also, whenever someone sends you a screenshot of a website as evidence or proof, bear in mind it could always have been modified, just like the following updated Google page!

The following is a screenshot of how a google page and its source code looks like:

Screenshot of a google page and it's source code

Debugging JavaScript code

Simply highlighting where an error occurs rarely is enough to be able to write qualitative and correct code. Sometimes no error is thrown, yet the results rendered on the screen are wrong or inaccurate. To better understand how your JavaScript code is executed, there's a very useful and helpful technique for debugging which is supported by Google Chrome's DevTool.

Adding a breakpoint

To begin debugging your code, you will need to add a breakpoint. A breakpoint is a temporary flag set in the source code which indicates to the browser to pause the execution of the script to then await further instructions by the developer. To set a breakpoint, all you have to do is to navigate to the **Source** panel and go into your loaded code file. In there, you will have the line number available on the left-hand side which will permit you to right-click on it to open up a number of options:

```
383        .attr('height', height + margins.top + margins.bottom)
384        .append("g")
385        .attr("transform", "translate(" + margins.left + "," + marg:
386
387            svg.selectAll("rect")
```

```
Blackbox script

Add breakpoint                     ")

Add conditional breakpoint...      function (d) {
                                   element

Never pause here                   , function (d) {
```

On the selected line number, you can add a breakpoint (indicated in blue), which can also be conditional (indicated in orange):

```
373        .tickFormat(formatScale);
374        var xAxis = d3.svg.axis()
375            .scale(xScale)
376            .orient("bottom");
377
378        var svg = d3.select($element.get(0)).selectAll('svg')
```
The breakpoint on line 378 will stop only if this expression is true:
`i=1`
```
379            .data([null])
380            .enter()
381            .append('svg')
382            .attr('width', width + margins.left + margins.right)
383            .attr('height', height + margins.top + margins.bottom)
384            .append("g")
385            .attr("transform", "translate(" + margins.left + "," + margi
386
387        svg.selectAll("rect")
388            .data(data)
389            .enter()
390            .append("rect")
```

Conditional breakpoint

Normal breakpoint

While the focus here is on debugging the script, you can freely also add breakpoints on to your DOM in the Elements panel when right-clicking on it as per the screenshot. This will allow you to break the execution of the code when DOMs are changing, which can be essential when debugging interactivity:

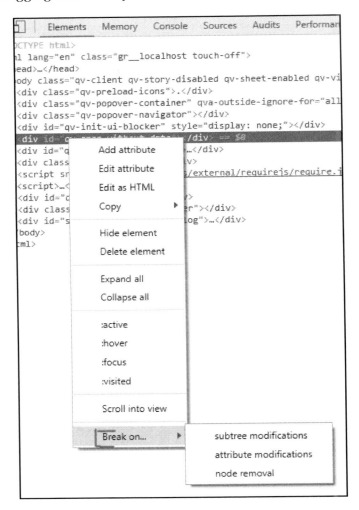

You can also create a breakpoint for the debugger by adding a `debugger` statement into your JavaScript code.

Debugging the breakpoint

When the breakpoint is added, all you need to do is to refresh your web page while keeping the Chrome DevTools open and wait for the code to execute. Once the breakpoint is activated, the browser will stop executing your code and prompt you for an action:

At the same time, Chrome DevTools will automatically jump into the script file where the breakpoint was activated and highlight to you the line of code. When in debug mode, the script editor will help you as much as possible, by showing you in light orange the evaluated variables and expressions that are being used in the code, as follows:

Now that the code is in debug mode, you typically have three options for how to proceed:

- **Inspect** the current state of the DOM, the $scope and variables, to see whether the code is being executed and behaving as expected. You can easily move over to the **Console** panel and you can investigate the state of the code by running the variables in there.

- **Modify** the code by manually executing code in the **Console** panel or by manipulating the DOM in the **Elements** panel. While not recommended, it can sometimes be helpful to quickly see how tiny changes affect the remaining execution of the script.

- **Run the debugger** by now executing the remaining code line by line. This is the most common use case when investigating the code for bugs and errors to see how and where they are occurring.

Running the debugger

Running the debugger gives you a couple of useful tools on how you like to continue executing your code after a break point to ensure you become efficient in discovering the error or bug. These tools are represented as icons when you are located in debug mode:

These are explained from left to right as follows:

- The **play** button (keyboard shortcut *F8*) resumes the script execution and will simply continue executing your code until it's finished or the next breakpoint is reached.
- The **curved arrow** (keyboard shortcut *F10*) will permit you to run the code and step over the current function call and pause again on the next available function. This is useful if you want to skip large function calls you are confident are working fine.
- The **bottom arrow** (keyboard shortcut *F11*) steps you into the next function call. Think of it as drilling down into the function and executing the code line by line. This is particularly useful if you want to thoroughly analyze a function or method.
- The **top arrow** (keyboard shortcut *Shift + F11*) steps you **out** of the existing function call. This is particularly useful when you have loops in your function and you wish to move over to the next part of your code without having to click your way through each iteration.
- The **crossed breakpoint** (keyboard shortcut *Ctrl + F8*) deactivates all your breakpoints and resumes executing the code.
- The **stop icon** lets you pause the code in the same fashion as breakpoints but on exceptions. Sometimes you may have a console error but have no idea where or how the exception was thrown. You can have the dev tools immediately break at uncaught or caught exceptions by clicking on this icon.

 It takes a while to get familiar with the Chrome DevTool debugging process, but it's worth investing the time to understand it properly as it can save you lots of nerves and development time further down the line when developing your code.

Some developers might have a preference for using `console.log()` in the script code for debugging purposes. While it can also help with the investigation, there are some caveats with it; for example, when a variable is modified and updated in due course of the script execution, `console.log` will display the last changed value, regardless of where it's positioned in the code. This can be misleading.

Inspecting the Qlik Sense API WebSocket

WebSockets are the main gateway for extensions, mashups, and web apps to communicate with the Qlik Engine via the APIs. Luckily, with Chrome DevTools, you are able to monitor the API calls and see what is being sent on any action and what the Qlik Engine returns as an object. For some, the Qlik Engine API can appear as a black box which does what it wants, and the poor documentation as of today does not help with it either. Inspecting the Qlik Sense API WebSocket communication helps to demystify the calls made, which facilitates the development efforts to a large extent. Also, the Qlik Engine API explorer, which is described in `Chapter 11`, *Working with the Qlik Dev Hub*, is very useful if you want to explore its methods.

To inspect the communication with the Qlik Engine, all you need to do is to navigate to the **Network** panel and select WS from the list of filters:

If you have not already started recording your network traffic, please do so by initiating recording. A red circle on the top left of the panel will indicate whether it's active.

Once the recording has begun, start interacting with your Qlik Sense app to fire API calls. If you click on the name of the WebSocket, located in the first column from the left-hand side called **Name**, a new window will open up and show you all available API calls, and whether or not they are outgoing or incoming:

In the overview, you can then conveniently select every single call, and inspect what JSON structure was sent to the Qlik Engine, and what JSON response the Qlik Engine returned. The following is an example of a request, and thereafter its corresponding response:

```
|{"jsonrpc":"2.0","id":55,"delta":true,"result":{"qLayout":[{"op":"add","path":"/","value":{"qInfo":{"qId":"ChAzpy",...   ...  00:47:02.904
|{"method":"GetListObjectData","handle":21,"params":["/qListObjectDef",[{"qTop":0,"qLeft":0,"qHeight":4,"qWi...   ...  00:47:03.396
|{"jsonrpc":"2.0","id":56,"delta":true,"result":{"qDataPages":[{"op":"add","path":"/","value":[{"qMatrix":[[{"qText":...   ...  00:47:03.446
|{"method":"GetLocaleInfo","handle":1,"params":[],"delta":false,"jsonrpc":"2.0","id":57}   ...  00:47:03.668
|{"jsonrpc":"2.0","id":57,"result":{"qReturn":{"qDecimalSep":".","qThousandSep":",","qListSep":",","qMoneyDeci...   ...  00:47:03.688

▼ {method: "GetListObjectData", handle: 21,…}
    delta: true
    handle: 21
    id: 56
    jsonrpc: "2.0"
    method: "GetListObjectData"
  ▼ params: ["/qListObjectDef", [{qTop: 0, qLeft: 0, qHeight: 4, qWidth: 1}]]
      0: "/qListObjectDef"
    ▼ 1: [{qTop: 0, qLeft: 0, qHeight: 4, qWidth: 1}]
      ▼ 0: {qTop: 0, qLeft: 0, qHeight: 4, qWidth: 1}
          qHeight: 4
          qLeft: 0
          qTop: 0
          qWidth: 1
```

This is the response:

```
|{"jsonrpc":"2.0","id":56,"delta":true,"result":{"qDataPages":[{"op":"add","path":"/","value":[{"qMatrix":[[{"qText":...   ...  00:47:03.446
|{"method":"GetLocaleInfo","handle":1,"params":[],"delta":false,"jsonrpc":"2.0","id":57}   ...  00:47:03.668
|{"jsonrpc":"2.0","id":57,"result":{"qReturn":{"qDecimalSep":".","qThousandSep":",","qListSep":",","qMoneyDeci...   ...  00:47:03.688

▼ {jsonrpc: "2.0", id: 56, delta: true, result: {qDataPages: [{op: "add", path: "/",…}]}}
    delta: true
    id: 56
    jsonrpc: "2.0"
  ▼ result: {qDataPages: [{op: "add", path: "/",…}]}
    ▼ qDataPages: [{op: "add", path: "/",…}]
      ▼ 0: {op: "add", path: "/",…}
          op: "add"
          path: "/"
        ▼ value: [{qMatrix: [[{qText: "1/2/2004", qNum: 37988, qElemNumber: 447, qState: "O"}],…], qTails: [],…}]
          ▼ 0: {qMatrix: [[{qText: "1/2/2004", qNum: 37988, qElemNumber: 447, qState: "O"}],…], qTails: [],…}
            ▶ qArea: {qLeft: 0, qTop: 0, qWidth: 1, qHeight: 4}
            ▶ qMatrix: [[{qText: "1/2/2004", qNum: 37988, qElemNumber: 447, qState: "O"}],…]
              qTails: []
```

The view of inspecting WebSocket network communication is of immense value when exploring the possibilities and functionality of the Qlik engine, which helps check whether or not the API calls were made correctly, and what the responding JSON structure looks like, for additional processing in the JavaScript code.

Summary

Coding in Qlik Sense requires a good understanding of web development and a knowledge of the relevant libraries. Especially for users who do not have a software development background, this chapter provides them with a crash course of what is relevant in Qlik Sense and why. The same applies to QlikView developers and consultants who might have a technical background in Qlik but are embarking on the web development journey for the very first time. This chapter, while extensive, provided you with a good understanding of the triangle of web development, which consists of CSS, JavaScript, and HTML. While it won't make you an expert straight away, you will generally be able to understand the lingo and the relationship between these three core languages.

As with many other programming languages, JavaScript, and web development benefit greatly from freely available open source libraries. Getting a little more technical, you were introduced to the most relevant JS-based libraries used in Qlik Sense and the chapter also explained how they work and why they are essential to Qlik Sense and to extended development on top of the Qlik API. You should be able to talk about AngularJS, D3, and RequireJS and, if required, know where to get additional training or knowledge.

To summarize the overview, this chapter showed you how debugging works when doing web development. It's an integral skill set to know how to quickly find your errors and fix them, as well as navigate through the produced code. Especially in Qlik, there will be a lot of dependencies on existing modules and codes, so being able to easily demystify the whole web app using Chrome's DevTools will take your fears away from web development and make it more fun and less frustrating to work with.

It's important to note, however, that this overview will not be able to turn you into an expert. It is high level and it's strongly advised to conduct additional reading or tutorials on JavaScript or the libraries to become more proficient at Qlik Sense. As much as reading helps, learning to code is best done when developing your own projects: play around, contribute to open source projects, and don't be afraid to delve into JavaScript-it will be very rewarding in the long term.

Equipped with an overview of how to code in Qlik Sense, the next chapters will introduce you to basic development of Qlik extensions and mashups where all of these concepts and libraries are used.

13

Creating Extensions in Qlik Sense

Extensions in Qlik Sense offer the beautiful opportunity to extend your Qlik Sense user experience by creating bespoke data visualizations, objects, or control elements that interact with the powerful Qlik data engine. It's mainly useful when you have a particular use case in mind, or you have seen a great visualization that you would like to implement in Qlik to visualize your data. Furthermore, sometimes advanced use cases exceed the native capabilities of Qlik Sense and require you to introduce custom objects to facilitate some niche requirements.

Luckily, with Qlik Sense and a basic knowledge of web development, this is not very difficult to achieve, and, with a little bit of practice, the possibilities on top of the Qlik Engine have no limits. To get you there, you have so far in this book internalized the basic concepts of web development, which will be vital to understanding this chapter. As such, it will not go into too much detail on how and why the code is used in specific ways. It will focus more on actually introducing you to web development but within Qlik Sense, bringing the structure of a Qlik extension closer to you and deepening your knowledge of Qlik APIs, in particular, the Extension API.

In detail, this chapter will cover the following relevant aspects:

- Structuring the code of your extension project
- Best practice and the dos and don'ts of extending your Qlik Sense apps
- Designing and creating a user-friendly property panel to change the settings of your charts dynamically

- The details of a `qHyperCube` structure, its definition, and the returned results
- A step-by-step guide to creating a D3 bar chart example from scratch
- A step-by-step guide to creating a drop-down component example from scratch for selecting filter values
- Introduction to some platforms where you can find useful and open source code for your projects

Structuring your code

It's always tempting to just go ahead and start coding right away, and I won't deny it's the most fun part of any project. However, as your extension projects grow and become more complicated, the technical debt of quick wins and fast fixes will take its toll. As such, it's important to begin each extension project by defining a proper code structure to ensure the project is prepared to scale.

To begin with, in each extension, you can expect to have the following basic files at a minimum. We'll be using MasteringQS as a sample extension name:

- `MasteringQS.qext` *(required)*
- `MasteringQS.js` *(required)*
- `MasteringQS.css` *(optional)*
- `wbfolder.wbl` *(optional)*

Name	Änderungsdatum	Typ	Größe
MasteringQS.css	31/12/2017 23:29	Kaskadierendes St...	0 KB
MasteringQS.js	31/12/2017 23:29	JScript-Skriptdatei	0 KB
MasteringQS.qext	31/12/2017 23:29	QEXT-Datei	0 KB
wbfolder.wbl	17/11/2017 03:50	WBL-Datei	1 KB

While some files are optional, for the purposes of this chapter, we will include them.

The .qext file

The .qext file is the definition file of each extension that defines its metadata and how it's being read by the Qlik Sense Repository as well as its Asset or Library Panel. This file ultimately determines how it's displayed on the left-hand panel within edit mode, and it's important to note that it has to have the same filename as the corresponding primary JavaScript file.

 The .qext file and main **JavaScript** of the extension must have the same name.

The qext file is a simple text file and, as such, can be edited with any notepad, and needs to define its metadata in a JSON format, for example:

```
{
    "name": "Mastering QS Example",
    "description": "This is a description",
    "preview": "masteringqs.png",
    "type": "visualization",
    "version": 1,
    "author": "Martin Mahler"
}
```

The preceding information is a shortened version of what can be defined in detail:

Name	Options	Description
name	N/A	Mandatory. Name of the visualization displayed in the library. It is recommended to use a unique name for the visualization to avoid interference with other visualizations that may have the same name.
type	N/A	Mandatory. Should always be *visualization*.
description	N/A	Description displayed in the library. The default is extension.
extension	✦	N/A

bar-chart-vertical	▮▮▮	N/A
line-chart	📈	N/A
pie-chart	◗	N/A
gauge-chart	◔	N/A
scatter-chart	⁖	N/A
text-image	**A**	N/A
table	▦	N/A
list	▤	N/A
filterpane	◰	N/A
treemap	▦	N/A
preview	[CustomImage].png	Defines the preview image to be used. The preview image is displayed in a popup when you select the visualization in the library. You can define a custom preview image file. It must be of .png file format. If the preview is undefined, the icon definition will be used.
version	NA	Defines your individual version handling of the extension. This setting is manually defined.
author	NA	Defines the author of the visualization. This parameter is manually assigned.

In addition to the preceding, you can freely leverage the .qext file to pass on additional information to the extension. While not used in Qlik Sense itself, they can later be called upon in the qHyperCube. Other metadata that is typically added is license, release date, home page, dependencies (QS version required to run), and so on.

The JavaScript file

This is the core JavaScript file, which is being picked up and read by Qlik Sense as well as your browser. It needs to carry the name of the extension as the name, and it needs to match the `.qext` file. Otherwise, it will not work. For loading the JavaScript file, RequireJS is being used, and, as such the following basic structure needs to be maintained:

```
define([],
    function() {
    return {
            paint: function ($element, layout) {
                $element.html("This is Mastering Qlik Sense");
            }
    };
});
```

This is a fundamental structure, which can be extended to include the following additional elements:

```
define([],
    function() {
    return {
            paint: function(){},
            resize: function(){},
            initialproperties: {},
            updateData: function(){}, //Feb 18'
            definition: properties,
            importProperties: function(){},
            showRequirements: function(){},
            support: {},
            getExportRawDataOptions: function(){},
            controller: [],
            template: HTMLtemplate,
            }
    };
});
```

Bear in mind that you should always decide whether you wish your extension to be implemented using Angular (using controller and template) or the `paint()` method. You shouldn't have both at the same time. Which one you end up choosing is up to you!

Having said that, it's highly recommended to use the AngularJS approach wherever possible as it's much more stable and controllable and has many more possibilities on offer.

The paint() method

The `paint()` method is used to render the visualization. It will be called every time the chart should be rendered (for example, when new selections have been made) or when the extension was resized.

It includes two main parameters:

- `$element`, which is the jQuery wrapper that contains the part where the visualization is rendered
- `layout`, which stores data and properties for the visualization, including metadata, as mentioned earlier

The resize method

The resize method is invoked whenever the elements on the Qlik Sense client are resized. In technical terms, it listens to the `resize()` event invoked by the API by calling `qlik.resize`.

Using `resize()` allows you to separate the treatment of a change in size and change in the model (data, properties, and selections).

If `resize()` is implemented, `paint()` is not called! Hence, you need to call `paint()` in your `resize()` function:

```
resize: function ($element, layout) {
    this.paint($element, layout);
},
```

initialProperties

`initialProperties` specifies the properties of your visualization or extension object when it is first created. You can use either the `qHyperCubeDef` or `qListObjectDef`, which will be elaborated on later in this chapter. One example of such a property setting is as follows:

```
initialProperties : {
    qHyperCubeDef : {
        qDimensions : [],
        qMeasures : [],
        qInitialDataFetch : [{
            qWidth : 2,
```

```
        qHeight : 50
    }]
  }
}
```

Naturally, you want to leave the `qDimensions` and `qMeasures` blocks empty, as you want to give the user the ability to define those via the property panel. However, the `qInitialDataFetch` property can be useful to be set at this point as it defines the size of the underlying data that the extension retrieves from the Qlik Engine.

More about the `qHyperCubeDef` and `qListObjectDef` structure can be found in the course of this chapter.

definition

`definition` is where the property panel is defined and rendered when the user is in **edit** mode. A separate section is dedicated to this, as it plays a very relevant role when building extensions as well as for the user experience.

importProperties

This is an advanced and unsupported method but it is sometimes required in certain scenarios. This method is called when you drag your extension over an existing one and **convert** it in the Qlik Sense Client.

Normally, the `qHyperCubeDef` definition is inherited from the existing object; however, sometimes additional settings are required. `importProperties` allows you to define default properties for the case when default properties are required in your extension that are not present in the existing object.

getExportRawDataOptions

The same as with `importProperties`, this is not officially supported, but this method is being called when you right-click on the object. Export settings or even add new features that become relevant on right-click can be implemented using this method.

support

`support` allows you to define which of the native Qlik Sense supporting features should be made available in the extension:

```
support: {
    snapshot: true,
    export: true,
    exportData: true
}
```

`snapshot` allows you to take snapshots, which can then be added to your Qlik Sense Stories.

`export` enables the exporting of your extension as an image, PDF, or PowerPoint. When set to `true`, the following options are available on right-click:

- Export as an image
- Export to PDF
- Export story to PowerPoint
- Export story to PDF

`ExportData` enables you to export the underlying HyperCube or list objects to XLS.

controller and template

`controller` and `template` are the standard AngularJS components required to render an extension using AngularJS. Both have already been comprehensively explained in Chapter 11, *Coding in Qlik Sense*.

When using AngularJS, the basic structure of your code compared to the `paint` approach looks as follows:

```
define(['text!./template.html'],
    function(template) {
    return {
        paint: function(){},
        resize: function(){},
        template: template,
        controller: ['$scope', '$element', function (scope, $element) {
            console.log("This is Mastering Qlik Sense");
        }
    };
});
```

The equivalent of `layout` in the `paint()` method can be found in `$scope.layout` object.

 It's important to note there's a downside to the AngularJS approach. In the previous example, the code will only run once and will not respond to resize or selection events, which is crucial if you wish to update your visualization based on the selections which are being made on the dashboard. As such, additional functions need to be added to the code which captures this event. On the bright side, this gives you more control of how the extension is rendered, including the ability to implement D3 transitions.

Loading Resources

When developing extensions within Qlik Sense, you can reference many already existing JavaScript libraries that are being loaded with the Qlik Sense AngularJS module and are presently available in your scope. You can load these resources at the top of your extension code, using the following approach:

```
define( [ /* dependencies */ ],
    function ( /* returned dependencies as arguments */ )
    { ... }
);
```

For example, if you wish to include jQuery or d3 in your extension, all you need to do is reference them in the definition part. Extending the previous code sample, it would look as follows:

```
define(['text!./template.html', 'jQuery', 'd3'],
    function(template, $, d3) {
        return {
            paint: function(){},
            resize: function(){},
            template: template,
            controller: ['$scope', '$element', function (scope, $element) {
                $element.html("This is Mastering Qlik Sense");
            }
        };
});
```

This would load the jQuery and d3 modules, which can then later be referenced in the code using the $ and d3 variables.

Make sure to keep the order of loaded reference libraries consistent with the order in which the variables are defined in the function(), for example: `function(template, $, d3)` mixing the order up is one of the most common errors.

Furthermore, you can use RequireJS to load many more resources of different kinds, such as the following:

- Style sheets / CSS files
- JavaScript libraries (see the previous example)
- Images
- Fonts
- Items from the content library

The most relevant local resources that can be loaded straightaway are the following:

- jQuery
- d3v4
- Qlik (to use the Engine API)
- AngularJS

When using local resources, be aware that you will need to import them when deploying your extension to a mashup or web application that is not hosted on the Qlik Sense server.

Bear in mind that the **Extension API** and the **Backend API** are automatically loaded and available, and they do not need to be explicitly referenced in the extension code.

The properties panel

The properties panel is, in the author's opinion, one of the most valuable things about extensions in Qlik Sense and the general extensibility of the product as a whole. The property panel is the configuration interface between the JavaScript code and the self-service user or developer.

As such, it is essential to leverage and understand the property definition file.

First and foremost, it is recommended and best practice to capture the property definition in a separate file and load it via RequireJS to your main JavaScript file. This is done fairly simply by creating a new JavaScript file in the folder structure, suggested to be called `properties.js`:

In the `MasteringQS.js` file, you load the properties module by defining it in the top of the file structure:

```
//MasteringQS.js
define(['./properties', 'text!./template.html'],
    function(properties, template) {
    return {
        definition: properties,
        paint: function(){},
        resize: function(){},
        template: template,
        controller: ['$scope', '$element', function (scope, $element) {
            $element.html("This is Mastering Qlik Sense");
        }]
    };
});
```

The `properties.js` file, on the other hand, needs to also include the RequireJS definition and return a definition object:

```
//properties.js
define([],
    function(){
        return {
            type: "items",
            component: "accordion",
            items: {
                dimensions: {
                    uses: "dimensions"
                },
                measures: {
```

```
                            uses: "measures"
                    },
                    sorting: {
                        uses: "sorting"
                    },
                    addons: {
                        uses: "addons"
                    },
                    settings: {
                        uses: "settings"
                    }
                }
            };
    });
```

That's all that is required, and the property definition file is loaded in your extension:

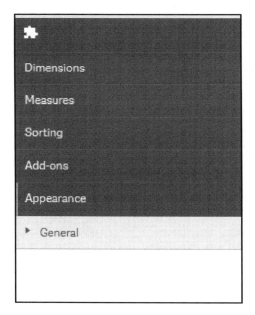

Reusable property components

Now, you might have noticed that the `properties.js` file content utilizes a lot of `uses` properties. These are Qlik's default reusable objects and allow you to quickly add most common properties panel settings to your extensions.

`dimensions` include the following properties:

- Ability to add/remove dimensions as an array
- Define the dimension or add a calculated dimension
- Dimension label
- Checkbox to include null values
- Dimension limitation options

`measures` include the following properties:

- Ability to add/remove measures as an array
- Define the measure
- Measure label
- Measure formatting settings

`sorting` includes the following properties:

- The ability to define the sort order of the dimensions, with multiple options on sort types (numerically, alphabetically)

`addons` include the following properties:

- Calculation conditions, which specify whether the extension object is calculated based on a condition
- Show/hide zero values

`settings` provide you with a predefined General tab, which includes the following properties:

- Show/hide titles
- Title, subtitle, footnote
- Show/hide details

It's recommended to use those properties wherever possible to save time when developing your components.

Defining custom property components

Ideally, you should implement every single thing that can change on your visualization as a setting for your users and developers. This permits reusability of your work and catering for multiple use cases, which means a higher return and value-add for your development work.

While the reusable Qlik property provides you with a head start, building a user-friendly and comprehensive property panel can be just as valuable as the extension itself. The following example is taken from the Vizlib Table property panel to illustrate the value-add of custom property components:

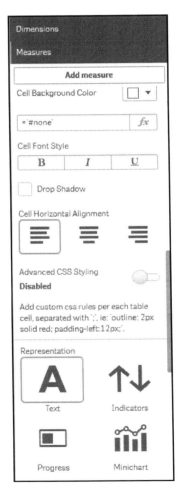

Thankfully, there are several available custom control components available to be used out of the box, which are all based on Qlik's Leonardo UI open source library and are described in this chapter.

The following on from the example structure from the `properties.js` file defined before, we are going to expand on the `settings` property, and extend it with an itemized list:

```
settings: {
    uses: "settings",
    items: {
        MyStringProp: {
        ref: "props.title",
        expression: "optional",
        label: "My string property",
        type: "string",
        component: "text box",
        defaultValue: "MyNewExtension"
        }
}
```

This is a sample string component that permits the user to define a string value property. Let's look at it in a bit more detail:

- `ref` defines the reference value of the property in the `qHyperCubeDef` within the extension. It's important that this value is unique and not reused for other properties, as this will cause your property panel to fail.

It is recommended to store all your properties in a separate object (props in this example) to avoid clashes with other native property settings.

- `expression` specifies whether this component can take on a Qlik expression. In this case, it is `"optional"`, but `"always"` is also available as an option. If empty or omitted, the component will not accept Qlik expressions.
- `label` represents the title of the component how it is represented in the property panel section.
- `type` defines the variable type of the property. It can be a string, number, integer, boolean, or object, and the component will ensure only valid types are entered.

- `defaultValue` defines the default value of the reference value.
- `component` defines which type of available control element is utilized to help the user set the reference value. If a component is empty, it automatically defaults to a textbox.

 As you can see, the custom properties are defined using the JSON format structure, and, as such, you need to be very careful with the use of your curly brackets and always ensure you are closing them appropriately. A good text editor (sublime for example) can help with the troubles

Custom components

To be able to create a user-friendly property panel, the full arsenal of **LUI (Leonardo UI)** icons is available to be implemented, such as arrays, buttons, checkboxes, drop-down lists, sliders, switch, button groups, and much more, which makes the setting of properties a straightforward thing.

In detail, the following components are available for use natively:

- Button
- Button group
- Checkbox
- Color-picker
- Drop-down list
- Input box/textbox
- Link
- Media
- Radio button
- Range slider
- Slider
- Switch
- Text
- Text area

We won't go too much into detail of each one of them, as these are described best on the official Qlik Sense site, but components can be grouped into sections and headers in the properties panel. Each of them exposes different configuration options to manipulate their behavior.

Taking the drop-down list, for example, it would look as follows, as defined in the property panel:

```
MasteringQSdrop-down: {
    type: "string",
    component: "drop-down",
    label: "Text Alignment",
    ref: "drop-downproperty",
    options: [{
        value: "v",
        label: "Vertical"
    }, {
        value: "h",
        label: "Horizontal"
    }],
    defaultValue: "v"
    },
}
```

Here is the result of the preceding code example:

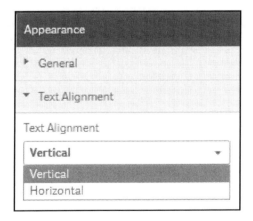

Creating your own components using AngularJS

Furthermore, if you require a very special component that is not available by default within Qlik Sense, you can easily embed your own AngularJS code and control how the property is set. Bear in mind that this is very advanced stuff, but to illustrate how this can be built, see the following example:

```
MasteringQSAngularComponent: {
    label: "AngularJS Component",
    type: "string",
    component: {
        template: '<div class="VizlibFilter-proppanel-title">{{label}}</div>',
        controller: ["$scope", "$element", function(scope, $element){
            scope.label = 'Hello there'
        }]
    }
}
```

This results in a fundamental text template:

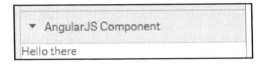

Creating your own components is undoubtedly advanced stuff and not really recommended, as the effort involved rarely justifies the value-add. Try using the native Qlik Sense property components as much as possible.

Using custom array items

Array items are particularly useful when you want to give the user the ability to dynamically define several items of the same kind in their visualizations. A good example use case for this is reference lines in a line chart. The user may not need reference lines at all or may want to add one, two, or multiple lines to their chart.

The custom array component helps you define the collection of reference lines into a JavaScript array, which can then be read by the extension code. The general structure, based on a reference line example, looks as follows:

```
settings: {
    uses: "settings",
    items: {
        horizontalReference: {
            type: "array",
            ref: "listItems",
            label: "Horizontal Reference Line",
            itemTitleRef: "reflabel",
            allowAdd: true,
            allowRemove: true,
            addTranslation: "Add Reference Line",
            items: {
                label: {
                    type: "string",
                    ref: "reflabel",
                    label: "Reference Line Label",
                    expression: "optional"
                },
                refvalue: {
                    label:"Reference Value",
                    type: "number",
                    ref: "refvalue"
                }
            }
        }
    }
}
```

The itemTitleRef value **must** reference the reflabel in the item list to make sure the correct title is used for the array time.

The result will look as follows:

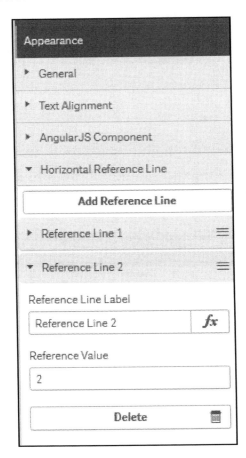

In the HyperCube, you can then read the resulting array:

```
>  scope.layout.listItems
<  ▼ (2) [{…}, {…}]
      ▶ 0: {reflabel: "Reference Line 1", refvalue: 1, cId: "AJWUS"}
      ▶ 1: {reflabel: "Reference Line 2", refvalue: 2, cId: "emyKutr"}
        length: 2
      ▶ __proto__: Array(0)
```

Qlik's HyperCube will be described later in the chapter.

The custom array component has several fields and settings, which are explained in detail in the following table:

Field	Description
type	This field is mandatory for array types and should always be defined as array.
label	Used for defining the label that is displayed in the property panel.
component	This field should not be used for array types.
ref	Name or ID used to reference a property.
itemTitleRef	Used for defining the title of the section items.
allowAdd	Boolean. Value true adds a button for adding new items.
allowRemove	Boolean. Value true adds a **Delete** button.
addTranslation	Used for defining a label of the button used to add new items.
allowMove	Boolean. true enables the ability to move the accordion item in the properties panel.

Unfortunately, the array component is considered to be *experimental* by Qlik as of the time of writing and may be subject to change or be removed in future releases.

Best practice on property panels

Working several years with Qlik Sense extensions, some best practices have been established, which are based on distilled experience covering the following:

- User experience
- Reusability of code
- Maintainability

User experience

Before you just crack on with adding tens of property settings, spend some time designing the user experience and the flow on how a user can navigate and meaningfully define its parameters. The purpose of a well-designed property panel is to promote reusability of the same code base for different use cases. User adoption is critical to the success of an extension, and it must be easy to use, with as little training as possible. Qlik Sense has powerful self-service capabilities, and for them to be appropriately leveraged, extension objects need to be just as easy to use.

As such, the following are some tips to focus on when working on the property panel, which will improve the user experience:

- Use Qlik Sense custom components, such as sliders, button groups, and drop-down lists as much as possible.
- Put the most relevant extension settings in the General Settings tabs. Split individual settings into sub-categories.
- Follow the user flow when defining extensions: they begin with dimensions, then metrics, then design and appearance. Make sure relevant settings are found in the respective sections of the property panel.
- If a user has to ask you where to find a particular property- rethink the property panel.
- If there is a discussion during requirements gathering whether a chart should have this feature or not-implement it as an option in the property panel and make it dynamic.

Expressions

Try to leverage the powerful associative Qlik Engine as much as you can by implementing your settings as expressions as much as possible. This will allow your users to use Qlik expressions, variables, and even dynamically define your chart properties using conditions. Variables, in particular, are a compelling reason to have each setting available set as an expression because you can then control settings of multiple charts of the same kind across an app or a collection of apps via variables—this reduces technical debt.

The challenge here lies in the fact that sliders, button groups, and other native custom components that improve the user experience do not support expressions. As such, one way to overcome the limitation is to use two components for each property, one for a user-friendly handling and another one sitting below, which is used to help define the property as an expression, for example:

```
fontSizeSlider: {
    type: "number",
    component: "slider",
    label: "Font Size (px)",
    ref: "FontSizeSliderValue",
    min: 10,
    max: 20,
    step: 1,
    defaultValue: 15
    change: function(prop){
        //Sets the fontSize variable based on the slider value.
        prop.fontSize = prop.FontSizeSliderValue
    }
},
fontSize: {
    type: "integer",
    expression: "optional",
    ref: "fontSize",
    defaultValue: 15
}
```

In the preceding example, you would then reference fontSize in the code.

Grouping your properties

Grouping helps to better organize your properties to the benefit of the end user as well as the developer.

Using variables in the properties panel

Earlier in the chapter, the `properties.js` file was described as holding all properties in one big JSON file. Try splitting that into its own segments and define them as variables which are later returned as a JSON file:

```
//properties.js
define([],
    function(){
        var dimensions = {
                uses: "dimensions"
            }
        var measures = {
                uses: "measures"
            }
        var sorting = {
                uses: "sorting"
            }
        var sorting = {
                uses: "sorting"
            }
        var addons= {
                uses: "addons"
            }
        var settings = {
                uses : "settings"
            }
    return {
        type: "item",
        component: "accordion",
        items: {
            dimension: dimensions,
            measures: measures,
            sorting: sorting,
            addons: addons,
            settings: settings
        }
    }
})
```

Defining related properties of objects

Rather than having entirely separate variables for every single property, try to logically group them into related objects, for example:

- `titlesettings.fontsize`

- `titlesettings.fontfamily`

- `titlesettings.show`

- `titlesettings.color`

- `titlesettings.bgcolor`

This will make the returned `layout` less messy and will help you find the properties faster.

Grouping properties in the panel

By organizing your property panel into items and allowing them to get groups, you can visually segregate your property panel:

```
FontProperties: {
    type: "items",
    label: 'Font Properties',
    grouped: true,
    items: {
      group1: {
        type:'items',
        items: {
          fontSizeSlider: {
            type: "number",
            component: "slider",
            label: "Font Size (px)",
            ref: "FontSizeSliderValue",
            min: 10,
            max: 20,
            step: 1,
            defaultValue: 15,
            change: function(prop){
                prop.fontSize = prop.FontSizeSliderValue
            }
          },
          fontSize: {
            type: "integer",
```

```
                expression: "optional",
                ref: "fontSize",
                defaultValue: 15
            }
        }
    },
    group2: {
        type:'items',
        items: {
          fontFamily: {
              label: "Font Family",
              type: "string",
              expression: "optional",
              ref: "fontfamily"
          }
        }
    }
  }
}
```

These will generate the following grouped view in the property panel:

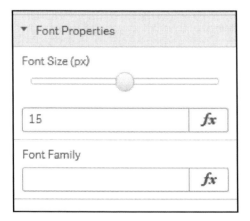

HyperCube

The HyperCube can be considered the heart of most visualizations. It's the cube definition provided to the Qlik Data Engine, which holds all information on which data is queried and how it is calculated. If selections are applied to a HyperCube, only the selected values are displayed.

A HyperCube can be visually imagined like a reqular Straight Table in Qlik, with a collection of dimensions and metrics as well as additional attributes.

As it's effectively describing how all data is processed, the `qHyperCubeDef` object plays a significant role in building visualizations or other components that heavily rely on the Qlik engine for calculation.

qHyperCubeDef

`qHyperCubeDef` is the definition object that is passed on to the Qlik Engine API to create a query for processing. Most visualizations built-in with Qlik Sense are based on a HyperCube definition on a root level, meaning the extension code is built around that.

A fundamental definition of a HyperCube looks as follows:

```
initialProperties: {
    version: 1.0,
    qHyperCubeDef: {
    qDimensions: [],
    qMeasures: [],
    qInitialDataFetch: [{
        qWidth: 2,
        qHeight: 50
    }]
  }
}
```

By default, most extensions will not have any dimensions or measures defined in their `initialProperties` to allow the user to achieve the same by adding dimensions and metric via the property panel.

 Always add `initialProperties` to define how many rows/columns are available in your JavaScript object.
When changing the `initialProperties`, remove and re-add your visualization extension; merely refreshing the page (*F5*) will not suffice.

The size of an actual HyperCube within the Qlik Engine is defined by the number of **resulting** rows after it has been calculated. Sometimes, even that can be huge, and as such, qInitialDataFetch allows you to determine how many of those data cells are returned to the extension code. It's defined using `qWidth` and `qHeight`.

The product of both *qWidth*qHeight* can never exceed 10,000 data cells. If you are required to return more than 10,000 data cells for a particular use case or visualizations, you will need to implement subsequent pagination in your code.

qHyperCubeDef properties

There are several high-level properties that can be used to help modify and specify the underlying HyperCube, even beyond the extent of dimensions and measure.

qDimensions

qDimensions defines the array of dimensions that will be used in the HyperCube. This is usually defined via the property panel, but it can also be done manually directly in the JSON file. The latter is only recommended for mashup usage when you are defining the visualization on the fly.

Further to the dimension name, you can also define settings, such as the following:

- qNullSuppression, which suppresses null values in the dimension
- qShowAll, which, if set to true, displays all dimension values, regardless of whether they are selected
- qCalcCond, which sets a calculation condition, which must be fulfilled for a dimension to be calculated
- qTotalLabel and qOtherLabel help to relabel the Other and Total labels in the returned HyperCube

If you are using the property panel to define dimensions, simply using those properties as reference values allows you to define them directly, for example:

```
suppressNulls: {
    type: "boolean",
    ref: "qNullSuppression",
    label: "Suppress Nulls",
    defaultValue: false
},
```

qMeasures

qMeasures is very similar to qDimensions but helps you define measures. The same as with the dimensions, they are usually defined via the property panel.

qInitialDataFetch

qInitialDataFetch has already been described previously and helps define how many data cells are initially retrieved from the calculated HyperCube.

qStateName

qStateName helps define the name of the alternate state, with $ (current selections) being the default one. Alternate states help create a virtual image of selections that are based on the same dataset but are not affected by selections made in other states. This is considered advanced stuff and is mostly utilized for comparative analysis purposes.

qInterColumnSortOrder

The qInterColumnSortOrder property helps define an inter-column sort order in the HyperCube. It is defined using an array of integers, for example, *[1,3,2,0]*, which specifies in which order the columns will be sorted.

qSuppressZero

qSuppressZero removes rows that have zero values across the entire HyperCube row, if set to true.

qSuppressMissing

qSuppressMissing removes rows that have missing values across the entire HyperCube row, if set to true.

qMode

qMode defines in what structure the HyperCube will be returned. By default, and for most relevant use cases, the data mode is returned in a straight table representation. Further advanced modes are available as follows:

- Pivot Table representation (qMode P)
- Stacked Table representation (qMode K)
- Tree representation (qMode T)

Those different representation types are advanced and return to you a pre-aggregated format of the underlying dimensions and measures, including subtotals.

qNoOfLeftDims

This property applies to pivot tables and stacked pivot tables.

In a Pivot Table structure, this setting is used to help define how many and which dimensions are set as rows, and which are pivoted horizontally. This is relatively advanced, and further documentation on this is available on Qlik Sense's help page.

qAlwaysFullyExpanded

This property applies to pivot tables and stacked pivot tables.

This property ensures cells are always expanded if set to true.

qMaxStackedCells

When in stacked mode (qMode is K), this defines the maximum number of cells for an initial data fetch (default is 5,000).

qPopulateMissing

Missing values or nulls are returned as hyphens (-) in the data model. qPopulateMissing replaces numerical nulls with 0 and string nulls with empty strings.

qShowTotalsAbove

If true, it returns the totals row on the first row of the HyperCube. They can also be retrieved from `qHyperCube.qGrandTotalRow[i].qNum`.

qIndentMode

This property applies to pivot tables and stacked pivot tables.

This property applies an indentation for pivot tables and allows you to change the `layout` of the table by adding an indentation to the beginning of each row.

qCalcCond

`qCalcCond` specifies a calculation condition for the whole HyperCube to calculate. This is particularly powerful when you are having wide tables with very complex calculations and you want to ensure that the user has filtered a subset of data before firing off the calculation to the Qlik engine. Heavy calculations not only take time to return but also build up RAM utilization on your Qlik Sense server.

qSortbyYValue

This property applies to pivot tables and stacked pivot tables.

`qSortbyYValue` enables sorting by ascending or descending order in the values of a measure.

Bear in mind that this collection of properties and settings is not entirely comprehensive and is subject to evolve with new releases of Qlik Sense. It is therefore recommended to always refer to the online documentation found at `http://help.qlik.com/en-US/sense-developer/November2017/Subsystems/EngineAPI/Content/GenericObject/PropertyLevel/HyperCubeDef.htm` to ensure you are using the most recent and correct definition.

Returned qHyperCube structure

Once the `qHyperCubeDef` is defined, either by a set of properties or via the property panel, the Qlik Engine then calculates the HyperCube on each selection and interaction with the Qlik engine. Once calculated, it then returns a `qHyperCube` structure in the `layout`, together with the results.

In our MasteringQS extension, the following example illustrates the returned calculated `qHyperCube` for a sample dimension and metric:

```
▼ Object 🔲
    FontSizeSliderValue: 15                            Property.js panel values
    dropdownproperty: "v"
  ▼ extensionMeta:
      author: "Martin Mahler"
      description: "This is a description"
      icon: "extension"                                Information
      isLibraryItem: true                              retrieved from
      isThirdParty: true                               the .qext file
      name: "Mastering QS Example"
      template: "MasteringQS"
      templateIconClassName: "icon-puzzle"
      type: "visualization"
      version: 1
    ▶ __proto__: Object
    fontSize: 15
    fontfamily: ""
    footnote: ""
  ▶ listItems: []
  ▼ qHyperCube:
    ▶ qDataPages: [{…}]
    ▶ qDimensionInfo: [{…}]                            qHyperCube containing:
    ▶ qEffectiveInterColumnSortOrder: (2) [0, 1]       1. Dimensions used
    ▶ qGrandTotalRow: [{…}]                            2. Metrics used
    ▶ qMeasureInfo: [{…}]                              3. Calculated data results
      qMode: "S"                                       (qDataPages)
      qNoOfLeftDims: -1
    ▶ qPivotDataPages: []
    ▶ qSize: {qcx: 2, qcy: 30}
    ▶ qStackedDataPages: []
    ▶ __proto__: Object
  ▶ qInfo: {qId: "LABLJzs", qType: "MasteringQS"}
  ▶ qSelectionInfo: {}
    showDetails: false
    showTitles: true
    subtitle: ""
    title: ""
    version: 1
    visualization: "MasteringQS"
    permissions: (...)
  ▶ get permissions: ƒ ()
  ▶ __proto__: Object
```

Having previously gone through the section on how to define a qHyperCube, you should now be able to recognize most of these objects and variables. Any property that begins with the letter q is a Qlik definition property; however, there are some additional ones that don't have the prefix (for example, title and subtitle).

Furthermore, together with the qHyperCube, the layout also returns information stored in the .qext file that can be retrieved via the extensionMeta object property. The same applies to the custom properties defined in the properties.js file, which are also returned in the layout ,together with the qHyperCube, for example, the fontSize, fontFamily, and so on.

For the beginning, three different objects are interesting:

- layout.qHyperCube.qDimensionInfo: Used dimensions
- layout.qHyperCube.qMeasureInfo: Used measures
- layout.qHyperCube.qDataPages: The result
- layout.qHyperCube.qSize: The page size

Of these three, the most relevant is, of course, qDataPages, which holds the calculated data:

```
▼ qDataPages: Array(1)
  ▼ 0:
    ▼ qArea:
      ▼ qHeight: 30
        qLeft: 0                              Returned Size of Data
        qTop: 0                               (2 columns & 30 rows)
        qWidth: 2
      ▶ __proto__: Object
    ▼ qMatrix: Array(30)          ←────────── Returned Data Set
      ▼ 0: Array(2)               ←────────── Row #1
        ▼ 0:
          qElemNumber: 21
          qNum: "NaN"
          qState: "O"
          qText: "1st Line Helpdesk"
        ▶ __proto__: Object              ⟍
        ▼ 1:                              ⟍  Cells
          qElemNumber: 0            ←─────
          qNum: 1344
          qState: "L"
          qText: "1344"
        ▶ __proto__: Object
        length: 2
      ▶ __proto__: Array(0)
    ▶ 1: (2) [{…}, {…}]            ←────────── Row #2
    ▶ 2: (2) [{…}, {…}]            ←────────── Row #3
```

If you expand the `qDataPages` node, you can see the following:

- `qDataPages` is an array
- the data is held within `qDataPages[0].qMatrix`, which is again an array of objects representing the rows, each again holding an array of some other objects representing the individual cells (columns for each row)

In turn, each cell holds the following information:

- `qText`, being the textual representation of its resulting value
- `qNum`, if numeric, will give you the numeric value
- If the cell is a dimension, `qElemNumber` will provide you with the internal ID of the dimension value, which can be used to make selections with `qState`, the selection state of the object

One typical challenge is to transform the `qDataPages.qMatrix` data into an array of objects of a different format for better processing in the extension code.

For example, if you know you will always only have one dimension value and one metric, transforming the data structure into something more friendly for your code can be done using JavaScript's `.map()` function, which looks as follows:

```
var data = [];
data = scope.layout.qHyperCube.qDataPages[0].qMatrix.map(function(d) {
return {
    dimensionvalue: d[0].qText,
    measurevalue: d[1].qNum
};
})
```

The result looks much friendlier:

```
▼ (30)
▼ [{…}, {…}, {…}, {…}, {…}, {…}, {…}, {…}, {…}, {…}, {…}, {…}, {…}, {
    ▶ 0: {dimensionvalue: "1st Line Helpdesk", measurevalue: 1344}
    ▶ 1: {dimensionvalue: "Aileen C. Millimaki", measurevalue: 192}
    ▶ 2: {dimensionvalue: "Aracelis K. Ranum", measurevalue: 11}
    ▶ 3: {dimensionvalue: "Carlita F. Glahn", measurevalue: 73}
    ▶ 4: {dimensionvalue: "Clifford H. Huxtable", measurevalue: 423}
    ▶ 5: {dimensionvalue: "Denver M. Navy", measurevalue: 237}
    ▶ 6: {dimensionvalue: "Dominic J. Breedlove", measurevalue: 45}
    ▶ 7: {dimensionvalue: "Gerardo E. Ferroni", measurevalue: 487}
    ▶ 8: {dimensionvalue: "Kenneth Z. Ruffonton", measurevalue: 9}
    ▶ 9: {dimensionvalue: "Kimbra C. Plasencia", measurevalue: 137}
    ▶ 10: {dimensionvalue: "Lamont R. Modest", measurevalue: 384}
    ▶ 11: {dimensionvalue: "Lowell E. Poet", measurevalue: 426}
    ▶ 12: {dimensionvalue: "Mitzi F. Pegler", measurevalue: 57}
    ▶ 13: {dimensionvalue: "Nathan C. Busterview", measurevalue: 297}
    ▶ 14: {dimensionvalue: "Patrice T. Gattie", measurevalue: 6}
    ▶ 15: {dimensionvalue: "Quincy B. Awnington", measurevalue: 62}
    ▶ 16: {dimensionvalue: "Ramiro L. Cheesman", measurevalue: 129}
    ▶ 17: {dimensionvalue: "Renita K. Vaksman", measurevalue: 25}
    ▶ 18: {dimensionvalue: "Revis D. Jackson", measurevalue: 137}
    ▶ 19: {dimensionvalue: "Robena E. Feister", measurevalue: 53}
    ▶ 20: {dimensionvalue: "Salley R. Reasons", measurevalue: 511}
```

qListObjectDef

The family of generic objects has provided qHyperCube with a sister called the qListObject. Unlike a HyperCube, a list object better serves the purposes of displaying one single dimension *without* any required calculation, meaning no metrics are required to be defined. As such, it is fairly straightforward to work the list objects, and their definition is very similar to the qHyperCube object, with some added extra properties but without measures.

The following code is an example of creating a qListObjectDef and writing the resulting list object into the console:

```
//DefineListObject
var obj = {
    "qDef": {
    "qFieldDefs": ["Case Owner"]
    },
    "qShowAlternatives" : true,
```

```
    "qInitialDataFetch": [{
        qTop : 0,
        qLeft : 0,
        qHeight : 10000,
        qWidth : 1
    }]
    };

var app = qlik.currApp(this);

//Create the listbox as a session object which will persist over the
//session and then be deleted.
app.createList(obj,function(listobject) {
  console.log(listobject)
})
```

This returns the following result:

```
▼ {qInfo: {…}, qSelectionInfo: {…}, qListObject: {…}} ▣
  ▶ qInfo: {qId: "MUFPPnE", qType: "mashup"}
  ▼ qListObject:
    ▼ qDataPages: Array(1)
      ▼ 0:
        ▶ qArea: {qLeft: 0, qTop: 0, qWidth: 1, qHeight: 29}
        ▶ qMatrix: (29) [Array(1), Array(1), Array(1), Array}
        ▶ qTails: []
        ▶ __proto__: Object
          length: 1
        ▶ __proto__: Array(0)
    ▼ qDimensionInfo:
        qApprMaxGlyphCount: 21
      ▶ qAttrDimInfo: []
      ▶ qAttrExprInfo: []
        qCardinal: 29
        qDimensionType: "D"
        qFallbackTitle: "Case Owner"
      ▶ qGroupFallbackTitles: ["Case Owner"]
      ▶ qGroupFieldDefs: ["Case Owner"]
        qGroupPos: 0
        qGrouping: "N"
        qIsAutoFormat: true
        qMax: 0
        qMin: 0
      ▶ qNumFormat: {qType: "U", qnDec: 0, qUseThou: 0}
        qSortIndicator: "N"
      ▶ qStateCounts: {qLocked: 0, qSelected: 0, qOption: 29
      ▶ qTags: (2) ["$ascii", "$text"]
      ▶ __proto__: Object
    ▶ qExpressions: []
    ▶ qSize: {qcx: 1, qcy: 29}
    ▶ __proto__: Object
  ▶ qSelectionInfo: {}
    permissions: (...)
  ▶ get permissions: ƒ ()
  ▶ __proto__: Object
```

It is a very similar structure to the qHyperCube, with its qDataPages, but with additional information on the retrieved dimension and list object.

On top of the classic properties already described for the qHyperCube earlier in this chapter, for a qListObject you can define the following settings:

- qAutoSortByState: Defines the sorting by state.
- qFrequencyMode: Defines the frequency mode used to calculate the frequency of a value in a list object. This parameter is optional and by default no frequency is returned (NX_FREQUENCY_NONE) value. Alternative values are NX_FREQUENCY_VALUE, NX_FREQUENCY_PERCENT, and NQ_FREQUENCY_RELATIVE.
- qShowAlternatives: If this is set to true, it will permit alternative values to be included in the returned qData. If set to false, no alternative values are displayed in qData. Values are excluded instead. qStateCounts counts excluded values as alternative values.

 It is important to note that, with a qListObject, all values are rendered, regardless of whether they have been excluded or not. If selections are applied to a list object, the selected values are displayed along with the excluded and the optional values.

qStringExpression and qValueExpression

For simpler, one-off calculations where you just want to leverage the power of the Qlik Sense engine, qStringExpression and qValueExpression are the little sisters of qHyperCube and qListObject. They work using the same concept as the rest but on a simpler level: all you need to do is define a Qlik expression, and the engine will return to you its result in a promise:

```
var app = qlik.currApp(this);
app.createGenericObject({
    user: {
        qStringExpression: "=OSUser()"
    },
    version: {
        qStringExpression: "=EngineVersion()"
    },
    fields: {
        qValueExpression: "=Count (DISTINCT $Field)"
    }
```

```
}, function ( reply ) {
   var str = "Version:" + reply.version +
      str+= " Number of Fields:"+reply.fields;
   if(reply.user) {
      str += " User:" + reply.user;
   }
   console.log(str)
}
```

Using those object definitions is very handy in conjunction with other objects, such as a
qHyperCube.

> The = sign in the string expression is not mandatory. Even if the = sign is
> not given, the expression is evaluated.
>
> A string expression is not evaluated if the expression is surrounded by
> pure quotes.

Example 1-bar chart

Now that you are familiar with the basic structure of an extension, the HyperCube, and
how to define useful properties, this section will cover building an example visualization
extension step by step using d3. It will quickly become very technical, so a good
understanding of previous chapters is required to follow why and how something is
implemented fully.

Bear in mind that, as with languages and their dialects, there are different ways to
implement the same results in coding. You are encouraged to explore different
implementations and to try out new ideas or methods that you are more comfortable with.

The example we will try to implement using d3 is a standard bar chart. We do
recognize Qlik Sense already comes with a sturdy bar chart that so this exercise will
replicate some of the basic functionality, but the steps of building d3-based
visualizations should be transferable to any other type of chart.

Requirements

A bar chart displays quantitative values for different categories, permitting the user to compare different categories with one another visually. The requirements here are to develop a bar chart that does the following:

- Supports one dimension and one metric
- Dynamically reads data from the Qlik engine
- Permits the user to change the color of the bars
- Supports selections
- Supports smooth transitions between selections
- Is responsive and automatically resizes based on the screen

Folder structure

Before we begin with the coding, we'll set up the folder structure to follow previously described best practices that have the property panel definition separated, as well as a dedicated file for the CSS styling. Bear in mind that, as this is an SVG-based extension, we will not be needing an AngularJS template:

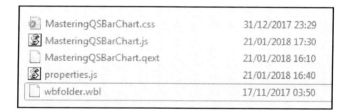

MasteringQSBarChart.css	31/12/2017 23:29
MasteringQSBarChart.js	21/01/2018 17:30
MasteringQSBarChart.qext	21/01/2018 16:10
properties.js	21/01/2018 16:40
wbfolder.wbl	17/11/2017 03:50

Also, make sure to include the bar-chart-vertical icon in your .qext file:

```
//MasteringQSBarChart.qext
{
"name": "Mastering QS bar chart Example",
"description": "This is a description",
"icon": "bar-chart-vertical",
"type": "visualization",
"version": 1,
"author": "Martin Mahler"
}
```

Property panel

The property panel will become very relevant in the case of the bar chart, or any other visualization, as you will want to provide the user with as many properties and settings as possible so they can update and style the chart to their liking, to appropriately support self-service analytics.

To begin with, we will utilize the native setting components and gradually add more settings as we develop the bar chart. As a starting point, we can add the Bar Color as the first setting, which will leverage Qlik's native color-component:

```
//properties.js
define([], function(){ return {
    type: "items",
    component: "accordion",
        items: {
        dimensions: {
            uses: "dimensions",
            min: 1,
            max: 1
        },
        measures: {
            uses: "measures",
            min: 1,
            max: 1
        },
        sorting: {
            uses: "sorting"
        },
        addons: {
            uses: "addons"
        },
        settings: {
            uses: "settings",
            items: {
            barColor: {
                label: "Bar Color",
                component: "color-picker",
                type: "object",
                dualOutput: true,
                schemaIgnore: true,
                ref: "barColor",
                defaultValue: {
                  index: -1,
                  color: "#657dbc"
```

```
            },
            show: function (layout) {
                return true
            }
        },
    }
}
};
});
```

This will result in the following property panel:

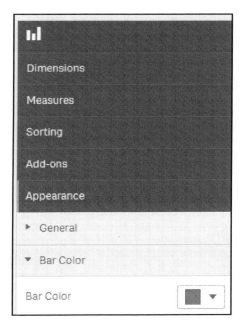

It makes sense to successively enrich the property panel as you develop rather than necessarily define everything from the beginning-things may change as you implement your visualizations with new ideas and user feedback. Remember, whenever it's ambiguous, how a setting or styling should be implemented, make it a dynamic property, and let the user decide.

Template

D3 visualizations are not driven by AngularJS and cannot be cleverly implemented using templates. You can, for example, utilize the template to declare directives. Remember, the DOMs are data-driven and dynamic and get appended based on the underlying data structure. However, defining a template is always necessary, which is why, in this example, we will use a plain placeholder `<div></div>` in the `template.html` file.

Let's get started-MasteringQSBarChart.js

Now that the folders and code structure are set, we can begin developing the bar chart visualization. With this particular bar chart example, we will be expecting to have at least one dimension and one metric. As such, we will need to define the `intialProperties` to ensure the `qHyperCube` will return a dataset, two columns wide with 5,000 rows, exhausting the cell limit of a `qHyperCube`:

```
//MasteringQSBarChart.js (snippet)
initialProperties : {
 qHyperCubeDef : {
 qDimensions : [],
 qMeasures : [],
 qInitialDataFetch : [{
  qWidth : 2,
  qHeight : 5000
 }]
 }
},
```

Furthermore, we will be organizing the JavaScript code into three parts serving different purposes:

- The `scope.prep()` function will prepare the DOM and SVG structure of the visualization so the visualization can be appended to Qlik Sense—*it will be called only once during the initial load of the screen.*
- The `scope.init()` function will initialize the chart, determine the width and height of the visualization, and position the *x* and *y*-axes—*it will be called at the beginning and then every time the screen size re-adjusts or resizes.*

- The `scope.getData()` function will retrieve the data from the `qHyperCube` and transform it in a way which can be readily consumed by the `scope.render()` function. It will also update the domain of the *x* and *y*-axes-*it will be called whenever the data updates.*
- The `scope.render()` function will render the visualization. Based on the returned `qHyperCube` data, it will create the SVG elements, the bars, using d3, and paint the chart on the initialized framework. It serves the same purpose as the `paint()` function; however, it offers more flexibility and control by saving values in the `$scope`—*it will be called whenever the data updates, including at the beginning when the initial dataset is calculated.*

> For more advanced implementations, it's recommended to collect all your developed functions and variables into your own object within the scope, for example, `$scope.masteringqsbarchart`, to avoid any ambiguity or unplanned collisions.

As such, the skeleton of the controller will look as follows:

```
//MasteringQSBarChart.js (snippet)
resize: function($element, layout){
    //Makes sure the chart is re-initialized when the object is
//resized.
    this.$scope.init(this.$scope.element, layout)
    this.$scope.render(scope.element, scope.layout)
},
controller: ['$scope', '$element', function (scope, $element) {
    scope.prep = function(scope, $element){
    //Prepares the SVG structure of the d3 visualization.
    //Initializes the chart once prepared
    scope.init(scope.element, scope.layout)
    };

    scope.init = function (element, layout){
    //Initializes the visualization, determines size of the chart
    //as well as its axis, ranges and domains
    //Renders the charts once initialized
    };

    scope.getData = function(layout){
       //Retrieves the data

    }
    scope.render = function(element, layout){
    //Takes the returned dataset and visualizes the bars
    }
```

```
  scope.prep(scope, $element);
  scope.getData(scope.layout);
  scope.render(scope.element, scope.layout)

  scope.backendApi.model.Validated.bind(function(a, b){
  //Listens for click events or other data
  //model changes to re-render the chart with the updated data.
     scope.getData(scope.layout);
     scope.render(scope.element, scope.layout)
  })
}]
```

Before moving on to the implementation of each function, please note a couple of points:

- To capture whether the extension is being resized on the screen (either manually or by changing the window size), the native `resize()` function is used for this purpose. After resizing, the width and height of the object need to be recalculated, which is why `$scope.init()` is called, and then `$scope.render()`.

- The controller only runs once. To ensure data changes to the bar chart are captured whenever the underlying Qlik data model updates, the native `scope.backendApi.model.Validated` watcher is used, and a function is bound to it.

 `scope.backendApi.model.Validated.bind(function(a, b){})` basically invokes the same behavior as the `paint()` function, but within the controller.

Preparing the SVG structure for the chart and the axis

As we are not creating a complex visualization with lots of functionality (yet), the preparation is relatively simple. However, it is still considered a good practice to separate one-off code executions from the remaining functions, or at least have a section within your code that covers that aspect in a segregated way.

In the case of the Mastering QS bar chart, the preparation will revolve around appending an SVG element to the extension div. This is achieved using the d3 function, as follows:

```
//MasteringQSBarChart.js - scope.prep() (snippet)
scope.svg = d3.select($element.children()[0])
    .append('svg')
```

```
scope.svg.append('g')
    .attr('class', 'canvas')

 scope.svg.append('g')
    .attr('class', 'x-axis')

scope.svg.append('g')
    .attr('class', 'y-axis')
```

With the SVG, we also added three g elements, which allow relevant elements to be grouped in the latter part of the code. This provides a better overview but also the ability to control some fixed styling via the classes.

This will create the following HTML structure:

```
▼<div class="qv-object-content ng-isolate-scope" qv-object-content component="object.con
  options="options" object="object" backend-api="object.backendApi" layout="layout" ext=
  "object.ext" selections-api="object.selectionsApi" tooltip-api="object.tooltipApi" throb
  api="object.throbberApi" on-init="onInit">
  ▼<div style="height: 100%; position: relative;" class="ng-scope">
    ▼<svg>
        <g class="canvas"></g>
        <g class="x-axis"></g>
        <g class="y-axis"></g>
      </svg>
    </div>
  </div>
</div>
</div>
```

Furthermore, we will also include the axis definitions into the preparation section to declare that our x-axis will be ordinal (categories) and our y-axis linear. These are created using the d3.svg.axis() function, as follows:

```
//MasteringQSBarChart.js - scope.prep() (snippet)
scope.x = d3.scale.ordinal()
scope.y = d3.scale.linear().nice();
scope.xAxis = d3.svg.axis()
scope.yAxis = d3.svg.axis();
```

Once the preparation is complete, we call the initialization function:

```
//MasteringQSBarChart.js - scope.prep() (snippet)
scope.init(scope.element, scope.layout)
```

Initializing the SVG chart

This part covers all the calculations around the settings and sizing of the visualization chart. This is where you can read your settings from the property panel.

In this particular example, in the initialization part, we will conduct three exercises:

- **Setting the width and height of the SVG**: `$element.width()` and `$element.height()` provide the dynamic width and height of the extension. To ensure the axis and other elements of the visualization have enough space on the canvas, we apply a margin and recalculate the width and height, less the margin, for visualization purposes:

```
//MasteringQSBarChart.js - scope.init() (snippet)
scope.margin = {top: 30, right: 30, bottom: 30, left: 50}
scpe.width = $element.width() - scope.margin.right -
scope.margin.left
scope.height = $element.height() - scope.margin.top -
scope.margin.bottom
```

- **(Re)positioning the canvas, and the *x*-axis and *y*-axis elements, based on the SVG's height and width**: The canvas and the axis are positioned relative to the parent SVG, based on the defined margins:

```
//MasteringQSBarChart.js - scope.init() (snippet)
scope.svg.select('.canvas')
  .attr('transform', 'translate('+scope.margin.left+',5)')

scope.svg.selectAll('.x-axis')
  .attr('transform',
'translate('+scope.margin.left+','+parseInt(scope.height+5)+')')

scope.svg.selectAll('.y-axis')
  .attr('transform', 'translate('+scope.margin.left+',5)')
```

It's worth mentioning we are deliberately moving all elements vertically by 5 px to ensure the *y*-axis tick values don't get cut off at the top.

- **Defining the *x*-axis and *y*-axis range**: An axis within d3 has two essential interval properties. One is the real range on the SVG canvas, set in pixels. The other one is the domain, which represents the min and max value of how the underlying data should be positioned within the range.

If, for example, the range is [0, 100px], and the domain [50,100], a data value of 50 will be positioned at the very bottom of the *y*-axis, and 75 will be placed in the middle of it. If a range does not make sense to be defined owing to an ordinal axis, you can use rangeRoundBands, which evenly spaces out the domain values:

```
//MasteringQSBarChart.js - scope.init() (snippet)
scope.y.range([scope.height, 0]);
scope.x.rangeRoundBands([0, scope.width], 0.1);
```

Furthermore, here is an excellent opportunity to define any other settings or properties that will be used when visualizing the data, for example, the bar color. Once the initialization is complete, the rendering function of the chart is ready to be called:

```
//MasteringQSBarChart.js - scope.init() (snippet)
scope.bar_color = layout.barColor.color;
```

Rendering the SVG chart

We have prepared the SVG elements, sized the canvas and the axis, as well as defining the ranges and properties of the chart. This part of the code focuses solely on the rendering part of the visualization.

Data preparation

To visualize data, you first need data. This is done by reading the returned qHyperCube and mapping the results to a convenient scope.data.

Furthermore, we will also leverage the same underlying dataset to return the names of the bar dimension values, which will then be used to populate the *x*-axis domain using scope.x.domain(scope.bars). Remember, the *x*-axis has an ordinal structure, so it can assume and work with discrete values.

To define the domain of the *y*-axis, we will assume 0 (zero) as the minimum value, and take the maximum available value from the data set, using d3.max. Bear in mind that you can also use layout.qHyperCube.qMeasureInfo[0].qMax to obtain the same amount directly from the qHyperCube.

The last bit revolves around defining the width of the bars that are to be rendered:

```
//MasteringQSBarChart.js - scope.getData() (snippet)
//Takes the returned dataset and visualizes the bars
 //Data prep
 scope.data = layout.qHyperCube.qDataPages[0].qMatrix.map(function(d, i,
arr){
         return {
             Bar: d[0].qText,
             BarID: d[0].qElemNumber,
             Value: d[1].qNum,
         }
 })
 scope.bars = layout.qHyperCube.qDataPages[0].qMatrix.map(function(d, i,
arr){
     return d[0].qText
 })
//x-Axis values
 scope.x.domain(scope.bars)
//y-Axis domain
 scope.y.domain([
     0,
     d3.max(scope.data, function(d){
         return d.Value;
     })
 ])
```

Data visualization (finally)

Next comes the actual visualizing of the data using bars. It's important to have some basic understanding of how to use D3.js as, otherwise, this part will mean very little to you.

Firstly, we define the bar's variable by selecting the canvas and possible rectangles, and then applying the updating dataset to it using the data() function:

```
//MasteringQSBarChart.js - scope.render() (snippet)

//Bar Width
 scope.bar_width = scope.width/scope.bars.length*0.8;

//Visualize Bars
 var bars = scope.svg.select('.canvas')
 .selectAll('rect')
 .data(scope.data)
```

Now it's time to enter the data and append the rect SVG elements to the canvas, and apply the settings and stylings of the bars based on their underlying data:

```
//MasteringQSBarChart.js - scope.render() (snippet)
//Enter
 bars
     .enter()
     .append("rect")
     .transition()
     .duration(300)
     .attr("class", "bar")
     .attr("elementid", function(d){
         return d.BarID
     })
     .attr('fill', scope.bar_color)
     .attr('width', scope.bar_width)
     .attr('x', function(d){
         return scope.x(d.Bar)
     })
     .attr('y', function(d){
         return scope.y(d.Value);
     })
     .attr('height', function(d){
         return scope.height-scope.y(d.Value);
     })
```

The physical *x* position in pixels is returned by our scope.x function, based on the predefined range and domain. The same applies to the *y*-axis; however, given it's a rectangle, it assumes two values: the *y* position and the height.

We want to ensure the bars are fully responsive and that they do the following:

- Resize when the screen size changes
- Are added and removed depending on the availability of the underlying data

Therefore, we will need to add code for the update() and exit() events.

The code to update the bar chart is very similar to the first one drawing the bars. However, it specifies which attributes and styles are updated, and you can apply a slick transition to them, as follows:

```
//MasteringQSBarChart.js - scope.render() (snippet)
//Update
 scope.svg.selectAll('rect')
     .attr("elementid", function(d){
         return d.BarID
```

```
    })
    .attr('fill', scope.bar_color)
    .attr('width', scope.bar_width)
    .attr('x', function(d){
        return scope.x(d.Bar)
    })
    .transition()
    .duration(300)
    .attr('y', function(d){
        return scope.y(d.Value);
    })
    .attr('height', function(d){
        return scope.height-scope.y(d.Value);
    })
```

And this is the `exit()` event, which simply removes bars that are no longer available based on the dataset:

```
//MasteringQSBarChart.js - scope.render() (snippet)
//Exit
 bars
     .exit()
     .remove();
```

Lastly, but equally important, is the rendering of the actual *x* and *y*-axes. No, they were not forgotten, but deliberately put to the end of the rendering code for a particular reason. Whichever element gets rendered last is the one that has the highest z index, for example, it overlaps the other objects. To ensure the axis is always visible and we do not have any ugly overlaps, the axis is rendered last:

```
//MasteringQSBarChart.js - scope.render() (snippet)
//Add x-axis
scope.svg.selectAll('.x-axis')
    .transition(300)
    .call(
        scope.xAxis
        .scale(scope.x)
        .orient('buttom')
        .ticks(20)
    )

//Add y-axis
scope.svg.selectAll('.y-axis')
    .transition(300)
    .call(
        scope.yAxis
        .scale(scope.y)
```

```
    .orient('left')
    .ticks(20)
)
```

Once everything is accomplished, you should be able to add the visualization to your Qlik Sense app, pick and choose one dimension and one metric, and see a MasteringQS bar chart on your screen, which looks similar to the following one:

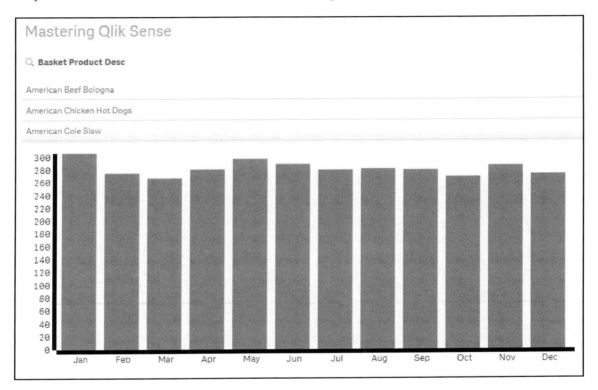

The chart will not only render but will also smoothly transition when making selections, adding a whole new layer of visualization dynamics, as the user can see how their values are updating and changing based on the filters they apply.

One thing, however, you will notice immediately is the thick lines and the missing ticks on the axes. This is because no CSS styling has been defined yet.

Styling your bar chart-MasteringQSBarChart.css

You should already know by now how powerful CSS is and how much you can style in your web page and Qlik Sense extension using it. Personally, I am a little bit in conflict with using too much CSS, and as such, this file as well will remain quite compact. The reason is that the styling of a visualization, in my opinion, should never be entirely fixed via CSS, but the user should be given the option to modify almost anything they see on the screen.

But in the case of d3, unless you apply some basic CSS styling to the axes, it will look ugly:

```
//MasteringQSBarChart.css
.qv-object-MasteringQSBarChart .y-axis path,
.qv-object-MasteringQSBarChart .x-axis path,
.qv-object-MasteringQSBarChart .y-axis line,
.qv-object-MasteringQSBarChart .x-axis line {
 fill: none;
 stroke: #000;
 stroke-width: 1px;
}
```

 Each extension will by default be wrapped in a Qlik Extension container, which is classed based on the extension name `qv-object-extensionname` class.

This will improve the design of the axes remarkably:

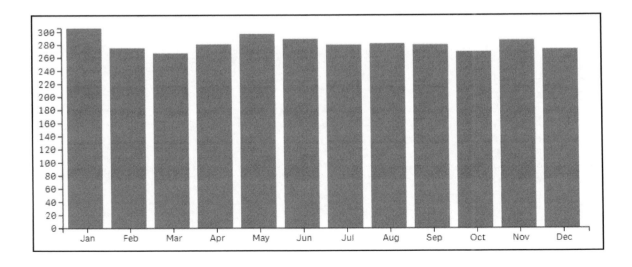

Adding selections to the bars in the chart

The beauty of Qlik Sense is that you can not only consume and visualize the data but also interact with it. The next step for the visualization then it becomes interactive by responding to click even on the individual bars. To achieve it, you first define the selection function in the scope. It should reside on the same level as `scope.prep()`, `scope.init()` and `scope.render()`:

```
//MasteringQSBarChart.js (snippet)
scope.selection = function(elementid){
    //Null, which carries elementid: -2, is not selectable
    if(elementid>=0){
      this.backendApi.selectValues(0, [elementid], false);
      //Multi-select
      //self.selectValues(0, [vElementId], false);
    }
  }
```

As you can see in the commented part, you can choose to either implement selections directly or by adding the option to support multi-select, which requires you to confirm the selections. Ideally, this becomes a setting in the property panel that permits you to check which selection mode should be applied. With the function, all you need to do now is to go back to your `scope.render()` and append another `.on("click")` function to your bars:

```
//MasteringQSBarChart.js - scope.render() (snippet)
//Update
 scope.svg.selectAll('rect')
 .on("click", function(d, e){
     scope.selection(d.BarID)
 })
 .attr("elementid", function(d){
     return d.BarID
 })
 .attr('fill', scope.bar_color)
 .attr('width', scope.bar_width)
 .attr('x', function(d){
     return scope.x(d.Bar)
 })
 .transition()
 .duration(300)
 .attr('y', function(d){
     return scope.y(d.Value);
 })
 .attr('height', function(d){
     return scope.height-scope.y(d.Value)
 })
```

Wrap-up

Developing the Mastering QS bar chart alongside the code examples step by step was a very quick introduction into how to build compelling visualizations on top of D3.js. Now that the skeleton is set up, you can proceed to use your imagination on any other requirements you can think of that you are missing in native Qlik Sense, or by implementing those odd use cases that your users have. What is important is to keep the structure of the code clean to ensure you can always quickly add new features without too much hassle. Given the rich selection of open source examples of D3 available on the web, being able to implement a visualization that reads from the Qlik engine, visualizes the results, and responds to user clicks is a very powerful skillset to have.

While this is only an introduction, I strongly encourage you to keep deepening your knowledge in this area, as you will be able to provide remarkable value to your users.

To summarize, please see next the complete runnable JavaScript code:

```
//MasteringQSBarchart.js
define(['d3', './properties', 'css!./MasteringQSBarChart.css'],
  function(d3, properties) {
  return {
      initialProperties : {
      qHyperCubeDef : {
      qDimensions : [],
      qMeasures : [],
      qInitialDataFetch : [{
          qWidth : 2,
          qHeight : 5000
      }]
    }
  },
  definition: properties,
  paint: function(){},
  resize: function($element, layout){
      //Makes sure the chart is re-initialized when the object is
//resized.
      this.$scope.init(this.$scope.element, layout)
      this.$scope.render(this.$scope.element, layout)
  },
  template: '<div></div>',
  controller: ['$scope', '$element', function (scope, $element) {
      scope.prep = function(scope, $element){
          console.log("PREP");
          //Prepares the SVG structure of the d3 visualization.
          //Initializes the chart once prepared
          scope.svg = d3.select($element.children()[0])
```

```
            .append('svg')
        scope.svg.append('g')
          .attr('class', 'canvas')
        scope.svg.append('g')
          .attr('class', 'x-axis')
        scope.svg.append('g')
          .attr('class', 'y-axis')
        scope.x = d3.scale.ordinal()
        scope.y = d3.scale.linear().nice();
        scope.xAxis = d3.svg.axis()
        scope.yAxis = d3.svg.axis();
        scope.init(scope.element, scope.layout)
    };
    scope.init = function (element, layout){
        console.log("INIT");
        //Initializes the visualization, determines size of the chart
        //as well as its axis, ranges and domains
        //Renders the charts once initialized
        scope.margin = {top: 30, right: 30, bottom: 30, left: 50}
        scope.width = $element.width() - scope.margin.right -
scope.margin.left
        scope.height = $element.height() - scope.margin.top -
scope.margin.bottom
        scope.svg
          .style('width', $element.width())
          .style('height', $element.height())

        scope.svg.select('.canvas')
          .attr('transform', 'translate('+scope.margin.left+',5)')
        scope.svg.selectAll('.x-axis')
          .attr('transform',
'translate('+scope.margin.left+','+parseInt(scope.height+5)+')')
        scope.x.rangeRoundBands([0, scope.width], 0.1);
        scope.svg.selectAll('.y-axis')
          .attr('transform', 'translate('+scope.margin.left+',5)')
        scope.y.range([scope.height, 0]);
        scope.bar_color = layout.barColor.color;
    };
    scope.getData = function(layout){
        console.log("GETDATA");
        //Takes the returned dataset and visualizes the bars
        //Data prep
        scope.data =
layout.qHyperCube.qDataPages[0].qMatrix.map(function(d, i, arr){
    return {
        Bar: d[0].qText,
        BarID: d[0].qElemNumber,
        Value: d[1].qNum,
```

```
        }
  })
     scope.bars =  layout.qHyperCube.qDataPages[0].qMatrix.map(function(d,
i, arr){
      return d[0].qText
  })
        //x-Axis values
        scope.x.domain(scope.bars)
        //y-Axis domain
        scope.y.domain([
          0,
          d3.max(scope.data, function(d){
             return d.Value;
          })
        ])
  }
     scope.render = function(element, layout){
         console.log("RENDER");
         //Bar Width
          scope.bar_width = scope.width/scope.bars.length*0.8;
         //Visualize Bars
          var bars = scope.svg.select('.canvas')
           .selectAll('rect')
           .data(scope.data)
         //Enter
          bars
            .enter()
            .append("rect")
            .transition()
            .duration(300)
            .attr("class", "bar")
            .attr("elementid", function(d){
               return d.BarID
          })
            .attr('fill', scope.bar_color)
            .attr('width', scope.bar_width)
            .attr('x', function(d){
               return scope.x(d.Bar)
             })
            .attr('y', function(d){
               return scope.y(d.Value);
            })
            .attr('height', function(d){
               return scope.height-scope.y(d.Value)
            })
         //Update
           scope.svg.selectAll('rect')
            .on("click", function(d, e){
```

```
            scope.selection(d.BarID)
      })
      .attr("elementid", function(d){
          return d.BarID
      })
    .attr('fill', scope.bar_color)
    .attr('width', scope.bar_width)
    .attr('x', function(d){
     return scope.x(d.Bar)
    })
    .transition()
    .duration(300)
    .attr('y', function(d){
     return scope.y(d.Value);
    })
    .attr('height', function(d){
     return scope.height-scope.y(d.Value)
    })
   //Exit
   bars
    .exit()
    .remove();

   //Add x-axis
   scope.svg.selectAll('.x-axis')
    .transition(300)
    .call(
        scope.xAxis
          .scale(scope.x)
          .orient('buttom')
          .ticks(20)
    )
   //Add y-axis
   scope.svg.selectAll('.y-axis')
    .transition(300)
    .call(
     scope.yAxis
       .scale(scope.y)
       .orient('left')
       .ticks(20)
    )
  }
  scope.selection = function(elementid){
      if (elementid >= 0) { // null is not selectabel (element -2)
          this.backendApi.selectValues(0, [elementid], false);
//Multi-select
          //self.selectValues(0, [vElementId], false);
      }
```

```
}
scope.prep(scope, $element);
scope.getData(scope.layout);
scope.render(scope.element, scope.layout)

scope.backendApi.model.Validated.bind(function(a, b){
    //Listens for click events or other data
    //model changes to re-render the chart with the updated data.
    scope.getData(scope.layout);
    scope.render(scope.element, scope.layout)
})
}]
  }
});
```

 Qlik is looking to improve the Extension API and with their February 2018 update have released a new method (similar to `paint()`) called `updateData()`. This permits `paint()` to finally becomes a stateless function, possibly removing the necessity to implement D3.js visualization using the AngularJS controller.

Example 2- drop-down list

While visualizations and control extensions are very similar and both rely on the same underlying libraries, building a control component as an example will highlight a different set of methods and objects that can be utilized to construct user-friendly components to interact with the app's data.

Requirements

To keep things simple, the requirements will be relatively straightforward to also illustrate that building simple extensions, such as a drop-down list, can be achieved in a short period of time. For the example, the requirements will be as follows:

- Display dimension values in a drop-down list, allowing the user to select one value at a time
- Give the user the ability to specify the chosen field themselves via the property panel

- Implement the ability to also show the frequency of dimension values in the data model
- Implement the setting to turn your drop-down list into read-only

Folder structure

The folder structure will be identical to the best practices already described and will see the property panel definition separated, and a dedicated file for the AngularJS template and the CSS styling:

Name	Änderungsdatum
MasteringQSDropdown.css	31/12/2017 23:29
MasteringQSDropdown.js	14/01/2018 18:13
MasteringQSDropdown.qext	14/01/2018 17:50
properties.js	14/01/2018 18:14
template.html	14/01/2018 18:01
wbfolder.wbl	17/11/2017 03:50

Property panel

As we already know which options and properties we wish to implement as a user option, defining the property panel for our drop-down list is fairly simple. We will utilize one expression component to help the user define their dimension, and two checkboxes to indicate whether to use one selected value and whether to apply read-only mode to the drop-down list. As we are not defining any calculations, we do not require any of the standard available properties, such as dimensions, measures, or add-ons. Keeping things simple, the property panel will look as follows:

```
//properties.js
define([], function(){
    return {
        type: "items",
        component: "accordion",
        items: {
            settings: {
            label: "Settings",
```

```
            type: "items",
            items: {
                MasteringQSdrop-down: {
                    type: "string",
                    label: "drop-down Field",
                    ref: "field",
                    expression: "optional"
                },
                includeFrequency: {
                    label: "Include Frequency",
                    ref: "includeFrequency",
                    type: "boolean",
                    defaultValue: false
                },
                ReadOnly: {
                    label: "Read Only",
                    ref: "readonly",
                    type: "boolean",
                    defaultValue: false
                }
            }
        }
    };
});
```

This, in Qlik Sense, will look as follows:

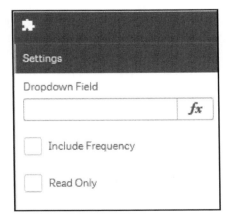

Template

A drop-down list is pretty much a user interface HTML element that can be implemented using `<select>` and `<option>` values. As this extension heavily relies on HTML, it's presenting a good use case to implement it using an AngularJS template.

As a result, we should try to implement an initial pre-populated version of a drop-down list in the template to first get to a good feeling of what we want it to look like, before connecting it to the engine.

To save time on styling, and to keep the drop-down object consistent with the rest of Qlik Sense's UI, we will make use of Leonardo UI's native drop-down list by defining the `template.html` file in the following way:

```
//template.html
<div>
<h4>Dimension Title</h4>
<select class="lui-select lui-select--gradient">
 <option value="1" selected>First</option>
 <option value="2">Second</option>
 <option value="3">Third</option>
</select>
</div>
```

This is the HTML output:

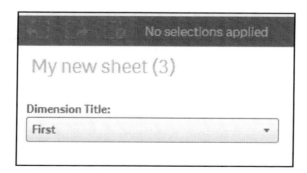

Before we dive into preparing and coding the template, let's first get to the main code in the next section and define all required variables to the scope.

Let's get started-MasteringQSdrop-down.js

The folder structure is defined, and so is the property panel and a basic idea of our desired HTML output. We can now get started with the coding. As we are not leveraging the dimensions and measure properties, we will not need to define `initialProperties`. Snapshots will be left out as well, as no one really needs to take screenshots of their drop-down elements for their Qlik Sense Story.

This will result in the JavaScript skeleton, which we will use to write our code in:

```
define(['qlik', './properties', 'text!./template.html',
'css!./MasteringQSdrop-down.css'],
function(qlik, properties, template) {
 return {
     snapshot: {
         canTakeSnapshot: false
     },
     definition: properties,
     paint: function(){},
     resize: function(){},
     template: template,
     controller: ['$scope', '$element', function (scope, $element) {
         //Code comes here
     }]
     }
});
```

Based on the requirements, as we need to display the drop-down filters, capture their states, and also to pass back selected drop-down values as selections to the Qlik Sense data model, we will need to define the following three variables for the dimension values:

- `title`
- `selection_state`
- `element_id`

As the first step, we will call the dimension values using a `qListObjectDef` object and retrieve them via the `createList` method:

```
//Get list of values
 var obj = {
     "qDef": {
     "qFieldDefs": [scope.layout.field]
     },
     "qInitialDataFetch": [{
         qTop : 0,
```

```
            qLeft : 0,
            qHeight : 10000,
            qWidth : 1
        }]
    };
    var app = qlik.currApp();
    //Create the listbox as a session object which will persist over the
    session and then be deleted.
    app.createList(obj,function(listobject) {
        //Dimension values values
    }
```

Now that the list object is created and returns its dimension values, it's time to define all required variables within the call:

```
    //Create the listbox as a session object which will persist over the
    session and then be deleted.
    app.createList(obj,function(listobject) {
        //Define dimension title
        scope.dimension_title =
    listobject.qListObject.qDimensionInfo.qFallbackTitle

        //Define Dimension value
        scope.dimension_values =
    listobject.qListObject.qDataPages[0].qMatrix.map(function(row){
        return {
            title: row[0].qText,
            element_id: row[0].qElemNumber,
            selection_state: row[0].qState
        }
    })
```

Everything that gets defined in the scope object can then be read by the AngularJS template.

Now that we have everything that we need in the scope let's go back to the template and explore how we can use the results of the dimension to create the dynamic drop-down list.

Starting with the dimension title, kept within `scope.dimension_title`, it can directly be read by the template by defining it, as it is using curly brackets: `{{dimension_title}}`.

For the drop-down list, we will need to utilize `ng-repeat`, as we wish to loop through all available dimension values and create separate HTML `<options>` tags for each one of them. This is achieved using `ng-repeat='value in dimension_values track by $index'`. Each repeated value can then be used to pull the `{{value.title}}`, and `{{value.element_id}}` as its option's value. The selection state will be defined as a class, as we can then later easily style those classes in the CSS file. The result looks as follows:

```
<div>
<h4>{{dimension_title}}:</h4>
<select class="lui-select lui-select--gradient">
    <option ng-repeat='value in dimension_values track by $index'
value="{{value.element_id}}"
class="state_{{value.selection_state}}">{{value.title}}</option>
</select>
</div>
```

And this now results in a beautiful dynamic drop-down list, which is defined by the property panel:

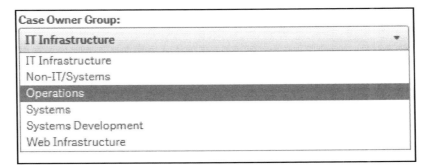

Adding selections

Now that we can successfully render the results of a defined dimension, the next step is to implement the feedback event: the ability for the user to make a selection.

This is achieved relatively quickly using AngularJS; all you need to do is the following:

1. Capture the selected value in the drop-down list
2. Set up a watcher, which is monitoring the value for changes
3. If the value changes, apply the new selection

Beginning with step 1, the selected value can be captured using AngularJS's `ng-model`, placed in the select tag of the HTML:

```
<select ng-model="selectedValue" class="lui-select lui-select--gradient">
     <option ng-repeat='value in dimension_values track by $index'
value="{{value.element_id}}"
class="state_{{value.selection_state}}">{{value.title}}</option>
</select>
```

If the options change, their underlying value (in this case, the `element_id`) will be assigned to `scope.selectedValue`, which can be read in the controller.

Step 2, in the controller, sets up the AngularJS watcher to watch the `selectedValue` for changes:

```
scope.$watch('selectedValue', function() {
     //I am watching selectedValue for changes
});
```

Now that it's set up, apply selections to the data model if the `selectedValue` has been updated:

```
scope.$watch('selectedValue', function() {
    if(typeof scope.selectedValue !== "undefined"){
       app.field(scope.layout.field)
        .select([parseInt(scope.selectedValue,10)])
    }
});
```

Using the Field API, selections are passed to the defined field using the `qElemNumber` of the dimension value.

`typeOf scope.selectedValue !== "undefined"` checks whether the `selectedValue` has an actual value. The watcher will get fired on the first rendering of the object, long before the dimension has been rendered. To avoid any errors in the code, we make sure the selection only gets fired if the selectedValue actually carries an `element_id`.
`parseInt(scope.selectedValue,10)` is required in this instance to pass the correct format to the Qlik Sense engine. The array element needs to be an integer; however, if it's being retrieved via the `<select>` element, it's a `string.parseInt()`, and then it transforms the string back to an integer.

Adding read-only mode

This one is easy, as we are already doing a check in the watcher to find out whether the `selectedValue` is undefined or not. As such, we can extend the conditional check to include whether the read-only property is true or false:

```
scope.$watch('selectedValue', function() {
    if(typeof scope.selectedValue !== "undefined"
&& !scope.layout.readonly){
        app.field(scope.layout.field)
            .select([parseInt(scope.selectedValue,10)])
    }
});
```

Showing the frequency

Sometimes it is useful to know how many times a dimension value occurs in the data model. It may give you an indication of its magnitude and whether it's worth selecting something in the first place. `qListObjectDef` supports the property to also return the frequency in `qDataPages`. All you need to do is to include it in the definition of the object:

```
//Get list of values
var obj = {
    "qDef": {
    "qFieldDefs": [scope.layout.field]
},
"qFrequencyMode": scope.layout.includeFrequency ?
"EQ_NX_FREQUENCY_VALUE" : "NX_FREQUENCY_NONE",
    "qInitialDataFetch": [{
        qTop : 0,
        qLeft : 0,
        qHeight : 10000,
        qWidth : 1
}]
};
```

If added, the list object will return the frequency as a separate value in its `cell` object:

```
//Define Dimension value
 scope.dimension_values =
listobject.qListObject.qDataPages[0].qMatrix.map(function(row){
    return {
        title: row[0].qText,
        element_id: row[0].qElemNumber,
        selection_state: row[0].qState,
```

```
        frequency: scope.layout.includeFrequency ? '- ' +
row[0].qFrequency : ''
        }
    })
```

And then, later in the template, you can include the frequency by just calling on the frequency value of the cell:

```
<div>
<h4>{{dimension_title}}:</h4>
<select ng-model="selectedValue" class="lui-select lui-select--gradient">
  <option ng-click="AddDateDimension(selectedDate)" ng-repeat='value in
dimension_values track by $index' value="{{value.element_id}}"
class="state_{{value.selection_state}}">{{value.title}}
{{value.frequency}}</option>
</select>
</div>
```

This will then display the frequency for each dimension value in the drop-down list, as shown in the following screenshot:

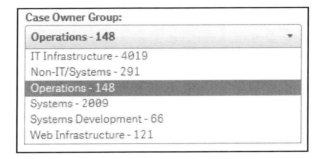

Styling your drop-down values

The self-created drop-down list seems to work brilliantly. The last step now is to style your listbox to be aware of the selection state using Qlik's green/gray/white logic based on the qState values of the dimension. The three states that can exist in our drop-down extension are the following:

- qState O: Available option to select, meant to be presented as is, unformatted
- qState S: Selected option, meant to be presented in Qlik green
- qState X: Excluded options, to be presented in gray

The only thing we need to do to achieve the desired formatting is to add CSS styles for the S and X states in our `MasteringQSdrop-down.CSS` file:

```
.qv-object-MasteringQSdrop-down .state_S {
 color: white;
 background-color: #42C24E;
}

.qv-object-MasteringQSdrop-down .state_X {
 color: #595959;
 background-color: #ddd;
}
```

The styling is, as a result, applied according to the selection state:

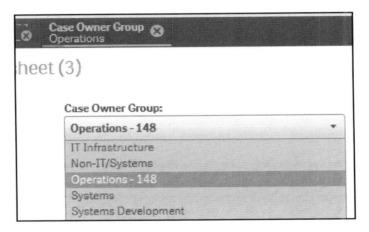

Wrap-up

Building simple widgets and components to better control your dashboard, as well as help your users navigate through your app can be fairly straightforward. Hopefully, now, with this step-by-step example, you will be more confident to have a go at JavaScript and build your own components, using AngularJS. Once you get to grips with it, you will be able to quickly achieve what you want, and you will be empowered to overcome the classic Qlik limitations.

Always make sure you are working in a structured way, as we did in this example, and bear in mind how the requirements could change in the future. Make as many features as possible available as an option in the property panel to save development costs.

Qlik Branch and other open source repositories

Why build something for yourself when it is already out there? Open source has seen a massive adoption over the past couple of years, where thousands of projects sprung out of nowhere and were made available to the community for free, to share knowledge and collaboratively develop code bases.

While you should technically be able to develop your code from scratch, conscious of time-to-market and efficiency, I am a firm believer of looking at what is already out there and taking some snippets of available code to speed up your development.

> Think of it as R&D-call it research and development or, maybe, rip off and duplicate.

The two most relevant platforms where you can find useful open source code for your projects are Qlik Branch, Qlik's open source platform with visualizations and components revolving exclusively around the Qlik APIs, and bl.ocks, which is a rich collection of open source visualizations based on d3.

Qlik Branch

Qlik Branch, as it defines itself, is a game-changing platform for web developers using Qlik's APIs to accelerate innovation in bringing the best ideas to market. Rooted in open source philosophy, all projects are freely distributed and modified, allowing faster collaboration and innovation.

The URL is `http://branch.qlik.com/` , and the website looks as follows:

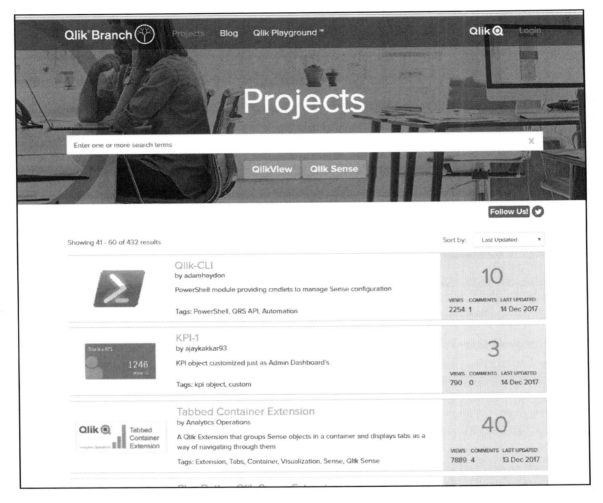

A screenshot of the website's home page

The positive thing about Branch is that you have a rich Qlik community contributing to various kind of projects based on top of the Qlik APIs, which are not necessarily visualizations only. You can find interesting integrations for WebSockets and PowerShell modules, as well as components to better control your Qlik Sense dashboards. It is a good collection of libraries to see how specific problems were solved using the Qlik Engine and how you can use the same code in your own projects.

The Qlik Branch page and community is actively supported by Qlik, and you have a dedicated Qlik Developer Relations team trying to promote projects in Branch, but they are also there to help you if you have got questions around the APIs. Furthermore, you can find exciting blogs on the latest endeavors in Qlik Branch, as well as exciting implementations on newly available features of Qlik as they are being released.

The downside of it is that the collection of projects is organized badly. They don't have categories for an easy browse, and they are not sorted based on a specific rank. Furthermore, as it's a relatively small open source community, the code is very often outdated or of low quality. It is therefore never recommended to use Qlik extensions from Branch, as they are in your Qlik Sense productions projects without an additional vetting exercise of whether they are stable enough to run on your latest Qlik Sense version. Given the pace at which Qlik releases its updates and upgrades to the APIs, unfortunately a large number of projects in Branch are buggy and outdated.

Nevertheless, it's an excellent platform to get ideas from and to copy snippets of code and see how others have technically solved similar challenges you may be facing.

bl.ocks-D3 open source platform

Bl.ocks (pronounced **Blocks**) is a simple viewer for sharing code examples hosted on GitHub Gist (`https://gist.github.com/`). As D3 examples are predominantly visualization examples, which can run on any browser, bl.ocks takes codes hosted on GitHub Gist and presents it in a more user-friendly way so users and developers can immediately see the resulting visualization output and the corresponding snippets, without the need to open or download any files.

Bl.ocks can be accessed via `http://bl.ocks.org` and shows you a minimalistic view of a collection of available projects:

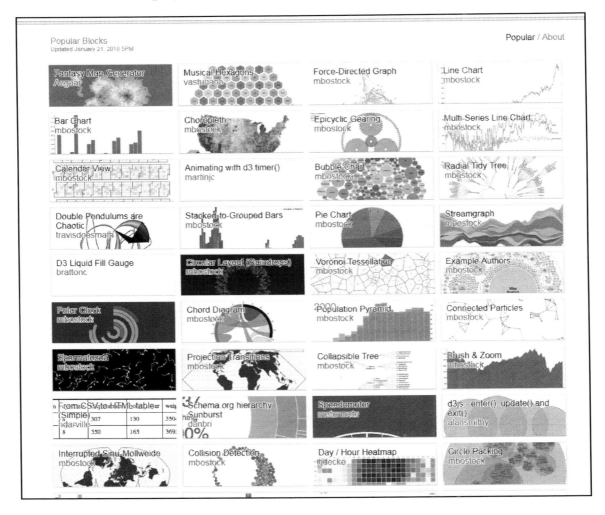

Collection of different Projects

You can view the full gallery of `http://bl.ocks.org` by going on the official d3 gallery page on GitHub at `https://github.com/d3/d3/wiki/Gallery`.

The good thing about those open source projects in D3 is the illustration that almost anything is possible to visualize using JavaScript, and it demonstrates how powerful the programming language is. Furthermore, the fact that you don't need to download and deploy code to see the result is a compelling asset, not only of JavaScript but also of D3.js.

The downside to all of this is that the examples are not integrated with Qlik Sense, and it is up to you to take snippets of D3.js code and incorporate them within your Qlik Sense extension and the Qlik APIs. It requires a bit of a learning curve to get up to speed with comfortably doing so but, eventually, it can become your source of powerful visualizations which, as we have mentioned several times already in this book, takes the possibilities of the Qlik platform on to another level.

Always remember to try to fully understand the code you are taking over from another open source project, as it will be up to you to support the code and the integration going forward.

Summary

The visualizations and components that come out of the box with Qlik Sense are, although improving with each version of Qlik Sense, somewhat limited. Very soon, as you progress with your Qlik Sense project, you will hit a brick wall of requirements coming from your user audience, which cannot be implemented using the native objects, and you will need to resort to either finding an existing open source project online that solves that particular requirement, or you will need to build a visualization or component yourself using the Extensions and Qlik APIs.

This chapter has covered in great depth the way in which an extension project is structured. It has described its files and highlighted some best practices on how to approach a new code project to be implemented within Qlik. Furthermore, the property panel and the Generic Objects structures were explored and explained for you to understand how to read user inputs, such as dimensions and metrics better, send them to the Qlik Engine for calculation, and processing, the results.

Qlik extensions can be leveraged for several use cases. The more obvious part is to find new or improved ways to visualize data,exploring the rich world of available D3.js libraries. On the other hand, extensions can also help you improve the user experience and the usability of your dashboards. As such, this chapter provided you with two comprehensive step-by-step examples on how to build extensions, one for visualization purposes (bar chart) and one to improve the usability of the dashboard by providing the user with a drop-down selector (drop-down list).

The chapter concluded by briefly describing other sources of where you can find the code to implement your Qlik Sense projects.

With the knowledge obtained, you should now be able to easily navigate through typical Qlik Sense extension code and understand how to build a user-friendly and intuitive property panel. You should be familiar with the results of a processed qHyperCube and know how to use the calculated data structure to visualize data using D3.js.

No data analytics requirements should appear impossible to you anymore and, by using the robust associative Qlik Engine API, you should now be able to deliver custom and tailor-made solutions to your users and customers.

While extensions can help you solve custom requirements, or challenges you face within Qlik Sense, the next chapter, on how to build a bespoke analytics app using the Mashup API, will show you that you can create anything you want on top of the Qlik Engine.

14
Integrating QS in Websites via Mashups

If working with Qlik Sense was a swimming competition, you would consider developing mashups a freestyle discipline. You are able to implement data analytics using the Qlik Engine in any way you like—you can work in the way most comfortable to you and use the libraries which you are the most skilled in. All frameworks are available for you to use, such as the previously described AngularJS, or a different one such as Vue.js or React.

You can leverage existing Qlik Sense visualization objects or use another third party library. It is entirely up to you and, with mashups, you can build compelling web applications designed to perfection using the full power of web technology.

With Mashup freedom comes great responsibility

With freedom comes great responsibility. While you can practically achieve anything using a Qlik Mashup, there are two important caveats to this approach:

- **Advanced web development skills are required** to implement mashups, and in particular, around web development. If you're not from that kind of background, building mashups is not simple, needing you to upskill in JavaScript, HTML, and CSS. Coding skills are necessary rather than simple configuration skills.
- **There is a lot that can go wrong,** and the introduction of technical debt will become expensive in the long run. This can be in the form of performance hits, newly added functionality which is difficult to maintain, or key-person-dependencies, where the developer becomes indispensable for the continuation of the project or app.

If you are still reading the introduction to this chapter despite its caveats, you are ready to continue.

While mashups are renowned for their impressive designs and added functionalities, this chapter will not focus on that aspect of using mashups in Qlik Sense, and will not be as much of a deep-dive. That is real web development, and it would go beyond the scope of this book. There are many other titles that will enable you to upskill in those areas, and I would not be surprised to see a new title being published focusing exclusively on mashups in Qlik Sense.

Instead, this chapter will focus on getting you up to speed on working with mashups swiftly, connecting to the Qlik Engine, and creating the necessary HyperCubes, as well as passing on field selection in the underlying app.

 We'll be using web apps and mashups as two distinct critical terminologies in this chapter, which might mean the same to some, but these are conceptually different in their implementation. **Mashups** are websites which are hosted by the Qlik Proxy and are more closely integrated with the Qlik Engine via the Mashup API. **Web apps**, on the other hand, are websites which are hosted outside of your Qlik infrastructure but are connected to the Qlik Engine and load objects from there.

The following is a list of topics that we will be covering in this chapter:

- Getting set up
- Connecting to the Qlik Engine
- Embedding objects
- Interacting with the Qlik Engine

Getting set up

Creating a mashup project is similar to building a new extension. You need a basic file structure, and as a bare minimum, an HTML file and, for best practices, a separate JavaScript and CSS file. These can either be created manually by moving the code structure to the extension folder or via the Dev Hub, which was explained in `Chapter 11`, *Working with the Qlik Dev Hub*.

Unlike extensions, which can be considered to be an add-on to Qlik Sense, where most of the relevant libraries and frameworks are already preloaded, mashups require you to load each required code base manually, which is done via the HTML file.

The mashup template in Qlik Dev Hub comes with absolute positioning and pre-layouts and pre-loads some of the relevant code, which is a good starting point for novices.

Connecting to the Qlik Engine

With mashups or web apps, the Qlik Engine sits outside of your project and is not accessible and loaded by default. The first step before doing anything else is to create a connection with the Qlik Engine, after which you can then continue to open a session and perform further actions on that app, such as:

- Opening a document/app
- Making selections
- Retrieving visualizations and apps

For using the Qlik Engine API, open a WebSocket to the engine. There may be a difference in the way you do this, depending on whether you are working with Qlik Sense Enterprise or Qlik Sense Desktop. In this chapter, we will also elaborate on how you can achieve a connection via enigma.js and the benefits of doing so.

Creating a connection

To create a connection using WebSockets, you first need to establish a new web socket communication line. To open a WebSocket to the engine, use one of the following URIs:

Qlik Sense Enterprise	Qlik Sense Desktop
`wss://server.domain.com:4747/app/` or `wss://server.domain.com[/virtual proxy]/app/`	`ws://localhost:4848/app`

Creating a Connection using WebSockets

In the case of Qlik Sense Desktop, all you need to do is define a WebSocket variable, including its connection string in the following way:

```
var ws = new WebSocket("ws://localhost:4848/app/");
```

Once the connection is opened and checking for `ws.open()`, you can call additional methods to the engine using `ws.send()`.

This example will retrieve the number of available documents in my Qlik Sense Desktop environment, and append them to an HTML list:

```
<html>
<body>
<ul id='docList'>
</ul>
</body>
</html>
<script>
var ws = new WebSocket("ws://localhost:4848/app/");
var request = {
    "handle": -1,
    "method": "GetDocList",
    "params": {},
    "outKey": -1,
    "id": 2
}
ws.onopen = function(event){
    ws.send(JSON.stringify(request));
    // Receive the response
    ws.onmessage = function (event) {
        var response = JSON.parse(event.data);
        if(response.method != ' OnConnected'){
            var docList = response.result.qDocList;
            var list = '';
            docList.forEach(function(doc){
                list += '<li>'+doc.qDocName+'</li>';
            })
            document.getElementById('docList').innerHTML = list;
        }
    }
}
</script>
```

The preceding example will produce the following output on your browser if you have Qlik Sense Desktop running in the background:

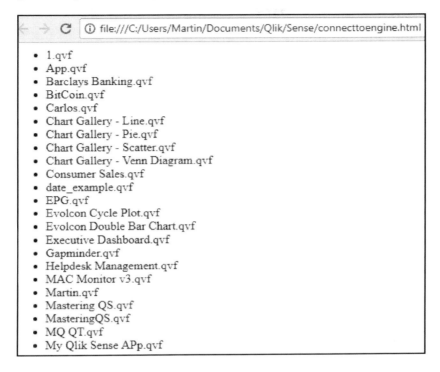

 All Engine methods and calls can be tested in a user-friendly way by exploring the Qlik Engine in the Dev Hub, as also described in `Chapter 11`, *Working with Qlik Sense Dev Hub*.

 A single WebSocket connection can be associated with only one engine session (consisting of the app context, plus the user). If you need to work with multiple apps, you must open a separate WebSocket for each one.

If you wish to create a WebSocket connection directly to an app, you can extend the configuration URL to include the application name, or in the case of the Qlik Sense Enterprise, the GUID. You can then use the method from the app class and any other classes as you continue to work with objects within the app.

```
var ws = new WebSocket("ws://localhost:4848/app/MasteringQlikSense.qvf");
```

Creating a Connection to the Qlik Server Engine

Connecting to the engine on a Qlik Sense environment is a little bit different as you will need to take care of authentication first. Authentication is handled in different ways, depending on how you have set up your server configuration, with the most common ones being:

- Ticketing
- Certificates
- Header authentication

Authentication also depends on where the code that is interacting with the Qlik Engine is running.

If your code is running on a trusted computer, authentication can be performed in several ways, depending on how your installation is configured and where the code is running:

- If you are running the code from a trusted computer, you can use certificates, which first need to be exported via the QMC
- If the code is running on a web browser, or certificates are not available, then you must authenticate via the virtual proxy of the server

Creating a connection using certificates

Certificates can be considered as a seal of trust, which allows you to communicate with the Qlik Engine directly with full permission. As such, only backend solutions ever have access to certificates, and you should guard how you distribute them carefully. To connect using certificates, you first need to export them via the QMC, which is a relatively easy thing to do:

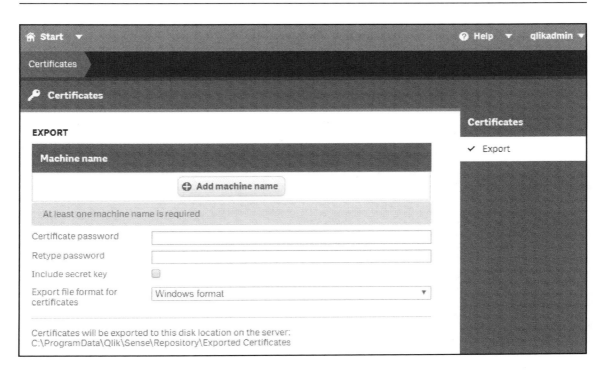

Once they are exported, you need to copy them to the folder where your project is located using the following code:

```
<html>
<body>
<h1>Mastering QS</h1>
</body>
<script>
var certPath =  path.join('C:', 'ProgramData', 'Qlik', 'Sense',
'Repository', 'Exported Certificates', '.Local Certificates');

var certificates = {
        cert: fs.readFileSync(path.resolve(certPath, 'client.pem')),
        key: fs.readFileSync(path.resolve(certPath, 'client_key.pem')),
        root: fs.readFileSync(path.resolve(certPath, 'root.pem'))
        };

// Open a WebSocket using the engine port (rather than going through the
proxy)
var ws = new WebSocket('wss://server.domain.com:4747/app/', {
        ca: certificates.root,
        cert: certificates.cert,
```

```
            key: certificates.key,
            headers: {
                          'X-Qlik-User':  'UserDirectory=internal;
UserId=sa_engine'
            }
            });
ws.onopen = function (event) {
 // Call your methods
}
</script>
```

Creating a connection using the Mashup API

Now, while connecting to the engine is a fundamental step to start interacting with Qlik, it's very low-level, connecting via WebSockets. For advanced use cases, the Mashup API is one way to help you get up to speed with a more developer-friendly abstraction layer.

As already described in Chapter 10, *Qlik Sense APIs Overview*, the Mashup API utilizes the qlik interface as an external interface to Qlik Sense, used for mashups and for including Qlik Sense objects in external web pages.

To load the qlik module, you first need to ensure RequireJS is available in your main project file. You will then have to specify the URL of your Qlik Sense environment, as well as the prefix of the virtual proxy, if there is one:

```
<html>
<body>
<h1>Mastering QS</h1>
</body>
</html>
<script
src="https://cdnjs.cloudflare.com/ajax/libs/require.js/2.3.5/require.min.js
">
<script>
//Prefix is used for when a virtual proxy is used with the browser.
var prefix = window.location.pathname.substr( 0,
window.location.pathname.toLowerCase().lastIndexOf( "/extensions" ) + 1 );

//Config for retrieving the qlik.js module from the Qlik Sense Server
var config = {
 host: window.location.hostname,
 prefix: prefix,
 port: window.location.port,
 isSecure: window.location.protocol === "https:"
};
```

```
require.config({
 baseUrl: (config.isSecure ? "https://" : "http://" ) + config.host +
(config.port ? ":" + config.port : "" ) + config.prefix + "resources"
});

require(["js/qlik"], function (qlik) {
 qlik.setOnError( function (error) {
 console.log(error);
 });
 //Open an App
 var app = qlik.openApp('MasteringQlikSense.qvf', config);
</script>
```

Once you have created the connection to an app, you can start leveraging the full API by conveniently creating HyperCubes, connecting to fields, passing selections, retrieving objects, and much more.

The Mashup API is intended for browser-based projects where authentication is handled in the same way as if you were going to open Qlik Sense. If you wish to use the Mashup API, or some parts of it, with a backend solution, you need to take care of authentication first.

Creating a connection using enigma.js

Enigma is Qlik's open-source promise wrapper for the engine. You can use enigma directly when you're in the Mashup API, or you can load it as a separate module. It's essential to also load the correct schema whenever you load enigma.js. The schema is a collection of the available API methods that can be utilized in each version of Qlik Sense. This means your schema needs to be in sync with your QS version.

When you are writing code from within the Mashup API, you can retrieve the correct schema directly from the list of available modules which are loaded together with qlik.js via 'autogenerated/qix/engine-api'.

The following example will connect to a Demo App using enigma.js and will retrieve a list of all available fields and write them out to the console:

```
define(function () {
  return function () {
    require(['qlik','enigma','autogenerated/qix/engine-api'], function
(qlik, enigma, schema) {
//The base config with all details filled in
var config = {
    schema: schema,
    appId: "My Demo App.qvf",
    session:{
        host:"localhost",
        port: 4848,
        prefix: "",
        unsecure: true,
    },
}
//Now that we have a config, use that to connect to the //QIX service.
enigma.getService("qix" , config).then(function(qlik){
    qlik.global.openApp(config.appId)
    //Open App
    qlik.global.openApp(config.appId).then(function(app){
        //Create SessionObject for FieldList
        app.createSessionObject( {
          qFieldListDef: {
              qShowSystem: false,
              qShowHidden: false,
              qShowSrcTables: true,
              qShowSemantic: true,
              qShowDerivedFields: true
          }, qInfo: {
              qId: "FieldList",
              qType: "FieldList"
          }
      } ).then( function(list) {
          return list.getLayout();
      } ).then( function(listLayout) {
          return listLayout.qFieldList.qItems;
      } ).then( function(fieldItems) {
        console.log(fieldItems)
      } );
      })
  }
})}})
```

From enigma.js version 2.x onwards, `getService('qix', config)` has been replaced with the `create(config)` method.

Embedding objects

The Qlik Engine itself is mighty, and establishing a connection to it is the first step before doing anything else. Once a connection is established, you'll then want to start embedding Qlik objects into your web apps or Qlik Sense mashup to leverage existing visualizations or already built apps.

Bringing Qlik objects into your mashup or website can be very simple, but depending on the level of required complexity, you can leverage more sophisticated methods to achieve the same outcome.

Being a true believer in keeping things as simple as necessary, we will introduce three methods for embedding charts, ordered by their technical complexity.

Single configurator

Some Qlik Gurus would not condone this approach for embedding Qlik Sense into web apps. However, the single configurator is the **most comfortable** and **most straightforward** way to integrate objects, or even full sheets, into another website or platform without having to write any code at all. It doesn't require any technical preparation or knowledge, as you are effectively only embedding a URL into an iFrame.

In short, an iFrame is an HTML document that is embedded inside another similar document on a website.

There are specific scenarios when using an iFrame within your pages is fine, such as when you have relatable, externally hosted content you wish to have on your page, as in the case of the Qlik Sense app.

However, the constant use of iFrames can affect your ability to customize your pages and provide a unified, coherent styling. For example, CSS styling on your site cannot modify content within an iFrame, because it is hosted elsewhere. As such, iFrames should not be used as an essential part of your site, but rather as a piece of content within it.

To generate a URL for the iFrame, you can use the highly dynamic single configurator you start with, the single prefix, and append a list of available parameters. This can be achieved either interactively, via the Dev Hub, or by just creating the URL yourself.

The basic URL of the single configurator is as follows:

- `http://localhost:4848/single` (Qlik Sense Desktop)
- `https://<ServerName>/single` (Qlik Server)

You then have the option to access a variety of objects with it, such as:

- A whole sheet
- A selection bar: Optionally, this object can be displayed at the top of the page
- A single visualization
- Master visualizations
- Snapshots

To access these objects, you need to supplement the URL with the following available parameters:

Parameter	Used for	Comment
`appid`	Retrieving the ID of a Qlik Sense app	If no `appid` is available, the file name will be listed.
`obj`	Retrieving the ID of a Qlik Sense visualization	If there is no `obj` and no sheet, the sheets and visualizations will be listed.
`sheet`	Retrieving the ID of a sheet in a Qlik Sense app	
`snapshot`	Retrieving the ID of a snapshot in a Qlik Sense app	

identity	Defining a session identity	If no identity is defined, the session and selection state will be shared with the client. When an identity is defined, it results in the creation of a separate session, and any selections made in that single feature does not affect a concurrent session in the Qlik Sense client.
opt	Defining options	This helps you define how the retrieved objects or sheet should behave. You can, for example, disable animations or interactions. Supported options are: • currsel: Displays the Selection bar • debug: Starts a JavaScript debugger (the debug option can only be defined in the URL) • noAnimate: Turns off animations • noInteraction: Turns off interactions If you want to define multiple options, you can separate them with a comma sign. For example: opt=noanimate,currsel
callback	Registering callbacks	This is the package name for callback functions, which returns the following callbacks: • window[callback package]onError: Called when an error occurs. The default is to use a JavaScript alert for errors. • window[callback package]onValid: Called when an object receives valid data from the Qlik Engine. • window[callback package]onRendered: Called when an object is rendered. Use test for testing, and use external for integration based on the Internet Explorer web component.
bookmark	Retrieving the ID of a bookmark in a Qlik Sense app	This is the ID of the bookmark to apply.

select	Field name and values to select	The field name and values define the selections to make. It is possible to determine multiple selected parameters. For example: `&select=Month,1,2,3,4&select=Item,Food` This example selects the months of January, February, March, and April, as well as Food Items. You have to define the number of numeric fields (Month, in the previous example); text will not work.

The following example will open the `Mastering QS.qvf` app and retrieve the sheet with the ID qAeJ with no interactions permitted and selections cleared out:

```
http://localhost:4848/single/?appid=Mastering
QS.qvf&obj=qAeJ&opt=nointeraction&select=clearall
```

If you wish to retrieve an object, with some default selections applied, the URL could look as follows:

```
http://localhost:4848/single/?appid=Mastering
QS.qvf&obj=qAeJ&select=Dim1,A,B&select=Dim3,X,Y
```

Once the URL is generated, you can now embed the object or sheet by adding it to an iFrame in the target web page. Make sure you do not forget to specify the width or height as the iFrame will otherwise default to a shrunken look. The following is the code to embed the object or sheet to an iFrame in the target web page:

```
<h1>Mastering QS Mashup Single Configurator Integration</h1>
<IFRAME
SRC="http://localhost:4848/single/?appid=Mastering
QS.qvf&obj=qAeJ&opt=nointeraction&select=clearall" width='100%'
height='100%'>
</IFRAME>
```

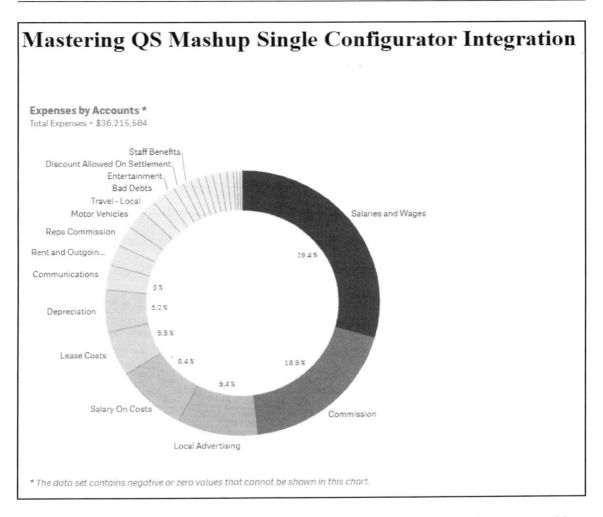

Mastering QS Mashup Single Configurator Integration

Expenses by Accounts *
Total Expenses = $36,215,504

Staff Benefits
Discount Allowed On Settlement
Entertainment
Bad Debts
Travel - Local
Motor Vehicles
Reps Commission
Rent and Outgoin...
Communications
Depreciation
Lease Costs
Salary On Costs
Local Advertising

Salaries and Wages
29.4 %
3 %
5.2 %
5.5 %
8.4 %
9.4 %
18.9 %
Commission

* The data set contains negative or zero values that cannot be shown in this chart.

And that's it—no technical skills or coding required. By using this approach, you can add Qlik Sense to SharePoint, JIVE, or any other platform which supports the iFrame DOM. The good thing about it is that the authentication is handled by a single configurator, so you do not need to apply any additional logic, and, as long as your users have Qlik Sense tokens allocated, they'll be able to view the produced sheet.

As a recommendation, before diving into coding, you should always explore whether the single configurator will suffice for a quick win.

Using the Object ID

Every object in Qlik Sense has an **Object ID**, which is a unique identifier for that particular virtual asset within the whole Qlik Sense environment. Using the Qlik App API, you can retrieve Qlik Sense objects directly from the Engine and embed them into the existing web page by inserting them into to a specified HTML element.

Not as easy as the single configurator, this approach requires you to create a connection to the Qlik Engine and then call the API programmatically. Furthermore, you will need to know the Object ID. With this method, however, you will have more control and flexibility over what the website looks like, especially regarding styling, overcoming the limitations of iFrames.

 The easiest way to retrieve the Object ID is to go to the Qlik Dev Hub and search for it using the single configurator explorer. Alternatively, you can also pick it up from the code using the element inspectors (advanced).

The following example will showcase how to open up the `Mastering QS.qvf` app and retrieve the same object as in the single configurator example, and display it within a defined DIV element:

```
<html>
<head>
 <link
href="https://<qlik_sense_servername>/resources/autogenerated/qlik-styl
es.css" rel="stylesheet">
 <script
src="https://<qlik_sense_servername>/resources/assets/external/requirej
s/require.js"></script>
 <script>

 var config = {
     host: 'localhost',
     prefix: '/',
     port: 443,
     isSecure: true
 };

 require.config({
  baseUrl: ( config.isSecure? "https://" : "http://" ) + config.host +
(config.port? ":" + config.port: "") + config.prefix + "resources"
  });

   require(["js/qlik"], function ( qlik ){
```

```
qlik.setOnError(function(error) {
    alert(error.message);
});

var appName = 'Mastering QS.qvf';
if (!app){
    //Get App
    app = qlik.openApp(appName, config);
    app.getObject("appObject", 'qAeJ');
}
});
</script>
</head>
<body>
<div class="qlik-embed" id="appObject"></div>
</body>
</html>
```

The `getObject` method also supports additional options such as the read-only mode and the ability to deactivate all interactions.

In detail, these are the available parameter references, as per the documentation:

Name	Type	Description		
`elem`	Element | String	Optional HTML element		
`id`	String	Object ID or `CurrentSelections` if used for Selections bar.		
`options`	Object	Optional.		
		Name	**Type**	**Description**
		`noInteraction`	Boolean	Set to true if you want to disable the interaction, including selections, in the visualization.
		`noSelections`	Boolean	Set to true if you want to disable selections in the visualization.

The world of Object IDs can, however, become a little bit more complicated depending on how you are using a visualization. Taking a bar chart, for example, you can have the object itself, or you can have it saved as a **Master Key Item**. Both will have a different Object ID, but then if you take snapshots of either the object or the Master Key Item, both snapshots will have different Object IDs as well. To make sure you get the right ID, you need to obtain it from various sources.

The following are three sources of the extension Object ID for the four cases discussed previously (considering AngularJS extensions here only):

- `$scope.layout.qInfo.qId`: Normal extension
- `$scope.layout.qExtendsId`: Extension as a Master Item
- `$scope.layout.sourceObjectId`: Extension snapshot on a story

Ralf Becher wrote a very useful blog post about this problem (`https://medium.com/@irregularbi/multiple-identities-in-qlik-sense-47083fda631a`), including a code snippet of the `getObjectId()` function for you to use in your projects.

Create visualizations on the fly

Embedding charts and objects into your web apps and mashups using `getObject()` is a perfectly viable method, but it carries three significant disadvantages:

- You need to manually create and maintain the object within the Qlik Sense app, which is an overhead
- You need to retrieve the Object ID somehow, and then, most likely, hard-code it into the mashup code if you wish to return a specific chart
- If you recreate the chart from scratch, you will then need to update the mashup with the new Object ID

Furthermore, you can only retrieve the objects as you cannot modify them further.

Precisely for these reasons, Qlik has released the ability to create visualizations on the fly. This allows you to programmatically define the dimensions, metrics, properties, and the chart type, and send it to the Qlik Engine to retrieve the chart object as a response. The Visualization API is driven by the `qlik.app.visualization` namespace, and can be used just like any other Qlik API we have described in this book so far.

An example of how to create a bar chart on the fly, with `Case Owner Group` as the dimension, and `=Avg([Case Duration Time])` as the expression, looks as follows:

```html
<html>
<head>
 <link
href="https://<qlik_sense_servername>/resources/autogenerated/qlik-styl
es.css" rel="stylesheet">
 <script
src="https://<qlik_sense_servername>/resources/assets/external/requirej
s/require.js"></script>
 <script>

 var config = {
     host: 'localhost',
     prefix: '/',
     port: 443,
     isSecure: true
 };

require.config({
 baseUrl: ( config.isSecure? "https://" : "http://" ) + config.host +
(config.port? ":" + config.port: "") + config.prefix + "resources"
 });

 require(["js/qlik"], function ( qlik ){
     qlik.setOnError(function(error) {
         alert(error.message);
     });

     var app = qlik.openApp('Mastering QS.qvf');
     app.visualization.create(
        'barchart',
        ["Case Owner Group","=Avg([Case Duration Time])"],
        {title:"Great on-the-fly barchart for Mastering QS"}
     ).then(function(bar){
         bar.show('appObject'); });
     });
 </script>
</head>
<body>
 <div class="qlik-embed" id="appObject"></div>
</body>
</html>
```

You can choose from a variety of available native visualizations, including custom extensions:

- Bar chart
- Boxplot
- Combo chart
- Distribution plot
- Gauge
- Histogram
- KPI
- Line chart
- Pie chart
- Pivot table
- Scatterplot
- Table
- List object
- Treemap
- Extension

The visualization API is compelling for many use cases, like when you wish to dynamically change the dimensions or metrics via your mashup or web app. Furthermore, as already discussed, it removes the need to create an object within the Qlik Sense app beforehand.

Interacting with the Engine

By now, you should know how to create a connection with the Qlik Engine, and how to embed nice looking visualizations in your web app or mashup to create a user-friendly dashboard sitting outside of the native Qlik Sense client. This section will now focus on interactivity, making selections in the data model, creating HyperCubes, connecting to fields, and most importantly, creating selection listeners for full duplex interactivity with both the Qlik App and the Qlik Engine.

Creating HyperCubes

The in-memory associative Qlik Engine is speedy and powerful when it comes to aggregating and calculating data on the fly. As such, it sometimes makes sense to leverage the Qlik Engine to calculate a dataset which you then process for a purpose other than visualizations. Alternatively, you could also build amazing, highly complex visualizations and utilize multiple HyperCubes to calculate the necessary data for them. HyperCubes are created using the `qlik.app.createCube(qHyperCubeDef, callback)` method. It's important to correctly define the `qHyperCubeDef` object before creating the cube, something which is explained in detail in `Chapter 13`, *Creating Extensions in Qlik Sense*.

The following example will create a HyperCube with the same dimensions as the ones in the example of creating visualizations on the fly, and will output the result to the HTML page as a list instead of visualizing it as a bar chart:

```
<html>
<head>
 <link
href="https://<qlik_sense_servername>/resources/autogenerated/qlik-styl
es.css" rel="stylesheet">
 <script
src="https://<qlik_sense_servername>/resources/assets/external/requirej
s/require.js"></script>
 <script>
 var config = {
     host: 'localhost',
     prefix: '/',
     port: 443,
     isSecure: true
 };

require.config({
 baseUrl: ( config.isSecure? "https://" : "http://" ) + config.host +
(config.port? ":" + config.port: "") + config.prefix + "resources"
 });

 require(["js/qlik"], function ( qlik ){
     qlik.setOnError(function(error) {
         alert(error.message);
     });

     var app = qlik.openApp('Mastering QS.qvf');
     app.createCube({
         qDimensions:[ {
             qDef:{
                 qFieldDefs : ["Case Owner Group"]
```

```
                    }
                }
            }],
            qMeasures:[{
                qDef:{
                    qDef : "=Avg([Case Duration Time])"
                }
            }],
            qInitialDataFetch:[{
                qTop: 0,
                qLeft: 0,
                qHeight: 20,
                qWidth: 3
            }]
    }, function(reply) {
        var str = "";
        $.each(reply.qHyperCube.qDataPages[0].qMatrix,
function(key, value) {
            str += '<li>' + value[0].qText + ':' + value[1].qText +
'</li>';
        });
        $('#list').html(str);
    });
 })
 </script>
</head>
<body>
 <ul class="qlik-list" id="list"></ul>
</body>
</html>
```

While the definition of the HyperCube and the coding of it might look cumbersome, the performance is instantaneous and, as such, creating HyperCubes in web apps or mashups can become a very powerful tool to calculate complex aggregations over a large amount of data in the backend with seamless integration, using the API to then render or process the results in the frontend.

Connecting to fields

Fields are the lists of available columns in the loaded data model within the app. While Qlik Sense is mostly focused around displaying or calculating data, interacting with the Qlik Data Model is equally as important, especially if you wish to pass selections to update the calculated dataset on your Qlik objects within your mashup or web app.

To connect to fields, all you need to do is use the Field API as part of the capabilities API, which goes by the namespace `qlik.app.field`. You can also use enigma.js.

Connecting to fields is reasonably straightforward once you have established a connection with the Qlik Engine, since you would only extend the `qlik.app`, which is shown in other examples provided in this chapter.

To make things a little more interesting, we'll create a compelling code example where we'll create two buttons, which will make a selection in a field, and clear selections, respectively:

```html
<html>
<head>
 <link
href="https://<qlik_sense_servername>/resources/autogenerated/qlik-styles.c
ss" rel="stylesheet">
 <script
src="https://<qlik_sense_servername>/resources/assets/external/requirejs/re
quire.js"></script>
 <script>
 var config = {
     host: 'localhost',
     prefix: '/',
     port: 443,
     isSecure: true
 };
require.config( {
 baseUrl: ( config.isSecure? "https://" : "http://" ) + config.host +
(config.port? ":" + config.port: "") + config.prefix + "resources"
 });

 require(["js/qlik"], function ( qlik ){
     qlik.setOnError(function(error) {
         alert(error.message);
     });
     var appName = 'Mastering QS.qvf';
     if (!app){
     //Get App
     app = qlik.openApp(appName, config);

     function makeSelection() {
        var field = app.field('Case Owner Group');
        field.selectAll(false)
     }

     function clearSelection() {
        var field = app.field('Case Owner Group');
        field.clear();
```

```
        }

      }
  });
  </script>
</head>
<body>
<button onclick="makeSelection()">Make Selection</button>
<button onclick="clearSelection()">Clear Selection</button>
</body>
</html>
```

Interacting with the Qlik data model and passing selections is a magnificent way to explore your data, which is why being familiar with connecting to fields is relevant for building compelling dashboards and adding value to the business user.

Creating a selection listener

Charts are being visualized, selections are being sent to the Qlik Engine by the user, and everything works brilliantly. In most cases, that's enough. But while Qlik Sense objects or charts are re-rendered and pushed every time the data model recalculates, other non-Qlik objects on the screen, sitting outside of Qlik, do not react.

Sometimes, what you need is a listener, which is basically a background function that fires off when a new data model change occurs, a filter is applied, or a reload occurs. These listeners can then fire functions to possibly connect the Qlik Engine model with other APIs and widgets on the screen.

The way to set up a listener is to bind a listener function to the selectionState() method. A code example of how this can be achieved can be seen as follows. The example will apply a listener to the selection state of an app and will output the current selections in real-time into the #QVSel HTML element:

```
//Code snippet kindly provided by Ralf Becher
var selState = app.selectionState();
 var listener = function () {
     $('#QVSel').html('');
     if (selState.selections.length > 0) {
         var selections = 'Selections:';
         $.each(selState.selections, function (i, s) {
             selections += '</br>';
             selections += s.fieldName + ': ';
             selections += s.selectedValues.map(function (e) {
                 return e.qName;
```

```
        }).join(', ');
      });
    $('#QVSel').html(selections);
}
//unregister the listener when no longer notification is needed.
//selState.OnData.unbind(listener);
};
//bind the listener
selState.OnData.bind(listener);
```

Summary

The world of mashups in Qlik Sense is a beautiful one. You can find fantastic and compelling examples on the internet, as well as blog posts on what is possible and achievable using the Qlik Sense API in a mashup. At the same time, it's also the most complex and challenging way to implement a data analytics project, compared to using the classic Qlik Sense client.

This chapter outlined the basics of using and building mashups or integrating Qlik Sense into web apps at a high level. It introduced ways to connect to, and authenticate with, the Qlik Engine from outside Qlik Sense, embed Qlik Sense objects into a web page, and interact with the Qlik App via the API passing on selections and reading selections. Enigma is also represented in this chapter as a way to move away from dependency on the mashup and capability APIs, and to work more directly with the Qlik Engine API.

With a solid understanding of web technologies and familiarity with the Qlik API, you should be able to comfortably build great web applications by leveraging data analytics. However, at the same time, you are moving away from Qlik Sense's self-service model, where users with relatively basic knowledge can quickly prototype applications. Time to market is longer using the mashup approach, and an advanced technical skill set is required to continue responding to user requirements and changes.

While it's seducing to approach a project with a mashup immediately, it's recommended to keep things simple where you can, and progress to more sophisticated data analytics implementations as and when it becomes necessary. As such, it's not uncommon to typically begin with a simple Qlik Sense app where the basics, such as the data modeling, basic visualizations, and a simple UI dashboard, can swiftly be implemented by a business analyst. Like the project, the underlying data model and the app will mature, and you can then make a case to switch over to a mashup, or even a web app, to improve the functionality and take the possibilities of the data analytics capabilities even further.

A more in-depth dive into mashups, advanced use cases, and examples would go beyond the scope of this book, and would almost justify a separate book specialized on this topic. If you wish to deepen your knowledge, it's highly recommended to do further reading on web technologies, such as AngularJS, JavaScript, HTML5, and CSS, and then spend some time familiarizing yourself even more with the Qlik API by looking at examples from Qlik Branch.

Other Books You May Enjoy

If you enjoyed this book, you may be interested in these other books by Packt:

Implementing Qlik Sense
Ganapati Hegde, Kaushik Solanki

ISBN: 9781786460448

- Understand the importance and expectations of a consultant's role
- Engage with the customer to understand the ir goals and future objectives
- Design the optimum architecture, using the best practices for the development and implementation of your projects
- Ensure successful adoption using real-life examples to make your learning complete
- Learn about the important stages of a Qlik project's life cycle

Learning Qlik Sense®: The Official Guide - Second Edition
Dr. Christopher Ilacqua, Dr. Henric Cronström, James Richardson

ISBN: 9781785887161

- Understand the vision behind the creation of Qlik Sense, and the promise that data discovery offers to you and your organization
- Get to grips with the life cycle of a Qlik Sense application
- Load and manage your data for app creation
- Visualize your data with Qlik Sense's engaging and informative graphing
- Administer your Qlik Sense system and monitor its security
- Build efficient and responsive Associative Models
- Extend the Qlik Analytic Platform with the Dev Hub
- Optimize Qlik Sense for sales, human resources, and demographic data discovery

Leave a review - let other readers know what you think

Please share your thoughts on this book with others by leaving a review on the site that you bought it from. If you purchased the book from Amazon, please leave us an honest review on this book's Amazon page. This is vital so that other potential readers can see and use your unbiased opinion to make purchasing decisions, we can understand what our customers think about our products, and our authors can see your feedback on the title that they have worked with Packt to create. It will only take a few minutes of your time, but is valuable to other potential customers, our authors, and Packt. Thank you!

Index

29565575R00282

Printed in Great Britain
by Amazon